CRITICAL SURVEY OF POETRY
Irish Poets

Editor

Rosemary M. Canfield Reisman
Charleston Southern University

SALEM PRESS
A Division of EBSCO Publishing, Ipswich, Massachusetts

Cover photo:
James Joyce (© Lebrecht Authors/Lebrecht Music & Arts/Corbis)

ISBN: 978-1-42983-661-6

CONTENTS

CONTRIBUTORS

James Lovic Allen
University of Hawaii at Hilo

David Barratt
Montreat College

Richard Bizot
University of North Florida

Neal Bowers
Iowa State University

Edmund J. Campion
University of Tennessee

Michael Case
Arizona State University

John R. Clark
University of South Florida

Caroline Collins
Quincy University

Desiree Dreeuws
Sunland, California

Welch D. Everman
University of Maine

Dennis Goldsberry
College of Charleston

John R. Griffin
*University of Southern
Colorado*

John Harty III
University of Florida

Sarah Hilbert
Pasadena, California

Miglena Ivanova
Coastal Carolina University

Philip K. Jason
*United States Naval
Academy*

Jeffry Jensen
Pasadena, California

Rebecca Kuzins
Pasadena, California

James Livingston
*Northern Michigan
University*

Archie K. Loss
*Pennsylvania State
University, Erie*

Arthur E. McGuinness
*University of California,
Davis*

Kevin McNeilly
*University of British
Columbia*

George O'Brien
Georgetown University

Robert M. Otten
Marymount University

Cóilín Owens
George Mason University

Charles H. Pullen
Queen's University

Paul Siegrist
Fort Hays State University

Eve Walsh Stoddard
St. Lawrence University

Andy K. Trevathan
University of Arkansas

IRISH POETRY

Ireland has a long and rich literary tradition in two languages. The Irish Gaelic language can be traced back to the Celts who settled in Ireland around 500 B.C.E, and the Irish language literary tradition is one of the oldest in Europe. In this tradition, the poet preserved the mythology of the culture; in fact, before Christianity came to the island, poets were also looked upon as prophets of sorts, thought to possess special powers. After the twelfth century Norman invasion, the English language was introduced to Ireland, and the resulting English dialect has become known as Irish English. Over the centuries, these two traditions have fought for supremacy in Ireland. By the nineteenth century, the Irish language was barely hanging on, but remarkably, it has survived until the present. In Ireland, history and literature have always been linked, and the country has produced many great writers, including such luminaries as Jonathan Swift, Oscar Wilde, William Butler Yeats, James Joyce, Samuel Beckett, and Seamus Heaney.

Born in Dublin in 1667, Swift is considered by many to be the greatest of all the satirists. During his lifetime, his word held much weight and those who crossed him did so at their peril. His talent for satire served him well in both poetry and prose. In poetry, his talents were best displayed when he remained raw and deliberately casual, and while he was not above composing verse that was less than scathing, Swift was at his vengeful best when he could go for the proverbial kill. In such blistering poems as "The Progress of Marriage," "The Lady's Dressing Room," and "A Beautiful Young Nymph Going to Bed," he does not hesitate to cause offense. The mocking tone of these poems emphatically tramples on all proper decorum.

EVERYTHING IRISH LEADS TO YEATS

Of a different temperament was the eighteenth century Irish writer Oliver Goldsmith. He is remembered for his work in a variety of genres, including poetry, long fiction, drama, and incisive nonfiction. In 1770, he published the extended pastoral poem *The Deserted Village*. A perceptive and touching portrait of rural life, the poem has retained its popularity due to its straightforward and uncluttered poetic style, as well as its nostalgia for a simpler time.

While Oscar Wilde's life and his writings in other genres overshadow his relatively small output of published poems, his poetry is still worth mentioning, if for no other reason than to reflect on the Romantic tradition that he proudly extended. New poetic horizons were soon to appear that Wilde would not be part of, but in such poems as *The Ballad of Reading Gaol* (1898), he speaks to man's capacity for cruelty, in a sense foreshadowing the events of the coming century.

William Butler Yeats cast an enormous shadow, not only on Irish poetry, but on the entire English-speaking world. In addition to being a well-respected poet, Yeats was a leading force behind the resurgence of Irish literature through the Celtic Revival. Much of the poetry that he wrote before the twentieth century included references to Celtic mythology. His best poems of this period were rich in the imagery that linked myth with place. He grew uneasy with the foggy vagueness that permeated his work during this time, however, and strived to bring his poetry into more focus. Yeats recognized the complexity of life and the imagination, a complexity that found its way into his poetry. He had a great thirst for literary traditions and a wide variety of philosophies, and schooled himself to be a great poet. Although his interests ran far and wide, he always remained centered in his Irishness as he grew into his role as a genius of the imagination. The literary world recognized his towering talent, and he was awarded the Nobel Prize in Literature in 1923. Yeats continued to push ahead and wrote some of his most brilliant poems after being honored by the Nobel Committee. During the 1920's, he wrote such masterpieces as "The Second Coming," "Leda and the Swan," "Sailing to Byzantium," and "Among School Children." Although not a revolutionary of poetic form, Yeats was able to capture the political and social turmoil in Ireland and the rest of the world in a way that still inspires repeated readings and close study. In addition to Yeats, other writers who were enthusiastic supporters of the Celtic Revival included Æ (pseudonym of George Russell), James Stephens, and Padraic Colum.

POETRY AFTER YEATS

Since Yeats's death in 1939, Irish poetry has flourished with a new breed of poet. While no less respectful of Yeats and what he gave to Ireland and to the literary world at large, poets such as Austin Clarke, Seamus Heaney, Patrick Kavanagh, Thomas Kinsella, John Montague, and Paul Muldoon have written about their island and its history in a less mystical way. Nature plays a significant, almost reverential, role in much of their poetry. Since the 1970's, Heaney has been considered the greatest Irish poet since Yeats, whether he has wanted the title or not. Born in rural Northern Ireland in the same year that Yeats died, Heaney has managed to craft quite a successful career as not only an award-winning poet but also a highly respected translator and intellectual. He won the Nobel Prize in Literature in 1995.

Ireland is also the birthplace of two of the most original writers of the twentieth century. While both James Joyce and Samuel Beckett are primarily considered masters of genres other than poetry, they have significantly contributed to the craft, each approaching composition from opposite ends of the spectrum. Joyce had a faith in language that he did not have in the world. The world was a tempestuous place where terrible things could, and usually did, befall even the most innocent of creatures. For Joyce, language was a refuge, a place removed from the chaos. As a modernist, Joyce relished how language could create meaning far removed from the everyday world, in poetry as well as in prose. Beckett recognized the same chaos, but for him, language was not the ultimate remedy. He did not believe that language would make life more bearable. While Joyce wove more words into his literary web, Beckett trimmed away all unnecessary verbiage, and won the Nobel Prize in Literature in 1969. Joyce and Beckett would eventually live in self-imposed exile from their homeland. Sadly, but perhaps appropriately, neither of them could live comfortably with Ireland or without.

Since the 1960's, a growing number of female poets from Ireland have struggled to gain recognition. Poets such as Eavan Boland, Catherine Walsh, Medbh McGuckian, and Eiléan Ní Chuilleanáin have raised a national consciousness and conversation about what it means to be a woman in Ireland, as well as a woman poet. While many social and cultural impediments continue to exist, these strong and resolute poets have not shrunk from the challenge at hand. Each, in her own way, has brought strength and dignity to Irish poetry and the land of their births.

Irish poetry has remained vital through the infusion of varied perspectives from its contemporary poets. While English has become the dominant language of most contemporary Irish poets, there are several, including Michael Davitt, Nuala Ní Dhomhnaill, and Michael Harnett, who have decided to express themselves in the Irish language. The rich tradition of Irish poetry seems to be as strong as ever, with its poets still speaking to a nation willing to listen.

Jeffry Jensen

BIBLIOGRAPHY

Garratt, Robert F. *Modern Irish Poetry: Tradition and Continuity from Yeats to Heaney.* Berkeley: University of California Press, 1986. Explores how Irish poetry has changed since the early twentieth century.

Johnston, Dillon. *Irish Poetry After Joyce.* 2d ed. Syracuse, N.Y.: Syracuse University Press, 1997. Presents an investigation of what Irish poetry has and may still become.

Kelleher, Margaret, and Philip O'Leary, eds. *The Cambridge History of Irish Literature.* 2 vols. New York: Cambridge University Press, 2006. A study of the rich history of Irish literature.

Kinsella, Thomas. *The Dual Tradition: An Essay on Poetry and Politics in Ireland.* Manchester: Carcanet, 1995. A study of Irish poetry, with special emphasis on the work of Yeats, Joyce, Beckett, and Austin Clarke.

Quinn, Justin. *The Cambridge Introduction to Modern Irish Poetry, 1800-2000.* Cambridge, England: Cambridge University Press, 2008. An overview of Ireland's poetic tradition.

Welch, Robert. *Irish Poetry from Moore to Yeats.* Gerrards Cross, England: C. Smythe, 1980. Discusses the evolution of Irish poetry.

Æ
George William Russell

Born: Lurgan, County Armagh, Ireland; April 10, 1867
Died: Bournemouth, England; July 17, 1935

OTHER LITERARY FORMS

In addition to his enormous amount of poetry, Æ (AY-ee) wrote pungent essays in almost every imaginable field, from literary criticism to politics, economics, and agriculture. These essays are collected in such volumes as *Some Irish Essays* (1906) and *The Living Torch* (1937). His interest in that department of letters would eventually lead him to become editor of *The Irish Homestead,* and later *The Irish Statesman.* He also tried his hand at fiction with *The Mask of Apollo, and Other Stories* (1904), ranging from the Asian-tinged "The Cave of Lillith" and "The Meditation of Ananda" to the Celtic-influenced "A Dream of Angus Oge," in which Æ characteristically blends East and West.

He also attempted drama with *Deirdre* (1902), the first important play to be performed by the company that was later to become the Irish National Theatre. Æ compiled his own spiritual autobiography, *The Candle of Vision* (1918), and in both it and *Song and Its Fountains* (1932), he attempted to explain his mysticism and poetic theory, which for him were one and the same. In *The National Being* (1916), Æ combines history with prophecy. *The Interpreters* (1922) consists of a dialogue among several characters typifying various positions in the Irish revolutionary movement—the heretic, the poet, the socialist, the historian, the aesthete, and the industrialist. In *The Avatars*

(1933), Æ created a "futurist fantasy" in which mythical heroes, or avatars, appear and spread joy wherever they go. They are removed by the authorities, but their cult grows through legends and artistic records.

In addition to his literary and journalistic work, Æ maintained an extensive correspondence, a part of which has been published in *Some Passages from the Letters of Æ to W. B. Yeats* (1936), *Æ's Letters to Mínánlabáin* (1937), and *Letters from Æ* (1961).

<h2 style="text-align:center">ACHIEVEMENTS</h2>

Æ's greatest contribution to Irish literature came from neither his artistic endeavors nor his journalistic and political involvement but rather from his unceasing kindness to younger writers. Frank O'Connor has said that Æ was the father of three generations of Irish poets. Among his discoveries were James Joyce, Padraic Colum, James Stephens, Frank O'Connor, Austin Clarke, and Patrick Kavanagh. As a poet, Æ is less known today for his own work, most of which is now out of print, than for his enormous influence on the younger generation, including William Butler Yeats. Although earlier critics grouped Æ with Yeats and John Millington Synge as one of the three major figures in the Irish Literary Revival, later criticism, such as Richard Finneran's *Anglo-Irish Literature* (1976), generally considers Æ among the lesser revival figures such as Lady Augusta Gregory, Oliver St. John Gogarty, and James Stephens.

It is difficult to select one artistic achievement for which Æ is remembered today, because so much of his work was indirect, involving the support of other artists, ideas, revivals, friendship, political expression, agriculture, economics, nationalism, mysticism, the Abbey Theatre, and art in general. Yeats's wife may have best summarized Æ's achievements when she told her husband that he was a better poet but that Æ was a saint.

<h2 style="text-align:center">BIOGRAPHY</h2>

The events of Æ's early years are somewhat obscure. He was born George William Russell into the Northern Irish Protestant family of Thomas Elias Russell and Mary Anne (Armstrong) Russell. When he was eleven, his family moved to Dublin, and Æ was educated at the Rathmines School. From 1880 to 1900, he attended the Dublin School of Art for a few months each year, where he met Yeats, a fellow student. Their long friendship was a troubled one, since Yeats felt that Æ never fulfilled his artistic potential.

Æ's first employment may have been as a clerk in a Guinness brewery, a job he soon quit. Painting was Æ's natural activity, but this was sacrificed because his family could not afford such luxuries, and he turned to literature. From 1890 to 1897, he worked in a warehouse twelve hours a day; in the evenings, he served as librarian of the Dublin Lodge of the Theosophical Society, where he lived. In the midst of all this, he still found time to publish his first two volumes of poetry, *Homeward* and *The Earth Breath, and Other Poems*.

The most important event in Æ's life occurred in 1887 when he discovered Theosophy. He had been a mystic from childhood, and becoming an ardent adherent, he utilized the principles of Theosophy. It was only after the death of Madame Blavatsky, the founder of the Theosophical Society, that he severed his official connection with Theosophy.

The mystic Æ later evolved into a philosopher and a political sage respected on both sides of the Atlantic. For his entire adult life, he was active in the cooperative agricultural movement of Sir Horace Plunkett's Irish Agricultural Organization Society and in the Home Rule movement.

Having achieved a certain security through his position as organizer in the Irish villages for Horace Plunkett, the agrarian reformer, Æ married Violet North. They had two sons, one of whom became an American citizen. Æ was never a domestic man because his variety of interests kept him busy and often away from home. When his health showed signs of deteriorating, Plunkett made him editor of the cooperative journal *The Irish Homestead*. In 1923, the journal merged with *The Irish Statesman*, with Æ again as editor; in 1930, however, the paper failed because of enormous legal expenses. Æ remained in Ireland until late in his life, when he toured the United States, and after the death of his wife, he spent most of his time abroad.

Æ was nearly six feet tall and became corpulent in old age. He had a russet beard, "mousecolored" hair, and blue-gray eyes covered by spectacles; he wore shabby clothes and was a perpetual pipe smoker. Æ looked like what he was—a thinker somewhere between a farmer and a mystical poet. In accord with Irish tradition, he was a great talker and an inspired speaker. His voice was mellow, with a strong north Irish accent. He painted all his life but never exhibited or sold his paintings, preferring instead to give them to his friends. Æ was intensely involved in the arts, but he always felt that people were more important, and he worked throughout his life for the welfare of humankind.

His pen name Æ (or A. E.) grew out of this tradition. It was originally Æon but a proofreader let it appear as Æ. Russell accepted the change and used it from that point on. Why Æon? John Eglinton recounted that Æ once made a drawing of the apparition in the Divine Mind of the idea of Heavenly Man. Unable to sleep one night, a voice gave him a title for his work, "Call it the Birth of Æon." His eye was caught by a passage in August Neander's *Allgemeine Geschichte der christlichen Religion und Kirche* (1825-1852; *General History of the Christian Religion and Church*, 1847-1855), on the doctrine of the Aeons. In a letter, he described the following elements of the word: *A*, the sound for God; *Æ*, the first divergence from *A; Au*, the sound continuity for a time; and *N*, change. Thus, Æon represents revolt from God, the soul's passage through its successive incarnations in humankind homeward to God, and finally God's amplification.

In 1935, Æ died from cancer at Bournemouth, England, his home after the death of his wife. Some years earlier he had written that the dead are happier than the living and that he did not fear death for himself or for others.

ANALYSIS

In his excellent introduction to *The Living Torch*, Monk Gibbon remarks that Æ's poetry began as that of a mystic and remained so to the end. Æ saw the poet not as an artisan of beauty but rather as a seer and prophet who derived a special authority from communion with the esoteric wisdom of the past. As Gibbon points out, Æ's poetry contains a beauty of thought and a sincerity of utterance, but in some poems, the form seems inadequate and the imagery vague.

Like other poets in the Irish Renaissance, Æ attempted to define Irishness in terms of the mysticism, reverie, and wavering rhythms of the Celtic Twilight, but his poetic voice remained a faint one. Some of Æ's best poetry is contained in his first two books: *Homeward* and *The Earth Breath, and Other Poems*. Some of his late work is also very good, but it is marred by a tendency to philosophize.

Æ will continue to have a place in literary history, but his prose and poetry are comparable only to the best imaginative work of the secondary figures of his day. Æ survives not as a painter or poet but as an exemplar of his age.

HOMEWARD

Æ's philosophy includes a pantheistic adoration of nature, and he argues that the important thing about Ireland is the primitiveness of the country and its people. The very title of *Homeward* indicates the author's attitude toward life. Ernest Boyd in his *Appreciations and Depreciations: Irish Literary Studies* (1918) has stated that "home" for Æ signifies the return of the soul to the oversoul, the spirit's absorption into the universal spirit—a doctrine that reflects his interest in Ralph Waldo Emerson, Henry David Thoreau, and Walt Whitman.

Homeward is a narrative of Æ's spiritual adventures, a record of the soul's search for the Infinite. Æ's poems are songs with sensuous, unearthly notes, records of the inner music of his life. They do not speak of humankind's mundane experiences but rather of those moments of divine vision and intuition when humankind's being dissolves into communion with the eternal. In that moment when the seer has come to his spiritual vision, he is truly at home.

Alone with nature, Æ beholds in his poetry the beauties of the phenomenal world, and through this experience, the poet is lifted toward participation in the eternal. The conditions that usually produce an exalted mood are those associated with morning or evening twilight, the quietude of the hills, and the silent, lonely countryside; such scenes are typical of both his poetry and his paintings. On innumerable occasions, the poet seeks the soft dusk of the mountains for meditation. Often his verses suggest the coming of daylight and the initial glories of sunlight as the seer pays homage to the light after a night of rapture on the mountainside.

However, solitude is not the sine qua non for Æ's visions. In "The City," his mood is unaltered by the change of setting. The poet's immortal eyes transfigure the mortal things of the city. The reader is reminded of another Metaphysical poet, T. S. Eliot, as Æ paints the gloom of the metropolis while managing to retain bright glimmers of hope.

Wayne Hall in his *Shadowy Heroes* (1980) has pointed out that, in recording his most intense experiences (his ecstatic visions), Æ produced his most notable work. The most successful poems in *Homeward* are "By the Margin of the Great Deep," "The Great Breath," and the sequence "Dusk," "Night," "Dawn," and "Day." "Dusk" begins at sunset, that special moment for poetic visions. At this early point in the volume, the vision of the speaker draws him away from domestic life and human contact toward "primeval being." Sunset also introduces "The Great Breath." The fading sky of this poem seems to suggest both a cosmic flower and an awareness that the death of beauty occasions its most complete fulfillment. This unstable insight, Hall points out, as with the paradox of spiritual union through physical separation in "By the Margin of the Great Deep," becomes more nearly resolved in the four-poem sequence. In "By the Margin of the Great Deep," rather than a sunset, chimney fires of the village mingle in the sky, signifying the merging of humanity within the vastness of God.

For Æ, night usually brings despair and the loss of vision, as in "The Dawn of Darkness." In "Waiting" the speaker can only hope that dawn will reawaken humanity to its former joy. In the poem "Night," however, Æ changes directions as night brings on a rebirth of spirit and beauty, a complete union of souls, while "Dawn" initiates a fragmentation of unity. In the light of common day, vision is lost but not entirely forgotten.

The sequence of poems from "Dusk" to "Day" succeeds far better than Æ's other attempts to link mortal pain with immortal vision. For Æ, to have a human spirit, a person must know sorrow. The path to wisdom is a road paved with the burdens of the world. Too often, however, he fails to integrate one world into the other, beyond the level of unconvincing abstraction.

OTHER MAJOR WORKS

LONG FICTION: *The Avatars*, 1933.

SHORT FICTION: *The Mask of Apollo, and Other Stories*, 1904.

PLAY: *Deirdre*, pr. 1902.

NONFICTION: *Some Irish Essays*, 1906; *The National Being*, 1916; *The Candle of Vision*, 1918; *The Interpreters*, 1922; *Song and Its Fountains*, 1932; *Some Passages from the Letters of Æ to W. B. Yeats*, 1936; *Æ's Letters to Mínánlabáin*, 1937; *The Living Torch*, 1937 (Monk Gibbon, editor); *Letters from Æ*, 1961.

MISCELLANEOUS: *The Descent of the Gods: Comprising the Mystical Writings of G. W. Russell "A.E.,"* 1988 (Raghavan Narasimhan Iyer and Nandini Iyer, editors).

BIBLIOGRAPHY

Allen, Nicholas. *George Russell (Æ) and the New Ireland, 1905-1930*. Portland, Oreg.: Four Courts Press, 2003. Looks at Æ and his relationship with Ireland.

Davis, Robert Bernard. *George William Russell ("Æ")*. Boston: Twayne, 1977. The first chapter sketches the external events of Æ. His varied interests are elaborated in six succeeding chapters, with focuses on the mystic, the poet, his drama and fiction, the economist, the statesman, and the critic. A brief conclusion assesses Æ's contributions. Provides a chronology, notes, an index, and an annotated, select bibliography.

Figgis, Darrell. *Æ, George W. Russell: A Study of a Man and a Nation*. San Rafael, Calif.: Coracle Press, 2008. A biography of Æ that looks at his poetic works and his contributions to Ireland.

Kain, Richard M., and James H. O'Brien. *George Russell (Æ)*. Lewisburg, Pa.: Bucknell University Press, 1976. The first three chapters, by Kain, present a biography of Æ by examining his personality, his early success, and his decline. The last two chapters, by O'Brien, examine Æ's interests in Theosophy and his work as a poet. Contains a chronology and a select bibliography.

Kuch, Peter. *Yeats and Æ: The Antagonism That Unites Dear Friends*. Totowa, N.J.: Barnes & Noble, 1986. This work examines the relationship between William Butler Yeats and George William Russell from their first meeting in art class to their split in 1908. Kuch provides excellent background on the inner workings of the London-Dublin esoteric worlds that shaped both men. Especially valuable is his ability to sort through the many branches of the esoteric tradition.

Loftus, Richard J. *Nationalism in Modern Anglo-Irish Poetry*. Madison: University of Wisconsin Press, 1964. Chapter 5, "The Land of Promise," is a substantial examination of Æ's attitudes toward Irish nationalism. His optimism turned to anger, then to disillusionment. Rarely did he include his private political feelings in his public verse. *The House of the Titans, and Other Poems* is analyzed for nationalistic implications. Supplemented by notes, a bibliography, and an index.

Mercier, Vivian. "Victorian Evangelicalism and the Anglo-Irish Literary Revival." In *Literature and the Changing Ireland*, edited by Peter Connolly. Totowa, N.J.: Barnes & Noble, 1982. Evangelicalism is examined as the background to Æ's career. His father made Æ aware of the power of conversion, which occurred away from evangelicalism to Theosophy for him. He helped to establish Theosophy as a sect similar in status to that of a Protestant evangelical group. Includes notes and an index.

Summerfield, Henry. *That Myriad-Minded Man: A Biography of George William Russell, "A. E.," 1867-1935*. Gerrards Cross, Ireland: Colin Smythe, 1975. Chapter 1 explains Russell's mysticism. His nationalism is then examined. Chapter 4 focuses on farm interests, and the following chapter describes his journalism from 1905 to 1914. Russell's pacifism is then posed against the violence of war in two chapters, and a final chapter covers his last years. Complemented by illustrations, notes, and an index.

John Harty, III

WILLIAM ALLINGHAM

Born: Ballyshannon, Ireland; March 19, 1824
Died: London, England; November 18, 1889

PRINCIPAL POETRY

Poems, 1850 (enlarged 1861)
Day and Night Songs, 1854 (revised and enlarged 1855 as *The Music Master, a Love Story, and Two Series of Day and Night Songs*)
Laurence Bloomfield in Ireland, 1864
Fifty Modern Poems, 1865
Songs, Ballads, and Stories, 1877
Evil May-Day, 1882
Blackberries Picked Off Many Bushes, 1884
Irish Songs and Poems, 1887
Rhymes for the Young Folk, 1887 (also known as *Robin Redbreast, and Other Verses*, 1930)
Flower Pieces, and Other Poems, 1888
Life and Phantasy, 1889
By the Way: Verses, Fragments, and Notes, 1912
The Poems of William Allingham, 1967 (John Hewitt, editor)

OTHER LITERARY FORMS

Although known primarily as a poet of light lyrics, William Allingham also wrote prose pieces and a diary. Few would deny that *William Allingham: A Diary* (1907) is one of the best literary diaries of the Victorian period. Primarily a product of his English years, it records conversations and encounters with an impressive array of eminent Victorian personalities. Alfred, Lord Tennyson, and Thomas Carlyle were intimates, and there is much about Robert Browning and Dante Gabriel Rossetti. Allingham's formal prose turns out to be surprisingly substantial. Starting in 1867, he wrote more than twenty travelogues for *Fraser's Magazine*. Narrated under the pseudonym Patricius Walker, the travelogues are notable for their expository emphasis. The traveler will sometimes pass opinion on what he has seen in his wanderings (Wales, Scotland, provincial England, parts of the Continent), but for the most part, he concentrates on describing scenery and reporting local customs and historical tidbits about the area. A selection of these pieces was later issued as *Rambles* (1873), while most of them were collected in the first two volumes of a posthumously published edition of his prose. The third volume of this work, *Varieties in Prose* (1893), contains Irish sketches and literary criticism.

ACHIEVEMENTS

William Allingham deserves the elusive label "Anglo-Irish." His reputation as a minor Victorian poet is largely the result of the popularity of a few frequently anthologized poems of Irish inspiration, subject matter, and sentiment. Like so many other "minor" literary figures, however, his historical significance goes beyond his accomplishment in any single genre. His foremost achievement is in lyric poetry. He had a knack for spinning songs and ballads. The most famous of these is "The Fairies," a delightful children's rhyme about the elvish world, which inevitably appears in anthologies of Irish verse. Also frequently anthologized is "The Winding Banks of Erne," a tender farewell to Ireland from an emigrant as he sets sail for the New World. Over the years, these two favorites have been included in most of the standard collections of Irish verse: Stopford A. Brooke and T. W. Rolleston's (1900), Padraic Colum's (1922), Lennox Robinson and Donagh MacDonagh's (1958), and Devin Garrity's (1965), among others. To complete their selection from Allingham's work, editors often include lyrics such as "A Dream" and "Four Ducks on a Pond," and ballads such as "Abbey Asaroe" and "The Maids of Elfin Mere."

A dozen or so preservable short poems from a canon of several hundred does not seem to be a very significant achievement. The quality of these poems is sufficiently high, however, to secure at least a minor position in Irish poetry, and, when he is considered in the light of Irish literary history, Allingham's stature grows substantially. As Ernest Boyd points out in *Ireland's Literary Renaissance* (1916), the third quarter of the nineteenth century was a transitional period in Irish literature, sandwiched between an earlier period of predominantly political verse and the later full renaissance led by William Butler Yeats and his circle. During this transitional period, there appeared a few poets who, though not of the first rank, were nevertheless serious, competent artists who celebrated Irish themes without lapsing into propaganda. Allingham was one of these, ranking alongside Aubry de Vere and just below Samuel Ferguson in importance. A country seeking to establish its cultural identity cannot afford to overlook the literary accomplishments of any of its native citizens. Allingham helped to set the stage for the later flowering of Irish verse, and his historical importance was recognized by poets of the Irish Renaissance, particularly Katherine Tynan, Yeats, Lionel Johnson, and Colum.

Yeats above all is responsible for securing Allingham's modest niche in literary history. In an article entitled "A Poet We Have Neglected," Yeats gave an appreciation of Allingham's Irish songs and ballads, noting the poet's facility at capturing ephemeral moods and moments. "It is time," he declared, "for us over here to claim him as our own, and give him his due place among our sacred poets; to range his books beside Davis, Mangum, and Ferguson." Four years later he was writing to Tynan that "you, Ferguson and Allingham are, I think, the Irish poets who have done the largest quantity of fine work." In 1905, he put together and published a small selection of Allingham's best poems (*Sixteen Poems by William Allingham*). More important than Yeats's service to Allingham's reputation, however, is Allingham's influence on Yeats's own poetry. In 1904, Yeats wrote to Mrs. Allingham, "I am sometimes inclined to believe that he was my own master in verse, starting me in the way I have gone whether for good or evil." Allingham's success with ballads and songs encouraged Yeats to explore those genres during the early part of his career, and specific borrowings have been noticed by critics.

Allingham's short verse deserves wider recognition than its slight representation in anthologies seems to warrant. It is true that an enormous amount of inferior work must be waded through, but a reading of his entire canon reveals several dozen poems worth keeping in addition to the well-known ones. There is, for example, an interesting series of poems all entitled "Aeolian Harp." Although these poems are inspired more by English poetic convention than by "Irish scenes and Irish faces" (Yeats's phrase), they are nevertheless fairly successful imitations of the type of reflective poem for which Samuel Taylor Coleridge is known. Some of the sonnets, such as "Autumnal Sonnet" and "Winter Cloud," are very expressive, and there is even a sparkling translation of "The Cicada" from the *Greek Anthology* (first century C.E.). The most judicious twentieth century selection of Allingham's poetry is found in Geoffrey Taylor's anthology *Irish Poets of the Nineteenth Century* (1951), which contains about fifty pages of his shorter poetry. A selection that appeared in 1967 (*The Poems of William Allingham*, edited by John Hewitt) contains about twenty shorter poems, plus excerpts from longer ones.

Allingham's second major achievement was *Laurence Bloomfield in Ireland*, a long narrative in verse about Irish tenant-landlord relations in the mid-nineteenth century. Many later critics, including Taylor and Alan Warner, place *Laurence Bloomfield in Ireland* first on the list of Allingham's achievements. Yeats castigated it, as he did all of Allingham's longer poetry, but William Gladstone praised it and even quoted from it in the House of Commons. After reading it, Ivan Turgenev told a mutual friend, "I never understood Ireland before!" Allingham himself considered *Laurence Bloomfield in Ireland* his best work. The poem's modest popularity was partly owing to its contemporary subject matter and partly to its artistic strengths. It ran through several editions during Allingham's lifetime.

His third major area of achievement is his prose, including travelogues, occasional pieces, and a diary. Critic Sean McMahon labels Allingham's posthumously published *William Allingham* his "greatest" work, ranking it above *Laurence Bloomfield in Ireland* and the lyrics.

BIOGRAPHY

William Allingham can be considered more quintessentially Anglo-Irish than other representatives of that breed because he was truly poised between the two spheres. In his first thirty-nine years, Ireland was his home; the last twenty-six were spent almost exclusively in England. Allingham's final visit to Ireland occurred as early as 1866, on the occasion of his father's funeral. The demarcation between the two lives, however, is not as clear as the mere circumstance of residence would seem to indicate. During the Irish years (1824-1863), he often visited England, where most of his friends and correspondents were. During the English years (1863-1889), his mind constantly returned to Ireland, as is evidenced in his writing and conversation.

Allingham was born in the western Ireland port town of Ballyshannon, County Donegal, situated at the mouth of the River Erne. Ballyshannon and vicinity would provide the setting for most of his well-known ballads and lyrics. His family was Protestant, having migrated from Hampshire more than two hundred years earlier. *William Allingham: A Diary* reports that his parents, William and Elizabeth, were both "undemonstrative," and his mother's early death in 1833 probably contributed to a curious personality trait observable in Allingham throughout his life—a simultaneous love of solitude and desire for companionship. "Has anyone walked alone as much as I?" he asked in his diary in 1865, and then immediately gave the counterpoint: "And who fonder of congenial company?"

His father, formerly a merchant, removed his son from a local boarding school at the age of thirteen and installed him as a clerk in the branch bank that he had managed for several years. Thenceforth Allingham educated himself at home during his spare time, no mean feat in the light of his later scholarship. When he was twenty-two, he secured a position in the Customs Service at eighty pounds a year, serving in Ballyshannon and other Ulster towns, and even for a short time on the Isle of Man. He assayed cargoes, visited shipwrecks, audited crew payrolls, no doubt did reams of paperwork, and, significantly, inspected fittings and provisions on immigrant ships heading for the United States. During those years he produced his first three volumes of poetry—*Poems, Day and Night Songs,* and *The Music Master, a Love Story, and Two Series of Day and Night Songs*—which, together, contain the core of his best ballads and lyrics.

Allingham's Irish period ended in 1863 when he transferred to the English port of Lymington, on the southern coast opposite the Isle of Wight. Long before this, however, he had become acquainted with England. Starting in 1847, he had made annual visits to London, eventually breaking into several different circles of artists. Through Leigh Hunt, Allingham met Carlyle; Coventry Patmore introduced him to Rossetti and the Pre-Raphaelites, as well as to Tennyson. During the early 1850's, he was especially intimate with Rossetti, "whose friendship," he wrote in a dedication to one volume of his collected works, "brightened many years of my life, and whom I never can forget." Rossetti's letters to Allingham are numerous, interesting, and accessible (*The Letters of Rossetti to Allingham,* 1897, G. B. Hill, editor). The intimacy with Tennyson and with Carlyle deepened after Allingham's transfer to England. In 1864, he published *Laurence Bloomfield in Ireland,* much revised from its original form in *Fraser's Magazine,* and in 1865, *Fifty Modern Poems.* The latter must be considered more a product of his Irish period.

In 1870, acting on Carlyle's advice, Allingham retired from the civil service to become subeditor of *Fraser's Magazine*, under J. A. Froude, whom he succeeded as editor in 1874. The same year he married Helen Paterson, an established watercolorist only half his age. They had three children. In 1879, Allingham retired permanently, moving to Witley, Surrey, in 1881, then to Hampstead in 1888, his final home. He had been awarded an annual civil pension of sixty pounds in 1864; it was increased to one hundred pounds in 1870. The last twenty years witnessed a decline in poetic output. *Songs, Ballads, and Stories* contains mostly work from previous volumes, though as a collection it may be the best single repository of Allingham's poetry. *Evil May-Day* will remain his least successful volume, mainly because of the heavy didactic nature of the title piece, which whines and frets in blank verse for some eight hundred lines. Ironically, the book also contains his most succinct lyric, the gemlike "Four Ducks on a Pond." His last major original production was *Blackberries Picked Off Many Bushes*, composed entirely of short aphoristic verse.

ANALYSIS

As a poet, William Allingham will remain known primarily for his lyrics and for *Laurence Bloomfield in Ireland*. He had a lyric voice of unusual charm. He had an eye alert to local beauty. He had a heart sensitive to those passing emotions and thoughts, which, in the aggregate, form the very fabric of human experience. The voices that moved his voice to sing were principally Irish, though not exclusively so. He chose to live the latter third of his life in England; his temperament was largely English; he derived his sense of literary community and artistic purpose from English sources. What poetic strengths he did have are a product of his love for England and Ireland. Those strengths should not be underrated. "I am genuine though not great," he once wrote to a friend, adding "and my time will come."

The chief strengths of Allingham's best lyrics and songs are their simplicity and musicality. His themes are the universal ones: the joys and frustrations of romantic love, the many faces of nature, the quality of country life, humankind's ultimate relation to an indecipherable universe, memories of happier times, the supernatural, and death. His simplicity of style is typified by the following stanza from "The Lighthouse":

> The plunging storm flies fierce against the pane,
> And thrills our cottage with redoubled shocks:
> The chimney mutters and the rafters strain;
> Without, the breakers roar along the rocks.

As he does here, Allingham commonly uses familiar rhyme schemes, keeps syntax straight, and restrains metaphor to an unusual degree. His syntactical purity is such that the only departures from normal word order permitted are entirely conventional poetic inversions ("Many fine things had I glimpse of"). Even then he manages to avoid the grosser sort of inversion, as when the main verb is delayed until the end of the line for mere rhyme's sake ("Loud larks in ether sing"). Implicitly in several poems, explicitly in personal conversations, Allingham criticized the convoluted style of Robert Browning's poetry, friend though he was. Instead, in poetry (see "The Lyric Muse") and prose (*Rambles*, "To Dean Prior"), he holds up Robert Herrick as a model of lyricism. Not too much should be made of that, however, since the serious Allingham would never imitate the cavalier element in Herrick's verse, although he did approve of its "elegant naivete." One might discern an elegance, certainly a gracefulness, in the naïve treatment of idyllic love in the opening lines of this untitled poem:

> Oh! were my Love a country lass,
> That I might see her every day,
> And sit with her on hedgerow grass
> Beneath a bough of may.

Here as elsewhere in his most successful lyrics, Allingham keeps diction simple. Surely the freshness of lines such as these has some value today.

WILLIAM ALLINGHAM

The musical element is so omnipresent in Allingham's poetry that the distinction between song, lyric, and ballad is sometimes obscured. Many of his enduring poems tend toward song. The musical element adds sweetness, or in some instances liveliness, to the simplicity of his poetry. *William Allingham* records a conversation with William Makepeace Thackeray, in which Allingham wholeheartedly agrees with the novelist's dictum, "I want poetry to be musical, to run sweetly." It is not always easy, however, to determine whether the musical charm of a particular song derives from meter, rhyme, phonetic effects, or from a combination of the three. From *William Allingham* and other prose writings it is apparent that Allingham considered meter to be the very soul of poetry. In fact, some of the most significant entries in his diary include those in which Tennyson and his Irish devotee discuss the technicalities of metrical effects. Lines such as "The pulse in his pillowed ear beat thick" ("The Goblin Child of Ballyshannon") echo Tennyson both metrically and phonetically. Repetition of the haunting place-name "Asaroe" in "Abbey Asaroe" shows that Allingham could choose a word for its rhythm and sound; its precise placement in each stanza shows a talent for emphasis. On the other hand, rhyme is a prominent feature of Allingham's verse. Triplets, internal rhyme, and refrains are not uncommon.

FAIRY POEMS

Sprightly music, such as that which makes children laugh and sing, contributes in part to the popularity of Allingham's beloved fairy poems. Justly most famous of these is "The Fairies," with its traditional opening:

Up the airy mountain,
Down the rushy glen,
We daren't go a-hunting
For fear of little men.

Others, however, are almost as highly cherished. "Prince Brightkin," a rather long narrative, has some brilliant touches of whimsicality. In "The Lepruchan," the wee shoemaker escapes his captors by blowing snuff in their faces. In "The Fairy Dialogue," mischievous sprites confound housewives attempting to do their daily chores. It should be noted, however, that much of Allingham's verse contains an opposite charm, that of sweet sadness. Many of his descriptive poems, as well as many of the romantic lyrics, are tinged with a sense of regret, of longing for something unattainable. Allingham could sing in a minor key. This tendency derives partly from personal temperament, partly from the fashion of the times, partly from literary imitation of the Graveyard school or even the Spasmodic school of poetry. He might be said to have anticipated the tone of voice adopted by writers of the Celtic Twilight. For example, one, "Aeolian Harp," opens and closes with the question, "O what is gone from us, we fancied ours?" Yeats so appreciated the way the poem enshrouds its *sic transit* theme with a meditative plaintiveness that he included it in his selection of Allingham's verse.

INFLUENCE OF BALLADS

Allingham wrote only a handful of ballads, but his work was sufficiently crucial to establish him as a modern pioneer in this form. During his Irish period, study of the local folk ballad became a sort of hobby. He listened to balladeers at country market fairs, transcribed lyrics and melodies, and collected anonymous broadsheet ballads sold by hawkers. Next, he produced his own ballads, printed and circulated them as anonymous ha'penny broadsheets (a few of which have survived), and had the pleasure of hearing them sung in the streets and cottages of Ireland. Later, Yeats, Colum, and other poets of the Irish Renaissance took up the genre. Five of Allingham's broadsheet ballads were collected in the volume of 1855, which also has a preface describing the difficulties of adapting peasant Anglo-Irish idiom to verse. The best of these are "Lovely Mary Donnelly" and "The Girl's Lamentation." There is in the former poem a blind fiddler who, although sad because he could not see the pretty lass, "blessed himself he wasn't deaf" on hearing her winsome voice. The girl's lament is for the perfidy of her lover and also for her own loss of chastity, since "a maid again I can never be/ Till the red rose blooms on the willow tree." A third broadside ballad, "Kate O' Ballyshanny," belongs with these two in quality. Allingham also wrote a few literary ballads, perhaps imitating Rossetti or the Romantic poets. The best of these are "The Maids of Elfinmere," "The Abbot of Innisfallen," "Squire Curtis," and "St. Margaret's Eve."

POETIC DETRACTIONS

Allingham liked Herrick's lyrics for their simplicity "without flatness." The problem with his own verse is that most of it is both simple and flat. His failings as a poet, which, in Sean McMahon's phrase, keep him entrenched "on the foothills of Parnassus," are largely ones common to his period. Victorian oppressive seriousness, mediocrity of thought, and gushy sentimentality too often invade his poetry. At times the effusion of emotion becomes embarrassingly urgent:

> Mine—Mine
> O Heart, it is thine—
> A look, a look of love!
> O wonder! O magical charm!
> Thou summer-night, silent and warm!

One is reminded of Percy Bysshe Shelley's "Indian Serenade." This tendency toward triteness extends past content into the realm of technique. For instance, eighteenth century poetic diction is resurrected and put to facile uses, so that one finds the earth to be "the whirling sphere," the night sky "the starry dome," and a field of wildflowers "the daisied lea."

Allingham's typical faults are magnified in his longer poems. "Evil May-Day" suffers especially from high seriousness. It is a philosophical discussion about the impact of science on traditional morality. The crisis of doubt, of the disorientation caused by a widespread questioning of creeds outworn, was a legitimate concern to Victorians, but Allingham's handling of it becomes painfully didactic. He treated the same issues more palatably in prose (see *Rambles*, "At Exeter," and "At Torquay"). "The Music Master," a tale about the tragic effects of prematurely severed love, suffers somewhat from sentimentality, but more so from lack of dramatic incident. Dante Gabriel Rossetti, who often asked Allingham for advice about his own poetry, wrote that "'The Music Master' is full of beauty and nobility, but I'm not sure it is not TOO noble or too resolutely healthy."

LAURENCE BLOOMFIELD IN IRELAND

The exception to this general awkwardness in the longer forms is *Laurence Bloomfield in Ireland*, which runs to nearly five thousand lines. Its fictionalized account of tenant-landlord relations provides a valuable sketch of economic and class struggles in rural Ireland a decade before the Land League and just before the first heated period of Fenian activity. The extreme right and extreme left are staked out by the reactionary landlords and the incendiary Ribbonmen respectively; the sensible, humane middle is occupied by Bloomfield (the ideal landlord) and the Dorans (the ideal peasant family). In outline form, the plot seems unpromisingly thin. Bloomfield, who has recently assumed control of his estate, is feeling his way cautiously into landlordism. He objects to the bigoted, self-servicing attitudes of the other landlords in the district, but as yet lacks the confidence to challenge the status quo. In addition, the secret societies are active in the district. Their activities, usually directed against the ruling class, range from the merely disruptive to the criminally violent. Neal Doran, a good lad, son of an aging tenant farmer, is drawn into the fringes of the insurgent movements. When he is arrested for fighting at a market fair, Pigot, the hardhearted agent for Bloomfield and other landlords, moves to evict the Dorans from the farm they had worked so hard to establish. It is then that Bloomfield acts decisively. Moved by the sight of the old man's grief, he dismisses Pigot, who is assassinated on his way home, and releases Doran. Time is telescoped in the latter section of the narrative: In the years to come, Bloomfield works hard at being the ideal landlord. He institutes revolutionary reforms, such as allowing tenants to buy their farms, and in general plays the enlightened, paternal ruler.

The poem's flaws are readily apparent. The lengthy coda, consisting of two whole books, seems tacked on, and occasionally a digression unnecessarily interrupts the flow of narrative. The poem was originally written under the pressure of monthly serial publication, which probably accounts for some of the structural flaws. After receiving proofs of book 12 from *Fraser's Magazine*, Allingham confided in *William Allingham*, "It's not properly compacted to plan, and never will be now." Another flaw is that Bloomfield, the central figure, is weakly drawn. The same might be said for the Dorans. Both are too pure to be believable. Nevertheless, a more pervasive and damaging problem is inconsistency in the quality of the verse.

The poem's strengths, however, far outweigh its weaknesses. In fact, virtually every modern critic writing on Allingham has given it high praise, particularly for its portraiture of Irish types and its many fine character sketches. The satiric portraits of the landlords in book 2 are worthy of Alexander Pope. A wide spectrum of types is surveyed, from the haughty aristocrat to the licentious absentee to the clever usurer who hides his exploitation behind a surface of unctuous piety. Less barbed but equally effective are the portraits of clergymen, especially Father John Adair. The poem is also strong in its close observation of Irish life. Depicting "every-day Irish affairs" was a "ticklish literary experiment" (preface, 1864 edition), but Allingham seems to have captured the essential fabric of life in his native Ballyshannon. To John Drinkwater, the poem is "second to none in the language as a description of peasant life and peasant nature" ("The Poetry of William Allingham," *New Ireland Review*, February, 1909). In this regard *Laurence Bloomfield in Ireland* is often compared to Oliver Goldsmith's "Deserted Village" and George Crabbe's "Borough." Allingham goes among the people, even into the most wretched hovel, showing their virtues and their vices. The description of the harvest fair in book 9 is alive with sights and sounds—the throngs of people, traders' disputes, beggars' blessings, the flourish of Her Majesty's recruiting party—a sort of poetic Irish version of William Powell Frith's *Derby Day* (1858).

Dealing with potentially flammable political material, Allingham strives for a precarious neutrality. Actually, however, this noncommittal position is a fusion of conservative and liberal elements. Allingham was not an advocate of home rule. He felt that Ireland did not yet have the political experience or the administrative skills to assume such responsibility. However, his advocacy of peasant proprietorship of land (or at least increased security of tenancy) puts him firmly in the liberal camp.

BLACKBERRIES PICKED OFF MANY BUSHES

After *Laurence Bloomfield in Ireland* and *Fifty Modern Poems*, the quality and quantity of Allingham's verse fall off sharply. Yeats and others have seen this atrophy as evidence that his Muse was essentially Irish. Undeniably, the only substantial, entirely new poetic work of the English period was *Blackberries Picked off Many Bushes*. Many of its aphorisms and short satiric rhymes are very good, but as a whole they lack brilliance, and it is likely that his reliance on abbreviated modes indicates a faltering confidence in the ability to create more ambitious poetry.

OTHER MAJOR WORKS

PLAY: *Ashby Manor*, pb. 1883.

NONFICTION: *Rambles*, 1873; *Varieties in Prose*, 1893 (3 volumes); *William Allingham: A Diary*, 1907.

BIBLIOGRAPHY

Cronin, Anthony. *Heritage Now: Irish Literature in the English Language*. New York: St. Martin's Press, 1983. An excellent, concise review of Allingham's life, work, and importance in the poetic canon. The significance of Allingham's Irish heritage and his love of London are well explained and vividly rendered. Cronin also includes assessments of Allingham's poetry by his contemporaries.

Howe, M. L. "Notes on the Allingham Canon." *Philological Quarterly* 12 (July, 1933): 290-297. Howe offers a distinctly personal critique of Allingham's work. He defends "The Fairies" from critics who labeled it hastily written, reveals the history behind "The Maids of Elfinmere," and untangles the relationships between Allingham, Dante Gabriel Rossetti, and William Morris. Howe also effectively argues the importance and grace of Allingham's overlooked dramas, essays, and short poems.

Hughes, Linda K. "The Poetics of Empire and Resistance: William Allingham's *Lawrence Bloomfield in Ireland*." *Victorian Poetry* 28, no. 2 (Summer, 1990): 103. Allingham's long narrative poem is discussed and analyzed in relation to the history of the English and the Irish peasants.

Husni, Samira Aghacy. "Incorrect References to William Allingham." *Notes and Queries* 30 (August, 1983): 296-298. An essential document for all Allingham scholars and students. Husni sets the record straight regarding common mistakes related to Allingham. These errors range from incorrect dates and titles of poems and books to generalizations about his poetry and relationships with contemporaries. Among those he finds guilty of errors are critics Katherine Tynan, Ifor Evans, and M. L. Howe.

Kavanagh, P. J. "Somewhat Surprising, Somewhat Surprised." *The Spectator* 283, no. 8941 (December 18, 1999): 71-72. A review of *William Allingham* with some biographical information about Allingham's relationship with Thomas Carlyle and Alfred, Lord Tennyson.

Quinn, Justin. *The Cambridge Introduction to Modern Irish Poetry, 1800-2000*. New York: Cambridge University Press, 2008. Provides an overview of the history and development of poetry in Ireland. Contains a chapter on Allingham, James Henry, and Samuel Ferguson.

Samuels Lasner, Mark. *William Allingham: A Biographical Study*. Philadelphia: Holmes, 1993. Samuels Lasner approaches Allingham by providing essential information with exceptionally rich notes on the production histories of the books, yet all this is presented in a humane style that serves as an excellent model of how to make an author bibliography both technically satisfactory and readable.

Warner, Allan. *William Allingham*. Lewisburg, Pa.: Bucknell University Press, 1975. Warner devotes his study to three aspects of Allingham: first, his narrative poem "Laurence Bloomfield in Ireland," second, his achievements as a lyric poet and writer of ballads and songs, and third, his prose as exemplified in *William Allingham*. In each of these areas, Warner illustrates Allingham's real powers of observation, imagination, and reflection.

Welch, Robert. *Irish Poetry from Moore to Yeats*. Totowa, N.J.: Barnes & Noble, 1980. Welch examines Allingham in the context of his contemporaries—such as Thomas Moore, Jeremiah Joseph Callanan, and James Clarence Mangan—and the Irish poetic tradition. He skillfully guides the reader toward an appreciation of Allingham's objectivity, love of common life, political common sense, appreciation of nature, and, most important to Welch, his warmth and humanity.

Michael Case

SAMUEL BECKETT

Born: Foxrock, near Dublin, Ireland; April 13, 1906
Died: Paris, France; December 22, 1989

PRINCIPAL POETRY
Whoroscope, 1930
Echo's Bones and Other Precipitates, 1935
Poems in English, 1961
Collected Poems in English and French, 1977

OTHER LITERARY FORMS

Samuel Beckett is far better known for his fiction and plays than for his poetry, even though it was as a poet that he began his writing career. In fact, Beckett explored almost every literary form, writing in English and in French. His early fiction, the collection of stories *More Pricks than Kicks* (1934) and the novels *Murphy* (1938) and *Watt* (1953), was written originally in English, but his best-known fiction, including the trilogy of *Molloy* (1951; English translation, 1955), *Malone meurt* (1951; *Malone Dies*, 1956), and *L'Innommable* (1953; *The Unnamable*, 1958), and *Comment c'est* (1961; *How It Is*, 1964) and *Le Dèpeupleur* (1971; *The Lost Ones*, 1972) were written and published originally in French. From the beginning, Beckett's greatest strength was as an innovator, writing prose works that do not seem to fit easily into traditional categories but instead extend the possibilities of contemporary fiction and have had a profound influence on the writers who have followed him.

Beckett was also a writer of plays, and when his name is mentioned, most people think of *En attendant Godot* (pb. 1952; *Waiting for Godot*, 1954). This difficult theatrical work met with astounding success on stages throughout the world, and it is still Beckett's best-known and most-discussed piece. Other works for the stage, *"Fin de partie," suivi de "Acte sans paroles"* (pr., pb. 1957; music by John Beckett; *Endgame: A Play in One Act, Followed by Act Without Words: A Mime for One Player*, 1958); *Krapp's Last Tape* (pr., pb. 1958), *Happy Days* (pr., pb. 1961), and *Rockaby* (pr., pb. 1981), to name only a few, have extended the possibilities of live theater. His *Collected Shorter Plays* was published in 1984.

Never content to restrict himself to a single medium, Beckett demonstrated that radio and television can serve as vehicles for serious drama with radio plays such as *All That Fall* (1957), *Cascando* (1963), and *Words and Music* (1962), and television scripts such as *Eh Joe* (1966; *Dis Joe*, 1967). Beckett also wrote the screenplay for the short movie *Film* (1965), produced and directed by Alan Schneider and starring Buster Keaton. Like the novels and the plays, these works for the mass media tapped new possibili-

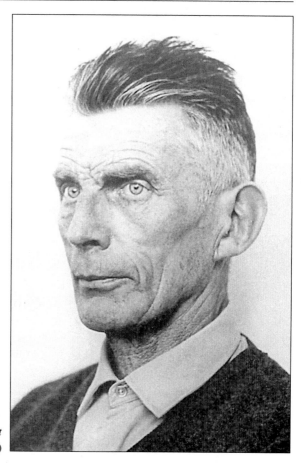

Samuel Beckett
(©The Nobel Foundation)

ties and pointed out new directions for younger writers.

Early in his career, Beckett also showed that he was a brilliant critic of the arts, writing on the fiction of James Joyce and Marcel Proust and on the paintings of his longtime friend Bram van Velde. In addition to translating his own works, he has translated those of other writers, including Robert Pinget, Paul Éluard, Alain Bosquet, and Sebastien Chamfort from the French and *An Anthology of Mexican Poetry* (1958) from the Spanish. His English version of Arthur Rimbaud's "Le Bateau ivre" (The Drunken Boat), done in the 1930's but lost for many years and rediscovered and published for the first time only in the 1977 *Collected Poems in English and French*, is masterful, but his best-known translation is of Guillaume Apollinaire's "Zone" (1972), a long poem that addresses many of Beckett's own themes and opens with a line that could well characterize Beckett's efforts in all forms: "In the end you are weary of this ancient world."

ACHIEVEMENTS

When the Swedish Academy selected Samuel Beckett to receive the Nobel Prize in Literature in 1969, the award only confirmed what critics and readers had known for some time: that he is one of the most important literary figures of the late twentieth century. Few authors in the history of literature have attracted as much critical attention as Beckett, and with good reason; he is both an important figure in his own right and a transitional thinker whose writings mark the end of modernism and the beginning of a new sensibility, postmodernism. The modernists of the early twentieth century—James Joyce, W. H. Auden, Virginia Woolf, Marcel Proust, and others—were stunned by the absurdity of their world. Previous generations had filled that world with philosophical, religious, and political meanings, but their orderly vision of reality no longer seemed to apply to life in the early twentieth century. The modernists lacked the faith of their forebears; they had experienced the chaos of the modern world with its potential for global war and the destruction of civilization, and they believed that the order of reality was a fiction, that life was unknowable. In response to their doubts, they turned literature in on itself, separating it from life, creating an art for its own sake. These writers trusted in language to create new meanings, new knowledge, and a separate, artistic human universe.

As a young man, Beckett also experienced this sense of absurdity and meaninglessness in the modern world, but unlike his modernist predecessors, he could not even muster faith in his art or in language. Thus, although Joyce could revel in the possibilities and textures of the written word, Beckett could not. Instead, he reduced his fictions, his plays, and his poems to the barest elements, and throughout his career, he tried to rejoin art and life in his own way. For the premodernists, art imitated the world beyond the human mind. The modernists rejected this idea of imitation, and so did Beckett. Instead, his art reflects the inner world, the world of the human voice, the only world human beings can ever really experience. In the premodern era, art was successful if it depicted some truth about the world. For the modernists, art succeeded only on its own terms, regardless of the world beyond the scope of the arts. For Beckett, art never succeeds. It is a necessary failure that never manages to link the inner mind to outer reality. As such, art is an exercise in courage, foredoomed to failure, like human life itself. Human beings are human beings not because they can give meaning to the world or because they can retreat into aesthetics but because they can recognize that their world is meaningless and that their lives are leading them only toward death; yet they must continue to live and strive. As a philosopher of failure, Beckett was the first thinker of the postmodern age.

BIOGRAPHY

Samuel Barclay Beckett grew up in a suburb of Dublin, Ireland, a Protestant in a Catholic country and therefore something of an exile in his own land. He attended Trinity College in Dublin, where he discovered his talent for languages and studied English,

French, and Italian. He taught for two terms at Campbell College in Belfast and then, in 1928, traveled to Paris, where he lectured in English at the ècole Normale Supèrieure. It was during this tenure that he met his countryman James Joyce. Beckett returned to Ireland to teach four terms at Trinity College, but in 1932, after much consideration and anguish, he left the teaching profession for good, convinced that he could not survive as a writer in academe. For the next five years, he wandered through Europe, and in 1937, he settled in Paris permanently. It was in Paris that Beckett died in 1989, at the age of eighty-three.

There were probably many reasons for Beckett's self-imposed exile and for his decision to write in a language not his by birth, but surely one reason was the influence of Joyce, who recommended exile for artists. It would be difficult to overestimate the effect that Joyce had on Beckett's life and work. In the late 1930's, the younger Irishman was an intimate member of Joyce's inner circle. He worked on a translation of Joyce's "Anna Livia Plurabelle" into French, took dictation for his friend, wrote a critical study of Joyce's writings, ran errands for the Irish master, and even attracted the romantic interest of Joyce's daughter, Lucia. Apparently, Joyce thought a great deal of Beckett, and Beckett looked on Joyce as a consummate master, so that it is possible he decided to write in French to avoid the language that, in his own mind, Joyce had all but exhausted.

As Beckett grew older and developed as a writer, Joyce's influence began to weaken, and in many ways, Beckett's later style—spare, flat, reduced to the barest elements—is the antithesis of Joyce's rich, punning, heavily textured prose. Beckett also rejected Joyce's "Irishness" in favor of characters and settings without specific nationality or history. In the early poetry, however, the influence of Joyce and Ireland is still strong, and, in fact, it was in his poems that Beckett first began to work through Joyce's voice and to discover his own.

ANALYSIS

Whoroscope was Samuel Beckett's first major publication. It is a long poem, written originally in English, and published in book form by Hours Press after winning a prize offered by the publisher for the best poem on the subject of time. The first-person narrator of the work is René Descartes, the seventeenth century French philosopher, mathematician, and scientist, and the poem is so full of obscure allusions to his life and times that, at the publisher's request, Beckett added a page and a half of notes to the ninety-eight-line piece. In fact, the notes are almost as interesting as the poem itself, and, without them, it is unlikely that the average reader would even recognize Descartes as the speaker.

WHOROSCOPE

Whoroscope is an important poem not only because it marked Beckett's official entry into the literary world but also because it introduced the basic themes that continued to occupy him as a writer and thinker. Clearly, Beckett himself recognized this fact, because he chose to keep this early work intact in the subsequent collections of his poetry, *Poems in English* and *Collected Poems in English and French*, which include all the works discussed here. In many ways, *Whoroscope* is quite unlike the author's later writings. The structure of the piece is open, without rhyme or regular meter. The poem shows the influence of the French surrealists in its associative juxtaposition of images, but the influence of Joyce is also apparent in the punning title and in the body of the text.

On first reading, it is not at all obvious that this is a poem about time. From the opening line, Descartes rambles on, apparently at random, about various events in his life, without respect for chronology or even historical accuracy. In the closing section, it becomes clear that the philosopher is on his deathbed and that his ramblings are the result of illness and fever. In a sense, his life is flashing before his eyes. He is trying to grasp the fullness of time at the moment of his death, and a closer reading shows that the sequence of memories is not random at all but associative, each a memory leading to the next—not in chronological order but in the order dictated by Descartes's subjective thought process.

In fact, the poem is very much about time—the time of a man's life and the attempt to recapture lost time in the instant before time runs out. The Joycean influence in Descartes's stream-of-consciousness narrative is evident, but it is also obvious that Beckett has learned a great deal from Marcel Proust's *À la recherche du temps perdu* (1913-1927; *Remembrance of Things Past*, 1922-1931), which the young Beckett knew well—so well, in fact, that in 1931 he published *Proust*, a book-length study of this French masterwork.

Whoroscope, then, is about time as the great destroyer, time that eats up a man's life and leads only to death. It is important to remember, however, that this poem is about the lifetime of a particular man, Descartes, and there is good reason for Beckett's choice of this philosopher as his narrator. Like Beckett himself, Descartes was a transitional figure, the founder of modern philosophy and the opponent of Aristotelian scholasticism. He and his contemporaries initiated a new age in Western civilization, and in his poem, Beckett pays tribute to other great thinkers such as Galileo and Francis Bacon, who directed Western thought into the era of science and rationalism.

Descartes was a great builder, but he was also a great destroyer of the philosophies of the past, and in the poem, he speaks with pride of "throwing/ Jesuits out of the skylight." He devoted his life to the development of a new system of thought, but, in so doing, he also undermined the Aristotelian metaphysics that had served as the basis of European philosophy for centuries. Ironically, while Descartes was destroying his predecessors, the time of his own life was destroying him.

This is one of the key themes of Beckett's work: the fact that death comes to all living things, without reason, without justice, regardless of whether one is innocent or guilty. As Beckett writes in a later, untitled poem, humanity lives "the space of a door/ that opens and shuts." Humans are born to die; they are dying even in the womb, losing time from the moment of conception, and there is nothing that can stop or even delay this process. Each person's life cancels itself, moment by moment.

The historical Descartes died while in the service of Queen Christina of Sweden, who forced the aging philosopher to call on her at five o'clock each morning although he had been in the habit of staying in bed until midday all his life. This change in his routine, coupled with the northern weather, led to his final illness. In the poem, the fictional Descartes refers to Queen Christina as "Rahab of the snows." Rahab was a biblical harlot mentioned in *La divina commedia* (c. 1320, 3 volumes; *The Divine Comedy*, 1802) of Dante (whom Beckett has called the only poet), and so it would seem that the queen is the "whore" of the title. In his notes to the poem, Beckett points out that Descartes kept his birthday a secret so that no astrologer could cast his horoscope. The philosopher was opposed to such mysticism, not only because it was unscientific but also because he felt that many people let their entire lives be dictated by astrology; he even knew of two young men who had allowed themselves to die simply because their horoscopes had predicted death for them. With this knowledge, the Joycean pun of the title becomes clear. Queen Christina, the harlot, has cast Descartes's death, which was present from the moment of his birth. His "whoroscope" is her prediction of his inevitable end.

This theme of the inevitability of death, of death as a necessary function of birth, runs through the poem in the form of a recurring motif. Again in the notes, Beckett explains that Descartes liked his morning omelette to be made from eggs that had been hatched from eight to ten days—that is, eggs in which the embryo was partially developed. Time and again in the poem he asks about his morning eggs: "How long did she womb it, the feathery one? . . . How rich she smells,/ this abortion of a fledgling!"

For Beckett, the egg is the symbol of the fetus conceived only to die, its brief span of life lived out in the instant between nonexistence and nonexistence. The time of the egg is the time of the philosopher as well. As with all human beings, Descartes is dying before he has even really lived, and like the fledgling in the egg, he is dying for no purpose, simply because that is the way things are.

Beckett explored the themes of the inevitability of death and the meaninglessness of life time and again in his works, but he has always coupled these themes with another: the necessity of going on, of raging against the inevitable, of refusing to accept humanity's fate. In the poem "Serena III," he insists that human beings must "keep on the move/ keep on the move," and in *Whoroscope*, he depicts Descartes first as angry, cursing his fate, then as begging for another chance at a life he has never managed to understand, a "second/ starless inscrutable hour." There is no reason for him to go on, and yet, as a human being, he must.

For Beckett, humans must die, but they must also live and think and speak, as Descartes does, even to the last possible instant. They must live in their own inner world, which is always dying, and they must also live in the outer world, which will live on after them and which, therefore, is not theirs. This theme of the conflict between the inner and the outer worlds that runs through Beckett's later work is present in *Whoroscope* as well. The very structure of the poem, which follows the philosopher's associative thinking, places the narrative within Descartes's inner mind, though in the end it moves to the outer world, to "Christina the ripper" and to her court physician, Weulles, who is attending to Descartes in his last moments. In his inner world, Descartes is alive and reliving his past, but it is the outer world that is leading him to inevitable death. Descartes devoted his life to trying to understand the outer world, but the very foundation of his thought, the dictum *Cogito, ergo sum* ("I think, therefore I am") trapped him within his own subjectivity, and generations of later philosophers have tried to understand how one can move from the certainty of the *cogito* to the world beyond which is not oneself. The *cogito*, the single point of certainty in the Cartesian philosophy of doubt, is the fulcrum of modern Western philosophy, and yet it restricts thinkers to their own inner worlds, to what Beckett calls, in his poem "The Vulture," "the sky/ of my skull."

For Beckett, it is impossible for humanity to come to know the world beyond the skull, that very world in which people must live and die. In the play *Endgame*, the characters Hamm and Clov live within a skull-like structure; Hamm is blind, and Clov can see the world only through two eyelike windows that restrict his vision. In the short novel *The Lost Ones*, an entire society lives and passes away within a huge white dome, a skull. In *Whoroscope*, Descartes can know his inner world, but the outer world remains "inscrutable." He knows that he thinks and, therefore, that he is, but he does not know why. He wants to know the truth and to speak it, but the *cogito* cannot lead him to knowledge of the outer world. In the poem, he mentions Saint Augustine, who also sought a single point of certainty in a world in which everything was open to question and found that the only thing he could be sure of was that he could be deceived. The Descartes of the poem states the Augustinian dictum as "Fallor, ergo sum!" ("I am deceived, therefore I am"). At the moment of death, this certainty seems truer to the philosopher than his own *cogito*. To be a human is to be deceived, to fail, and, for a human being, courage is the courage to fail. Humans are human only insofar as they know that failure is inevitable and yet keep going in spite of that knowledge.

ECHO'S BONES AND OTHER PRECIPITATES

Another important Beckett theme surfaces only briefly in *Whoroscope* but becomes the main focus of the author's second collection of poems, *Echo's Bones and Other Precipitates*: the theme of the impossibility of love in the face of absurdity and death. For Beckett, love is another of humankind's basic needs, as important as the quest for meaning, and as futile. The Descartes poem touched on the theme only briefly, in the philosopher's memory of a little cross-eyed girl who was his childhood playmate and who reminds him of his only daughter, Francine, who died of scarlet fever at the age of six. The implication is that love always ends, if not now, then later; and, like the rest of life, love is both essential and hopeless, necessary and frightening. Knowing that love is impossible, pretending that it is not, humanity loves, and that love is the source of human pain but also of human life.

The poems of *Echo's Bones and Other Precipitates* differ from *Whoroscope* not only because they focus on love but also because the narrator is not a fictional version of a historical character but the author himself. The title of the collection comes from Ovid's *Metamorphoses* (c. 8 C.E.; English translation, 1567), from the story of Echo, who, after being spurned by Narcissus, lets herself wither away until only her bones and voice remain. The connection between Ovid's tale and Beckett's theme of love is clear, but the story of Echo also provides the poet with two of his favorite images: the inevitability of death and the survival of the voice.

Most of the titles and forms of the poems in this collection are based on the songs of the troubadours, which Beckett knew well and which attracted him no doubt because they were songs of love and, often, of loss, and also because the troubadours were usually wanderers and exiles, like Beckett himself and like the narrators of most of these poems. The work "Enueg I" draws its title from the traditional Provençal lament or complaint, and as might be expected, it is a complaint of love. In the poem, the narrator leaves the nursing home where his beloved is dying of tuberculosis ("Exeo in a spasm/ tired of my darling's red sputum") and wanders through Dublin, traveling in a wide circle. He finds that the world is full of images of death ("a dying barge," "the stillborn evening," "the tattered sky like an ink of pestilence") and that he cannot forget his beloved or the fate of their love. Of course, these signs of death are not really present in the outer world; they reflect the narrator's inner life, the only life he can know, and, like Descartes, he rages against what he knows to be true as his own blood forms a "clot of anger."

There is no romance in Beckett's lament, only the all-encompassing awareness of mortality. Love and romance are like "the silk of the seas and the arctic flowers/ that do not exist," figments of the imagination that lose all sense of reality in the face of "the banner of meat bleeding."

The narrator keeps moving, however, and throughout the poem he has contact with others, with a small boy and "a wearish old man," an archetypal Beckett character, "scuttling along between a crutch and a stick,/ his stump caught up horribly, like a claw, under his breech, smoking." These meetings show the continuing possibility of human contact, even in a dying world; they also make clear the need for going on even in the face of futility. Perhaps the others, like the narrator, are also moving in circles, but circular movement is still movement, and even the old man, crippled and in pain, does not remain motionless, does not give up.

"Sanies I" is also modeled on a Provençal form; the title is derived from a Latin term meaning "morbid discharge." For Beckett, writing is such a discharge, a residue, a "precipitate." It is a by-product of living and dying, but it is also that which remains, like Echo's voice.

Like the narrator of "Enueg I," the narrator of "Sanies I" is a wanderer in the process of completing a circle; in this case, he is returning home to Ireland after traveling in Europe, apparently in Germany, for his speech is full of Germanic terms. Like later Beckett protagonists, he rides a bicycle, and he describes himself as "a Ritter," a German knight, and, therefore, a somewhat ironic hero, though perhaps the only kind of hero who remains in the postmodern age: the hero who keeps moving. He has been wandering for a long time, and he says that he is "müüüüüüüüde now." The German "müde" means "tired," but the extended "ü" sound also gives a sense of boredom, an essential element in most of Beckett's work. Clearly, the narrator is both tired and bored, and, as a result, he is "bound for home like a good boy." Thinking about home and his parents, he recalls his birth and longs for that sweet oblivion of the womb: "Ah to be back in the caul now with no trusts/ no fingers no spoilt love."

This is a key passage. "The caul" to which the narrator would like to return is a fetal membrane covering the head, and according to folklore, the child who is born with a caul is born to good luck. The implication here, however, is that the best of luck is never to have been born at all and, therefore, to have avoided "trusts" and "spoilt loves," those exercises in futility. The unborn child also has "no fingers," and one without fingers cannot, and therefore need not, travel on a bicycle as the narrator does. Even better, one without fingers cannot write, no matter how strongly he might feel the need to do so.

Of course, the narrator no longer has the option of not being born. He is "tired now hair ebbing gums ebbing ebbing home," and yet he approaches his hometown like a "Stürmer," German slang for "lady-killer." It would seem that, despite his "spoilt loves," he is prepared for love again, and indeed, he sees his beloved waiting for him. "I see main verb at last/ her whom alone in the accusative/ I have dismounted to love." In German, the "main verb" comes at the end of the sentence, and in this sentence that word is "love." At the last moment, however, the narrator sends the girl away ("get along with you now"), refusing to make the mistake his parents made by bringing another being into the world. Although one cannot return to the peace of the womb, one can at least refuse to pass on the curse of life to another.

If "Sanies I" is about nonexistence in the womb (the Cartesian egg), and if "Enueg I" is about nonexistence in the tomb, the title poem of the collection brings these two notions together. "Echo's Bones" is a short lyric that restates Beckett's key themes in capsule form. The first word of the poem is "asylum," a reference to the womb, but this is an "asylum under my tread," a shelter underground, a tomb. Like those in the womb, those in the tomb are beyond the confusions and pains of living now that they have run the gauntlet of life, "the gantelope of sense and nonsense." Only now, in death, are they free to be themselves, "taken by the maggots for what they are," and what they are is fleshless bone, without love or dreams and without the need to keep striving. The title of the poem, however, is a reminder that something more than bone remains: the voice. The words may be only a "morbid discharge," but, like Echo's voice, they survive.

"SOMETHING THERE"

Leaping ahead four decades to "Something There," a poem composed in 1974, the reader finds that the author's voice has changed, although his key themes remain. Here the lines are short and direct, flat and prosaic. There are no obscure allusions, no Joycean puns. The "something there" of the title is "something outside/ the head," and this contrast of inner and outer worlds returns the reader to *Whoroscope* and to the Cartesian dilemma of subjectivity that cannot reach beyond itself. The poem tries to reach that "something" in the only way it can, through words, but "at the faint sound so brief/ it is gone." The reality beyond the inner mind disappears as soon as the words of the mind try to grasp it, and so language, in the end, describes only the inner world, which becomes something like a womb and a tomb in the midst of life. The inner world is not life, and although humanity cannot reach beyond its inner self to comprehend the "something outside/ the head," still it must try to do so, and the sign of its failure is language, the voice that always remains.

One can argue that Beckett's view of existence is largely negative. However, it is important to remember that he was influenced greatly by the medieval theologians who argued that truth, in the person of God, is beyond positive statement and that humankind can know the truth only in the negative, by describing what it is not. Beckett seems to have taken the same approach. It is true that he wrote about the curse of life, but he did so beautifully, raging against the inevitability of silence. The beauty of his work is the beauty of the human will to live in the face of death. Beckett sings the praises of those who say, with the nameless, formless, faceless narrator of *The Unnamable*, "I can't go on, I'll go on."

OTHER MAJOR WORKS

LONG FICTION: *Murphy*, 1938; *Malone meurt*, 1951 (*Malone Dies*, 1956); *Molloy*, 1951 (English translation, 1955); *L'Innommable*, 1953 (*The Unnamable*, 1958); *Watt*, 1953; *Comment c'est*, 1961 (*How It Is*, 1964); *Mercier et Camier*, 1970 (*Mercier and Camier*, 1974); *Le Dépeupleur*, 1971 (*The Lost Ones*, 1972); *Company*, 1980; *Mal vu mal dit*, 1981 (*Ill Seen Ill Said*, 1981); *Worstward Ho*, 1983.

SHORT FICTION: *More Pricks than Kicks*, 1934; *Nouvelles et textes pour rien*, 1955 (*Stories and Texts for Nothing*, 1967); *No's Knife: Prose, 1947-1966*, 1967; *First Love, and Other Shorts*, 1974; *Pour finir encore et autres foirades*, 1976 (*Fizzles*, 1976; also known as *For to Yet Again*, 1976); *Four Novellas*, 1977 (also known as *The Expelled, and Other Novellas*, 1980); *Collected Short Prose*, 1991.

PLAYS: *En attendant Godot*, pb. 1952 (*Waiting for Godot*, 1954); *"Fin de partie,"* suivi de *"Acte sans paroles,"* pr., pb. 1957 (music by John Beckett; *"Endgame: A Play in One Act,"* Followed by *"Act Without Words: A Mime for One Player,"* 1958); *Krapp's Last Tape*, pr., pb. 1958; *Act Without Words II*, pr., pb. 1960 (one-act mime); *Happy Days*, pr., pb. 1961; *Play*, pr., pb. 1963 (English translation, 1964); *Come and Go: Dramaticule*, pr., pb. 1965 (one scene; English translation, 1967); *Not I*, pr. 1972;

Ends and Odds, pb. 1976; *Footfalls*, pr., pb. 1976; *That Time*, pr., pb. 1976; *A Piece of Monologue*, pr., pb. 1979; *Ohio Impromptu*, pr., pb. 1981; *Rockaby*, pr., pb. 1981; *Catastrophe*, pr. 1982; *Company*, pr. 1983; *Plays*, pb. 1984; *Complete Dramatic Works*, 1986; *Eleutheria*, pb. 1995.

SCREENPLAY: *Film*, 1965.

TELEPLAYS: *Eh Joe*, 1966 (*Dis Joe*, 1967); *Tryst*, 1976; *Shades*, 1977; *Quad*, 1981.

RADIO PLAYS: *All That Fall*, 1957, 1968; *Embers*, 1959; *Words and Music*, 1962 (music by John Beckett); *Cascando*, 1963 (music by Marcel Mihalovici).

NONFICTION: *Proust*, 1931; *The Letters of Samuel Beckett: Vol. 1, 1929-1940*, 2009 (Martha Dow Fehsenfeld and Lois More Overbeck, editors).

TRANSLATION: *An Anthology of Mexican Poetry*, 1958 (Octavio Paz, editor).

MISCELLANEOUS: *I Can't Go On, I'll Go On: A Selection from Samuel Beckett's Work*, 1976 (Richard Seaver, editor).

BIBLIOGRAPHY

Bair, Deirdre. *Samuel Beckett: A Biography*. 1978. Reprint. New York: Simon & Schuster, 1993. Although Beckett was often reluctant to talk about himself, he cooperated with Bair. It is the fullest, most helpful version of his life in print, and to know his life is to understand his art. The criticism of the specific texts is often limited, but Bair is very good at putting the work in conjunction with Beckett's very odd life.

Birkett, Jennifer, and Kate Ince, eds. *Samuel Beckett*. New York: Longman, 2000. A collection of criticism of Beckett's works. Bibliography and index.

Brater, Enoch. *The Essential Samuel Beckett: An Illustrated Biography*. New York: Thames & Hudson, 2003. A general biography of Beckett that provides information on how his life affected his works.

Carey, Phyllis, and Ed Jewinski, eds. *Re: Joyce'n Beckett*. New York: Fordham University Press, 1992. This collection of essays examines the relationship between Joyce and Beckett.

Cronin, Anthony. *Samuel Beckett: The Last Modernist*. New York: HarperCollins, 1996. A fully documented and detailed biography of Beckett, describing his involvement in the Paris literary scene, his response to winning the Nobel Prize, and his overall literary career.

Kenner, Hugh. *Reader's Guide to Samuel Beckett*. Syracuse, N.Y.: Syracuse University Press, 1996. Kenner, a well-known commentator on Beckett, places Beckett in the Irish tradition and assesses his part in the movement of experimental literature.

Knowlson, James. *Damned to Fame: The Life of Samuel Beckett*. New York: Simon & Schuster, 1996. A comprehensive biography with much new material, detailed notes, and bibliography.

McDonald, Ronan. *Samuel Beckett: The Life and the Work*. Dublin: Dublin Stationery Office, 2005. A general biography of Beckett that looks at his literary works.

Pattie, David. *The Complete Critical Guide to Samuel Beckett.* New York: Routledge, 2000. A reference volume that combines biographical information with critical analysis of Beckett's literary works. Bibliography and index.

Pilling, John, ed. *The Cambridge Companion to Beckett.* New York: Cambridge University Press, 1994. A comprehensive reference work that provides considerable information about the life and works of Beckett. Bibliography and indexes.

Welch D. Everman

EAVAN BOLAND

Born: Dublin, Ireland; September 24, 1944

PRINCIPAL POETRY

Twenty-three Poems, 1962
New Territory, 1967
The War Horse, 1975
In Her Own Image, 1980
Introducing Eavan Boland, 1981 (reprint of *The War Horse* and *In Her Own Image*)
Night Feed, 1982
The Journey, and Other Poems, 1983
Selected Poems, 1989
Outside History: Selected Poems, 1980-1990, 1990
In a Time of Violence, 1994
Collected Poems, 1995 (pb. in U.S. as *An Origin Like Water: Collected Poems, 1967-1987*, 1996)
The Lost Land, 1998
Against Love Poetry, 2001
Code, 2001
Three Irish Poets, 2003 (with Paula Meehan and Mary O'Malley; Boland, editor)
New Collected Poems, 2005
Domestic Violence, 2007
New Collected Poems, 2008

OTHER LITERARY FORMS

Eavan Boland (BOW-lahnd) collaborated with Micheál Mac Liammóir on the critical study *W. B. Yeats and His World* (1971). Boland has contributed essays in journals such as the *American Poetry Review*; she also has reviewed for the *Irish Times* and has published a volume of prose called *Object Lessons: The Life of the Woman and the Poet in Our Time* (1995). With Mark Strand, she prepared the anthology *The Making of a Poem: A Norton Anthology of Poetic Forms* (2000).

ACHIEVEMENTS

Ireland has produced a generation of distinguished poets since 1960, and the most celebrated of them have been men. Of this group of poets, Seamus Heaney is the best known to American audiences, but the reputations of Thomas Kinsella, Derek Mahon, Michael Longley, Paul Muldoon, and Tom Paulin continue to grow. Poetry by contemporary Irishwomen is also a significant part of the Irish literary scene. Eavan Boland is one of a group of notable women poets including Medbh McGuckian, Eithne Strong, and Eiléan Ní Chuilleanáin. In an essay published in 1987, "The Woman Poet: Her Dilemma," Boland indicates her particular concern with the special problems of being a woman and a poet. Male stereotypes about the role of women in society continue to be very strong in Ireland and make Irishwomen less confident about their creative abilities. Women also must contend with another potentially depersonalizing pressure, that of feminist ideology, which urges women toward another sort of conformity. Boland and the other female Irish poets previously mentioned have managed to overcome both obstacles and develop personal voices.

Boland has served as a member of the board of the Irish Arts Council and a member of the Irish Academy of Letters. Her honors and awards include the American Ireland Fund Literary Award (1994), the Lannan Literary Award for Poetry (1994), the Bucknell Medal of Distinction from Bucknell University (2000), the Smartt Family Foundation Prize for *Against Love Poetry*, the John Frederick Nims Memorial Prize from *Poetry* magazine (2002), the John William Corrington Award for Literary Excellence from Centenary College of Louisiana (2002-2003), and the James Boatwright III Prize for Poetry from *Shenandoah* (2006) for "Violence Against Women."

BIOGRAPHY

Eavan Boland was born on September 24, 1944, in Dublin, Ireland. Her parents were Frederick Boland and Frances Kelly Boland. Her father was a distinguished Irish diplomat who served as Irish ambassador to Great Britain (1950-1956) and to the United States (1956-1964). Her mother was a painter who had studied in Paris in the 1930's. Boland's interest in painting as a subject for poetry can be traced to her mother's encouragement. Because of her father's diplomatic career, Boland was educated in Dublin, London, and New York. From 1962 to 1966, she attended Trinity College, Dublin; beginning in 1967, she taught at Trinity College for a year. In 1968, she received the Macauley Fellowship for poetry.

In the 1980's, Boland reviewed regularly for the arts section of the *Irish Times*. In 1987, she held a visiting fellowship at Bowdoin College. She married Kevin Casey, a novelist, with whom she had two children: Sarah, born in 1975, and Eavan, born in 1978.

Boland began writing poetry in Dublin in the early 1960's. She recalls this early period: ". . . scribbling poems in boarding school, reading [William Butler] Yeats after lights out, revelling in the poetry on the course. . . . Dublin was a coherent space then, a small circumference in which to . . . become a poet. . . . The last European city. The last literary smallholding." After her marriage, Boland left the academic world and moved into the suburbs of Dublin to become "wife, mother, and housewife." *In Her Own Image* and *Night Feed* focus on Boland's domestic life in the suburbs and especially on her sense of womanhood. In the 1990's, Boland taught at several universities in the United

States. In 1995, she became a professor at Stanford University, where she has served as Bella Mabury and Eloise Mabury Knapp Professor in the Humanities as well as the Melvin and Bill Lane Professor and chair of the creative writing program.

ANALYSIS

Hearth and history provide a context for the poetry of Eavan Boland. She is inspired by both the domestic and the cultural. Her subjects are the alienating suburban places that encourage people to forget their cultural roots, her children with their typically Irish names, demystified horses in Dublin streets that can still evoke the old glories from time to time, and the old Irish stories themselves, which at times may be vivid and evocative and at others may be nostalgic in nature. Boland's distinctly female perspective is achieved in several poems about painting that note the dominance of male painters—such as Jan van Eyck, Edgar Degas, Jean Auguste Dominique Ingres, and Pierre-Auguste Renoir—in the history of art from the Renaissance to the Impressionists. Women were painted by these artists in traditional domestic or agrarian postures. Boland perceives women as far less sanitized and submissive. Her collection *In Her Own Image* introduces such taboo subjects as anorexia, mastectomy, masturbation, and menstruation.

NIGHT FEED

Two of Boland's works, *In Her Own Image* and *Night Feed*, deal exclusively with the subject of women. *Night Feed* for the most part examines suburban women and positively chronicles the daily routine of a Dublin homemaker. The book has poems about diapers, washing machines, and feeding babies. The cover has an idyllic drawing of a mother feeding a child. However, *In Her Own Image*, published two years before *Night Feed*, seems written by a different person. Its candid and detailed treatment of taboo subjects contrasts sharply with the idyllic world of *Night Feed*. Boland's ability to present both worlds testifies to her poetic maturity.

The need for connection is a major theme in Boland's poetry. Aware of traditional connections in Irish and classical myths, she longs for an earlier period when such ties came instinctively. Her sense of loss with respect to these traditional connections extends beyond mythology to Irish history as well, even to Irish history in the twentieth century. Modern-day Dubliners have been cut off from the sustaining power of myth and history. Their lives, therefore, seem empty and superficial. Surrounded with the shards of a lost culture, they cannot piece these pieces together into a coherent system.

The alienation of modern urban Irish people from their cultural roots is the subject of Boland's "The New Pastoral" (from *Night Feed*). She considers alienation from a woman's perspective. Aware of the myths that have traditionally sustained males, Boland desires equivalent myths for females. She longs for a "new pastoral" that will celebrate women's ideals, but she finds none. She encounters many domestic "signs," but they do not "signify" for her. She has a vague sense of once having participated in a coherent ritual, of having "danced once/ on a frieze." Now, however, she has no access to the myth. Men seem to have easier access to their cultural roots than women do. The legends of the cavemen contain flint, fire, and wheel, which allowed man "to read his world." Later in history, men had pastoral poems to define and celebrate their place in the world. A woman has no similar defining and consoling rituals and possesses no equivalent cultural signs. She seems a "displaced person/ in a pastoral chaos," unable to create a "new pastoral." Surrounded by domestic signs, "lamb's knuckle," "the washer," "a stink/ of nappies," "the greasy/ bacon flitch," she still has no access to myth. Hints of connection do not provide a unified myth:

> I feel
> there was a past,
> there was a pastoral
> and these
> chance sights—
> what are they all
> but late amnesias
> of a rite
> I danced once
> on a frieze?

The final image of the dancer on the frieze echoes both John Keats's Grecian urn and William Butler Yeats's dancers and golden bird. The contemporary poet, however, has lost contact. Paradoxically, the poem constitutes the "new pastoral," which it claims is beyond its reach. The final allusion to the dancer on the frieze transforms the mundane objects of domestic life into something more significant, something sacred.

Boland seems in conflict over whether women should simply conform to male stereotypes for women or should resist these pressures to lead "lesser lives," to attend to "hearth not history." Many poems in *Night Feed* accept this "lesser" destiny, poems such as "Night Feed," "Hymn," and "In the Garden." The several poems in this volume that deal with paintings, "Domestic Interior," "Fruit on a Straight-Sided Tray," "Degas's Laundresses," "Woman Posing (After Ingres)," "On Renoir's *The Grape-Pickers*," all deal with paintings by male painters that portray women in traditional domestic or rural roles. The women in these paintings appear content with their "lesser lives." Poems such as "It's a Woman's World" seem less accepting, however, more in the spirit of *In Her Own Image*, which vigorously rejects basing one's identity on male stereotypes. "It's a Woman's World" complements "The New Pastoral" in its desire for a balance between hearth and history.

> as far as history goes
> we were never
> on the scene of the crime. . . .

And still no page
scores the low music
of our outrage.

Women have had no important roles in history, Boland asserts. They produce "low music," rather than heroic music. Nevertheless, women can have an intuitive connection with their own "starry mystery," their own cosmic identity. The women in those paintings, apparently pursuing their "lesser lives," may have a sense of "greater lives." The male world (including male artists) must be kept in the dark about this, must keep believing that nothing mythic is being experienced.

That woman there,
craned to the starry mystery
is merely getting a breath
of evening air,
while this one here—
her mouth
a burning plume—
she's no fire-eater,
just my frosty neighbour
coming home.

IN HER OWN IMAGE

The "woman's world" and the "starry mysteries" are presented far less romantically in *In Her Own Image*. The poems in this volume refuse to conform to male stereotypes of woman as happy domestic partner. They explore male-female conflicts in the deepest and most intimate psychic places. The title *In Her Own Image* indicates the volume's concern with the problem of identity. Boland wishes to be an individual, free to determine her own life, but other forces seek to control her, to make her conform to female stereotypes. A woman should be perfect, unchanging, youthful, pure—in short, she should be ideal. Male-dominated society does not wish women to explore their own deepest desires. Women transform these social messages into the voice of their own consciences, or, in Sigmund Freud's terms, their own superegos: "Thou shalt not get fat!" "Thou shalt not get old!" "Thou shalt not get curious."

These naysaying inner voices dominate the first three poems of *In Her Own Image*: "Tirade for the Mimic Muse," "In Her Own Image," and "In His Own Image." The "mimic muse" in the first poem urges the speaker to "make up," to conceal aging with cosmetics. The illustration for this poem shows a chubby and unkempt woman gazing into a mirror and seeing a perfect version of herself—thin, unwrinkled, and physically fit. The phrase "her own image" in the second poem refers to another idealization, the "image" of perfection that the speaker carries around inside herself. She finally frees herself from this psychic burden by planting the image outside in the garden. The illustration shows a naked woman bending over a small coffin.

The third poem, "In His Own Image," considers the pressures of a husband's expectations on a wife's sense of self. The speaker in this third poem does not try to reshape her features with makeup. She is battered into a new shape by a drunken husband. No illustration appears with this poem.

The speaker's "tirade" in "Tirade for the Mimic Muse" begins at once and establishes the intensely hostile tone of much of *In Her Own Image*: "I've caught you out. You slut. You fat trout." She despises the impulse in herself to conform to a stereotype, to disguise the physical signs of time passing: "the lizarding of eyelids," "the whiskering of nipples," and "the slow betrayals of our bedroom mirrors." In the final section of the poem, the authentic self has suppressed those conforming impulses: "I, who mazed my way to womanhood/ Through all your halls of mirrors, making faces." Now the mirror's glass is cracked. The speaker promises a true vision of the world, but the vision will not be idyllic: "I will show you true reflections, terrors." Terrors preoccupy Boland for much of this book.

"In Her Own Image" and "In His Own Image" deal with different aspects of the "perfect woman." The first poem has a much less hostile tone than does "Tirade for the Mimic Muse." The speaker seems less threatened by the self-image from which she wishes to distance herself. Images of gold and amethyst and jasmine run through the poem. Despite the less hostile tone, Boland regards this "image" as a burdensome idealization that must be purged for psychic health: "She is not myself/ anymore." The speaker plants this "image" in the garden outside: "I will bed her,/ She will bloom there," safely removed from consciousness. The poem "In His Own Image" is full of anxiety. The speaker cannot find her center, her identity. Potential signs of identity lie all around her, but she cannot interpret them:

> Celery feathers, . . .
> bacon flitch, . . .
> kettle's paunch, . . .
> these were all I had to go on, . . .
> meagre proofs of myself.

A drunken husband responds to his wife's identity crisis by pounding her into his own desired "shape."

> He splits my lip with his fist,
> shadows my eye with a blow,
> knuckles my neck to its proper angle.
> What a perfectionist!
> His are a sculptor's hands:
> they summon
> form from the void,

they bring
me to myself again.
I am a new woman.

How different are these two methods of coping with psychic conflict. In "In Her Own Image," the speaker plants her old self lovingly in the garden. In "In His Own Image," the drunken husband reshapes his wife's features with violent hands. The wife in the second poem says that she is now a "new woman." If one reads this volume as a single poem, as Boland evidently intends that one should (all the illustrations have the same person as their subject), one understands that the desperate tone of other poems in the book derives from the suffering of this reshaped "new woman," a victim of male exploitation.

The next four poems of *In Her Own Image* deal with very private subjects familiar to women but not often treated in published poems: anorexia, mastectomy, masturbation, and menstruation. Both the poems and Constance Hart's drawings are startlingly frank. The poet wants readers to experience "woman" in a more complete way, to realize the dark side of being female. The poems further illustrate Boland's sense of alienation from cultural myths or myths of identity. She desires connections, but she knows that she is unlikely to have them. She is therefore left with images that signify chaos rather than coherence, absence rather than presence, emptiness rather than fullness.

Two of the four poems, "Anorexia" and "Mastectomy," read like field reports from the battle of the sexes. The other two poems, "Solitary" and "Menses," have a female perspective but are also full of conflict. In the illustrations for "Anorexia," a very determined and extremely thin naked woman, arms folded, looks disapprovingly at a fat woman lolling on a couch. An anorectic woman continues to believe that she is fat, despite being a virtual skeleton. Boland introduces a religious level in the first three lines: "Flesh is heretic./ My body is a witch./ I am burning it." The conviction that her body is a witch runs through the whole poem. Here, in an extreme form, is the traditional Roman Catholic view that soul and body are separate. The body must be punished because since the Fall, it has been the dwelling place of the devil. The soul must suppress the body in order for the soul to be saved. This tradition provides the anorectic with a religious reason for starving herself. In this poem, she revels in the opportunity to "torch" her body: "Now the bitch is burning." A presence even more disturbing than the witch is introduced in the second half of the poem, a ghostly male presence whom the anorectic speaker desires to please. To please this unnamed male presence, the speaker must become thin, so thin that she can somehow return to the womb imagined here paradoxically as male: "I will slip/ back into him again/ as if I had never been away." This return to the male womb will atone for the sin of being born a woman, with "hips and breasts/ and lips and heat/ and sweat and fat and greed."

In "Mastectomy," male-female conflict predominates. Male surgeons, envious of a woman's breasts (an effective transformation of the male-centered Freudian paradigm), cut off a breast and carry it away with them. The shocking drawing shows one gowned male surgeon passing the breast on a serving dish to another gowned male surgeon. The woman who has experienced this physical and psychological violation cries despairingly "I flatten to their looting." The sympathetic words of the surgeon before the operation belie the sinister act of removing the breast. It can now become part of male fantasy, as a symbol of primal nourishment and primal home:

> So they have taken off
> what slaked them first,
> what they have hated since:
> blue-veined
> white-domed
> home
> of wonder
> and the wetness
> of their dreams.

The next two poems, "Solitary" and "Menses," deal with equally private aspects of a woman's life, autoeroticism and menstruation. "Solitary" has a celebratory attitude toward self-arousal. The drawing shows a relaxed naked female figure lying on her stomach. Religious imagery is used in this poem as it is in "Anorexia," but here the body is worshiped rather than feared. The only negative aspect of "Solitary" is its solitude. The female speaker is unconnected with another person. Solitary pleasures are intense but less so than the pleasures of intercourse. The reader is taken on a journey from arousal to orgasm to postorgasmic tranquility. The religious language at first seems gratuitous but then perfectly appropriate. The speaker affirms the holiness of her body: "An oratory of dark,/ a chapel of unreason." She has a few moments of panic as the old words of warning flash into her mind: "You could die for this./ The gods could make you blind." These warnings do not deter her, however, from this sacred rite:

> how my cry
> blasphemes
> light and dark,
> screams
> land from sea,
> makes word flesh
> that now makes me
> animal.

During this period of arousal and climax, her "flesh summers," but then it returns again to winter: "I winter/ into sleep."

"Menses" deals with the private act of menstruation. A cosmic female voice addresses the speaker as menstruation begins, attempting to focus her attention solely on the natural powers working in her body. The speaker resists this effort. She feels simultaneously "sick of it" and drawn to this process. She struggles to retain her freedom. "Only my mind is free," she says. Her body is taken over by tidal forces. "I am bloated with her waters./ I am barren with her blood." At the end of the poem, the speaker seems more accepting of this natural cycle. She reflects on two other cycles that she has experienced, childbirth and intercourse. All three cycles, she begins to see, make her a new person: "I am bright and original."

The final three poems of *In Her Own Image*, "Witching," "Exhibitionist," and "Making-up," return to the theme that "Myths/ are made by men" (from "Making-up"). Much of a woman's life is spent reacting to male stereotypes. In "Witching," Boland further explores the idea of woman-as-witch, which was introduced in "Anorexia." Historically, women accused by men of being witches were doomed. The charges were usually either trumped-up or trivial. Boland's witch fantasizes about turning the table on her male persecutors and burning them first:

> I will
> reserve
> their arson,
> make
> a pyre
> of my haunch . . .
> the stench
> of my crotch

It is a grim but fitting fate for these male witch-burners.

Another stereotype, woman-as-stripper, is treated in the poem "Exhibitionist." This poem has the last accompanying drawing, a vulnerable young woman pulling her dress up over her head and naked to those watching her, perhaps as Boland feels naked toward those who have read through this volume. The male observers in "Exhibitionist" have in mind only gratifying their lusts. The speaker detests this exploitation and hopes to have a deeper impact on these leering males, hopes to touch them spiritually with her shining flesh:

> my dark plan:
> Into the gutter
> of their lusts
> I burn
> the shine
> of my flesh.

The final poem, "Making-up," returns to the theme of "Tirade for the Mimic Muse," that women must alter their appearances to please men, but that men have no such demands placed on them. The poem rehearses a litany of transformations of the speaker's "naked face." "Myths/ are made by men," this poem asserts. The goddesses men imagine can never be completely captured by that "naked face." A woman's natural appearance inevitably has flaws. Women are encouraged by men to disguise these flaws to make themselves look perfect. From these "rouge pots," a goddess comes forth, at least in men's eyes. Women should really know better.

> Mine are the rouge pots,
> the hot pinks, . . .
> out of which
> I dawn.

Boland is determined to make poetry out of her domestic life. *In Her Own Image* and *Night Feed* indicate that she has turned to the very ordinary subjects of hearth, rather than to the larger subjects of history, which she explored in her earlier volumes *New Territory* and *The War Horse*. In "The Woman Poet: Her Dilemma," Boland admits to uncertainty about this new orientation. She is encouraged especially, however, by the example of French and Dutch genre painters, whose work she calls "unglamorous, workaday, authentic," possessing both ordinariness and vision: "The hare in its muslin bag, the crusty loaf, the women fixed between menial tasks and human dreams." In her own equally ordinary domestic life, she believes that she has found a personal voice.

THE JOURNEY, AND OTHER POEMS

Boland's next major collection, *The Journey, and Other Poems*, explores more fully the poetic implications of this uncertainty. *In Her Own Image* and *Night Feed* offer opposed accounts of Boland's concerns as a woman and a writer, the former vehemently critical and openly outraged at sexual injustices, the latter more generously idyllic and positive about the domestic side of her femininity. In *The Journey, and Other Poems*, Boland incorporates this ambivalence into the fabric of her poems, channeling the tension between her contrary aspects into an antithetical lyric energy; each piece, that is, derives its form and force from a doubleness in the poet's mind, an impulse to be at once critical and affirmative. Instead of lamenting her inner confusions and contradictions, however, Boland builds a new sense of the lyric poem and engages with renewed vigor the vexed questions of gender, tradition, and myth that characterize her work.

The collection is divided into three sections, forming a triptych. In traditional religious painting, a triptych is composed of three canvases, side by side, the outer two either elaborating on or visually supporting the central portion, which usually contains the main subject of the work. In *The Journey, and Other Poems*, the first and third sections comment on, refocus, and expand the thematically dense matter of the central section, which contains "The Journey"—one of Boland's finest lyric achievements—and its "Envoi." Furthermore, Boland uses the structure of the triptych to underscore the ambivalence she feels. In the first section, the reader encounters memorial and idyll; in the third section, the reader finds the opposite, a vehement critique of inherited sexual mores and the patriarchal "tradition." Only in the central portion of the volume, "The Journey," does Boland take on both aspects at once and attempt, not to reconcile one to the other, but to reanimate and reenergize what she calls a dying, diminished poetic language.

The volume opens with "I Remember," a nostalgic tribute to the poet's mother. Boland recalls her mother's studio and her own almost irrepressible need, as a child exploring that room, "to touch, to handle, to dismantle it,/ the mystery." Boland longs for the mystery of innocence and the childlike wonder of a lost time—before the harsh realities of Irish economics and suburban alienation had taken root—when the world seemed balanced, "composed," and beautiful; but in the poem, that world is veiled and hidden from her, like the otherworldly elegance of her mother's "French Empire chairs" over which opaque cotton sheets have been draped. Similarly, in "The Oral Tradition," in which Boland overhears two women exchanging gossip—figures who, emblematically, "were standing in shadow"—she longs for "a musical sub-text," an "oral song" that seems only to express itself in "fragments and innuendoes," which nevertheless resonate with "a sense/ suddenly of truth." Boland wants to discover the archetypal "truth" buried under opaque surfaces, and, as she says in "Suburban Woman: A Detail," to find traces of the lost "goddess" within her instinctive, feminine memory. She expresses her need to be "healed into myth" through poetry and to recover the deeply ingrained, basic "patterns" of her womanhood.

The third section works negatively, upsetting traditional myths of the archetypal feminine. In "Listen. This Is the Noise of Myth," Boland starts to recount a "story" of a man and a woman setting the stage for a traditional version of domestic order, but she becomes self-conscious and critical, calling her own methods into question, making her characters—especially the woman—into "fugitives" from their traditional roles. Boland proposes to "set truth to rights," defiantly dismantling the old stories. She laments that even she must put "the same mirrors on the old magic" and return to the "old romances." Despite the sweet lure of storytelling, Boland wants to remake her own role as an author, and though she finds herself repeatedly thwarted by the "consolations of the craft," she struggles on.

Several poems in the third section echo Boland's other work. "Tirade for the Lyric Muse" recalls her "Tirade for the Mimic Muse," but here the subject is plastic surgery. The speaker addresses a sister "in the crime," an epithet that suggests a fellow poet, but one who, in Boland's view, has betrayed herself and her implicit commitment to "truth" by having the ordinary "surface" of her face altered to conform to a false notion of "skin deep" beauty. The true "music" of poetry, for Boland, cannot be captured by outward conformity to the "cruel" standards of a male world. Poems such as "Fond Memory" and "An Irish Childhood in England: 1951" respond to lyrics such as "I Remember" in the first section, rejecting nostalgia and finding in Boland's own indelible Irishness a sense of exile and insecurity. To be an English-speaking Irish native is to be a perpetual outcast. Irishness, for Boland, represents her own inability to settle on a given set of values or a certain appearance of "truth"; her nationality, paradoxically, undermines easy acceptance of the safe "myths" she craves.

If the first section works to rediscover the force of myth and the last section to dismantle the false safety net of traditional roles, the central portion—"The Journey"—springs directly from a double impulse. "The Journey" is a dream-vision, a description of a mental journey to the underworld undertaken in the poet's dreams. Many medieval poets, including Geoffrey Chaucer, wrote dream-visions. Like these poets, Boland depicts herself falling asleep over an open book of classical poetry. This connection to tradition, both medieval and ancient, is important to the poem, which describes a poetics, an account of how poems are or ought to be written. Boland searches for a new, vital form of writing. She begins by stating angrily that "there has never . . . been a poem to an antibiotic. . . ." She questions what is the proper subject for poetry, introducing antibiotics as something about which no one would bother to write. She espouses the ordinary and the domestic rather than the ethereal of the "unblemished" as a basis for poetry. To heal people and to repair their diminished relationship to "the language," poetry must look with renewed energy to the particulars of everyday life.

In her dream, Boland descends with Sappho—the greatest ancient female poet, whom she has been reading—to the land of the dead, where she meets the ghosts of mothers and housewives, women in whose experiences Boland has been trying to discover her mythical roots. Boland pleads with her mentor to let her "be their witnesses," but she is told that what she has seen is "beyond speech." She awakens, only to find "nothing was changed," despite her vision of "truth," and she weeps. This poetic "misery," taken up in the poem's "Envoi," comes from disappointment at being incapable of resuscitating the lost myths of womanhood, the anxiety of trying to bless "the ordinary" or to sanctify "the common" without the comfort of a traditionally sanctioned muse. Boland's work, to revive the feminine in poetry, results in a difficult mixture of discovery, desire, dissatisfaction, and rage. "The Journey" is a complex poem, and one of Boland's best works. It expresses both a naïve, dreamy faith in the power of myth and "truth" and a severe self-consciousness that calls the elements of her feminine identity into question. The ability to dwell poetically on such a problematic duplicity in a single poem truly indicates Boland's literary accomplishment.

IN A TIME OF VIOLENCE AND THE LOST LAND

Similar concerns, sometimes more deeply and darkly wrought, sometimes inscribed with a tonic humor, permeate Boland's poems of the 1990's. *In a Time of Violence* uses unusual and risky strategies to clarify the personal/political weave in Boland's vision. All those who lack autonomy are ultimately susceptible to victimhood and violence.

This equation pertains to gender, nationhood, and any other form of identification. In *The Lost Land*, she continues to explore the issues and emotions of those who are victims of exile and colonialism. These are especially the burdens of "Colony," a major poem that makes up the first half of the book. Colonization, Boland says, is not just an act of governments, but an act of individuals—any exercise of power and dominance at the expense of the independence of others. It even applies to the relationships of parents and children, husbands and wives. These echoes weave their way more noticeably through the shorter poems in the collection. Along with the losses of place that Boland records—"place" having political, cultural, and psychic significance—she expresses here the loss of motherhood—another "place" of position that vanishes with time. Boland's constantly growing artistry, her ability to fasten on the telling concrete detail, and her hard-won personal and public authority make this collection outstanding.

AGAINST LOVE POETRY

Against Love Poetry deftly reconciles the sacrifice of freedom necessary for a lasting marriage with "the idea of women's freedom." If such a move seems unexpected or contradictory, it nonetheless arises from the same impulse as Boland's earlier work: the desire to delineate the true experience of women's lives. The book's first half, a section entitled "Marriage," clarifies the book's title. The sentimental ideal of romantic love, by now a well-known part of the poetic tradition, cannot begin to render adequately the truths of married life: "It is to mark the contradictions of a daily love that I have written this. Against love poetry." Throughout the volume, Boland draws on history, myths, folktales, and memory, continually subverting clichéd versions of romantic love in favor of a more complex, if often more stark, reality. For example, the poem "Quarantine," the fourth poem in the "Marriage" section, follows the route of a married couple walking during the Irish potato famine. Ultimately, after the man struggles unsuccessfully to keep his ill wife warm, both die "Of cold. Of hunger. Of the toxins of a whole history." Here the narrative shifts, echoing the book's title briefly to declare that "There is no place here for the inexact/ praise of the easy graces and sensuality of the body." What is important, the poem emphasizes, is the ordinary yet striking reality of what happens: "Their death together in the winter of 1847. Also what they suffered. How they lived./ And what there is between a man and a woman./ And in which darkness it can best be proved."

As in her earlier work, Boland continues to blend personal history, folktale, and classical myth to overturn past and present stereotypes of women's lives. "Called," an entry in the section half of the book, describes the author's unsuccessful search for the grave of her grandmother who died young. With Boland's resolve to "face this landscape/ and look at it as she was looked upon:// Unloved because unknown./ Unknown because unnamed," the familiar landmarks are stripped away, the earth returns to its essences, and the poet drives home as constellations appear, "some of them twisted into women."

Even as Boland notes the vital role of women within the cosmos, those who "single-handedly holding high the dome/ and curve and horizon of today and tomorrow," she acknowledges the pain of being marginalized: "All the ships looking up to them./ All the compasses made true by them./ All the night skies named for their sorrow." Not surprisingly, in "Suburban Woman: Another Detail," she aptly describes her writing as the process of selecting words "from the earth,/ from the root, from the faraway/ oils and essence of elegy:/ Bitter. And close to the bone."

Interestingly, Boland extends her range of subjects to include poetry about the little-known accomplishments of historical women from the remote and recent past. The first poem in the "Marriage" section portrays Hester Bateman, a British silversmith who in the nineteenth century took on the trade of her husband, engraving marriage spoons for an Irish customer. In the book's second section, "Code," Boland directly addresses Grace Murray Hopper, who verified the computer language known as COBOL: "Let there be language—/ even if we use it differently:/ I never made it timeless as you have./ I never made it numerate as you did." In both poems, Boland identifies strongly with her protagonists, demonstrating the ability of the woman artist to create the future and to reconcile oppositions: "composing this/ to show you how the world begins again:/ One word at a time./ One woman to another" ("Code").

DOMESTIC VIOLENCE

In *Domestic Violence*, the late-night quarrels of a neighbor couple, the sectarian strife that erupted in Ireland in the 1960's, the poet's personal history, and the plight of Irish women become inextricably entwined. The title poem recalls how Boland and her husband, then newly married, watched the civil unrest known as the Troubles unfold in the grainy images of a small black-and-white television set, "which gave them back as gray and grayer tears/ and killings, killings, killings,/ then moonlight-colored funerals." In the same section, another poem, "How It Was Once in Our Country," evokes Ireland's turbulent history from previous centuries, relating the story of a mermaid who, according to some storytellers, "must have witnessed deaths" and remained below the water "to escape the screams." As always, there is the note of exile: "What we know is this/ (and this is all we know): we are now/ and we will always be from now on—/ for all I know have always been—// exiles in our own country."

In the book's second section, Boland explores both past and present as she considers "last things," pondering what she will bequeath to her daughters. "Inheritance" expresses the poet's regret that she never learned the crafts of her predecessors: "the lace bobbin with its braided mesh,/ its oat-straw pillow and the wheat-colored shawl/ knitted in one season/ to imitate another." She also recalls a long night of tending to her first child: "When dawn came I held my hand over the absence of fever,/ over skin which had stopped burning, as if I knew the secrets of health and air, as if I understood them// and listened to the silence/ and thought, I must have learned that somewhere." In the entries that conclude this section, the poet's voice becomes more strident. "Windfall," an imagined rendering of the funeral for the grandmother whose grave she could not locate, describes "the coffin of a young woman/ who has left five children behind. There will be no obituary." The tragedy resides not only in her ancestor's unrecorded death, but also the insidious ways that language can be appropriated to justify ignoring lives that a culture or a country may consider insignificant:

> We say *Mother Nature* when all we intend is
> a woman was let die, out of sight, in a fever ward.
>
> Now say *Mother Ireland* when all that you mean is
> there is no need to record this death in history.

In "Letters to the Dead," the "signs and marks" used to inscribe ancient Egyptian pottery laid at the entrance of tombs become the poet's telling metaphor for a similar communication with her own ancestors. Ultimately, however, Boland's frank question reaches deep into Irish history:

> How many daughters stood alone at a grave,
> and thought this of their mothers' lives?
> That they were young in a country that hated
>   a woman's body.
> That they grew old in a country that hated a
>   woman's body
>
> They asked for the counsel of the dead.
> They asked for the power of the dead.
> These are my letters to the dead.

In a similar poem, "Violence Against Women," Boland mourns the female casualties of the Industrial Revolution, "women who died here who never lived:// mindless, sexless, birthless, only sunned/ by shadows, only dressed in muslin." For the poet, they resemble "shepherdesses of the English pastoral" trapped in traditional poetry, "waiting for the return of an English April/ that never came and never will again." Boland's closure questions and indicts the cultural and historical institutions that so often connive in the fate of women like Boland's grandmother.

Like her fellow poet and countryman Heaney, Boland's poetry has become a search for the images, symbols, and language that could adequately, realistically portray the struggles of women throughout history and her own pain at feeling like an exile in her own country. Throughout a career of patiently and carefully crafting poems, Boland has achieved an eloquence that is truly superlative.

OTHER MAJOR WORKS

NONFICTION: *W. B. Yeats and His World*, 1971 (with Micheál Mac Liammóir); *Object Lessons: The Life of the Woman and the Poet in Our Time*, 1995.

TRANSLATION: *After Every War: Twentieth-century Women Poets*, 2004.

EDITED TEXT: *The Making of a Poem: A Norton Anthology of Poetic Forms*, 2000 (with Mark Strand).

BIBLIOGRAPHY

Boland, Eavan. Interview by Patty O'Connell. *Poets and Writers* 22 (November/December, 1995). A lengthy conversation that ranges through Irish and American poetry, Dublin as an image in Boland's work, her mother, and poetry workshops.

Collins, Floyd. "Auspicious Beginnings and Sure Arrivals: Beth Ann Fennelly and Eavan Boland." *West Branch* 52 (Spring, 2003): 108-123. Contains an excellent discussion of *Against Love Poetry* and a comparison of Boland and Beth Ann Fennelly.

Constantakis, Sara, ed. *Poetry for Students*. Vol. 31. Detroit: Thomson/Gale Group, 2010. Contains an analysis of Boland's "Outside History."

Gonzalez, Alexander G., ed. *Contemporary Irish Women Poets: Some Male Perspectives*. Westport, Conn.: Greenwood Press, 1999. Enthusiastic responses by male critics to a wide range of Irish women poets include two strong essays on Boland: Thomas C. Foster's "In from the Margin: Eavan Boland's 'Outside History' Sequence" and Peter Kupillas's "Bringing It All Back Home: Unity and Meaning in Eavan Boland's 'Domestic Interior' Sequence."

Haberstroh, Patricia Boyle. *Women Creating Women: Contemporary Irish Women Poets*. Syracuse, N.Y.: Syracuse University Press, 1996. Compares Boland, Eithne Strong, Eiléan Ní Chuilleanáin, Medbh McGuckian, and Nuala Ní Dhomhnaill.

Keen, Paul. "The Doubled Edge: Identity and Alterity in the Poetry of Eavan Boland and Nuala Ní Dhomhnaill." *Mosaic* 33, no. 3 (2000): 14-34. Setting his investigation within the political and cultural upheavals in contemporary Ireland, Keen attends to Boland's theoretical writings to approach her poems. He sees her as rewriting Irish myths about the country and women rather than subverting them. Several key poems are examined with clarity and compassionate care. The comparative approach is fruitful.

McElroy, James. "The Contemporary Fe/Male Poet: A Preliminary Reading." In *New Irish Writing*, edited by James Brophy and Eamon Grennan. Boston: Twayne, 1989. McElroy defends Boland against critical charges of "stridency" and overstatement, arguing that her recurrent confrontations with the Irish domestic woman constitute a crucial part of her poetics of recovery and renewal, and that her willful reiterations of "female miseries" form a powerful catalog of matters that must be treated emphatically if Irish poetry is to recover its potency.

Randolph, Jody Allen, ed. *Eavan Boland: A Critical Companion*. New York: Norton,

2008. This volume, one of the first book-length studies of Boland, includes poetry and prose by Boland, interviews with her, and criticism of her work.

Villar-Argáiz, Pilar. *Eavan Boland's Evolution as an Irish Woman Poet: An Outsider Within an Outsider's Culture.* Lewiston, N.Y.: Edwin Mellen Press, 2007. Focuses on Boland as a female poet, presenting analysis of male-female relationships in her poetry. Includes an analysis of "Anorexic."

_____. *The Poetry of Eavan Boland: A Postcolonial Reading.* Dublin: Maunsel, 2008. This volume places Boland squarely within the context of postcolonial literature.

Kevin McNeilly; Arthur E. McGuinness; Philip K. Jason
Updated by Caroline Collins

AUSTIN CLARKE

Born: Dublin, Ireland; May 9, 1896
Died: Dublin, Ireland; March 19, 1974

PRINCIPAL POETRY

The Vengeance of Fionn, 1917 (based on the Irish Saga "Pursuit of Diarmid and
    Grainne")
The Fires of Baal, 1921
The Sword of the West, 1921
The Cattledrive in Connaught, and Other Poems, 1925 (based on the prologue to
    Tain bo Cuailnge)
Pilgrimage, and Other Poems, 1929
The Collected Poems of Austin Clarke, 1936
Night and Morning, 1938
Ancient Lights, 1955
Too Great a Vine: Poems and Satires, 1957
The Horse-Eaters: Poems and Satires, 1960
Collected Later Poems, 1961
Forget-Me-Not, 1962
Flight to Africa, and Other Poems, 1963
Mnemosyne Lay in Dust, 1966
Old-Fashioned Pilgrimage, and Other Poems, 1967
The Echo at Coole, and Other Poems, 1968
Orphide, and Other Poems, 1970
Tiresias: A Poem, 1971
The Wooing of Becfolay, 1973
Collected Poems, 1974
The Selected Poems, 1976

OTHER LITERARY FORMS

Besides his epic, narrative, and lyric poetry, Austin Clarke published three novels,
two volumes of autobiography, some twenty verse plays, and a large volume of journalistic essays and literary reviews for newspaper and radio. He also delivered a number of
radio lectures on literary topics and gave interviews on his own life and work on Irish
radio and television.

ACHIEVEMENTS

In a poetic career that spanned more than fifty years, Austin Clarke was a leading figure in the "second generation" of the Irish Literary Revival (also known as the Celtic

Revival). Most of his career can be understood as a response to the aims of that movement: to celebrate the heroic legends of ancient Ireland, to bring the compositional technique of the bardic poets into modern English verse, and to bring poetry and humor together in a socially liberating way on the modern stage.

Clarke's earliest efforts to write epic poems on pre-Christian Ireland were not generally successful, although his first poems do have passages of startling color and lyric beauty that presage his later work. When, in the 1930's, he turned to early medieval ("Celtic Romanesque") Ireland, he found his métier, both in poetry and in fiction. To the celebration of the myth of a vigorous indigenous culture in which Christian ascetic and pagan hedonist coexisted, he bent his own disciplined efforts. Unlike William Butler Yeats and most of the leading writers of the Revival, Clarke had direct access to the language of the ancient literature and worked to reproduce its rich sound in modern English. In this effort he was uniquely successful among modern Irish poets.

In his later years, Clarke turned to satirizing the domestic scene, living to see cultural changes remedy many of his complaints about Irish life. Although he wrote in obscurity through most of his career, in his later life, Clarke was belatedly recognized by several institutions: He was awarded an honorary D.Litt. in 1966 from Trinity College, received the Gregory Medal in 1968 from the Irish Academy of Letters, and was the "Writer in Profile" on Radio Telifís Éireann in 1968.

BIOGRAPHY

Austin Clarke was born into a large, middle-class, Catholic, Dublin family on May 9, 1896. He was educated by the Jesuits at Belvedere College and earned a B.A. and an M.A. in English literature from University College, Dublin, in 1916 and 1917, and he was appointed assistant lecturer there in 1917. In his formative years, he was heavily impressed by the Irish Literary Revival, especially Douglas Hyde's Gaelic League and Yeats's Abbey Theatre, and his political imagination was fired by the Easter Rising of 1916. In 1920, following a brief civil marriage to Geraldine Cummins, he was dismissed from his university post; shortly thereafter, he emigrated to London and began to write his epic poems on heroic subjects drawn from the ancient literature of Ireland.

In 1930, Clarke married Nora Walker, with whom he had three sons, and between 1929 and 1938, he wrote a number of verse plays and two novels—both banned in Ireland—before returning permanently to Ireland in 1937. Since in his creative career and national literary allegiance he was from the beginning a disciple of Yeats, he was sorely disappointed to be omitted from *The Oxford Book of Modern Verse* that Yeats edited in 1936. Nevertheless, with the publication of *Night and Morning*, Clarke began a new and public phase in his creative career: The following year, he began his regular broadcasts on poetry on Radio Éireann and started to write book reviews for *The Irish Times*. Between 1939 and 1942, he was president of Irish PEN and cofounder (with Robert Farren) of the Dublin Verse-Speaking Society and the Lyric Theatre Company. Subsequently, his verse plays were produced at the Abbey and on Radio Éireann. Clarke's prolonged creative silence in the early 1950's seems, in retrospect, oddly appropriate to the depressed state of Ireland, where heavy emigration and strict censorship seemed to conspire in lowering public morale. However, as if he were anticipating the economic revival, he published *Ancient Lights* in 1955. Here began a new phase in his poetic career, that of a waspish commentator on contemporary events, composing dozens of occasional poems, some of which can lay claim to a reader's attention beyond their particular origins. Between 1955 and his death, a collection of these pieces appeared every two or three years, as well as two volumes of autobiography. His public profile was maintained through his radio broadcasts, his regular reviews in *The Irish Times*, his attendance at many PEN conferences, and his visits to the United States and the Soviet Union. In 1972, he was nominated for the Nobel Prize in Literature. He died on March 19, 1974, shortly after the publication of his *Collected Poems*.

ANALYSIS

The first phase of Austin Clarke's poetic career, 1917 to 1925, produced four epic poems that are little more than apprentice work. Drawing on Celtic and biblical texts, they betray too easily the influences of Yeats, Sir Samuel Ferguson, and other pioneers of the Revival. Considerably overwritten and psychologically unsure, only in patches do they reveal Clarke's real talent: his close understanding of the original text and a penchant for erotic humor and evocative lyrical descriptions of nature. The major preoccupations of his permanent work did not appear until he assimilated these earliest influences.

Clarke's difficulties with religious faith, rejection of Catholic doctrine, and an unfulfilled need for spiritual consolation provide the theme and tension in the poems from *Pilgrimage, and Other Poems* and *Night and Morning*. These poems arise from the conflicts between the mores of modern Irish Catholicism and Clarke's desire for emotional and sexual fulfillment. These poems, therefore, mark a departure from his earlier work in that they are personal and contemporary in theme, yet they are also designedly Irish, in setting and technique.

In searching for a vehicle to express his personal religious conflicts while keeping faith in his commitment to the Irish Literary Revival, Clarke found an alternative to Yeats's heroic, pre-Christian age: the "Celtic Romanesque," the medieval period in Irish history when the Christian Church founded by Saint Patrick was renowned for its asceticism, its indigenous monastic tradition, its scholastic discipline, its missionary zeal, and the brilliance of its art (metalwork, illuminated manuscripts, sculpture, and devotional and nature poetry). Although this civilization contained within it many of the same tensions that bedeviled Clarke's world—those between the Christian ideal and the claims of the flesh, between Christian faith and pagan hedonism—it appealed to his imagination because of his perception of its independence from Roman authority, the separation of ecclesiastical and secular spheres, and its respect for artistic excellence. This view of the period is selective and romanticized but is sufficient in that it serves his artistic purposes.

Clarke's poetry is Irish also in a particular, technical sense: in its emulation of the complex sound patterns of Gaelic verse, called *rime riche*. In this endeavor, he was following the example set by Douglas Hyde in his translations of folk songs and by the poems of Thomas MacDonagh. This technique employs a variety of rhyming and assonantal devices so that a pattern of rhymes echoes through the middles and ends of lines, playing off unaccented as well as accented syllables. Relatively easy to manage in Gaelic poetry because of the sound structure of the language, *rime riche* requires considerable dexterity in English. However, Clarke diligently embraced this challenge, sometimes producing results that were little more than technical exercises or impenetrably obscure, but often producing works of unusual virtuosity and limpid beauty. Clarke summed up his approach in his answer to Robert Frost's inquiry about the kind of verse he wrote: "I load myself with chains and I try to get out of them." To which came the shocked reply: "Good Lord! You can't have many readers."

Indeed, Clarke is neither a popular nor an easy poet. Despite his considerable output (his *Collected Poems* runs to some 550 pages), his reputation stands firmly on a select number of these. Of his early narrative poems, adaptations of Celtic epic tales, only a few passages transcend the prevailing verbal clutter.

PILGRIMAGE, AND OTHER POEMS

With the publication of *Pilgrimage, and Other Poems*, however, the focus narrowed, and the subjects are realized with startling clarity. Perhaps the most representative and accomplished poem in this volume is the lyric "Celibacy." This treatment of a hermit's struggle with lust combines Clarke's personal conflicts with the Catholic Church's sexual teachings and his sympathy with the hermit's spiritual calling in a finely controlled, ironic commentary on the contemporary Irish suspicion of sex. Clarke achieves this irony through a series of images that juxtapose the monk's self-conscious heroism to his unconscious self-indulgence. The rhyming and assonantal patterns in this poem are an early example of the successful use of the sound patterns borrowed from Gaelic models that became one of the distinctive characteristics of his work.

NIGHT AND MORNING

With the publication of *Night and Morning*, there is a considerable consolidation of power. In this collection of sterling consistency, Clarke succeeds in harnessing the historical elements to his personal voice and vision. In the exposition of the central theme of the drama of racial conscience, he shows himself to be basically a religious poet. The central problems faced here are the burden to the contemporary generation of a body of truth received from the centuries of suffering and refinement, the limitations of religious faith in an age of sexual and spiritual freedom, and the conflicts arising from a sympathy with and a criticism of the ordinary citizen. Clarke's own position is always ambivalent. While he seems to throw down the gauntlet to the dogmatic Church, his challenge is never wholehearted: He is too unsure of his position outside the institution he ostensibly abjures. This ambivalence is borne out in the fine title poem in this volume, in the implications of the Christian imagery of the Passion, the candle, the celebration of the Mass, the Incarnation, and the double lightning of faith and reason. A confessional poem, "Night and Morning" protests the difficulties in maintaining an adult faith in the Christian message in a skeptical age. Although it criticizes the lack of an intellectual stiffening in modern Irish Catholicism and ostensibly yearns for the medieval age when faith and reason were reconciled, the poem's passion implies an allegiance to the Church that is more emotional than intellectual. These ambiguities are deftly conveyed by the title, design, tone, and imagery of the poem.

Almost every poem in this volume shows Clarke at his best, especially "Martha Blake," "The Straying Student," and "The Jewels." In "Martha Blake," a portrait of a devout daily communicant, Clarke manages multiple points of view with lucidity and ease. From one perspective, Martha's blind faith is depicted as heroic and personally valid; from another, Martha is not very aware of the beauty of the natural world around her, although she experiences it vicariously through the ardor of her religious feelings; from a third, as in the superb final stanza, the poet shares with his readers a simultaneous double perspective that balances outer and inner visions, natural and supernatural grace. The ambiguity and irony that permeate this last stanza are handled with a sensitivity that, considering the anguish and anger of so much of his religious verse, reveals a startling degree of sympathy for ordinary, sincere Christians. He sees that a passionate nature may be concealed, and may be fulfilling itself, beneath the appearances of a simple devotion.

ANCIENT LIGHTS

When, after a long silence, *Ancient Lights* appeared in 1955, Clarke had turned from his earlier historical and personal mode to a public and satirical posture. These poems comment wittily on current issues controversial in the Ireland of the early 1950's: the mediocrity and piety of public life, "scandalous" women's fashions, the domination of Irish public opinion by the Catholic Church, the "rhythm" method of birth control, and the incipient public health program. Many of these poems may appear quaint and require annotations even for a post-Vatican II Irish audience. The lead poem, "Celebrations," for example, in criticizing the smug piety of postrevolutionary Ireland, focuses on the Eucharistic Congress held in Dublin in 1932. The poem is studded with references to the Easter Rising of 1916, its heroic antecedents and its promise for the new nation. These are set in ironic contrast with the jobbing latter-day politicians who have made too easy an accommodation with the Church and have thus replaced the British with a native oppression. Clarke vehemently excoriates the manner in which the public purse is made to subscribe to Church-mandated institutions. Despite its highly compressed content, this poem succeeds in making a direct statement on an important public issue. Unfortunately, the same is not true of many of Clarke's subsequent satires, which degenerate into bickering over inconsequential subjects, turn on cheap puns, or lapse into doubtful taste.

This cannot be said, however, of the title poem of this volume, one of Clarke's best achievements. Autobiographical and literally confessional, it can be profitably read in conjunction with his memoir, *Twice 'Round the Black Church: Early Memories of Ireland and England* (1962), especially pages 138-139. It begins with the familiar Clarke landscape of Catholic Dublin and the conflict between adolescent sex and conscience. Having made a less than full confession, the persona guiltily skulks outside, pursued by a superstitious fear of retribution.

Emerging into the light like an uncaged bird, in a moment reminiscent of that experienced by James Joyce's Stephen Daedalus on the beach, the protagonist experiences an epiphany of natural grace that sweeps his sexual guilt away. The Church-induced phobias accumulated over the centuries drop away in a moment of creative self-assertion. This experience is confirmed in nature's own manner: driven by a heavy shower into the doorway of the Protestant black church (for the full significance of the breaking of this sectarian taboo, see again his memoir), he experiences a spiritual catharsis as he observes the furious downpour channeled, contained, and disposed by roof, pipe, and sewer. With the sun's reappearance, he is born again in a moment of triumphant, articulate joy.

The narrative direction, tonal variety, and especially the virtuosity of the final stanza establish this poem as one of Clarke's finest creations. It weaves nostalgia, humor, horror, vision, and euphoria into a series of epiphanies that prepare the reader for the powerful conclusion. This last stanza combines the images of penance with baptism in a flood of images that are precisely observed and fraught with the spiritual significance for which the reader has been prepared. It should be noted, however, that even here Clarke's resolution is consciously qualified: The cowlings and downpipes are ecclesiastical, and the flood's roar announces the removal of but "half our heavens." Nevertheless, in the control and energy of its images and sound patterns, the poem realizes many of Clarke's objectives in undertaking to write poetry that dramatizes the proverbial tensions between art, religion, and nature in the national conscience.

SATIRE AND IRONY

In the nineteen years following the publication of *Ancient Lights*, Clarke produced a continuous stream of satires on occasional issues, few of which rise above their origins. They are often hasty in judgment, turgid almost beyond retrieval, or purely formal exercises. These later volumes express a feeling of alienation from modern Ireland, in its particular mix of piety and materialism. Always mindful of the myths lying behind Irish life, his critique begins to lose its currency and sounds quixotically conservative. Then in the early 1960's, with the arrival of industrialization in Ireland, relative prosperity, and the Church reforms following Vatican II, many of Clarke's criticisms of Irish life become inapplicable and his latter-day eroticism sounds excessively self-conscious and often in poor taste. Nevertheless, some of his later lyrics, such as "Japanese Print," and translations from the Irish are quite successful: lightly ironic, relaxed, matching the spirit of their originals.

MNEMOSYNE LAY IN DUST

The most impressive personal poem of this last phase in his career is the confessional *Mnemosyne Lay in Dust*. Based on his experiences during a lengthy stay at a mental institution some forty years before, it recrosses the battleground between his inherited Jansenism and his personal brand of secular humanism. In harrowing, cacophonic verse, the poem describes the tortured hallucinations, the electric shock treatment, the amnesia, the pain of rejection by "Margaret" (his first wife), the contemplated suicide, and the eventual rejection of religious taboos for a life directed to the development of reason and human feeling. For all its extraordinary energy, however, this poem lacks the consistency and finish of his shorter treatments of the same dilemma.

FINAL PHASE

The last phase of Clarke's poetic career produced a group of poems on erotic subjects that affirm, once again, his belief in the full right to indulge in life's pleasures. The best of these—such as "Anacreontic" and "The Healing of Mis"—are remarkably forthright and witty and are not marred by the residual guilt of his earlier forays into this subject.

Clarke's oeuvre is by turns brilliant and gauche. Learned and cranky, tortured and tender, his work moves with extraordinary commitment within a narrow range of concerns. His quarrels with Irish Catholicism and the new Irish state, his preoccupation with problems of sexuality and with Irish myth and history, and his technical emulation of Irish-language models set him firmly at the center of Irish poetry after Yeats. These considerations place him outside the modernist movement. In Ireland, he has been more highly rated by literary historians than by the younger generation of poets. Recognition abroad is coming late: In about twenty poems, he has escaped from his largely self-imposed chains to gain the attention of the world at large.

OTHER MAJOR WORKS

LONG FICTION: *The Bright Temptation*, 1932, 1973; *The Singing Men at Cashel*, 1936; *The Sun Dances at Easter*, 1952.

PLAYS: *The Son of Learning*, pr., pb. 1927 (pr. 1930 as *The Hunger Demon*); *The*

Flame, pb. 1930; *Sister Eucharia*, pr., pb. 1939; *Black Fast*, pb. 1941; *As the Crow Flies*, pr. 1942 (radio play), pr. 1948 (staged); *The Kiss*, pr. 1942; *The Plot Is Ready*, pr. 1943; *The Viscount of Blarney*, pr., pb. 1944; *The Second Kiss*, pr., pb. 1946; *The Plot Succeeds*, pr., pb. 1950; *The Moment Next to Nothing*, pr., pb. 1953; *Collected Plays*, pb. 1963; *The Student from Salamanca*, pr. 1966; *Two Interludes Adapted from Cervantes: "The Student from Salamanca" and "The Silent Lover,"* pb. 1968; *The Impuritans: A Play in One Act Freely Adapted from the Short Story "Young Goodman Brown" by Nathaniel Hawthorne*, pb. 1972; *The Visitation*, pb. 1974; *The Third Kiss*, pb. 1976; *Liberty Lane*, pb. 1978.

NONFICTION: *Poetry in Modern Ireland*, 1951; *Twice 'Round the Black Church: Early Memories of Ireland and England*, 1962; *A Penny in the Clouds: More Memories of Ireland and England*, 1968; *The Celtic Twilight and the Nineties*, 1969; *Growing Up Stupid Under the Union Jack: A Memoir*, 1980.

BIBLIOGRAPHY

Algoo-Baksh, Stella. *Austin C. Clarke: A Biography*. Toronto, Ont.: ECW Press, 1994. Combines a narrative of Clarke's life with thoughtful interpretations of some of his major works. Gives a portrait of his public persona but few details of his personal life. Includes bibliographical references and index.

Corcoran, Neil. *Poets of Modern Ireland*. Carbondale: Southern Illinois University Press, 1999. Contains an essay on Clarke, which focuses on his poetic achievements.

Garratt, Robert F. *Modern Irish Poetry: Tradition Continuity from Yeats to Heaney*. Berkeley: University of California Press, 1986. Devotes a chapter to Clarke, the main figure of transition for twentieth century Irish poetry. Clarke's early poetry followed William Butler Yeats in retelling Irish myths, his middle work focused on medievalism, and his later poems echoed James Joyce in their critical analysis of religion. Contains an index and select bibliography that includes material on Clarke.

Halpern, Susan. *Austin Clarke: His Life and Work*. Dublin: Dolmen Press, 1974. This survey of Clarke's prolific output in prose and verse concentrates on the verse. Substantial bibliography.

Harmon, Maurice. *Austin Clarke, 1896-1974: A Critical Introduction*. Dublin: Wolfhound Press, 1989. The introduction covers the life of Clarke, the contexts for his writing, his Catholicism, and his participation in nationalist movements. Two phases are then examined: first, his prose, drama, and poetry from 1916 to 1938; second, his sustained work in poetry, short and long, from 1955 to 1974. Supplemented by a portrait, notes, a bibliography, and an index.

Irish University Review 4 (Spring, 1974). This special issue on Clarke contains a detailed account of his involvement with, and artistic contributions to, the Dublin Verse-Speaking Society and the Lyric Theatre Company, and it provides a complete list of the two organizations' productions.

Murphy, Daniel. "Disarmed, a Malcontent." In *Imagination and Religion in Anglo-Irish Literature, 1930-1980*. Blackrock, Ireland: Irish Academic Press, 1987. Analyzes Clarke's lyrics and satires. Also examines religious tensions in *Mnemosyne Lay in Dust*, reviews Clarke's use of history, examines Clarke's satirical style, and finally sketches Clarke's use of nature. The chapter is supplemented by notes and a bibliography. The book contains an index.

Ricigliano, Lorraine. *Austin Clarke: A Reference Guide*. New York: Maxwell Macmillan International, 1993. A chronology of the major works by Clarke; an alphabetical list of all the individual poems and plays in the volumes cited; and a secondary bibliography, also arranged chronologically from 1918 to 1992, with descriptive annotations.

Schirmer, Gregory A. *The Poetry of Austin Clarke*. Notre Dame, Ind.: University of Notre Dame Press, 1983. A critique of Clarke's poetry. Bibliography and index.

Tapping, G. Craig. *Austin Clarke: A Study of His Writings*. Dublin: Academy Press, 1981. After calling Clarke's tradition "modern classicism," Tapping sketches a background of Romanticism to "Celto-Romanesque." Five chapters study the poetic drama, the novels, the poetry from 1938 to 1961, the poetry of the 1960's, and the new poems as treatments of old myths. Augmented by bibliographies, notes, an appendix, and an index.

Cóilín Owens

PADRAIC COLUM

Born: County Longford, Ireland; December 8, 1881
Died: Enfield, Connecticut; January 11, 1972

<small>PRINCIPAL POETRY</small>
Wild Earth: A Book of Verse, 1907
Dramatic Legends, and Other Poems, 1922
Creatures, 1927
Way of the Cross, 1927
Old Pastures, 1930
Poems, 1932
The Story of Lowry Main, 1937
Flower Pieces: New Poems, 1938
The Collected Poems of Padraic Colum, 1953
The Vegetable Kingdom, 1954
Ten Poems, 1957
Irish Elegies, 1958
The Poet's Circuits: Collected Poems of Ireland, 1960
Images of Departure, 1969
Selected Poems of Padraic Colum, 1989 (Sanford Sternlicht, editor)

<small>OTHER LITERARY FORMS</small>

Padraic Colum (KAWL-uhm) was a prolific writer who expressed himself in many different genres during the first seven decades of the twentieth century. He helped found the Abbey Theatre in Dublin with William Butler Yeats, and he wrote three major plays: *The Land* (pr., pb. 1905), *The Fiddler's House* (pr., pb. 1907), and *Thomas Muskerry* (pr., pb. 1910). All three plays deal with the dignity of Irish farmers. He wrote numerous short stories; two major novels, *Castle Conquer* (1923) and *The Flying Swans* (1957); and numerous essays on Irish history and politics. After his immigration to the United States in 1914 with his wife, Mary Colum, he became especially famous for his elegant retelling of folk tales for children. Some of his most admired books for children are *The King of Ireland's Son* (1916), *The Golden Fleece and the Heroes Who Lived Before Achilles* (1921), and *Legends of Hawaii* (1937).

<small>ACHIEVEMENTS</small>

Unlike other great writers of the literary movement called the Irish Renaissance (also the Celtic Revival), such as William Butler Yeats, Lady Augusta Gregory, and James Joyce, who were his friends, Padraic Colum was from a peasant background. He under-

Padraic Colum
(Library of Congress)

stood profoundly the beliefs and moral values of Irish farmers. Although he moved to the United States in 1914, his thoughts never really left the Irish countryside of his youth. In his poetry and prose, he wrote in a deceptively simple style. His poetry captured the simple dignity of Irish peasants, whose emotions and struggles he presented as representations of the rich diversity of human experience. Some of his poems, including "An Old Woman of the Roads" and "A Cradle Song," have been learned by heart by generations of Irish and Irish American students. His poetry is immediately accessible to young readers, but more mature readers also appreciate the simple eloquence and evocative power of his poems. He captured the essence of Irish folklore and popular culture and transmitted to readers its profound universality. He became a member of the American Academy of Arts and Letters in 1948 and served as chancellor for the Academy of American Poets from 1950 to 1951. In 1952, Colum won an Academy of American Poets Fellowship. He received the Gregory Medal of the Irish Academy of Letters in 1953 and the Regina Medal in 1961.

BIOGRAPHY

Padraic Colum was born in a workhouse in Ireland's County Longford on December 8, 1881. His original name was Patrick Columb, but in his early twenties, he changed his name to Padraic Colum to make it sound more Irish and less English. He was the first of eight children born to Susan and Patrick Columb. During his youth, he learned about Irish folklore and traditions by listening to the oral tales told by those who lived in County Longford. He never wavered in his commitment both to the Catholic faith of his ancestors and to the values of Irish peasant culture. His formal education ended when he was sixteen, and he was in many ways a self-educated man.

His family moved to Dublin in 1891, and after his studies ended, Colum became a clerk for the Irish railroads. He soon developed a deep interest in Gaelic culture and discovered his abilities as a writer. With the encouragement of Yeats and Lady Augusta Gregory, he wrote plays for the newly founded Abbey Theatre in Dublin as well as lyric poetry. A monetary grant in 1908 from American businessman Thomas Kelly enabled Colum to resign from his job with the railroads and to concentrate solely on his writing. From then on, Colum earned his living as a writer. He married Mary Maguire in 1912, and they moved to the United States two years later.

While in the United States, the Colums often wrote together. They were popular lecturers and visiting professors at various American universities, especially at Columbia University, where they taught literature for many years. They spent most of their time in New York City, but they traveled frequently. Although they had no children, Colum earned his living largely by retelling folktales for children. These books were enormously popular. In 1924, the provincial legislature in Hawaii decided to preserve traditional Hawaiian folktales, and it decided that Colum was the most qualified person to undertake this project. The Colums spent two years in Hawaii, where Padraic learned Hawaiian and became so erudite in Hawaiian culture that he gave numerous lectures on Hawaiian history and culture in Honolulu's Bishop Museum.

During his nearly six decades in the United States, Colum remained a prolific writer. He was a humble man who preferred speaking about his wife and their numerous fellow writers, especially their close friend James Joyce, to talking about himself. One year after Mary's death in 1957, Colum completed a biography the two of them had been writing of Joyce, which he titled *Our Friend James Joyce*. At that time Colum began receiving care from his nephew Emmet Greene, who assisted him in his many trips around the New York area. Although Colum never wrote an autobiography, American scholar Zack Bowen recorded a series of interviews with him in the 1960's. In the interviews, Colum spoke extensively of his literary career. Bowen relied on these interviews for his 1970 biography of Colum, and he donated these tapes to the library of the State University of New York, Binghamton, which houses Colum's papers. Colum died in a nursing home in Connecticut on January 11, 1972. His body was flown to Ireland, where he was buried next to his beloved Mary.

ANALYSIS

In nineteenth century British and American plays, a common character type was the "stage Irishman." This artificial Irish character was not very bright or sensitive. He tended to be a buffoon whose major interest in life was drinking. These plays revealed no understanding of the harsh reality of colonial rule and economic exploitation in rural Ireland. Until the very end of the nineteenth century, Catholics could not own land in Ireland, and farmers were forced to pay rent to absentee landlords. A desire for stability and a profound love of the land were deeply felt by Irish peasants. Padraic Colum expressed their feelings in a poetic voice that was authentic.

"AN OLD WOMAN OF THE ROADS"

Colum's 1907 book *Wild Earth* includes some of his most admired poems. The very title suggests that generations of Irish peasants had resisted British efforts to suppress their culture and their Catholic faith. One of Colum's most famous early poems is "An Old Woman of the Roads." Its title refers to so-called tinkers, itinerant peddlers who traveled the roads of Ireland in their wagons and sold their goods. Because of their trade, tinkers did not develop roots in a specific village. In this twenty-four-line poem, which is composed of six four-line stanzas, the old woman speaks in the first person. She is a humble but proud woman with simple desires. She dreams of having a house with a hearth, heated by sod, in which she could have a bed and a dresser. She imagines that this house would also be her store, in which she could display her goods to eager customers. She is tired of endless traveling in her wagon, and she dreams of stability, which she associates with peace. Like almost all Irish peasants, she is deeply committed to the Catholic faith that gives her the strength to endure suffering with quiet dignity. In the final stanza, the old woman realizes that she may never have a house in this life, but she still dreams of paradise, where she will be "out of the wind's and the rain's way." As she travels the roads of Ireland, she prays to God "night and day."

As for other Irish peasants, God's presence in their daily lives and the resurrection are realities that she does not question. She is tired of the constant struggle to survive in abject poverty, but she never forgets that God loves her, and she believes that she will eventually return to her true "house" in heaven. With many different uses of the word *house*, Colum enables his readers to appreciate the quiet dignity and profound spirituality of ordinary Irish people. It is not at all surprising that "An Old Woman of the Roads" remains a poem beloved by generations of Irish readers and readers of Irish descent.

"A CRADLE SONG"

Another 1907 poem that has remained popular is the sixteen-line poem "A Cradle Song." As in "An Old Woman of the Roads," each stanza contains four lines of free verse. The scene evoked in this poem is universal. Parents around the world sing to their babies to calm them and to help them sleep. Just as in "An Old Woman of the Roads,"

Colum includes a clear religious reference because the mother of whom he speaks in "A Cradle Song" is the Virgin Mary.

Colum transfers the infancy of Christ to an Irish country setting, and he refers to Mary by the Irish term of endearment "Mavourneen," which means "darling." The Gospel according to Saint Matthew tells how three wise men, or magi, came to adore the infant Jesus just after Mary had given birth. In "A Cradle Song," Colum transforms these wise men into "men from the fields" whom a new mother has invited to come see her infant son, whom she has protected with "her mantle of blue." The great respect due Christ and all babies and mothers requires that the "men from the fields" enter the house "gently" and "softly," lest they disturb the mother or child. Colum evokes the poverty of these surroundings by pointing out that the floor in this house is cold, and farm animals are "peering" at the mother and baby "across the half door." Despite the lack of material comfort, the mother is happy because she is experiencing the miracle of a new life. In this poem, Colum expresses very eloquently to his readers the incredible joy that new life brings.

"ROGER CASEMENT"

Colum wrote several elegies in praise of distinguished Irish people who had died. His most famous elegy was for the Irish patriot Roger David Casement (1864-1916), whom the British hanged on a charge of treason. Colum and others who favored Irish independence from Great Britain never believed the accusations against Casement, whom they considered to be a martyr. This elegy contains two eight-line stanzas. Four of the sixteen lines contain the Gaelic words for mourning, "ochone, och, ochone, ochone!" One could translate the word *ochone* as "alas," but these are words people say at an Irish country burial. Casement was hanged in a British jail, but Colum imagines that Irish peasants have reserved for him the honors owed to a worthy person who has left this earth to spend eternity in heaven. Colum states that those who respect Roger Casement's memory are not respectable English people named Smith, Murray, or Cecil, who approved of the execution of an Irish hero, but rather "outcast peoples . . . who laboured fearfully." These social outcasts, whom the British disdain and with whom Colum identifies, will "lift" Casement "for the eyes of God to see."

Although Casement was executed for treason, Colum reminds his readers that although a colonial power can reduce individuals to silence by killing them, it can never destroy in the minds of ordinary people the martyr's dignity. Casement's heroism in the face of death serves only to remind Irish people of his "noble stature . . . courtesy and kindliness" that Colum evokes in this very powerful elegy.

"AFTER SPEAKING OF ONE WHO DIED A LONG TIME BEFORE"

Although Colum wrote poems of very high quality for seventy years, just three years before his death, he completed an extraordinary collection of twenty poems, titled *Images of Departure*. These exquisite poems express the joy of life felt by an eighty-eight-year-old poet who had survived his wife and almost all his friends. Perhaps the finest poem in this collection is the twenty-four-line poem "After Speaking of One Who Died a Long Time Before." This short poem is composed of an eleven-line stanza and a thirteen-line stanza. He links his personal loss of his beloved wife and best friend, Mary, with the "tenderness and grief" simultaneously felt by people when they think of dead loved ones who profoundly touched their lives. Near the very end of his long life, Colum still demonstrated his masterful ability to use ordinary words and images to help his readers appreciate the rich complexity of human emotions.

OTHER MAJOR WORKS

LONG FICTION: *Castle Conquer*, 1923; *The Flying Swans*, 1957.

SHORT FICTION: *Selected Short Stories of Padraic Colum*, 1985 (Sanford Sternlicht, editor).

PLAYS: *The Children of Lir*, pb. 1901 (one act); *Broken Soil*, pr. 1903 (revised as *The Fiddler's House*, pr., pb. 1907); *The Land*, pr., pb. 1905; *The Miracle of the Corn*, pr. 1908; *The Destruction of the Hostel*, pr. 1910; *Thomas Muskerry*, pr., pb. 1910; *The Desert*, pb. 1912 (revised as *Mogu the Wanderer: Or, The Desert*, pb. 1917); *The Betrayal*, pr. 1914; *Three Plays*, 1916, 1925, 1963 (includes *The Land*, *The Fiddler's House*, and *Thomas Muskerry*); *The Grasshopper*, pr. 1917 (adaptation of Eduard Keyserling's play *Ein Frühlingsofer*); *Balloon*, pb. 1929; *Moytura: A Play for Dancers*, pr., pb. 1963; *The Challengers*, pr. 1966 (3 one-act plays: *Monasterboice*, *Glendalough*, and *Cloughoughter*); *Carricknabauna*, pr. 1967 (also as *The Road Round Ireland*); *Selected Plays of Padraic Colum*, 1986 (includes *The Land*, *The Betrayal*, *Glendalough*, and *Monasterboice*; Sternlicht, editor).

SCREENPLAY: *Hansel and Gretel*, 1954 (adaptation of Engelbert Humperdinck's opera).

NONFICTION: *My Irish Year*, 1912; *The Road Round Ireland*, 1926; *Cross Roads in Ireland*, 1930; *A Half-Day's Ride: Or, Estates in Corsica*, 1932; *Our Friend James Joyce*, 1958 (with Mary Colum); *Ourselves Alone: The Story of Arthur Griffith and the Origin of the Irish Free State*, 1959.

CHILDREN'S LITERATURE: *A Boy in Eirinn*, 1913; *The King of Ireland's Son*, 1916; *The Adventures of Odysseus*, 1918; *The Boy Who Knew What the Birds Said*, 1918; *The Girl Who Sat by the Ashes*, 1919; *The Boy Apprenticed to an Enchanter*, 1920; *The Children of Odin*, 1920; *The Golden Fleece and the Heroes Who Lived Before Achilles*, 1921; *The Children Who Followed the Piper*, 1922; *At the Gateways of the Day*, 1924; *The Island of the Mighty: Being the Hero Stories of Celtic Britain Retold from the Mabinogion*, 1924; *Six Who Were Left in a Shoe*, 1924; *The Bright Islands*, 1925; *The Forge in the Forest*, 1925; *The Voyagers: Being Legends and Romances of Atlantic Discovery*, 1925; *The Fountain of Youth: Stories to Be Told*, 1927; *Orpheus: Myths of the World*, 1930; *The Big Tree of Bunlahy: Stories of My Own Countryside*, 1933; *The White Sparrow*, 1933; *The Legend of Saint Columba*, 1935; *Legends of Hawaii*, 1937;

Where the Winds Never Blew and the Cocks Never Crew, 1940; *The Frenzied Prince: Being Heroic Stories of Ancient Ireland*, 1943; *A Treasury of Irish Folklore*, 1954; *Story Telling, New and Old*, 1961; *The Stone of Victory, and Other Tales of Padraic Colum*, 1966.

BIBLIOGRAPHY

Bowen, Zack. *Padraic Colum: A Biographical-Critical Introduction.* Carbondale: Southern Illinois University Press, 1970. This excellent introduction to Colum's works was based on a careful study of his writings but also on extensive interviews between Colum and Zack Bowen in the 1960's.

Colum, Mary. *Life and the Dream.* Garden City, N.Y.: Doubleday, 1947. A firsthand account by Colum's wife of the impact of the Irish Literary Revival. The events and personalities of that creative period are regarded nostalgically and rather uncritically.

Hogan, Robert, Richard Burnham, and Daniel P. Poteet. *The Rise of the Realists.* Atlantic Highlands, N.J.: Humanities Press, 1979. This volume concentrates on the years of Colum's involvement with the Abbey Theatre and the national theater movement. Although it focuses on the plays, it sheds light on Colum's poetry.

Journal of Irish Literature 2, no. 1 (January, 1973). This special issue on Colum contains a miscellany of Colum material, including tributes from a number of Irish scholars, a substantial interview, and articles surveying Colum's achievements. Also included is a portfolio of work by Colum, including two plays, poems for children and other verse, and various prose pieces, one of which is a self-portrait.

Murphy, Ann. "Appreciation: Padraic Colum (1881-1972), National Poet." *Eire-Ireland: A Journal of Irish Studies* 17, no. 4 (Winter, 1982): 128-147. A thoughtful essay that describes well the important place of Colum in twentieth century Irish poetry.

Murray, Christopher. "Padraic Colum's *The Land* and Cultural Nationalism." *Hungarian Journal of English and American Studies* 2, no. 2 (1996): 5-15. A short but accurate description of Colum's support for Irish independence from Great Britain.

"Poet to the Eye, Giant in the Canon." *Irish Times*, December 11, 2006, p. 14. This article, written after the 135th birthday of the poet, argues that Colum's skills as a poet should be more highly recognized.

Sternlicht, Sanford. *Padraic Colum.* Boston: Twayne, 1985. An introductory study of Colum's long life and various literary achievements. Much attention is given to the poems. Also contains a detailed chapter on the prose and another on Colum's works of mythology, which are associated with his children's writing. Includes a chronology and a bibliography.

_____. "Padraic Colum: Poet of the 1960's." *Colby Literary Quarterly* 25, no. 4 (1989): 253-257. A short but insightful analysis of *Images of Departure* elegies written by Colum in the 1960's.

Edmund J. Campion

GEORGE DARLEY

Born: Dublin, Ireland; 1795
Died: London, England; November 23, 1846

PRINCIPAL POETRY
The Errors of Ecstasie: A Dramatic Poem with Other Pieces, 1822
Nepenthe, 1835
Poems of the Late George Darley, 1890
The Complete Poetical Works of George Darley, 1908 (Ramsey Colles, editor)

OTHER LITERARY FORMS

George Darley might be called a literary hack. The profession of writer in the early nineteenth century was a precarious one, and Darley tried his hand at most of the popular literary forms of his time. Although his work was usually unsigned, in keeping with the tradition of anonymous reviewing and publishing at the time, Darley can be credited with lyrical dramas, or masques, in the Elizabethan style, and a large number of reviews of art exhibits and current plays.

Among Darley's major literary works were a series of "dramatic" poems, *Sylvia: Or, The May Queen, a Lyrical Drama* (pb. 1827); and two tragedies: *Thomas à Becket: A Dramatic Chronicle in Five Acts* (pb. 1840) and *Ethelstan: Or, The Battle of Brunaburh, a Dramatic Chronicle in Five Acts* (pb. 1841). The titles of Darley's dramatic pieces suggest that they were written to be publicly staged, but none ever made it to the theater. Finally, Darley's letters should be noted as a highly valuable commentary on the life of a professional writer at a critical phase in English literature. His letters, even more than his various essays on literature and art, provide a useful series of insights into the events and problems of the era. In spite of Darley's shy disposition, he met many of the most famous poets and critics of his time, read widely in the literature of his day, and was a fair commentator on many pressing social issues.

It should be noted that Darley spent his last five years writing scientific textbooks for the use of students of secondary age. He may also have written a *Life of Virgil*, which is ascribed to him in the British Museum catalog.

ACHIEVEMENTS

George Darley never attained the recognition for his poetry and dramatic works that he earnestly sought throughout most of his adult life, although he pretended to be indifferent to the poetic fame that invariably eluded him and demanded that his friends be unsparing of his feelings in making their comments on his work. In truth, his poetry was seldom reviewed or even noticed by anyone outside the immediate circle of his friends.

It is difficult to find references to his ideas or to his poetry in anything but the most exhaustive surveys of English Romanticism. Still, within the circle of Darley's friends, he was regarded as something of a poetic genius—the poet who would bring forth a new era of poetry. Charles Lamb, Thomas Lovell Beddoes, and John Clare were enthusiastic readers of his work and did their best to secure attention from the critical reviews. Even the proverbially churlish Thomas Carlyle remarked that Darley was one of the few poets of his day who really understood the spirit of Elizabethan tragedy, to the extent of being able to imitate it with any kind of success. Despite these favorable opinions, Darley never achieved more than a marginal place among the English poets of the early nineteenth century.

It was only some forty years after his death that readers took up Darley's poetry with interest. Part of this interest derived from the Celtic renaissance, but part also derived from Darley's ultimate claims to be read as a good minor poet.

BIOGRAPHY

George Darley was born in Dublin, Ireland, in 1795. He was the oldest of seven children of Arthur and Mary Darley. His parents were of the upper class, and for unknown reasons went to America for an extended visit when Darley was about three. The boy was reared by his grandfather, and he always referred to this period of his life as the "sunshine of the breast." At this time in his life, Darley acquired an extreme stammer, so severe that even in his later years, his closest friends could scarcely make out what he was saying. The stammer may have been important in determining his later career as a poet, and it partly accounts for one of the most common themes in the poetry: the isolation of the poet.

In 1815, Darley entered Trinity College, Dublin. He apparently made few friends there and, curiously, never mentioned the school in his later correspondence. The stammer interfered with his examinations, but he received his degree in 1820 and immediately left for London. Despite his speech defect and chronic shyness, Darley made friends with a number of writers who were emerging in the 1820's. His friends encouraged his work, and the letters he exchanged with such poets as Clare and Beddoes reveal their high regard for his work.

Darley spent almost ten years in London working at various literary and scientific projects, but late in 1830, he determined to go to France. He wrote occasional essays on art for the *Athenaeum* and (perhaps) another journal, titled *The Original*, but there are few records of his life in Paris or his tours to Italy. It is significant, however, that several members of the Darley family were, for a while, reunited. The older brothers toured Italy together, and later Germany. Darley had always been sickly and generally poor, but he was a good tourist, and the letters from this period are among his best.

Darley continued to review books on various subjects for the *Athenaeum*, earning a reputation for extreme severity. He adopted the role in his private life of a vivacious and often bitter critic; he died in November, 1846, having never revisited Ireland, which constituted the one subject that was above criticism.

ANALYSIS

George Darley's best poetry is the work of a man seeking escape from the world. The sorrows of his life—his poverty and his lack of recognition—are for the most part not present in his poetry. Many of his poems are about love, beautiful women, and the death of innocent women. This preoccupation suggests one of the more common Romantic motifs: the separation between a desirable realm of creativity and fertility and the sterile existence of the poet's life. In Darley's love poems, there is a continuing search for perfection—the perfect woman, the perfect love. These poems show the influence of the Cavalier poet Thomas Carew, and it might be noted that one of Darley's most successful poems ("It Is Not Beauty I Demand") was published in the *London Magazine* with the name Carew appended to it. The fraud was not discovered until much later, after Francis Palgrave had included the poem in *The Golden Treasury*.

The women in Darley's poems are not the sentimental idols of so much nineteenth century love poetry, yet these lyrics are marred by Darley's frequent use of Elizabethan clichés: lips as red as roses, breasts as white as snow, hair as golden as the sun. In setting and theme as well, Darley's love poems are excessively conventional.

NATURE POEMS

In his nature poetry, Darley was able to achieve a more authentic style and tone. His early years in the Irish countryside had given him an almost pantheistic appreciation of nature as the ultimate source of comfort; many of his nature poems border on a kind of religious veneration. It is nature that comforts humanity, not the Church; it is nature that speaks with an "unerring voice" and will, if attended to, provide humans with the lessons in morality that they require.

"A Country Sunday," one of Darley's finest nature poems, illustrates this idea of God-in-nature. The poem, given its reference to Sunday, is curiously barren of any directly religious references. It is the sun that gives joy and the wind that serves as the vehicle of prayer. Nature serves as the great link between humanity's sordid existence and heaven.

"IT IS NOT BEAUTY I DEMAND"

In several of the lyric poems the themes of nature and love are fused. "It Is Not Beauty I Demand"—Darley's one assuredly great poem—illustrates the blending of nature and love, though the intent of the poet is to raise human love to a level beyond anything that might be found in nature. Darley's method is to use many of the standard phrases about women's beauty ("a crystal brow"; "starry eyes"; "lips that seem on roses fed") in a series of ten rapidly moving quatrains, with eight beats to each line, and a simple rhyme scheme of *abab cdcd* through the whole of the poem. The quatrains move rapidly, in part because Darley uses the syntax and diction of one who is speaking directly to his reader.

In "It Is Not Beauty I Demand," the natural beauties of the perfect woman are rejected as mere ornaments, or "gauds." In the fourth stanza, Darley breaks from the Cavalier tradition of "all for love" and inserts a fairly traditional moral into the poem. Thus, the red lips are rejected because they lead to destruction, like the red coral "beneath the ocean stream" upon which the "adventurer" perishes. The same moral argument is continued in the following stanzas, in which the white cheeks of the woman are rejected because they incite "hot youths to fields of blood." Even the greatest symbol of female beauty— "Helen's breast"—is rejected because Helen's beauty provoked war and suffering.

Darley's ideal woman would be a companion, a comforter, one with "a tender heart" and "loyal mind." Despite Darley's obvious affinities in this poem with Carew and other Cavalier poets, the poem represents a rejection of the Cavalier ideals of going off to battle to prove one's love and honor; it also represents a challenge to the rich sensuality of much Romantic poetry. With its emphasis on the intellectual virtues of women and the pleasures of companionship (versus sex), "It Is Not Beauty I Demand" is an affirmation of the ideals of love and marriage associated with the Victorians.

VERSE DRAMAS VERSUS LYRICS

Mention must be made of Darley's two tragedies, which in spite of their obvious failure as stage plays represent his most sustained creative effort. Darley had always been an enthusiastic reader of William Shakespeare and other Elizabethan dramatists; one of the most striking themes in his dramatic reviews was the death of tragedy in his own time. He was especially sickened by the rise and popularity of domestic tragedy; he reviewed one of the most popular tragedies of his time (*Ion*) in an almost savage manner for its sentimentality. Darley was not able to reverse the tendencies of Victorian playwriting, but his two tragedies, *Thomas à Becket* and *Ethelstan*, whatever their shortcomings as plays (they can be characterized as dramatic verse), illustrate what he thought a tragedy ought to be. He invoked the Elizabethan ideal of a man in high place who is brought to his death through his own error and the malice of others. Darley, however, was not able to write dialogue, and his characters are much given to lengthy, histrionic speeches. In many instances, the speeches cover entire scenes. As far as the plays have merit, they serve to illustrate the Victorian preoccupation with the "great man." Darley's heroes and villains are indeed on the heroic scale, but they lack credibility and the blank verse is frequently bathetic.

By contrast, Darley's lyrics, his only lasting achievement, have a genuine but limited appeal. His speech impediment, aloofness, and chronic shyness seemed to have forced him into a career that would serve as a natural release to his emotions. In his poetry, Darley created a world of fantasy, of benevolent nature and beautiful maidens, an ordered universe that the poet never found in real life.

OTHER MAJOR WORKS

PLAYS: *Sylvia: Or, The May Queen, a Lyrical Drama*, pb. 1827; *Thomas à Becket: A Dramatic Chronicle in Five Acts*, pb. 1840; *Ethelstan: Or, The Battle of Brunaburh, a Dramatic Chronicle in Five Acts*, pb. 1841.

NONFICTION: *The Life and Letters of George Darley*, 1928 (Claude Abbott, editor of letters).

BIBLIOGRAPHY

Abbott, Claude Colleer, ed. *The Life and Letters of George Darley, Poet and Critic.* 1928. Reprint. Oxford, England: Clarendon Press, 1967. A rare biography of Darley, which presents him as a poet and critic of distinction. Includes a full analysis of Darley's lyric poetry and of his major work *Nepenthe*. Notes the weakness in the structure of his work and suggests that it should be read as a series of lyric episodes expressing the theme of spiritual adventure. Includes a complete bibliography of works by Darley.

Bloom, Harold. *The Visionary Company: A Reading of English Romantic Poetry.* 1961. Rev. ed. Ithaca, N.Y.: Cornell University Press, 1971. This brief analysis is important because Bloom is one of the most influential of modern literary critics. He pays Darley a high compliment by including him in the "visionary company" of Romantic poets. Includes a reading of *Nepenthe*, which Bloom sees as a quest-romance in the tradition of Percy Bysshe Shelley's *Alastor* (1816) and John Keats's *Endymion: A Poetic Romance* (1818).

Brisman, Leslie. *Romantic Origins.* Ithaca, N.Y.: Cornell University Press, 1978. The most extensive treatment of Darley by a modern critic, although it makes difficult reading. Brisman argues that Darley's awareness of his rank as a minor poet provides him with a recurring theme: He deliberately cultivates a "myth of weakness." This is particularly noticeable in *Nepenthe*, a poem in which Darley transforms the romantic quest "into a search for images of poetic diminutiveness."

Heath-Stubbs, John F. *The Darkling Plain: A Study of the Later Fortunes of Romanticism in English Poetry from George Darley to W. B. Yeats.* 1950. Reprint. Philadelphia: R. West, 1977. Perhaps the best brief overview of Darley's work, particularly *Nepenthe*. Heath-Stubbs links *Nepenthe* to works by Keats and Shelley, and also those by William Blake. Argues that in its "continuous intensity of lyrical music and vivid imagery" *Nepenthe* is unlike any other poem of similar length in English.

Jack, Ian. *English Literature, 1815-1832.* Oxford, England: Clarendon Press, 1963. Brief assessment in which Jack argues that Darley was a better critic than he was poet. Of his poetry, Darley's lyrics are superior to his long poems, although his diction was often flawed. He may, however, have had an influence on Alfred, Lord Tennyson. One of Darley's weaknesses was that he did not have anything original to say.

John R. Griffin

OLIVER GOLDSMITH

Born: Pallas, County Longford(?), Ireland; November 10, 1728 or 1730
Died: London, England; April 4, 1774

PRINCIPAL POETRY
"An Elegy on the Glory of Her Sex: Mrs. Mary Blaize," 1759
"The Logicians Refuted," 1759
The Traveller: Or, A Prospect of Society, 1764
"Edwin and Angelina," 1765
"An Elegy on the Death of a Mad Dog," 1766
The Deserted Village, 1770
"Threnodia Augustalis," 1772
"Retaliation," 1774
The Haunch of Venison: A Poetical Epistle to Lord Clare, 1776
"The Captivity: An Oratoria," pb. 1820 (wr. 1764)

OTHER LITERARY FORMS

Like Joseph Addison, Samuel Johnson, and other eighteenth century writers, Oliver Goldsmith did not confine himself to one genre. Besides poetry, Goldsmith wrote two comedies, a novel, periodical essays, a collection of letters, popular histories of England and Rome, and several biographical sketches. By the 1760's, literature had become a commercial enterprise, and successful authorship meant writing what the public would read. Goldsmith could write fluently on a wide variety of subjects, even when his knowledge of some of them was superficial. He was especially skillful at adapting another's work to his audience's interests: Many of his short poems are imitations of foreign models, and the collection of fictional letters, *The Citizen of the World* (1762), is an adaptation of Montesquieu's *Persian Letters* (1721). Both his collected works and his letters are available in modern editions.

ACHIEVEMENTS

Oliver Goldsmith used his fluent pen to write himself out of obscurity. Like many other eighteenth century writers, he progressed from hackwork to authorship—and along the way did something to raise the level of hackwork. His life and career demonstrate the transition that occurred in British literature as commercial publishing gradually replaced patronage as the chief support of writers.

Goldsmith is both one of the most characteristic and one of the best English writers of the late 1700's. His *The Vicar of Wakefield* (1766), for example, both reflects the taste of the period for sentimental fiction and maintains itself as a minor classic today. His

Oliver Goldsmith
(Library of Congress)

The Deserted Village is likewise a typical pastoral of the period and a landmark of English poetry. In his own time, Goldsmith reflected an important new sensibility in English culture: an awareness of Britain as part of a European community with which it shared problems and attitudes. This new view is evident in *The Traveller*, which contrasts the great states of Europe to understand the character of each nation more than to trumpet British superiority; this cosmopolitan spirit also shapes the letters of *The Citizen of the World*, which analyze English society through a Chinese visitor's eyes.

Even without a historical interest, many readers still find Goldsmith enjoyable for his style and his comedy. Goldsmith is one of the masters of the middle style; no reader has to work hard at his informal, almost conversational prose and poetry. Although his pieces are often filled with social observation, Goldsmith's human and humorous observations of people make his work accessible and pleasurable even to those who never met a lord or made the Grand Tour. His characters and perceptions are rooted in universal experiences.

BIOGRAPHY

Although David Garrick's epigrammatic remark that Oliver Goldsmith "wrote like an angel, but talk's like poor Poll" exaggerates his social awkwardness, it does contain an important indicator. Before Goldsmith discovered authorship, his life had been all trial and mostly error.

As the second son of an Irish clergyman, Goldsmith could not look forward to independent means; most of the family resources went to increase the dowry of a sister. Nature seems to have been equally parsimonious toward him: Childhood disease, natural indolence, and physical ungainliness left him prey to his classmates' teasing and his schoolmasters' scorn. His later days at Trinity College in Dublin were no better: He got into trouble with administrators, ran away, but returned to earn a low bachelor's degree in 1749.

For the next ten years, Goldsmith seemed at a complete loss for direction. He toyed with the idea of running away to America, but instead applied for ordination in the Church of England. Emphatically rejected by the local bishop, Goldsmith went in 1751 to study medicine at the University of Leyden. After mild attention to his studies, Goldsmith toured Europe, sometimes with the dignity of a "foreign student" and sometimes with the poverty of a wandering minstrel. Returning to London in 1756, he successively failed at teaching and at getting a medical appointment in the navy. He found work as a proofreader for the novelist-printer Samuel Richardson and as a hack writer for the bookseller Griffiths. To raise money, Goldsmith began writing *An Enquiry into the Present State of Polite Learning in Europe*, for which he found a publisher in 1759.

This lively account of the contemporary intellectual world won him attention from two literary entrepreneurs, Tobias Smollett and John Newbery, who gave him regular work on a variety of periodical papers writing essays, biographies, and a few poems. These labors brought him important acquaintances and the opportunity for greater success.

The year 1764 was a watershed for Goldsmith. First, he was admitted to the Literary Club, which brought together such luminaries as the actor David Garrick, the painter Joshua Reynolds, the politician Edmund Burke, and the writer Samuel Johnson. Second, he published *The Traveller*, which established him in the public's mind as one of the foremost poets of the day.

The success of *The Traveller* brought Goldsmith the first substantial income of his career, but because he never was capable of careful financial management, he continued to do piecework as well as to engage in serious projects. The last decade of his life saw a remarkable output of rapidly written general works, haphazardly compiled anthologies, as well as his best poem, a novel, and two plays. Whatever effort he put into a project, his name on the title page enormously increased chances for a brisk sale.

Goldsmith wrote practically until the hour of his death. His last effort was the poem "Retaliation," a verse response to Garrick's teasing epigram. Goldsmith died on April 4, 1774, the victim of both a fever and the remedy prescribed to cure it.

ANALYSIS

Eighteenth century poets viewed themselves primarily in relation to their audience. They acted as intermediaries between the audience and some higher truth: divine providence, the majesty of state, or the ideal world described by art. In his verse, Oliver Goldsmith made two self-appointments: first as arbiter of literature for a society that had largely lost its ability to appreciate poetry and second as commentator on social changes. Arbitrating poetic ideals and offering social commentary were not separate activities, Goldsmith thought, because readers who could not discriminate real feeling in poetry were likewise not likely to observe the world around them accurately. Again, like other eighteenth century poets, Goldsmith expressed his concerns in both comic and serious works. The comic efforts tease readers back from excesses; the serious ones urge them to return to the norm. These trends are clearest in Goldsmith's best poems, two mock elegies, the didactic *The Traveller* and the pastoral *The Deserted Village*.

COMIC ELEGIES

Thomas Gray's "Elegy Written in a Country Churchyard" (1751) had started a fashion in poetry for sentimental reflections on occasions of death. This impulse, although quite natural, found further expression in lamenting the end of persons and things not traditionally the subjects of public mourning. (Gray himself parodied the fashion he had started with an ode on the death of a favorite cat who drowned while trying to snare a goldfish.) Goldsmith attacked this proliferation of laments in the *Critical Review* in 1759. Citing the corruption of the elegy, Goldsmith judged that his peers thought flattery, bombast, and sorrow sufficient ingredients to compose a moving poem. He also teased the popular mode of elegies with several mock versions; the best of these are "An Elegy on the Glory of Her Sex: Mrs. Mary Blaize" and "An Elegy on the Death of a Mad Dog." No other poems so well illustrate Goldsmith's comic ability.

Adapted from an older French poem, "An Elegy on the Glory of Her Sex: Mrs. Mary Blaize" laments with tongue in cheek the passing of a one-time strumpet turned pawnbroker. The poem's narrator strives hard to attribute conventional virtues of charity and probity to her, only to admit in the last line of each stanza to some qualification of the lady's virtue:

> She strove the neighbourhood to please,
> With manners wondrous winning,
> And never follow'd wicked ways,—
> *Unless when she was sinning.*

"An Elegy on the Death of a Mad Dog," which first appeared as a song in *The Vicar of Wakefield*, makes a similar point about the perversion of elegiac conventions by telling of a "kind and gentle" man who befriended a dog "of low degree." At first they get along well, then the dog, "to gain some private ends," goes mad and bites the man. The townspeople lament that this good man must die a wretched death, betrayed by the ungrateful cur that he has trusted. In the final stanza, however, the poet twists the reader's sentimental expectation of a tragic ending: Instead of the man, it is the dog that dies.

THE TRAVELLER

Goldsmith had more serious issues to lay before his audience. His first major poem, *The Traveller*, attempts a philosophic survey of European life, showing, he declared in the dedication, that "there may be equal happiness in states that are governed differently from our own; that every state has a particular principle of happiness, and that this principle in each may be carried to a mischievous excess."

Condensing observations made on his trip to Europe into one moment, Goldsmith describes himself seated on a mountaintop in the Alps, from which he can look across to the great states of Europe: Italy, Switzerland, France, Holland, and Britain. Each land reveals to the poet's eye its special blessing—and its liability.

Italy, bountifully supplied by Nature and once the seat of empire, has been exhausted by the pursuit and burden of wealth; now peasant huts arise where once imperial buildings stood. Switzerland, less endowed by Nature, produces a self-reliant and hardy race that has few wants but cannot develop "the gentler morals" that are a hallmark of a refined culture. France, dedicated to the graces of civilized life, has developed the most brilliant society in Europe but one which is prey to ostentation and vanity. Holland, claimed from the sea by an industrious people, devotes its energies to commerce and trade that now accumulates superfluous treasure "that engenders craft and fraud." England, which Nature has treated neither too richly nor too miserly, is the home of Liberty and Freedom, which allow people to rule themselves; but self-rule in excess becomes party strife and colonial ambition.

Because every human society is imperfect, Goldsmith concludes, people must remember that human happiness is seldom regulated by laws or royal edicts. Since each of us is "to ourselves in every place consigned," the constant in life must be the "smooth current of domestic joy."

The Traveller echoes Goldsmith's favorite poets of the preceding generations and of his own time. Like Joseph Addison's "A Letter from Italy" (1703), it comments on England's political state by contrast with that of other European powers. Like Alexander Pope's *An Essay on Man* (1733-1734), it enunciates a philosophic principle in verse. Like Samuel Johnson's *The Vanity of Human Wishes* (1749), it concludes with the assertion that human happiness is determined by individual, not social experience. As derivative as *The Traveller* is, however, Goldsmith's poem is still his own. Less nationalistic than Addison's, less systematizing than Pope's, and less tragic than Johnson's, Goldsmith's poem possesses the graceful ease of the periodical essay whose tone is conversational and whose form mixes personal observation with public pronouncement. *The Traveller* is cast as an epistle to the poet's brother and as an account of the years of wandering that have led the poet to this meditation on human experience. The interest moves easily and naturally from the poet's wanderings to his social meditations, observations, and finally to philosophic insight. In the dedication to *The Traveller*, Goldsmith also laments the decay of poetry in a society verging on the "extremes of refinement."

By echoing the themes and forms of earlier poets, Goldsmith offers his readers a return to the poetry of an age that brought the "greatest perfection" of the language. As he observed in *An History of England in a Series of Letters from a Nobleman to His Son* (1764), modern poets have only added finery to the muse's dress, not outfitted her anew.

THE DESERTED VILLAGE

The Deserted Village, 430 lines long, repeats the mixture of personal observation and public utterance. This time the topic is closer to home, the depopulation of the countryside because of a series of Enclosure Acts that turned formerly common village lands into private farms worked only for well-to-do landlords. Goldsmith observes that enclosure drives "a bold peasantry, their country's pride" into the city or away to the colonies. The poem is at once a lament for a lost way of life and a call to society to awaken to a danger.

The first 114 lines describe the poet's relationship to Auburn, the "loveliest village of the plain," an abstract, idealized version of Goldsmith's boyhood home. The poet recalls Auburn as a place of innocence where his youth was so happy that work and play were scarcely distinguishable. Now, like other villages, Auburn is "to hastening ills a prey"; these ills are trade, the growth of wealth, and the peasantry's departure from the land. The decline of Auburn darkens not only the poet's memory and civic pride but his hopes as well. Auburn was to be his place of retirement from life's cares where he might "die at home at last."

In the next 140 lines, the narrator surveys the buildings and inhabitants of Auburn: the church and the parsonage where the minister, "unpracticed he to fawn, or seek for power," kept a refuge to feed a hungry beggar, talk with an old soldier, and comfort the dying; the schoolhouse where the master, "a man severe and stern to view," shared with his pupils "the love he bore to learning"; and finally, the inn whose neat and trim interior played host to "greybeard mirth and smiling toil."

An equally long section then describes the present sad condition of Auburn. Imagining the village as a beautiful girl who turns increasingly to fashionable dress and cosmetics as her natural bloom fades, Goldsmith recounts how the "sons of wealth" force the peasantry off the land to build splendid estates with striking vistas. The displaced villagers trek to the cities, where pleasure seduces them from innocence or crime overcomes their honesty, or to the colonies, where a fiercer climate than England's threatens their lives. The section ends with a poignant description of families uprooted and friends or lovers separated as the people depart the village. With them "rural virtues leave the land."

The final section of the poem invokes "Sweet Poetry," which, like the inhabitants of Auburn, is being driven from the land. The poet hopes that poetry will nevertheless continue "to aid truth with [its] persuasive train" and teach humanity the age-old lesson that wealth ultimately destroys the simple virtues that bind people to the land and to one another.

The Deserted Village emphasizes that moral by a striking departure from literary convention. As a pastoral, the poem ought to persuade readers of the countryside's charms and goodness; as a pastoral it should express the ideals of peaceful virtue, harmony with nature, and productive use of the land that were commonplaces since classical Greek poetry. Goldsmith's poem presents these familiar ideas, but as a lament and a warning that the pastoral ideal is slipping away. Bound by tradition to use the conventions but unable to disguise the truth, the poet seeks to arouse rather than soothe the reader's imagination.

One of Goldsmith's most moving poetic devices in *The Deserted Village* is the catalog. At four crucial places, the narrative slows to allow leisurely description; these descriptive catalogs are composed of grammatically and metrically similar lines. The device is an elaboration of the neoclassical practice of balancing and paralleling couplets; its effect is to intensify the emotional impact of the passage. The catalog of the inn's furnishings is the most vivid of these passages and illustrates Goldsmith at his best.

FLAWED EXPERIMENTS

Trying his hand at many different styles and pieces, Goldsmith inevitably failed at some. "Threnodia Augustalis," for example, a poem mourning the death of the princess dowager of Wales, falls victim to the bombast and pomposity that Goldsmith laughed at in other elegiac poems. It shows how increasingly difficult had become the task of making poetic praise of the aristocracy sound convincing in an age when middle- and lower-class life was providing rich materials for the essay and the novel.

Another flawed poem is "Edwin and Angelina," a ballad of the type becoming more popular as the century progressed. Readers were drawn to this genre of folk poetry for its mysterious happenings in remote and romantic locations. Goldsmith tried to mix these qualities with the didactic strain of *The Traveller* and *The Deserted Village*. He tells of young lovers, separated by a cruel parent, who later meet while both are in disguise. The joy of their reunion is delayed while each delivers a long moral dissertation on the necessity of steadfast virtue and trust in Providence.

"The Captivity: An Oratorio" is a more ambitious treatment of the same theme but equally unsuccessful. Goldsmith makes a promising start by using the Israelite bondage in Babylon—a subject hardly ever treated in the literature of the age—as the frame for his moral, but he simply does not have a poetic vocabulary capable of describing spiritual anguish. When, early in the poem, a prophet urges the Israelites to repent and "offer up a tear," the poem has reached its deepest point of profundity.

OTHER MAJOR WORKS

LONG FICTION: *The Vicar of Wakefield*, 1766.

SHORT FICTION: *The Citizen of the World*, 1762 (collection of fictional letters first published in *The Public Ledger*, 1760-1761).

PLAYS: *The Good-Natured Man*, pr., pb. 1768; *She Stoops to Conquer: Or, The Mistakes of a Night*, pr., pb. 1773.

NONFICTION: *The Bee*, 1759 (essays); *An Enquiry into the Present State of Polite Learning in Europe*, 1759; *The Life of Richard Nash of Bath*, 1762; *An History of England in a Series of Letters from a Nobleman to His Son*, 1764 (2 volumes); *Life of Henry St. John, Lord Viscount Bolingbroke*, 1770; *Life of Thomas Parnell*, 1770; *An History of the Earth, and Animated Nature*, 1774 (8 volumes; unfinished).

MISCELLANEOUS: *The Collected Works of Oliver Goldsmith*, 1966 (5 volumes; Arthur Friedman, editor).

BIBLIOGRAPHY

Dixon, Peter. *Oliver Goldsmith Revisited*. Boston: Twayne, 1991. An updated introduction to the life and works of Goldsmith.

Hopkins, Robert H. *The True Genius of Oliver Goldsmith*. Baltimore: The Johns Hopkins University Press, 1969. Hopkins interprets Goldsmith not in the traditional view as a sentimental humanist but as a master of satire and irony. The chapter "Augustanisms and the Moral Basis for Goldsmith's Art" delineates the social, intellectual, and literary context in which Goldsmith wrote. Hopkins devotes a chapter each to Goldsmith's crafts of persuasion, satire, and humor.

Kazmin, Roman. "Oliver Goldsmith's *The Traveller* and *The Deserted Village*: Moral Economy of Landscape Representation." *English Studies* 87, no. 6 (December, 2006): 65. A critical study of Goldsmith's view of England's social problems.

Lucy, Séan, ed. *Goldsmith: The Gentle Master*. Cork, Ireland: Cork University Press, 1984. This short but useful collection of essays provides interesting biographical material on Goldsmith, as well as critical comment on his works.

Lytton Sells, Arthur. *Oliver Goldsmith: His Life and Works*. New York: Barnes and Noble, 1974. This volume is divided into two sections on Goldsmith's life and works, respectively. Individual chapters focus on particular facets of Goldsmith's work ("The Critic," "The Journalist," "The Biographer") and also feature more detailed studies of major works. Contains an extended discussion of Goldsmith as dramatist and poet.

Mikhail, E. H., ed. *Goldsmith: Interviews and Recollections*. New York: St. Martin's Press, 1993. Contains interviews with Goldsmith's friends and associates. Includes bibliographical references and index.

Quintana, Richard. *Oliver Goldsmith: A Georgian Study*. New York: Macmillan, 1967. This work incorporates biography and criticism in a readable account of Goldsmith's colorful life and his development as a writer. Goldsmith's many literary genres are discussed in depth, with chapters on his poetry, drama, essays, and fiction. A lengthy appendix offers notes on Goldsmith's lesser writings, such as his biographical and historical works.

Rousseau, G. S., ed. *Goldsmith: The Critical Heritage*. London: Routledge & Kegan Paul, 1974. A record of critical comment on Goldsmith, this volume is organized by particular works with an additional section on Goldsmith's life and general works. This anthology extends only as far as 1912, but pieces by Goldsmith's contemporaries, such as Sir Joshua Reynolds's sketch of Goldsmith's character, and by later critics such as William Hazlitt and Washington Irving, offer interesting perspectives on Goldsmith's place in literary history.

Swarbrick, Andrew, ed. *The Art of Oliver Goldsmith*. Totowa, N.J.: Barnes and Noble, 1984. This excellent collection of ten essays offers a wide-ranging survey of the works of Goldsmith. Essays treat individual works (*The Citizen of the World, The Deserted Village, The Traveller*), as well as more general topics such as the literary context in which Goldsmith wrote, the elements of classicism in his works, and his place in the Anglo-Irish literary tradition.

Worth, Katharine. *Sheridan and Goldsmith*. New York: St. Martin's Press, 1992. Worth compares and contrasts the lives and works of Goldsmith and Richard Brinsley Sheridan. Bibliography and index.

Robert M. Otten

EAMON GRENNAN

Born: Dublin, Ireland; November 13, 1941

OTHER LITERARY FORMS

Although Eamon Grennan (GREH-nahn) is celebrated principally for his poetry collections, he also is a respected critic and translator of Irish poetry. He has written reviews for *Dublin Magazine, Irish Times, Poetry Ireland Review, Poetry London, The New Republic*, and the *Times Literary Supplement* on various topics, including new Irish writing, the plays of George Fitzmaurice, medieval Irish lyrics, James Joyce, and Irish poetry since Patrick Kavanagh. He has penned a major work on Irish poetry in the twentieth century and translated several important poetic works.

ACHIEVEMENTS

Eamon Grennan is recognized by many fellow poets for his uncanny constructions of bicultural, international poetic works. In 2003, he received the Lenore Marshall Poetry Prize for his *Still Life with Waterfall*. Commenting on the award, poet Robert Wrigley referred to Grennan's ability to reward the reader by means of clarification across international and cultural barriers. Grennan also received the PEN Award for Poetry in Translation (1997), for *Selected Poems of Giacomo Leopardi* (1995). Leopardi is widely considered as the greatest lyric poet in the Italian literary tradition. Grennan is cited for his unique ability to translate Leopardi's work into a modern English form that exactly mimics the original intonation. Grennan has also received the James Boatwright III Prize for Poetry (1995) and Pushcart Prizes (1997, 2001, 2002, 2005), and "The Curve" was included in *The Best American Poetry, 2006*, edited by Billy Collins and David Lehman. He has made many personal appearances at poetic events, including the Writers Institute on March 13, 1997, for a Commemoration of the Irish Famine and Celebration of Irish Literature with Peter Quinn.

BIOGRAPHY

Eamon Grennan was born in Dublin in 1941. He attended a boarding school in a Cistercian monastery. He did his undergraduate studies at University College in Dublin, where he became acquainted with fellow poets Derek Mahon and Eavan Boland. Afterward, he spent one year in Rome before coming to the United States in 1964. He earned his doctoral degree at Harvard. In 1974, he became the Dexter M. Ferry, Jr., Professor of English at Vassar College, and remained in that position until his retirement in 2004.

Grennan published *Wildly for Days*, his first collection of poems, in 1983. He has a long and distinguished record of publications and is known for his attention to the lyrical and cerebral qualities of his works. Former U.S. poet laureate Collins has remarked on Grennan's generous, telluric, and sensual works, which deal openly and compassionately with the complexity of being human.

Grennan has settled in the United States but returns frequently to Ireland. Like his poetry, he shares components of both cultures, often blending American experience with Irish recollection. He twice returned to Ireland for limited periods, in 1977 and 1981. It was in Ireland that he began writing poetry, and he states that Gaelic poetry became a dominant force in his need to produce poems that echo this unique linguistic sound. Grennan embraces his status of alien resident in the United States, stating that he prefers to live at a distance from the land he occupies, as this gives his work an angle that cannot otherwise be achieved.

ANALYSIS

Eamon Grennan writes of a magical world that lies before the eyes of all his readers—the natural world of bugs, bees, deer, wind, dolphins, dunes, waves, and any other element in nature he chooses. He does so in a manner that interweaves a natural sensuality with the eroticism of humans and in nature. His poems combine his native and adopted lands, Ireland and the United States. His intimate descriptions of the occupants with whom all people share Earth are presented through a sort of memory looking-glass that views his world through his unique form of "bilingual" English.

Grennan leads the reader of his poems down a verbal and poetic nature trail that not only winds its way through the intricate lives of insects and animals and through earth and light, but also brings the reader face-to-face with the complexity of human nature and experience. The organic world he describes is seldom tranquil. His observations often remind the reader of the brutal realities that exist in the natural world. To the natural world, he juxtaposes the parallel human world, especially the erotic one, which is also sublime, but full of challenge, decay, and erosion. Whether Grennan speaks of the thick and frosty light that illuminates Cobble Bay, the lethal radiance of an errant star, or a dead otter rotting by the tide line, he sheds light on the human world and people's lives much as an inspirational sunrise lights up one's soul. That is, his poems illuminate people's lives by confirming the profound beauty and brutal reality of a world people often overlook. Grennan describes with sincere reverence the spirituality embedded in the natural world.

AS IF IT MATTERS

In *As if It Matters*, Grennan demonstrates the interconnectedness between the human realm and the natural world. The often violent human interaction with nature is asserted in his memory of the simple and subtle act of a friend chopping wood. The friend finds a sense of freedom in the act, but the tree, so violently split apart in providing the wood, is just one of various examples in this collection that point out the often tragic consequences of human domination of the natural world. Other poems reflect on how nature also participates, without regret, in the ongoing destruction of self and others that is the final and unavoidable means of balancing out day-to-day existence on earth. These poems of first-person meditations are often shrouded in references to various forms of light, wind, rain, flames, and vividly contrasted colors. In "Endangered Species," this mixture of elements from the natural environment mingles with the stark human gaze on that world. Typical of Grennan's works, it draws on seemingly unconscious human observation of an equally indifferent plant, animal, and climatological realm. Although the almost endless references to untold utopian happenings tend to blur Grennan's decisive descriptions, the poems are masterfully insightful.

STILL LIFE WITH WATERFALL

In *Still Life with Waterfall*, Grennan successfully combines astute comments on personal moments of love with an almost erotic gaze on the seemingly least important acts that occur within nature. He subtly links the love and necessity of human existence with the unconsciousness of nature and, by analogy, sheds light on people's unrealized connectivity with the natural world in which they live. The poems weave together a realm of frost, fire, marshland, tangled branches, and animal sounds (both gentle and alarming), and the interplay of predator and prey with human reality. In "Detail," the man hunting is juxtaposed to the hawk that simply snatches the robin in flight. Both acts, seemingly harsh, are presented as uncomplicated realities within the natural environment of humans and animals. The human becomes less human and, somehow, more natural. Grennan takes the reader to a point where trivial moments such as the nearly unheard hatching of bird eggs or the intimate gaze of a deer that looks for a reason to run become fused with human observation (in "Grid"). The poet filters these glimpses of reality with his bicultural and individual viewpoint and leaves the reader with a new way of integrating the outer world in which people live with the inner world that all people possess.

RELATIONS

In *Relations*, which collects poems from earlier volumes and presents new poems written between 1993 and 1995, the poet continues his observations of the analogy between human existence and that of the other realms of the planet: the flora, fauna, land, and climate of Earth. His words reflect a lifetime of scrutinizing the physical world. He infuses this surveillance of life's minor events with remarkable meaning. For example, in "Compass Reading," his description of a cat contemplating the slow death of its victim leads the reader to a very human analogy, that is, our own mortality. In this collection, Grennan includes many poems that examine human love in its more basic and physical forms. His reflection on the girl who remains in his memory by means of her connectedness with nature and physical love draws a powerful response from the reader. In "Muse, Maybe," he presents visions of the girl who was kissed in a graveyard, her warm skin beneath a raincoat, a woman of shadows and half-lights who is worn like a mask in his mind. The natural world of light, darkness, rain, and inevitable death is one of Grennan's most repeated themes. The poet remains faithful to his personal gazes of nature that reveal his inner self, and ours. For example, in "Swifts over Dublin," the swifts that twist, kiss, and soar are seen with human delight. Nonetheless, their cavorting in the full flush of summer is beyond the author's real-time life. They bring awareness of the human yearning for the eternal moment. This is a remarkable collection of poems that invite the reader to look within by means of lucidly presented examinations of the least remarkable events within the natural world.

OTHER MAJOR WORK

NONFICTION: *Facing the Music: Irish Poetry in the Twentieth Century*, 1999.

TRANSLATIONS: *Selected Poems of Giacomo Leopardi*, 1995; *Oedipus at Colonus*, 2004 (with Rachel Kitzinger; of Sophocles).

BIBLIOGRAPHY

Baker, Timothy. "'Something Secret and Still': Silence in the Poetry of Eamon Grennan." *Mosaic* 42, no. 4 (December, 2009): 45-63. Compares Grennan to Yves Bonnefoy and examines how his poetry "reveals the world through notions of silence and absence."

Boran, Pat. *Flowing, Still: Irish Poets on Irish Poetry*. Syracuse, N.Y.: Dedalus Press, 2009. The introduction presents a thoughtful and well-organized overview of Irish poets and poetry. It is quite useful for understanding the place of Irish poetry in the modern world. Grennan's section, "That Blank Mouth: Secrecy, Shibboleths, and Silence in Northern Irish Poetry," gives the reader insight into his unique ability to present the ordinary as extraordinary. Includes bibliographical references and index.

Brophy, James D. *Contemporary Irish Writing*. Boston: Twayne, 1983. The section by Grennan, "That Always Raised Voice," presents his own description of the poet's personal presence in his works. Contains a general review of modern Irish poetry and prose. Includes an extensive bibliography.

Collins, Billy, and David Lehman, eds. *The Best American Poetry, 2006*. New York: Scribner Poetry, 2006. Grennan's "The Curve" demonstrates his ability to present his American viewpoint without abandoning his Irish ancestry. It is this unique style of intercultural writing that helps to differentiate Grennan from other poets. Includes bibliography.

Fleming, Deborah. "The Common Ground of Eamon Grennan." *Éire-Ireland* 28, no. 4 (Winter, 1993): 133-149. Discusses Grennan's simple but profound approach to poetry that involves linking the natural world to that of human experience and aspiration. The viewpoint presented is distinctly Irish.

Greening, John. Review of *Selected and New Poems*. *Times Literary Supplement*, April 13, 2001. Gives the reader a brief but interesting review of Grennan's *Selected and New Poems*.

Grennan, Eamon. "When Language Fails." Interview by William Walsh. *Kenyon Review* 28, no. 3 (Summer, 2006): 125-141. Grennan talks about the craft of poetry and how living abroad has affected him.

Hacht, Anne Marie, and David Kelly, eds. *Poetry for Students*. Vol. 21. Detroit: Thomson/Gale, 2005. Analyzes Grennan's "Station," about leaving his son at the station. Contains the poem, summary, themes, style, historical context, critical overview, and criticism. Includes bibliography and index.

Johnston, Fred. Review of *So It Goes*. *Irish Times*, February 17, 1996, p. 9. Presents an insightful review. Again, the viewpoint is from Ireland, but the international mixture of Irish and American experience is examined.

Kenneally, Michael. *Poetry in Contemporary Irish Literature*. Gerrards Cross, Buckinghamshire, England: Colin Smythe, 1995. Grennan's segment, "Foreign Relations: Irish and International Poetry," explores the international and intercultural approach that he uses in much of his poetry. The introduction to the book provides an overview of modern Irish poetry. Includes bibliography and index.

Paul Siegrist

SEAMUS HEANEY

Born: Mossbawn, County Derry, Northern Ireland; April 13, 1939

OTHER LITERARY FORMS

Preoccupations: Selected Prose, 1968-1978 (1980) is a collection of memoirs, lectures, reviews, and essays in which Seamus Heaney (HEE-nee) accounts for his development as a poet. *The Government of the Tongue: The T. S. Eliot Memorial Lectures, and Other Critical Writings* (1988) similarly gathers reviews and lectures that elaborate on his views on the relationship between society and poetry.

ACHIEVEMENTS

Seamus Heaney's work has been recognized with some of the most prestigious honors in literary circles. Perhaps his most impressive award came in 1995, when he won the Nobel Prize in Literature. For *Death of a Naturalist*, he won the Eric Gregory Award in 1966, the Cholomondeley Award in 1967, and both the Somerset Maugham Award and the Geoffrey Faber Memorial Prize in 1968. He also won the Poetry Book Society Choice citation for *Door into the Dark* in 1969, the Irish Academy of Letters award in 1971, the Writer in Residence Award from the American Irish Foundation and the Denis Devlin Award (both for *Wintering Out*) in 1973, the E. M. Forster Award, election to the American Academy and Institute of Arts and Letters in 1975, and the W. H. Smith Award, the Duff Cooper Memorial Prize, and a Poetry Book Society Choice citation, all in 1976 for *North*.

In 1982, Heaney was awarded honorary degrees by Fordham University and Queen's University of Belfast; the two universities noted particularly that his reflection of the troubles of Northern Ireland in his poetry had universal application. He then received a Los Angeles Times Book Prize nomination in 1984, as well as the PEN Translation Prize for Poetry in 1985, both for *Sweeney Astray*. He won the Whitbread Award in 1987 for *The Haw Lantern*, the Lannan Literary Award for Poetry in 1990, a Premio Internazionale Mondello in 1993, the Whitbread Award in 1996 for *The Spirit Level*, and the *Irish Times* Award in 1999 for *Opened Ground*. In 1999, he won the Whitbread Award for poetry and book of the year for his translation of the epic Anglo-Saxon poem *Beowulf*, which was considered groundbreaking in its use of the modern idiom. He received the Truman Capote Literary Award in 2003, the T. S. Eliot Prize for Poetry in 2006 for *District and Circle*, and the David Cohen Prize in 2009.

BIOGRAPHY

Seamus Justin Heaney was born into a Roman Catholic farming family in rural Country Derry, Northern Ireland (Ulster), the predominantly Protestant and industrial province of the United Kingdom on the island of Ireland. Much of his boyhood was spent on a farm, one border of which was formed by a stream that also divided Ulster from Eire, the predominantly Catholic Republic of Ireland. As a schoolboy, he won scholarships, first at the age of eleven to St. Colomb's College, a Catholic preparatory school, and then to Queen's University, Belfast, from which he graduated in 1961 with a first class honors degree in English. There he joined a group of young poets working under the direction of creative writers on the faculty.

He began his professional career as a secondary school English teacher, after which he went into teacher education, eventually joining the English faculty of Queen's in 1966. In 1965, he married Marie Devlin; they would have two sons and a daughter. When civil dissension broke out in Ulster in 1969, eventually leading to martial law, Heaney, as a Catholic-reared poet, became increasingly uncomfortable. In 1972, he relocated to a manor in the Eire countryside to write full time, although he also became a faculty member of a college in Dublin. Beginning in 1979, he adopted the practice of accepting academic appointments at various American universities and spending the rest of the year in Dublin. In 1986, he was appointed Boylston Professor of Rhetoric and Oratory at Harvard University, and in 1989, he became professor of poetry at Oxford University. To accommodate both positions, he split his time between a home in Dublin and one in Boston. In August, 2006, he suffered a stroke but has recovered.

ANALYSIS

Almost from the beginning of his poetic career, Seamus Heaney gained public recognition for poems rooted deep in the soil of Northern Ireland and flowering in subtle rhythms and nuanced verbal melodies. In many respects, he pursues a return to poetry's foundations in Romantic meditations on nature and explorations of the triple relationship among words, emotions, and the imagination. Heaney's distinctive quality as a poet is that he is at once parochial and universal, grounded in particular localities and microcultures yet branching out to touch every reader. Strangely, this unusual "here and everywhere" note remains with him even when he changes the basic subject matter of his poetry, as he has done frequently. His command of what William Blake called "minute particularity" allows him to conjure up a sense of the universal even when focusing on a distinct individuality—to see "a world in a grain of sand." He makes the unique seem familiar. Because his success at this was recognized early, he was quickly branded with the label "greatest Irish poet since Yeats"—an appellation that, however laudatory, creates intolerable pressure and unrealizable expectations. Neo-Romantic he certainly is, but not in William Butler Yeats's vein; Heaney is less mythic, less apocalyptic, less mystical, and much more material and elemental.

In many respects Heaney's art is conservative, especially in technique. Unlike the forms of the iconoclastic leading poets of the first half of the twentieth century—T. S. Eliot, E. E. Cummings, Wallace Stevens, Ezra Pound, William Carlos Williams, and Dylan Thomas—Heaney's meters, figures, diction, and textures are all relatively straightforward. Also in contrast, his poetry is not "difficult" as theirs was; his sentences generally employ standard syntax. Nevertheless, he is a master technician with an ear for fine and subtle verbal melodies. Instead of breaking with the past, his poems much more often depend on forging links; his music often harks back to that of William Wordsworth, John Milton, or Edmund Spenser. However, his diction is common and Irish as well as formal and English. Colloquial speech patterns of the brogue often counterpoint stately cadences of British rhetoric. The combination produces a varied music, blending the different strains in his personal history and in the history of his people and his region. His best poems ring in the memory with echoes of modulated phrase and evocative sound patterns. He has probed the Irish conscience and discovered a way to express it in the English language, to render the Irish soul afresh.

DEATH OF A NATURALIST

Heaney's first book, *Death of a Naturalist*, laid the groundwork for his achievement. Centered firmly in the country scenes of his youth, these poems declare both his personal heritage from generations of Irish farm laborers and his emancipation from it, acquired by the mastery of a foreign tradition, the literature of the English. His art is Irish in origins and inspiration and English by training. The result is a surprisingly uniform and rich amalgam that incorporates much of Ulster's complex mix of cultures. The poems become what Heaney at the time hoped was possible for his region: the preservation of both Irish and English traditions by a fusion that transcended either of them separately.

"Digging," a celebrated poem from this volume, illustrates this idea. It memorializes the typical work he associated with his father's and grandfather's generations (and, by implication, those of their ancestors): cutting turf, digging. He deliberately contrasts their tool of choice, the spade, with his, the pen: "I've no spade to follow men like them." By his instrument, he can raise their labor into art, in the process ennobling them.

"Follower" similarly contrasts his labor with his father's. It captures in paced phrases and exact images his father's skill at and identification with plowing. This was the ancestral craft of the Heaneys; it makes his father what he is. As a result, it serves as the model of what young Seamus believed he should grow up to become. Sent instead to school, however, he was not reared to the plow and could never do more than hobble in his father's wake. The poem ends in a complex and disturbing image:

> But today
> It is my father who keeps stumbling
> Behind me, and will not go away.

The meaning is clear and manifold. His father stumbles intellectually—because the son has climbed beyond him—and culturally, for he will never be able to reach this point or even appreciate it. His father also stumbles merely physically, as the older generation does, and he must be cared for by his son when he cannot care for himself. Finally, his father is a clog at Heaney's heels, hindering him by his heritage: The poet will never be able to evade his father's influence.

DOOR INTO THE DARK

Three years later, *Door into the Dark* found Heaney continuing to explore this material from his upbringing, but it also showed him expanding his range and developing new moral insights. Increasingly he began sensing that the various pasts in his heritage—of family, race, and religion—were reincarnating themselves in the present, that the history of the people was recapitulating itself. This insight bound present and past indissolubly together. What unfolded in the here and now, then, became part of a gradually evolving theme and variations, revealing itself in event and place.

Some of the poems in this volume accordingly focus on events and occupations illustrating continuity in the Irish experience. "Thatcher," for example, celebrates an ancient Irish craft: thatching roofs out of by-products and discards. The fabric of the poem beautifully reflects and incorporates its subject, for its rhythms and rhymes form parallel patterns that imitate one another and interlock, although the dovetailing is not exact. Left unstated in the poem is an implied theme: The craft of the poet is equally ancient and equally intricate. A similar interweaving of past and present occurs in "The Wife's Tale," in which the persona—a farm woman—re-creates simply the routine of laying out a field lunch for laborers during threshing. The narrative is matter-of-fact and prosaic, detached and unemotional, and unspecific in time: It could be almost anytime, a reiterative action. Her action thus binds the generations together, suggesting the sameness of human life regardless of time. The poem also subtly depicts the interdependence of husband and wife—he fights and plants, she nourishes and supports—and their failure to merge completely: "And that was it. I'd come and he had shown me,/ So I belonged no further to the work."

A number of the poems in this volume are simply musings on travels in Ireland and on the Continent. At first it is easy to pass over these pieces because the simple, undramatic language and quiet tone do not attract much attention. In fact, however, these meditations are extremely important in the evolution of Heaney's poetic orientation, for they document his growing awareness of place as a determinant of sensibility. For Heaney, a person's surroundings, particularly the environment of his or her growing-up years, become the context to which he or she instinctively refers new experiences for evaluation. They become the norms of consciousness, the images from which the individual forms values. In "The Peninsula," for example, the persona spends a day touring the scenes of his youth. He discovers upon return that he still has "nothing to say," but he realizes that henceforth he will "uncode all landscapes/ By this." In "Night Drive," the speaker, driving through France and thinking of his love in Italy, finds his "ordinariness" renewed by simple things such as signposts and realizes that the same thing is happening to her. Environment forms and frames consciousness.

More important, it also frames historical consciousness, the intersection of the past with the present in the individual. In the poems that first document this idea, Heaney announces what is to be a major theme: the inescapable presence of the past. This emerges in "Requiem for the Croppies," a long-after-the-fact elegy for the insurrectionist Catholic peasants—designated "croppies" because in the 1790's they cropped their hair to indicate their support of the French revolutionaries—who were slaughtered by the thousands at Vinegar Hill at the end of the uprising of 1798.

The poem, a simple sonnet, quietly recalls the mood of that campaign, in which unarmed, uneducated plowboys terrorized the great estates of the absent English overlords until they were hemmed in and mowed down by cavalry and cannon. At first, the rebellion was a romp; finally, it became a nightmare and a shame. The poem documents this in one encircling image: The ultimate harvest of the battle is the spilled barley, carried for food, which sprouts from the mass graves the following summer. A better symbol of futility and helplessness could hardly be found. Written in 1969, the year of the recurrence of the Troubles (ethnic conflicts in Ulster between Protestant unionists and Cath-

olic secessionists), the poem both marks Heaney's allegiances—he was reared Catholic—and records his dismay over the renewal of pointless violence. Significantly,
Heaney left Belfast for good in that year, although his major motive was to devote
himself to writing full time.

"BOGLAND"

In the same year, Heaney encountered the book *The Bog People* (1969) by the eth-
nologist and anthropologist P. V. Glob. This account of a race of Iron Age peoples who
inhabited the boglands of northern Europe in the dark past, before the Indo-European
migrations of the first millennium B.C.E., was based largely on excavated remains of
bodies that had been preserved by immersion in bogs. The photographs of these bodies
particularly fired Heaney's imagination, especially because many of them had been
ritualistically sacrificed.

Since the newspapers and magazines had recently been saturated with atrocity pun-
ishments and murders, often involving equally primitive rituals, Heaney postulated a
connection between the two, forged by the history of terrorism between clans and religions in Northern Ireland: Modern Ulster, despite centuries of alterations in its facade
and supposed progress in its politics and civilization, was populated by a race different
only in accidentals from its Iron Age progenitors. The same elemental passions and ata-
vistic fears seethed beneath a deceptively civilized surface. Furthermore, those ancient
dark mysteries that precipitated the superstitious sacrifices had not been superseded by
civilization; they had merely receded into the background. Unsuspected, they continued
to be inherited in the blood. Although he nowhere uses the Jungian terminology,
Heaney seems to subscribe to the idea of the collective unconscious, the reservoir of
instinctive, intuitive behavior acquired genetically.

These ideas bear first fruit in "Bogland," in which he invents a powerful metaphor
for another of his central themes. He visualizes his kind, his culture, as centered on a
bog: "Our unfenced country/ Is bog that keeps crusting/ Between the sights of the sun."
The bog simultaneously buries and preserves, destroys and reconstitutes. Through it,
the past becomes continuous with the present, represented in it. The bog records all generations of humanity that have grown up alongside it, disclosing continuous occupation:
"Every layer they strip/ Seems camped on before."

The bog is also an analogue of the human mind, which similarly buries and preserves, and which inherits the entire weight of the past. Furthermore, both have fathom-
less depths, brooding pools, and nameless terrors bubbling up from unplumbed regions.
The bog becomes the perfect image of the inexplicable in the self and in society as a
whole. Further, it provides Heaney with a device for illustrating the force behind the violence and a means of distancing himself from it. The bog becomes a link with humankind's preconscious, reptilian past: "The bogholes might be Atlantic seepage./ The wet
centre is bottomless."

WINTERING OUT

Heaney's third book, *Wintering Out*, secured his early reputation. Like his first two books, it is rooted in his homeland, but it also includes poems of departure. Places precisely realized play a large part in it; in particular, these places declare themselves through their ancient names. Heaney spins music out of them:

> *Anahorish*, soft gradient
> of consonant, vowel meadow,
>
> after-image of lamps
> swung through the yards
> on winter evenings.

Brough, Derrygarve, Ballyshannon voice related melodies, weaving together past and present, counterpointing also with English names: Castledawson, Upperlands. The two languages together stitch the present out of the past.

The volume opens with "Bog Oak," which Heaney makes into a symbol for his bog world: It is a relic from the past, wood preserved in a bog where no oaks now stand, excavated to make rafters for new buildings. Furthermore, it is saturated with the bog, so that images of past centuries may be imprinted in it, as on film, to be released as the wood is used and thus to redirect the present. In one more way, then, the past is reincarnated. Dreaming that the oak images will bring him contact with the spirits of past poets, Heaney reminds his readers that the history of poetry is also a means of realizing the past in the present.

Other species of the Irish environment also participate in this process of continuity. "Gifts of Rain," for example, memorializes the omnipresent threat of rain in the Irish weather, but it also makes the rain into a stream flowing through everything, a liquid voice from the past: "Soft voices of the dead/ Are whispering by the shore." It becomes a solvent of the Irish experience.

This awareness of and openness to all aspects of life, especially the dark and the violent, leads Heaney to treat some topics in this volume that are quite different from his past choices. Among them is one of the more inexplicable incidents of human cruelty: infanticide by mothers, or maternal rejection of infants. "Limbo" considers an infant drowned shortly after birth and netted by salmon fishermen. Heaney dispassionately records the ironies, beginning with the simple suggestion that this child's baptism was in fact murder, the most extreme sacrilege, although he fully sympathizes with the mother's agony. Still, the child died without baptism; hence, it is ineligible for Heaven and must be relegated to Limbo, a place of painless exile, according to orthodox Catholic doctrine. Such a conclusion, however, is so unjust that it seems incompatible with any God who claims to incarnate love: "Even Christ's palms, unhealed,/ Smart and cannot fish here."

Similarly, "Bye-Child" re-creates the perspective of a child shut up by his mother in a henhouse, without vital human contact. The inscription states that he could not speak. Heaney seems astounded that anyone could deny a human the possibility of communication: to be human is to communicate. This child, as a result, becomes in turn a curiosity, a rodent, an alien, a "moon man"—nothing human. Still, his response to his rescuers reveals an attempt to communicate, to reach "beyond love."

The experience that apparently enabled Heaney to contemplate such events took place through Glob's *The Bog People*. He was so struck by the images of some of the recovered bodies—particularly those sacrificed in earth mother rites and those punished for crimes—that he wrote poems about them. The first, the three-part "The Tolland Man," first published in *Wintering Out*, has become one of his most widely reprinted poems. Heaney first describes the body, now displayed at the Natural History Museum at Århus, Denmark, and briefly alludes to his fate: Given a last meal, he was hauled in a tumbril to the bog, strangled, and deposited as a consort to the bog goddess, who needed a male to guarantee another season of fertility. In the second section, Heaney suggests that the ritual makes as much sense as the retaliatory, ritualistic executions of the Troubles; the current practice is as likely to improve germination. The third section establishes a link between survivors and victims, past and present. It implies that all humans are equally involved, equally responsible, if only by complicity or failure to act. Heaney suggests that senseless violence and complacent acceptance of it are both parts of human nature.

STATIONS

Heaney's next book, *Stations*, marked both an advance and a setback. The advance was compound, both formal and topical. Formally, the book consists of a series of prose poems; topically, they all deal with the experience of growing up rural and Catholic in an industrialized, Protestant-dominated culture. The title *Stations* alludes to this: The events detailed here constitute the contemporary equivalent of the Stations of the Cross, the sufferings Christ endured in his passion and death; moreover, they are the way stations of modern education, the stopping points of the soul. The poems show Heaney returning to his childhood to identify and document his indoctrination into the complicity he finds unacceptable in *Wintering Out*. In all these ways, the book celebrates gains.

The individual poems of *Stations* are less successful and less uniform than his earlier work. They disclose an artificiality, a staginess, a contrived quality formerly absent. They also depend on a good bit of private information for comprehension. In some respects, this is curious, because Heaney managed to avoid any hint of these weaknesses elsewhere, either in his poetry or in the retrospective prose that also dates from around this time. To an extent, this uneasiness must be associated with his private uncertainty during this period, when he was trying to justify his leaving Ulster rather than staying to take a stand. Whatever the reason, it left the poetry of the same time intact.

NORTH

His second book of 1975, *North*, capitalized on his previous successes; significantly, the title indicates that all these poems still focus on the poet's Ulster experiences. The book includes more meditations on place and place-names, such as "Mossbawn"; there are also a few more nature pieces and reminiscences. Far and away the majority of the collection, however, deals with the cultural conflict of the North, the pagan heritage of Ireland, and the continuity of past and present through the mediation of the bog people. A series based on bone fragments from the past supplements the bog material. Practically all of Heaney's best-known poems are found in this volume.

This is the first of Heaney's books that is more than a mere collection. The order and arrangement are designed to create an integrated reading experience; groupings reflect, refract, and diffuse patterns and themes. The basic structure of the book is twofold, with each part using distinctive verse forms. Part 1 focuses on the "North" of northern Europe from the time of its first population to the present. The basic verse is the taut, unrhymed or off-rhymed quatrain developed for *Wintering Out*; much of the diction is formal or archaic, and the atmosphere is solemn and austere. Part 2 takes "North" as contemporary Ulster. The root verse is the standard pentametric rhymed quatrain; the diction and tone are informal and playful. The polarity seems to reflect the two kinds of poetry Heaney describes repeatedly in *Preoccupations*: poetry that is "made" and poetry that is "given."

Some of the poems in part 1 actually fall partly outside this overly neat division. "Funeral Rites," an often-praised poem, joins the urgency of funerals during the Troubles with the legacy of pagan burials. The theme of the poem is that the frequent occurrence of funerals today has cheapened them: they lack the impact of ancient funerals, when death still meant something, still could be beautiful, and still could give promise of resurrection. The title poem also crosses the established border of the book. It centers on the imagination of the poet in the present, where he must work with what he finds—which falls far short of the epic standards of the past. Voices out of the water advise him to search the past of the race and express it through the roots of his language.

The center of part 1 is the past. Here the bog poems take precedence. There are six of them, all powerful. "The Grauballe Man" depicts another victim of the bog mother cult, this one written as if the persona were in the presence of the body. Heaney arranges a series of metaphors drawn from biology to create the image of the body, then inserts the line "The head lifts"—and the body seems to come alive before the mind's eye. The persona explicitly denies that this can be called a "corpse." Previously, seen only in photographs, the man seemed dead, "bruised like a forceps baby." Now he is "hung in the scales/ with beauty and atrocity"—he has taken on the life of enduring art yet also testifies to humanity's eternal and ongoing depravity. Violence creates beauty, and vice versa.

"Punishment" portrays another category of victim among the bog people. According to the Roman historian Tacitus, the ancestral Germans punished women taken in adultery by shaving off their hair and immersing them naked in the bog, weighed down with stones and logs, until they drowned. This barely postpubescent girl of Heaney's poem illustrates the practice: undernourished, shaved, and blindfolded, she has no visible wounds. The persona sees her as a "scapegoat," a figure of terror: "her shaved head/ like a stubble of black corn." However, she was also "beautiful," one who could arouse love. Nevertheless, he recognizes that had he been present, he "would have cast . . ./ the stones of silence," in an allusion to the New Testament story of the woman taken in adultery. Heaney asserts that all human beings comply with the practices of their tribe, and then he finds the perfect modern parallel. In the early 1970's, young Catholic women who consorted with British soldiers were punished similarly by the Irish Republican Army: They were shaved, tarred, feathered, and chained to public railings. Again all spectators comply, and the past, the primitive past, is present.

In "Strange Fruit," Heaney borrows the metaphor in the title from an African American civil rights protest song, in which "strange fruit" refers to the bodies of lynched blacks hanging from gallows. The fruit in the poem is ancient: an accidentally preserved severed head of a young woman. Here there is no justification in ritual; the woman is simply the victim of random violence or tribal conflict. Heaney, as before, suggests that exhuming the head from its bog grave is equivalent to restoring it to life and beauty. This time, however, he finds the consolation of art itself disturbing. He adds a new note, alluding to another Roman historian: "Diodorus Siculus confessed/ His gradual ease among the likes of this." Multiple atrocities generate complacency as well as complicity. Thus this girl stops short of beauty; far from attractive, she has "eyeholes blank as pools in the old workings." This is an image of the forlorn, the abandoned. These black eyeholes—lacking eyes—still outstare "what had begun to feel like reverence." Tolerating atrocities may not be the state human beings finally want to reach.

FIELD WORK

Heaney's next book, *Field Work*, poses a series of questions, mostly dealing with the relationship between art and social conscience. The questions cast doubts on both the attitude he had adopted toward contemporary violence and the resolution to which he had come about his life. Still, the answers he finds basically confirm his decisions. He chooses here the path of civilization, of art, the "field work" of the practicing artist. At the balancing point of this book rest the Glanmore sonnets, a series of ten sonnets reflecting his life at the country estate of Glanmore, County Wicklow, his retreat after Belfast. In terms of subject matter, he returns overtly to the natural settings and homely ways of his first two books. In this work, however, he is much more concerned with the poetic temperament, its influences, and its relation to society.

Accordingly, several of the sounds trace the parallels between Heaney and other figures who used rural solitude to comment on society: the Roman poets Horace and

Vergil, the mythical Irish hero Sweeney, and the English poet Wordsworth. The sonnets themselves are the densest, most intricate poems he had written to this point, rich and finely fashioned, delicate and subtle. Typical is sonnet 5, which commemorates the elderberry bush that served as refuge for the poet as a boy; he shapes it and his reminiscences about it into a symbol of his searches into the roots of language and memory.

Another major section of the book is devoted to elegies—three for victims of civil violence, three for fellow poets, and one for a relative killed in World War I. These are more conventional poems of mourning than his earlier meditations, which lamented but also accepted. They reflect a sense of absolute and final loss, the senseless wasting away that the pace of modern life leads people to take for granted, anger that so much good should be squandered so casually. Still, death is relentless and undiscriminating, taking the small with the great: "You were not keyed or pitched like these true-blue ones/ Though all of you consort now underground."

SWEENEY ASTRAY

After *Field Work* Heaney moved for a while in a different direction. *Sweeney Astray* is an adaptation of the medieval Gaelic epic *Buile Suibhne*. Heaney had long been fascinated by the character of Sweeney, at once king and poet, and had used him as one of the persona's alter egos in *Field Work*. In the poem, Sweeney fails in a quest and suffers the curse of Saint Ronan, the peacemaker, after repeatedly violating truces and killing one of the saint's clerics. Already nicknamed "Mad" because of his battle rages, Sweeney is now transformed into a bird and driven into the wilderness, doomed to be hunted by humans and beasts alike and to suffer delusions. The poem is more an anthology of rhapsodic songs and laments made by Sweeney in his exile than the standard heroic quest-poem. It is easy to detect the sources of Heaney's fascination, which include the easily overlooked rhyme of Sweeney's name with his own—the kind of thing he would spot immediately. Like Heaney, Sweeney is driven out of a violent society, though given to violence himself; he feels a natural kinship with animals, birds, trees, plants, and the things of the wild; he identifies with the places of his exile; and he senses the elemental divine pulse beating in and unifying everything. Furthermore, he represents the wounded imagination, in love with and repelled by the ways of humans in the world.

Although widely praised and honored, *Sweeney Astray* seems to have fallen short of Heaney's expectations. It did receive some hostile reviews, from Irish critics who did not really believe that English is a suitable medium for anything Gaelic and English critics who viewed Irish writers as plotting a hostile takeover of things British. The extent of Heaney's disappointment appears in the layout of *New Selected Poems, 1966-1987*, in which this book is the most scantily represented of his major works, being given only sixteen pages as against sixty-six for *Station Island* and forty-four for *North*. Clearly, it is more difficult to cull from a continuous sequence than from a collection; yet it is also true that ever since the publication of *North*, Heaney had paid considerable attention to the organization of his books, so that, theoretically at least, excerpting should be difficult from any of them.

STATION ISLAND

Station Island is Heaney's amplest, most diversified, and most highly integrated book of poems. It consists essentially of three parts: a collection of separate lyrics, many family-centered and some combined into mini-sequences; the title sequence, centered on Station Island, also called St. Patrick's Purgatory, in west Ireland, a favorite Irish pilgrimage site; and a series named "Sweeney Redivivus," in which he creates new poems through the persona of the poet-hero brought back to life in himself and committed to reveal what remains of the past in the here and now. The lyrics show Heaney experimenting with new line lengths, new forms, and new approaches. They include meditations reminiscent of W. H. Auden, such as "Chekhov on Sakhalin," and a series on found objects called "Shelf Life"; both provide him with occasions for discovering unexpected epiphanies.

Similarly, the Sweeney poems disclose Heaney deepening his vision. The identification with his mythic predecessor required by the translation brings him to a new vantage point: He realizes that perceptive and imaginative as Sweeney was, deeply as he penetrated to the soul of things, he still remained alien from the bulk of the people, and he had not changed much. Heaney writes out of a new humility and also now out of relief. He concludes that he need not blame himself for having abandoned his people in the Troubles. They were not really his people, in retrospect; his values were not theirs. He could not accomplish much for them that would last, thus it was better to pursue his poetry.

The title series also teaches him that lesson, though in a different way. It is Heaney's major triumph, consolidating and drawing on strengths he had been establishing since early in his career. It is the quintessential place-poem, for Station Island has many places and provides multiple occasions for poetry. Situated on Lough Derg in County Tipperary, Eire, the island was originally a primitive settlement; in the eighth or ninth century it became a locus of pilgrimage, renowned as a place of penitence. A number of foundation rings remain, the relics of either monastic cells or primitive dwellings. Devotees complete the act of repentance by making a circuit of these, kneeling and praying at each in turn, and by this act gaining remission of punishment for past sins.

Heaney bases his cycle on the persona's return to the island in middle age. Although by this point in his life he was an unbeliever, he finds the island well populated with souls eager to establish common ground with the living. For the devout, St. Patrick's Purgatory is a place of personal repentance, expiation, and rectification. For the literary, as a purgatorial site it has a forerunner in Dante's *Purgatorio* (in *La divina commedia*, c. 1320; *The Divine Comedy*, 1802). Heaney uses the experience as a poetic examination of conscience, a Catholic devotional exercise: He reviews his career as a poet, attempting to determine once again the proper relationship between poetry and society. In this process, he gains assistance and insight from the attendant ghosts, who include a number of figures from his private and literary past, notably including James Joyce. Heaney records their conversations, often weaving their voices together in terza rima, the verse form used by Dante. In the twelfth and last poem, Joyce advises Heaney to follow his lead in concentrating on art and ignoring the politics of the moment.

THE HAW LANTERN

The Haw Lantern continues in the direction mapped out in *Station Island*. It is among the slightest of Heaney's collections: thirty-one poems in fifty-two pages. His topics, too, are rather commonplace: hailstones, alphabets, fishing lures, a peacock's feather, and (in the title poem) the fruit of the hawthorn. Heaney transforms this brilliant red winter fruit metaphorically into a lantern, an instrument for seeing and for measuring human values. Commonly used for hedging in the British Isles, this thorny shrub becomes a means of testing human integrity in the daily situations that finally count. The book also contains another of Heaney's trademark sequences. "Clearances," a set of eight sonnets written to commemorate the death of Heaney's mother, moves him to another stage in the definition of his poetic character. Symbolically, this constitutes Heaney's prayer at his mother's deathbed, bonding him to the past and committing him to the future. It also sets him apart from Joyce, his spiritual mentor, who made his refusal to pray at his mother's bedside a pivotal scene in *A Portrait of the Artist As a Young Man* (1916) and *Ulysses* (1922).

SEEING THINGS

Despite being an active writer and continuing to produce published collections, Heaney seemed to move toward poetry that had a decidedly "later" feel about it beginning in the 1990's, as if the poet were consistently revisiting old scenes, revising opinions, refining thoughts once had, and critiquing versions of self presented in previous poems. In *Seeing Things*, Heaney appears to reach for a lightness, moving away from the thickets of alliteration and sensuality found in the early work or the harsh minimal realities of the bog period or even the casual sublimities of daily life found in both *Field Work* and, to a lesser extent, *The Haw Lantern*.

THE SPIRIT LEVEL AND OPENED GROUND

The Spirit Level explores the themes of politics, humanism, and nature. It includes in its composition a plea for hope, innocence, and balance, and to seek eventually that "bubble for the spirit level." Here he balances the personal with the universal, as well as the process of life to death, in an attempt to seek an equilibrium. *Opened Ground* provides a comprehensive overview of his poetry from 1966 to 1996, with works from the 1990's heavily represented: Much of *The Spirit Level* is reproduced here. By chronologically following his progression as a poet, readers can discern Heaney's peculiar wistful and earthy mixture of rural reverie and high public speech and see how his interests broaden in the middle and later poems when the poet seeks out Greek myths, Irish epics, and Scandinavian archaeological digs to look for correlatives appropriate for his meditations.

ELECTRIC LIGHT

Perhaps Heaney's most reflective collection during this period is *Electric Light*. Using a compilation of poetic genres and styles—including eclogue, elegy, epigram, yarn, meditation, and ecstatic lyric—Heaney meditates on the origins and inevitable ending of his life and art. His array of verse styles showcases Heaney's will and ability to speak of many kinds of experiences to many kinds of reader. Above all, his awareness of his aging, from which he turns away in memory and looks past in poems about death, gives the collection special coherence and expression. In "The Gaeltacht," modeled on a poem by Dante, he examines his literary fame, his desire for release from it, and a return to primal things. Heaney wishes he were in the Gaeltacht, a Gaelic-speaking region of northwestern Ireland, with one of his old pals "and that it was again nineteen sixty." Then other friends now old or dead would also be with them "talking Irish."

He also celebrates nature with a range of poems that explore landscapes, such as his birthplace of Northern Ireland, imprinted by human life, its meanings and violence handed down through the generations. Heaney's use of dialect and feeling-laden place-names distinctly help convey this theme. Notable literary figures make appearances here as well: He elegizes the Russian poet Joseph Brodsky, offers translations of Vergil and the Russian poet Alexander Pushkin, and has memorial poems for the Polish poet Zbigniew Herbert and American translator Robert Fitzgerald.

DISTRICT AND CIRCLE

District and Circle contains forty-four poems and several short prose pieces, including "One Christmas Day in the Morning" and "Fiddleheads." The poems differ significantly in structure and topic, and Heaney's poetic rhythms vary widely between the classical and contemporary. The poet employs many familiar themes evident in his previous work, such as remembrances of his rural Irish childhood, the lives of country folk, and Catholicism and the Catholic rites, but the poems all relate to the collective theme of memory.

The opening poem, "The Turnip-Snedder," a relatively short poem about an ancient turnip-mashing machine, is constructed as ten unrhymed couplets. The rhythm within the poem varies between and against the two-beat line and extends even further by Heaney's pairing of phrases throughout. The exact year of the poem is not noted, but the nostalgia-infused image of rural life and farmwork suggests a time when the agrarian lifestyle involved hard physical labor. Farmwork is the topic of several other poems in this collection.

"District and Circle," the title poem, has a more urban setting, involving train stations and rail travel. The poem is constructed as five stanzas of fourteen lines, except the third stanza, which is thirteen lines. This use of the fourteen-line stanza could be seen as Heaney's modern interpretation of a sonnet since he also combines the fourteen-line stanza with iambic pentameter. "District and Circle" places the speaker of the poem in an underground train station, waiting along with other travelers, and evokes an image of the jostle inherent in mass transit. The poem also addresses themes of identity and of isolation, even while in a familiar setting such as a crowded train station.

Heaney's tendency to retool the sonnet form also is evident in the poem "In Iowa," which depicts an old Mennonite mowing machine covered with snow. This poem consists of three unrhymed quatrains and a final couplet, which serves as the turn, or volta. Like other contemporary poets, Heaney incorporates the Petrarchan form in a modern narrative poetic structure. Within "In Iowa," Heaney takes certain artistic liberties that are not restricted by the strict metrical or rhyme schemes associated with the traditional Petrarchan form.

In this collection, Heaney recalls the people and sights of the rural Ireland of his childhood. Some of the poems within are overtly nostalgic, while others are imbued with a more subtle message elevating the agrarian lifestyle.

OTHER MAJOR WORKS

NONFICTION: *Preoccupations: Selected Prose, 1968-1978*, 1980; *The Government of the Tongue: The T. S. Eliot Memorial Lectures, and Other Critical Writings*, 1988 (pb. in U.S. with the subtitle *Selected Prose, 1978-1987*, 1989); *The Redress of Poetry*, 1995; *Homage to Robert Frost*, 1996 (with Joseph Brodsky and Derek Walcott); *Seamus Heaney in Conversation with Karl Miller*, 2000; *Sounding Lines: The Art of Translating Poetry*, 2000 (with Robert Hass); *Finders Keepers: Selected Prose, 1971-2001*, 2002; *Stepping Stones: Interviews with Seamus Heaney*, 2008 (with Dennis O'Driscoll).

TRANSLATIONS: *The Midnight Verdict*, 1993 (of Ovid and Brian Merriman); *Beowulf: A New Verse Translation*, 1999; *Diary of One Who Vanished*, 1999 (of song cycle by Leos Janacek of poems by Ozef Kalda).

EDITED TEXTS: *The Rattle Bag: An Anthology of Poetry*, 1982 (with Ted Hughes); *The Essential Wordsworth*, 1988; *The School Bag*, 1997 (with Hughes).

BIBLIOGRAPHY

Brandes, Rand, and Michael J. Durkan, eds. *Seamus Heaney: A Bibliography, 1959-2003*. London: Faber and Faber, 2008. Bibliography of the poet's works provides a good starting point for research.

Cavanagh, Michael. *Professing Poetry: Seamus Heaney's Poetics*. Washington, D.C.: Catholic University of America Press, 2009. Provides extensive analysis of the critical essays written by Heaney to discern his theory of poetics.

Collins, Floyd. *Seamus Heaney: The Crisis of Identity*. Newark: University of Delaware Press, 2003. A fine introduction to the poet's expertise and style.

Crowder, A. B., and Jason David Hall, eds. *Seamus Heaney: Poet, Critic, Translator*. New York: Palgrave Macmillan, 2007. These twelve essays address not only Heaney's poetry but also Heaney's criticism and translations.

Hall, Jason David. *Seamus Heaney's Rhythmic Contract*. New York: Palgrave Macmillan, 2009. An examination of Heaney's poetry that focuses on its structure and place it in the context of mid-twentieth century theories of meter and rhythm.

McCarthy, Conor. *Seamus Heaney and Medieval Poetry*. Rochester, N.Y.: Boydell & Brewer, 2008. Examines how Heaney translated medieval poetry and otherwise incorporated it into his poetry.

Moloney, Karen Marguerite. *Seamus Heaney and the Emblems of Hope*. Columbia: University of Missouri Press, 2007. An extensively researched study of Heaney's poetry and his theme of the Celtic fertility myth of kings marrying goddesses. Informative and easy to read.

O'Brien, Eugene. *Seamus Heaney and the Place of Writing*. Gainesville: University Press of Florida, 2002. Analyzes Heaney's attitude toward place and home and its relevance to Irish identity.

O'Donoghue, Bernard, ed. *The Cambridge Companion to Seamus Heaney*. New York: Cambridge University Press, 2009. A collection of essays that cover the life and works of Heaney, examining topics such as the Irish influence, the poet and medieval literature, and the poet as a critic.

Vendler, Helen Hennessy. *Seamus Heaney*. Cambridge, Mass.: Harvard University Press, 2000. Whereas other books on Heaney have dwelt chiefly on the biographical, geographical, and political aspects of his writing, this book looks squarely and deeply at Heaney's poetry as art.

James Livingston; Sarah Hilbert
Updated by Andy K. Trevathan

JAMES JOYCE

Born: Dublin, Ireland; February 2, 1882
Died: Zurich, Switzerland; January 13, 1941

PRINCIPAL POETRY
Chamber Music, 1907
Pomes Penyeach, 1927
"Ecce Puer," 1932
Collected Poems, 1936

OTHER LITERARY FORMS

Although James Joyce published poetry throughout his career (*Chamber Music*, a group of thirty-six related poems, was in fact his first published book), it is for his novels and short stories that he is primarily known. These works include *Dubliners* (1914), a volume of short stories describing what Joyce saw as the moral paralysis of his countrymen; *A Portrait of the Artist as a Young Man* (1916), a heavily autobiographical account of the growing up of a writer in Ireland at the end of the nineteenth century and the beginning of the twentieth; *Ulysses* (1922), a novel set in Dublin in 1904, recounting the day-long adventures of Leopold Bloom, a modern-day Odysseus who is both advertising man and cuckold, Stephen Dedalus, the young artist of *A Portrait of the Artist as a Young Man* now grown somewhat older, and Molly Bloom, Leopold's earthy wife; and *Finnegans Wake* (1939), Joyce's last published work, not a novel at all in the conventional sense, but a world in itself, built of many languages and inhabited by the paradigmatic Earwicker family.

ACHIEVEMENTS

James Joyce's prose works established his reputation as the most influential writer of fiction of his generation and led English prose fiction from Victorianism into modernism and beyond. To this body of work, Joyce's poetry is an addendum of less interest in itself than it is in relationship to the other, more important, work. At the same time, in the analysis of Joyce's achievement, it is impossible to ignore anything that he wrote, and the poetry, for which Joyce reserved some of his most personal utterances, has its place along with the play *Exiles* (pb. 1918)—now seen as more important than it once was—and the essays, letters, and notebooks.

BIOGRAPHY

The life of James Augustine Aloysius Joyce is interwoven so inextricably with his work that to consider one requires considering the other. The definitive biography of

Oliver Goldsmith
(Library of Congress)

Joyce, by Richard Ellmann, is as strong in its interpretation of Joyce's work as it is of his life. If Joyce, as Ellmann suggests in that biography, tended to see things through words, readers must try to see him through his words—the words of his work—as well as through the facts of his life.

Joyce was born into a family whose fortunes were in decline, the first child to live in the match of a man who drank too much and accumulated too many debts and a woman whose family the Joyces considered beneath them. John Joyce, James's father, became the model for Stephen's father both in *A Portrait of the Artist as a Young Man* and in *Ulysses*, where he is one of the most memorable characters, and also a model for H. C. Earwicker in *Finnegans Wake*. If Joyce's father seemed not to understand his son's work or even to show much interest in it during his lifetime, that work has become a surer form of immortality for him than anything he ever did himself.

Joyce was educated at Clongowes Wood College, a Jesuit school not far from Dublin that he memorialized in *A Portrait of the Artist as a Young Man*, and later at Belvedere College, also Jesuit, in Dublin. In 1898, on his graduation from Belvedere, he entered

University College, Dublin. At this point in his life, increasingly rebellious against the values of his home and society, Joyce did his first writing for publication. He graduated from the university with a degree in modern languages in 1902 and then left Dublin for Paris to study medicine. That, however, quickly gave way to Joyce's real desire to write, and he entered a difficult period in which he turned to teaching to earn a living. The problems of the father had become the problems of the son, but during this period Joyce wrote some of his best earlier poems, including what is now the final piece in the *Chamber Music* sequence. With the death of his mother imminent in April, 1903, Joyce returned to Dublin, where, the following winter, he began to write the first draft of *A Portrait of the Artist as a Young Man* (known as *Stephen Hero*).

By far the most important event after Joyce's return to Ireland, however, was his meeting in June, 1904, with the woman who was to become his mate for the rest of his life, Nora Barnacle, whose roots (like those of the family Joyce) were in Galway, the westernmost county in Ireland. If Joyce's mother's family had seemed too low for the Joyces, Nora's family was even lower on the social scale, but Joyce, like Stephen Dedalus, was to escape the net of convention and take the woman he loved away from Ireland to live in a succession of temporary residences on the Continent while he established himself as a major writer. The model, at least in part, for Molly Bloom and also for Anna Livia Plurabelle, Nora, not Joyce's legal wife until 1931, was the mother of their two children—Giorgio, born in 1905, and Lucia, born in 1907—and Joyce's main emotional support for almost four decades.

From the time Joyce and Nora moved to the Continent until the outbreak of World War I, they lived chiefly in Trieste, a port city in northeastern Italy that in appearance seemed more Austrian than Italian; there Joyce taught English in a Berlitz School, and wrote; he returned to Ireland only twice, in 1909 and again in 1912, for what turned out to be his last visit. With the outbreak of the war, Joyce and his family moved to Zurich, which was neutral ground, and in 1920—after a brief sojourn once again in Trieste—moved to Paris, where they were to remain until the fall of France twenty years later.

Paris in the 1920's, Ernest Hemingway was to write years later, was a "moveable feast," but Joyce, as always, was a selective diner, an integral part of the literary life of Paris at that time, yet aloof from it, imaginatively dwelling in the Dublin of 1904, the year he had met Nora. Having published *Chamber Music, Dubliners, A Portrait of the Artist as a Young Man,* and *Exiles,* Joyce had embarked on his most ambitious project to date—a treatment in detail of one day in Dublin—June 16, 1904—and the adventures of a modern-day Odysseus, Leopold Bloom, ultimately to be his greatest single achievement in characterization. The serialization of *Ulysses* had begun in 1918; its publication in book form waited until Joyce's fortieth birthday, on February 2, 1922. Because of publication difficulties resulting from censorship, Joyce did not realize much financially from the book until later in his life, and remained dependent on a succession of patrons and subscribers not only for its initial publication but also for his livelihood. With its publication, however—difficult though it was to achieve—came the recognition of Joyce as the greatest living novelist in English, a master stylist who had managed (as such major figures as T. S. Eliot and Ezra Pound were quick to see) to give the modern experience a historical dimension that so many realistic novels had lacked.

As recognition of *Ulysses* came, Joyce characteristically moved on to something different (in a sense, in his published work he almost never repeated himself, in style or in form, though he dealt continuously with certain themes), publishing in 1924 the first portion of what for years was termed "Work in Progress" and then ultimately became *Finnegans Wake*. This novel broke new ground in the same way *Ulysses* did, in its rendering of unconscious universal experiences and in its use of language; but it took much longer for it to achieve general recognition as a masterpiece. Plagued throughout his lifetime by financial problems, health problems (especially with his eyes), and family problems (his daughter's mental health was always fragile, and she has lived most of her life in a sanatorium), Joyce remains the prime example of the artist as exile.

ANALYSIS

Chamber Music appeared in 1907, but James Joyce had been working on the poems that comprise the volume for some time before that date. As early as 1905, he had worked out a plan for the poems, different from the one finally devised for the 1907 version but perhaps more revealing of the thematic content of the poetry. With the addition of several poems not in the 1905 scheme, *Chamber Music* came to thirty-six poems of varying lengths and forms, the work of a young man who had already largely abandoned poetry in favor of prose fiction.

CHAMBER MUSIC

In many ways the poems of *Chamber Music* are typical of the period in which they were written. The poetry of the late nineteenth century in English has a hothouse quality; like the French Symbolists, who—next to the English Romantics—provided the chief inspiration throughout this period, the poets of the fin de siècle eschewed ordinary life in favor of an aesthetic ideal. This was in fact the final flowering of the ideal of art for art's sake so important to nineteenth century literature and art, an attitude that the young Joyce flirted with and ultimately abandoned, satirizing it in the pages of *A Portrait of the Artist as a Young Man*. In the poems of *Chamber Music*, however, the satire is less easy to detect, and fin de siècle themes provide the basis of many of the poems in the sequence. The dominant note of the poetry of the fin de siècle is one of weariness or sadness, the favorite time dusk or night, the favorite stance one of retreat; in Joyce's *Chamber Music* poems, as later in *A Portrait of the Artist as a Young Man*, such favorite attitudes are questioned but not totally rejected. If the final note is one of anger or bitterness rather than simply of sadness or despair, there is still a strong enough taste of the latter to mark the poems—even the celebrated number XXXVI—as the work of a young man who has grown up in the last important moment of aestheticism. Even so, the experience of the young man who is the principal speaker of the sequence of poems seems ultimately to toughen him in a way more typical of Joyce than of the poetry of the fin de siècle.

In Joyce's 1905 sequence, the personas of the poems are more easily perceived, the themes developed in them clearer, as William York Tindall was first to point out at length in his 1954 edition of *Chamber Music*. In that sequence there are thirty-four poems, designated first in the following list, with the numbers from the 1907 edition in Roman numerals in parentheses immediately after: 1 (XXI), 2 (I), 3 (III), 4 (II), 5 (IV), 6 (V), 7 (VIII), 8 (VII), 9 (IX), 10 (XVII), 11 (XVIII), 12 (VI), 13 (X), 14 (XX), 15 (XIII), 16 (XI), 17 (XIV), 18 (XIX), 19 (XV), 20 (XXIII), 21 (XXIV), 22 (XVI), 23 (XXXI), 24 (XXII), 25 (XXVI), 26 (XII), 27 (XXVII), 28 (XXVIII), 29 (XXV), 30 (XXIX), 31 (XXXII), 32 (XXX), 33 (XXXIII), and 34 (XXXIV).

This sequence has certain important features. Poem 1 (XXI) introduces the young man of the sequence, a sort of romantic rebel in the tradition of the Shelleyan hero, a "high unconsortable one" more in love with himself than with anyone else. This theme of aloofness and narcissism is struck in several poems following this one—in 2 (I), 3 (III), and 4 (II)—but by 5 (IV) the young man has not only become the speaker of the poem, but he has also found someone to love. Poem 6 (V) gives her a name— Goldenhair—and establishes the theme of the next group of poems: the young man in pursuit of Goldenhair, in the traditional rites of courtship. In 7 (VIII), he pursues her through the "green wood," and in 8 (VII), he sees her among the apple trees, vernal settings for these ancient rites. In 9 (IX), however, he cannot find her, and 10 (XVII) explains why: Here the third persona of the sequence is introduced—the rival who is a friend of the young man and who, at the same time, is threatening his relationship with Goldenhair: "He is a stranger to me now/ Who was my friend." Poem 11 (XVIII), addressed both to Goldenhair and to the rival, complains of the failure of friends and suggests that another woman may well give the young man succor. As the poems proceed, this other woman takes on a variety of connotations, until finally, in 17 (XIV) the young man imagines his union with her in terms suggesting that she has combined characteristics, in Tindall's words, "of church, mother, muse, nation, and soul." After 17, the poems do variations on the themes of separation and lost love, ending in 33 (XXXIII) and 34 (XXXIV) on a decidedly wintry note: "The voice of the winter/ Is heard at the door./ O sleep, for the winter/ Is crying, 'Sleep no more.'"

This pattern of love challenged by a rival and ending in bitter or mixed feelings occurs elsewhere in Joyce's work, most notably in *A Portrait of the Artist as a Young Man* and in the play *Exiles*, where, as a test of a relationship, it provides the major theme. *Chamber Music* thus becomes an early working out of this theme, though Joyce ultimately agreed to an ordering of the poems (devised by his brother Stanislaus) different from the one of 1905—allowing for an ending on a much stronger note with poem

XXXVI, beginning "I hear an army charging upon the land," which was not part of the 1905 sequence at all and which suggests an attitude that is more than simply passive or accepting on the part of the young man. These little poems, while carrying the weight of themes developed more completely in Joyce's later work, are also lyrics light and fresh enough to serve as the basis of songs. Joyce himself set a number of them to music, and over the years they have been set by many other composers as well.

Poem 16 (XI) illustrates the technique of the lyrics of *Chamber Music*. The diction is simple but frequently archaic—note the use of "thee" and "thy," "hast" and "doth," in keeping with much of the lyric poetry of the 1890's—and the tone light and songlike, with touches of irony apparent only in the last few lines of the second stanza. This irony is heralded in line 9 by the verb "unzone," which stands out in a poem of otherwise simple diction. Like many such words in these poems, "unzone" is unusual for the accuracy with which it is used (compare, for example, "innumerous" in poem 19 [XV]), Joyce returning to its original meaning of "encircle" or "surround," derived by way of the Latin *zone* from Greek *zona*, or "girdle." What is frequently most distinctive about Joyce's choice of words, in prose as well as in poetry, is their accuracy. In this context, the contrast between the formality of "unzone" and the "girlish bosom" of the next line, reinforced by the irony in other poems of the series dealing with the wooing of Goldenhair, makes the reader question her innocence if not the young man's intentions.

The repetition of the opening lines of 16 is another notable feature of the series. In 12 (VI) one can see the same quality on a somewhat larger scale, the final line pointing back to the beginning of the poem. If the poems of *Chamber Music* are relatively simply lyrics, they have their own complexities and ambiguities, as this poem shows. The "bosom" of the first stanza is conceivably Goldenhair's, but may also be interpreted as that of mother or church. "Austerities," like "bosom" used twice in the poem, in particular leads the reader to think so, the bosom or heart leading to an ascetic, not hedonistic, form of satisfaction for the young man. In this poem, the young man flees from the relationship with Goldenhair and seeks other means of satisfaction. The language of the poem creates irony through repetition, forcing the reader to reexamine the premises of the relationship described. If this technique is much simpler than the one Joyce employed in his prose masterpieces, it is certainly a technique of the same order.

POMES PENYEACH

In 1927, Joyce published a second volume of poetry with the unassuming title *Pomes Penyeach*. The occasion for the volume was largely negative; stung by criticism of "Work in Progress" from people such as Ezra Pound, who had been so supportive of *Ulysses*, Joyce wished to show that he could also produce a relatively simple volume of lyrics. However, the lyrics were too simple for the taste of the time, and the volume went largely ignored; Pound himself suggested that Joyce should have reserved the poems for the Bible or the family album. This criticism now seems unfair, or at least out of proportion. The thirteen poems of *Pomes Penyeach* do not in any sense break new ground in English poetry, but they provide a kind of personal comment on Joyce's private life that is not easy to find in the prose works, and some of them are also simply good lyrics in the manner of *Chamber Music*.

The poems represent work of a period of approximately twenty years, beginning with "Tilly," composed in 1903 just after Joyce's mother's death, and ending with "A Prayer" of 1923, though stylistically they are of a piece. In this poetry, Joyce favored a diction and tone that seemed archaic by the late 1920's, and he did so without any of the irony apparent or at least incipient in certain poems of *Chamber Music*. If the mood of these poems did not suit the times in which they appeared, neither did it seem to suit the style of the supreme punster of "Work in Progress." They provide the single instance in Joyce's published work of an anachronism—a work that looks back in style and tone, in this case to the poetry of Joyce's youth and young manhood, rather than forward in time—and this accounts in part for their unenthusiastic reception.

In *Pomes Penyeach*, the poems occur in roughly the order of their composition, and may be grouped according to subject matter. Some celebrate Joyce's feelings toward his children, as in "A Flower Given to My Daughter" or "On the Beach at Fontana," while others refer to feelings provoked in him by women he fancied himself to be in love with, either in the Trieste period or in Zurich during World War I. Some poems suggest certain of the prose works, such as "She Weeps over Rahoon" with its echoes of the long story "The Dead," written some five years before the poem. The final poem of the group, "A Prayer," returns to the mood of the darker poems in *Chamber Music* and to the image of woman as vampire that occurs so frequently in the poetry and art of the fin de siècle. It also suggests the strain of masochism that shows itself so often in Joyce's work in connection with sensuous pleasure. All in all, these lyrics provide an engaging record of various moods of Joyce as he passed into middle age, tempered by the public reputation he had acquired by that time.

"A Flower Given to My Daughter" and "A Prayer" illustrate the extremity of mood and variety of technique of these poems. In the first, the inverted word order and quaint diction of the poem—"sere" is the best example of the latter—do not keep the last line from being extremely touching, in part because it is so realistic a description. Joyce manages in the best of *Pomes Penyeach* to find just such a strong line with which to end, establishing a kind of contrast between the somewhat antique technique of the poem and conclusions remarkable for their simplicity and strength. "A Prayer" is far more dramatic in tone, but here the long lines and the rolling words ("remembering" followed by "pitying") also carry the reader into the joy become anguish of the final lines. In these poems as in others of the group, Joyce seems to be using the style and tone of another time with sometimes deadly effect—a conscious archaism rather than the more distanced irony of some of the poems of *Chamber Music*.

"ECCE PUER"

In 1932, Joyce published his last poem, "Ecce Puer," a touching commemoration of two occasions—the death of his father and the birth of his grandson and namesake Stephen James Joyce, the son of Giorgio and his wife, Helen. "Tilly," the first item of *Pomes Penyeach*, was written on the occasion of the death of his mother and is in many ways the strongest of the group; "Ecce Puer"—written just after the death of John Joyce—is even stronger. For felt emotion conveyed, it has no equal among Joyce's works in this form, and its concluding stanza is all the more touching for its echoes of the theme of paternity so important to *Ulysses*—"A child is sleeping:/ An old man gone./ O, father forsaken,/ Forgive your son!" In fact, the poem was completed not many days after the tenth anniversary of the publication of *Ulysses*, which provides yet a third occasion for its composition.

SATIRIC POEMS

In addition to *Chamber Music*, *Pomes Penyeach*, and "Ecce Puer," Joyce published occasional broadsides—satiric poems to express his unhappiness over various literary matters. These include "The Holy Office" (1904) (now the rarest of all the published works of Joyce), an attack on the Irish literary movement by a young writer who already knew that his work was to be essentially different from theirs, and "Gas from a Burner" (1912), an attack on the Dublin publisher who ultimately burned the proofs of *Dubliners* rather than print what he considered an indecent book.

Finally, in *A Portrait of the Artist as a Young Man*, one of the crucial moments occurs (in the final part of the book) when Stephen Dedalus composes a poem in the form of a villanelle. This poem, while technically not Joyce's, represents as sure a comment as Joyce ever made on the aestheticism of the 1890's, and thus stands in contrast with *Pomes Penyeach*, which echoes the themes and tones of that time.

Joyce's poetry was ultimately expressed most fully in his prose works, where the traditional distinctions between poetry and prose are effectively blurred. Perhaps in the end, his lyric poetry is best viewed as a minor expression—almost a form of relaxation—of a master stylist in prose.

OTHER MAJOR WORKS

LONG FICTION: *A Portrait of the Artist as a Young Man*, 1914-1915 (serial), 1916 (book); *Ulysses*, 1922; *Finnegans Wake*, 1939; *Stephen Hero*, 1944 (Theodore Spencer, editor).

SHORT FICTION: *Dubliners*, 1914.

PLAY: *Exiles*, pb. 1918.

NONFICTION: *Letters of James Joyce*, 1957-1966 (3 volumes); *The Critical Writings of James Joyce*, 1959; *Selected Letters of James Joyce*, 1975 (Richard Ellmann, editor); *The James Joyce Archives*, 1977-1979 (64 volumes); *On Ibsen*, 1999; *Occasional, Critical, and Political Writing*, 2000.

BIBLIOGRAPHY

Attridge, Derek, ed. *The Cambridge Companion to James Joyce.* New York: Cambridge University Press, 1990. A collection of eleven essays by eminent contemporary Joyce scholars. Surveys the Joyce phenomenon from cultural, textual, and critical standpoints. A valuable aid and stimulus, containing a chronology of Joyce's life and annotated bibliography.

Blades, John. *How to Study James Joyce.* Houndmills, England: Macmillan, 1996. An excellent study guide for students of Joyce. Includes bibliographical reference, outlines, and syllabi.

Bulson, Eric. *The Cambridge Introduction to James Joyce.* New York: Cambridge University Press, 2006. A work on Joyce that is divided into his life, his works, and the critical reception.

Ellmann, Richard. *James Joyce.* 1959. 2d ed. New York: Oxford University Press, 1984. The definitive biography, generally regarded as the last word on its subject's life and widely considered as the greatest literary biography of the twentieth century. Copiously annotated and well illustrated, particularly in the 1984 edition.

Jones, Ellen Carol, and Morris Beja, eds. *Twenty-first Joyce.* Gainesville: University Press of Florida, 2004. This useful reference work collects thirteen scholarly essays written by Joyce experts. Part of the University Press of Florida James Joyce series.

McCourt, John. *James Joyce: A Passionate Exile.* New York: St. Martin's Press, 2001. Photos and sketches embellish this account of the life, times, relationships, and works of Joyce. Excellent introductory text, particularly for its illustrations.

Potts, Willard. *Joyce and the Two Irelands.* Austin: University of Texas, 2001. Potts aligns Joyce with Catholic nativists, arguing that, while the novelist rejected Catholicism, his treatment of independence and industrialization betrays a sympathy for Irish nationalism.

Stewart, Bruce. *James Joyce.* New York: Oxford University Press, 2007. A biography of Joyce that looks at his life and works.

Strathern, Paul. *James Joyce in Ninety Minutes.* Chicago: I. R. Dee, 2005. A biography of Joyce that attempts to explain his life and works in an easily understandable manner.

Theall, Donald F. *James Joyce's Techno-Poetics.* Toronto, Ont.: University of Toronto Press, 1997. Representative of a new wing of Joyce studies, Theall's work examines Joyce as a progenitor of today's cyberculture. Includes bibliography and index.

Archie K. Loss

PATRICK KAVANAGH

Born: Inniskeen, Ireland; October 21, 1904
Died: Dublin, Ireland; November 30, 1967

PRINCIPAL POETRY
Ploughman, and Other Poems, 1936
The Great Hunger, 1942
A Soul for Sale, 1947
Recent Poems, 1958
Come Dance with Kitty Stobling, and Other Poems, 1960
Collected Poems, 1964
The Complete Poems of Patrick Kavanagh, 1972 (Peter Kavanagh, editor)

OTHER LITERARY FORMS

Three fictional autobiographies—*The Green Fool* (1938), *Tarry Flynn* (1948), and *By Night Unstarred* (1977)—are based on the years Patrick Kavanagh (KAV-uh-nuh) spent in County Monaghan. The latter part of *By Night Unstarred* pursues his life into Dublin. Various prose essays and occasional pieces can be found in *Collected Prose* (1967) and *November Haggard: Uncollected Prose and Verse of Patrick Kavanagh* (1971). *Kavanagh's Weekly*, a magazine that published thirteen issues between April 12 and July 15, 1952, contains a variety of fiction, commentary, and verse that was written under various pseudonyms but is almost all Kavanagh's own work (reprinted, 1981). *Lapped Furrows: Correspondence, 1933-1967* (1969) and *Love's Tortured Headland* (1974) reprint correspondence and other documents between 1933 and 1967. After the poet's death, his brother Peter edited and published his work, and Peter's biography, *Sacred Keeper* (1980), contains a number of previously unpublished or unreprinted documents. Despite the claims of various titles, Kavanagh's work remains uncollected. A poem ("The Gambler") was adapted for ballet in 1961, and *Tarry Flynn* was dramatized in 1966; each was performed at the Abbey Theatre.

ACHIEVEMENTS

Despite handicaps of poverty, physical drudgery, and isolation, Patrick Kavanagh became the leading figure in the "second generation" of the Irish Literary Revival. He practically reinvented the literary language in which rural Ireland was to be portrayed. Bypassing William Butler Yeats, John Millington Synge, and Lady Augusta Gregory, he returned for a literary model to a fellow Ulsterman, William Carleton, and to his own experience of country life as a subject. He invested his fiction and poetry with fresh regional humor that did not sentimentalize or condescend to its characters. His vision is fundamentally religious, imbued with a Catholic sacramental view of nature. His various criticisms of Irish life and institutions arise from an unrefined but genuine spirituality. The quality of Kavanagh's work is uneven, and his public attitudes are inconsistent. Even so, the sincerity of his best work, its confidence in its own natural springs, its apparent artlessness, its celebration of local character, place, and mode of expression, make him the most widely felt literary influence on the poets of contemporary Ireland, most significantly on those with similar backgrounds, such as John Montague and Seamus Heaney.

BIOGRAPHY

Patrick Kavanagh was the fourth of ten children of James Kavanagh, a shoemaker, and his wife, Bridget. The Kavanagh home was in Mucker, a townland of Inniskeen, County Monaghan, near the Armagh (and now Northern Ireland) border. The boy attended Kednaminsha National School until he was thirteen, when he was apprenticed to his father's trade. Later, he worked a small farm purchased in the nearby townland of Shancoduff. His first literary influences were the school anthologies that featured Henry Wadsworth Longfellow, Charles Kingsley, William Allingham, Alfred, Lord Tennyson, Robert Louis Stevenson, and Thomas Moore, and his earliest poems were written in school notebooks. As he worked on his small farm, he nurtured his taste on magazines picked up at fairs in the town of Dundalk. His keen observations of country life, its customs, characters, and speech patterns, together with his growing awareness of his sensitivity that set him apart from his peers, are well set forth in his account of his early life, *The Green Fool*. Many of his early poems appeared in the 1930's in *The Irish Statesman*, whose editor, Æ (George William Russell), was the first to recognize and cultivate the peasant poet. Æ introduced him to modern world literature, providing him with books, advice, payment, and introductions to the Irish literary establishment. Of the books given him by Æ, *Gil Blas of Santillane* (1715, 1724, 1735), *Ulysses* (1922), and *Moby Dick: Or, The Whale* (1851) remained the classics most revered by Kavanagh.

After he moved to Dublin in 1939, he supported himself as a journalist. Throughout the 1940's, he wrote book and film reviews, a range of critical and human interest pieces, city diaries, and various pieces for *The Irish Press* (as "Piers Plowman"), *The Standard*, *The Irish Times*, and *Envoy*. During that time, the long poem *The Great Hunger*, his second poetry collection, *A Soul for Sale*, and the novel *Tarry Flynn* appeared, so that following the deaths of Yeats (1939) and James Joyce (1941), he emerged as the central figure in Irish literary life. His most ambitious journalistic venture was in 1952 when, with his brother's financial and managerial assistance, he produced *Kavanagh's Weekly*, which ran for thirteen issues (April 12-July 5). This production comprises the fullest expression of Kavanagh's "savage indignation" at the mediocrity of Irish life and letters. It is useful as a document of the Dublin ethos in the early 1950's and in reading Kavanagh's poetry of the same period. In October, 1952, *The Leader* responded—in a spirit typical of the infamous factionalism of Dublin's literary politics—with a malicious "Profile," which prompted Kavanagh to file suit for libel. Following a celebrated trial, which Kavanagh lost, he fell dangerously ill with lung cancer.

He made a dramatic physical recovery, however, which in turn revivified his creative powers. This second birth resulted in a group of poems—mainly sonnets—written in 1955 and 1956—set in and around the Rialto Hospital and by the Grand Canal, Dublin, and published in *Recent Poems* and *Come Dance with Kitty Stobling, and Other Poems*. Thereafter he went into a slow decline, physically and creatively. In April, 1967, he married Katherine Moloney, but he died the following November. He is buried in Inniskeen.

His brother Peter (twelve years his junior) was Kavanagh's constant correspondent, financier, confidant, critic, and promoter. He edited and published many works arising from this fraternal collaboration, including *Lapped Furrows*; *November Haggard*; *The Complete Poems of Patrick Kavanagh*, which supersedes and corrects *Collected Poems*; a bibliography, *Garden of the Golden Apples* (1972); and a documentary biography, *Sacred Keeper*. Despite its title, *Collected Prose* contains only a sampling of Kavanagh's prose works.

ANALYSIS

Although he frequently and vehemently denied it, Patrick Kavanagh was a distinctively Irish poet. He had already formed his own voice by the time he discovered—or was discovered by—the Celtic Revival and became a leading figure in the second generation. Kavanagh was not a Celtic mythologizer such as William Butler Yeats, a conscious dialectician such as J. M. Synge, a folklorist such as Lady Gregory, an etymologist such as James Joyce, or a Gaelic revivalist such as Douglas Hyde. He felt and wrote with less historical or political consciousness than his progenitors. His gifts and temperament made him an outsider in Inniskeen, his lack of formal education and social grooming excluded him from Dublin's middle-class literary coteries, and his moral sensibility excluded him from Bohemia.

Yet in retrospect, Kavanagh emerges as the dominant Irish literary personality between 1940 and 1960. Although he admired each of the Revival's pioneers for particular qualities, he regarded the Irish Literary Revival in the main as an English-inspired hoax. The romanticized peasant, for example, he considered the product of Protestant condescension, and he felt that too many writers of little talent had misunderstood the nature of Yeats's and Joyce's genius and achievements, so that the quality of Irishness replaced sincerity.

Against a pastiche of literary fashions that misrepresented the peasant, attempted the revival of the Irish language, and promoted nationalism in letters and in politics, Kavanagh posited his own belief in himself, in his powers of observation, and his intimate knowledge of the actual lives of country people. Kavanagh's subsequent popular success in Ireland and his influence on the third generation are attributable to several distinct characteristics: his parochialism, which he defined as "confidence in the social and artistic validity of his own parish"; his directness, the apparent offhandedness of his work, and his freedom from literary posing; his deep Catholicism, which went beyond sentimentality and dogma; his imaginative sympathy for the ordinary experiences of country people; his comedy; his repose; his contemplative appreciation of the world as revelation; and his sincerity, his approval of feelings arising only from a depth of spirit. Although he has often been admired for one or more of these virtues, and although his manner often masked these qualities, they must be taken as a whole in accounting for his character as a poet. He disdained the epithet Irish poet, yet shares with each of the pioneers of the Revival one or more signally Irish characteristics.

Kavanagh's creative development followed three stages: first, the works of intimacy with and disengagement from the "stony grey soil" of parochial Monaghan; second, the works that show his involvements with Dublin or national cultural issues; and third, his "rebirth" in the post-1955 reconciliation of public and private selves, when rural parish and national capital find mutual repose.

Kavanagh's two most successful fictional works, *The Green Fool* and *Tarry Flynn*, provide a rich lode of documentation of their author's country background and the growth of his sensibility. Some of his finest lyrics come from this period, along with his magnum opus, *The Great Hunger*. All these works are set in the same few townlands, and the theme is the revelation of grace in ordinary things and tasks. Through these poems, and from *The Green Fool* to *Tarry Flynn*, the poet's confidence in his own visionary gifts progressively deepens, even though the expression is often uncertain. In a handful of lyrics, however, such as "Ploughman," "Inniskeen Road: July Evening," "A Christmas Childhood," "Spraying the Potatoes," "Shancoduff," and "Epic," Kavanagh's technique realizes his intentions. In each of these, the chance appearances belie the deft design, and the natural voice of the countryman is heard for the first time since Carleton in Irish literature.

"SHANCODUFF"

"Shancoduff" (In *The Complete Poems of Patrick Kavanagh*) is one of Kavanagh's most successful expressions of his parochial voice and is a representative early poem. The small farmer's pride in his bare holding is seemingly disquieted by a casual comment from passing strangers: "By heavens he must be poor." Until this uninvited, materialistic contrast with other places intrudes, this little world, although uncomfortable, has been endurable. Now it may not be so.

Before the cattle drovers assess the farm, the readers have seen it through the eyes of its owner, and they do not need to be told that he is a poet. With him they have first observed these hills' exemplary, incomparable introspection (lines 1-7). Even as his readers are being invited to contemplate the hills' ontological self-sufficiency, however, the poet, by necessity a maker of comparisons, introduces mythological and geographical allusions from the larger world. Even though these references—to Lot's wife, the Alps, and the Matterhorn—ostensibly imply his sympathy with his property's self-justification, their very statement admits some kind of comparison and betrays the principle it proposes. This and the irony in "fondle" arrange the scene for the dour pragmatism of the jobbers. Shancoduff is very poor land, poets do make poor farmers, or farmers make poor poets, and the eavesdropping owner-farmer-poet seems disconcerted. The question in line 16 is slyly rhetorical, however; the poet's evident disdain for the jobbers implies that his heart may not be quite so "badly shaken."

The poem operates by a set of contrasts that set the cold, wet, dark, ungainly native places against apparently more positive reflections from the outside. Earth and water oppose air and fire; Saint Patrick's see of Armagh (and/or ancient Ulster's adjacent capital of Emhain Macha) is a counterattraction to the foreign cities of dubious renown—Sodom, Rome, London, even perhaps Tokyo. The gauche place-names of Kavanagh's parish do not seem to invite tourists, yet they combine in shaping the poet's attitude to these humble townlands and the design of the poem (see also "Old Black Pocket"; "Glassdrummond," "Streamy/Green Little Hill"; "Featherna," "Streamy"; with the "Big Forth" they compose an ancient, native estate).

"Shancoduff" uses seasonal, biblical, and religious images to suggest his parochial independence from urban cultures, while foreshadowing several motifs that run through Kavanagh's later works: his distrust of cities and critics, his investment of local dialect or commonplace phrases with larger, often mystical, reference, his disdain for positivist assessments, and his cutting irony. Yet, despite the representative nature of its content, it must be admitted that by its total coherence and clarity this poem stands out from most of his work.

THE GREAT HUNGER

The Great Hunger is Kavanagh's most ambitious poem and is one of signal importance in the literature of modern Ireland. First published in 1942, it is 756 lines long, in fourteen sections. It narrates the life of Patrick Maguire, a peasant farmer whose life is thwarted by physical poverty, Jansenism, and the lack of imagination. The poem is Kavanagh's most extensive rebuke to the idealization of the peasant: A report "from the other side of the ditch," it has great reportorial force. For just as it describes the degradation of the rural poor, it also projects Maguire sympathetically as a figure of keen self-awareness and spiritual potential. Maguire's anguish is muffled and extended by his procrastination, the dull round of gossip, gambling, and masturbation. The Church distorts his natural religious sensibilities into patterns of guilt, which, together with his mother's hold on the farm, conspire to justify his pusillanimity. Woman is the embodiment of life's potentialities, and Maguire's failure to marry is thus the social expression of his spiritual retardation.

The title recalls the potato famine of 1845 to 1847, when starvation and disease ravaged the population and caused long-term psychological and social harm. The mood of the people turned pessimistic as they accepted the disaster as a judgment from an angry deity, and they turned penurious. This historical catastrophe had a deeply depressing effect on rural life, enlarged the power of the Church, reduced national self-confidence, and led to the disuse of the native language and the loss of the gaiety and spontaneity for which the Irish had been renowned. Kavanagh's poem reflects several of these effects with unflinching honesty.

The poem is a tour de force of descriptive writing, technical variation, and complex tonal control. In the modernist mode, it uses the rhythms and idioms of jazz, nursery rhymes, ballads, the Hiberno-English dialect, the Bible, the pastoral, and the theater, with only occasional lapses in momentum. The poet stands at very little distance from his subject; the tone is somber to bitter. Kavanagh shows compassion rather than condescension toward his protagonist; the humor is grim and restrained. *The Great Hunger* suffers by its occasional stridency, but its urgency and commitment do not diminish it as much as its author would have readers think when he later disowned it as "lacking the nobility and repose of poetry" (*Self-Portrait*).

By the time Kavanagh had made that statement, he had gone through some important changes in spirit. Even though *The Great Hunger* established his reputation in Dublin's literary life, he suffered from lack of patronage and managed to survive only by journalism. That activity he undertook with zest and courage—witness *Kavanagh's Weekly*—but it brought to the fore some of his insecurities that found expression in flailing abuse of his rivals and in sententious dogma on a range of public issues. As the objects of his satirical verses changed, the central vision began to disintegrate. The bitter libel suit against *The Leader* was a personal disaster. His bout with lung cancer took him close to death, and his creative energies had reached their nadir. His remarkable physical recovery, however, led to a spiritual revivification on the banks of the Grand Canal, Dublin, in the year following the summer of 1955.

RECENT POEMS AND COME DANCE WITH KITTY STOBLING, AND OTHER POEMS

This reinvigoration of spirit is reflected in a group of sonnets published in *Recent Poems* and *Come Dance with Kitty Stobling, and Other Poems*, notably the title poem of the latter, along with "Canal Bank Walk," "The Hospital," and "Lines Written on a Seat on the Grand Canal." As his various accounts (notably in *Self-Portrait*) of this experience testify, Kavanagh rediscovered his original capacities to see, accept, and celebrate the ordinary. In these poems, the original innocence of the Monaghan fields graces his experience of Dublin, mediated by his hospitalization and the repose offered by the environment of the Grand Canal. Kavanagh purged these poems of many defects that had marred his previous work—contentiousness, self-pity, shrill engagement in passing events, messianic compulsions—all of which arose from relative shallows.

In "Lines Written on a Seat on the Grand Canal," for example, there is a nicely balanced irony in the mock-heroic view of self, which is deftly subsumed by the natural grace observed in the setting. The artificial roar is drowned by the seasonal silence. The well-tempered voice of the poet commands original simplicities with easy assurance. The poet's memorial, "just a canal-bank seat for the passer-by," summarizes Kavanagh's testament: his acknowledgment of Yeats, his self-definition as observer, namer, and diviner, and his humility as no more than a "part of nature." The countryman, the poet, the visionary, the Irishman, and the citizen are finally reconciled to one another. Although the poem appears to mirror the persona's affection of indifference, its taut conclusion indicates that casualness has not been easily won.

The accomplishment of these late poems notwithstanding, Kavanagh retained a sense of defeat to the end of his career. He never overcame a defensiveness arising from his deprived youth. He rarely reconciled his feelings for his Monaghan sources and his need for a Dublin audience. His *The Complete Poems of Patrick Kavanagh* shows how small a proportion of his total production is truly successful. Nevertheless, his impact on Irish cultural life is large, and this is attributable to the color of his personality, the humor of his prose, and his unsentimental social criticism, as much as to his poetic oeuvre.

OTHER MAJOR WORKS

LONG FICTION: *The Green Fool*, 1938; *Tarry Flynn*, 1948; *By Night Unstarred*, 1977.

PLAY: *Tarry Flynn*, pr. 1966.

NONFICTION: *Lapped Furrows: Correspondence, 1933-1967*, 1969 (with Peter Kavanagh); *Love's Tortured Headland*, 1974 (with Peter Kavanagh and others); *A Poet's Country: Selected Prose*, 2003 (Antoinette Quinn, editor).

MISCELLANEOUS: *Kavanagh's Weekly*, 1952, serial (1981, facsimile); *Self-Portrait*, 1964; *Collected Prose*, 1967; *November Haggard: Uncollected Prose and Verse of Patrick Kavanagh*, 1971 (Peter Kavanagh, editor).

BIBLIOGRAPHY

Agnew, Una. *The Mystical Imagination of Patrick Kavanagh*. Blackrock, County Dublin, Ireland: Columba Press, 1998. A critical study of selected works by Kavanagh. Includes bibliographical references and indexes.

Garratt, Robert F. *Modern Irish Poetry: Tradition and Continuity from Yeats to Heaney*. Berkeley: University of California Press, 1986. The chapter devoted to Kavanagh is divided into four parts: his criticism of the Irish Literary Revival and revisionist reading of William Butler Yeats, his early poetic realism, his poetic rebirth in the "Canal Bank" poems, and the development of his influential poetics of the local and familiar, which influenced the next generation.

Heaney, Seamus. *The Government of the Tongue*. New York: Farrar, Straus and Giroux,

1988. This collection of prose by Kavanagh's most famous successor contains a lecture in which Kavanagh's poetry is seen in two stages: the "real topographical presence" of the early poems, followed by the "luminous spaces" of the late poems. The essay shows the importance of Kavanagh for younger Irish poets in the words of one of the best.

Kavanagh, Peter. *Sacred Keeper: A Biography of Patrick Kavanagh.* The Curragh, Ireland: Goldsmith Press, 1980. This partisan biography by the poet's devoted brother claims to avoid the lies and legends of "the eccentric, the drunkard, the *enfant terrible* of Dublin" in favor of the facts, lovingly recorded in a pastiche of letters, poems, photographs, articles, and reminiscences.

Nemo, John. *Patrick Kavanagh.* Boston: Twayne, 1979. Provides a useful overview of Kavanagh's life and work, along with a chronology and a bibliography. The examination of the poetry is thorough and authoritative.

Quinn, Antoinette. *Patrick Kavanagh.* Syracuse, N.Y.: Syracuse University Press, 1991. A critical assessment of Kavanagh's oeuvre. Includes bibliographical references and indexes.

Ryan, John. *Remembering How We Stood: Bohemian Dublin at Mid-century.* New York: Taplinger, 1975. A chapter of this colorful, if respectful, memoir captures "Paddy Kavanagh," the picturesque eccentric and pub crawler, in the local atmosphere of literary Dublin from 1945 to 1955. Entertaining and anecdotal but not thoroughly reliable.

Smith, Stan, ed. *Patrick Kavanagh.* Portland, Oreg.: Irish Academic Press, 2009. A collection of essays about Kavanagh that cover the reception of his early and later poetry and his identity as an Irish writer.

Warner, Alan. *Clay Is the Word: Patrick Kavanagh, 1904-1967.* Dublin: Dolmen Press, 1973. The first full-length study and the best introduction to Kavanagh, Warner's book is engaging in tone, discursive in method, and speculative in its conclusions. Makes use of reminiscences of those who knew the poet as well as literary analyses of the poems. Includes bibliography.

Cóilín Owens

THOMAS KINSELLA

Born: Dublin, Ireland; May 4, 1928

PRINCIPAL POETRY

The Starlit Eye, 1952
Three Legendary Sonnets, 1952
The Death of a Queen, 1956
Poems, 1956
Another September, 1958, 1962
Moralities, 1960
Poems and Translations, 1961
Downstream, 1962
Six Irish Poets, 1962
Wormwood, 1966
Nightwalker, and Other Poems, 1968
Poems, 1968 (with Douglas Livingstone and Anne Sexton)
Tear, 1969
Butcher's Dozen, 1972
Finistere, 1972
Notes from the Land of the Dead, and Other Poems, 1972
A Selected Life, 1972
The Good Fight: A Poem for the Tenth Anniversary of the Death of John F. Kennedy,
    1973
New Poems, 1973
Selected Poems, 1956-1968, 1973
Vertical Man, 1973
One, 1974
A Technical Supplement, 1976
The Messenger, 1978
Song of the Night, and Other Poems, 1978
Fifteen Dead, 1979
One, and Other Poems, 1979
Peppercanister Poems, 1972-1978, 1979
Poems, 1956-1973, 1979
One Fond Embrace, 1981, 1988
Her Vertical Smile, 1985
Songs of the Psyche, 1985
St. Catherine's Clock, 1987

Blood and Family, 1988
Poems from Centre City, 1990
Madonna, and Other Poems, 1991
Open Court, 1991
From Centre City, 1994
Collected Poems, 1956-1994, 1996
The Pen Shop, 1997
The Familiar, 1999
Godhead, 1999
Citizen of the World, 2000
Littlebody, 2000
Collected Poems, 1956-2001, 2001, 2006
Belief and Unbelief, 2007
Man of War, 2007
Selected Poems, Poems 1956-2006, 2007

OTHER LITERARY FORMS

In addition to his own poetry, Thomas Kinsella (kihn-SEH-luh) has published a large body of verse translated from the Irish. This work is most notably embodied in *The Táin* (1969), his celebrated version of the eighth century Irish epic *Táin bó Cuailnge*, and in *An Duanaire, 1600-1900: Poems of the Dispossessed* (1981; with Sean O Tuama). ("An duanaire," literally translated, means "the poemery.") An appreciation of the significance that Kinsella attaches to the Irish-language tradition of Irish poetry and the magnitude of his commitment to it is crucial to an overall sense of his achievement. His introduction to *The New Oxford Book of Irish Verse* (1986), which he edited, provides convenient access to Kinsella's thinking on the subject of the Irish-language poetic tradition. The attitude expressed in that introduction recapitulates earlier statements contained in the poet's small but influential body of cultural criticism.

ACHIEVEMENTS

Thomas Kinsella is one of the most important Irish poets to emerge since the end of World War II. By means of a restlessly experimental formal and aesthetic sense, broadly conceived themes, and relentless self-scrutiny and self-exposure, his work has raised him above his contemporaries in the Republic of Ireland and placed him in the forefront of his generation of poets writing in English.

In the context of contemporary Irish poetry, his work has an unwonted syntactical density, complexity of imagery, and dramatic intensity. Since modern Irish poetry in English is noted more for lyric grace than for tough-minded plumbing of existential depths, Kinsella's poetry gains in importance because of its originality. Its essential inimitableness, in turn, commands respect by virtue of the tenacity of vision it embodies.

In recognition of his uniqueness and commitment, Kinsella has received widespread critical acclaim and has won the Guinness Poetry Award in 1958 for *Another September* and the Irish Arts Council Triennial Book Award in 1961 for *Poems and Translations*. He is a four-time winner of the Denis Devlin Memorial Award, in 1964-1966, 1967-1969, 1988, and 1994. He has also held two Guggenheim Fellowships. In 1983, along with Sean O Tuama, he received the American Book Award from the Before Columbus Foundation. In 2007, he was awarded the rarely given Freedom of the City of Dublin. He has received honorary doctorates from the University of Turin and the National University of Ireland.

BIOGRAPHY

Thomas Kinsella was born in Dublin on May 4, 1928. His family background is typical of the vast majority of native Dubliners—Catholic in religious affiliation, left-tending Nationalist in politics and lower-middle class in social standing, the kind of background detailed with such loving despair by one of Kinsella's favorite authors, James Joyce, in the stories of *Dubliners* (1914). Kinsella's father worked at the Guinness brewery and was active in labor union matters.

Educated at local day schools, Kinsella received a scholarship to attend University College, Dublin, to read for a science degree. Before graduation, however, he left to become a member of the Irish civil service, in which he had a successful career as a bureaucrat, rising to the rank of assistant principal officer in the Department of Finance.

Kinsella left the civil service in 1965 to become artist-in-residence at Southern Illinois University. In 1970, he was appointed to a professorship of English at Temple University, a position he retained until 1990. In the end, he taught for one semester a year at Temple, spending the rest of the year in Dublin running the Peppercanister Press.

Founded in 1972, Peppercanister is the poet's private press. It was established, in the poet's own words, "with the purpose of issuing occasional special items." As well as being a notable addition to the illustrious private and small tradition of Irish publishing, Peppercanister has allowed Kinsella to produce long poems on single themes and to carry out fascinating exercises in the area of the poetic sequence. It has also allowed him to use it as a work in progress and to avoid using literary magazines to bring out new poems. He also has used it for critical and cultural statements in prose.

In 1976, Kinsella founded Temple University's School of Irish Tradition in Dublin, enabling him to continue dividing his time between the United States and Ireland. Since his retirement from teaching in 1990, he has continued his direction of Peppercanister Press, as well as the Dolmen and Cuala Presses, both in Dublin. He established a pattern of living part of the year in County Wicklow and the rest in Philadelphia.

ANALYSIS

From the outset of his career, Thomas Kinsella has shown an unremitting preoccupation with large themes. Love, death, time, and various ancillary imponderables are persistently at the forefront of Kinsella's poetic activity. Such concerns beset all poets, no doubt, as well as all thinking beings. More often than not, Kinsella grapples with these overwhelming subjects without the alleviating disguise of metaphor, and he confronts them without the consolations of philosophy. Their reality consists of the profundity of the poet's human—and hence, frequently baffled and outraged—experience of them.

Even in Kinsella's early love lyrics, it is impossible for the poet merely to celebrate the emotion. He cannot view his subject without being aware of its problematical character—its temporariness and changeability. Thus, to identify Kinsella's themes, while initially informative, may ultimately be misleading. It seems more illuminating to consider his preoccupations, which a reader may label time or death, as zones of the poet's psychic experience, and to recognize that a Kinsella poem is, typically, an anatomy of psychic experience, a rhetorical reexperiencing, rather than a particularly conclusive recounting. Such a view would seem to be borne out by the forms that his poems typically assume. Their fractured look and inconsistent verse patterns (unavoidably but not imitatively reproducing the prosody of T. S. Eliot and Ezra Pound) suggest an idea still developing. As Kinsella writes in "Worker in Mirror, at His Bench": "No, it has no practical application./ I am simply trying to understand something/ —states of peace nursed out of wreckage./ The peace of fullness, not emptiness."

An immediate implication of this approach to poetry is that it owes little or nothing to the poet's Irish heritage. His concerns are common to all humanity, and while the conspicuous modernism of his technique has, in point of historical fact, some Irish avatars (the unjustly neglected Denis Devlin comes to mind), these are of less significance for a sense of Kinsella's achievement and development than the manner in which he has availed himself of the whole canon of Anglo-American poetry. In fact, an interesting case could be made for Kinsella's poetry being an adventitious, promiscuous coalescence of the preoccupations of poets since the dawn of Romanticism. Such a case might well produce the judgment that one of the bases for Kinsella's general importance to the history of poetry in the postwar period is that his verse is a sustained attempt to inaugurate a post-Romantic poetic that would neither merely debunk its predecessor's fatal charms (as perhaps Eliot desired to do) nor provide them with a new repertoire of gestures and disguises (which seems to have been Pound's project). The effect of this judgment would be to place Kinsella in the company of another great Irish anti-Romantic of twentieth century literature, Samuel Beckett.

A more far-reaching implication of Kinsella's technique is that it provides direct access to the metaphysical core of those preoccupations. Often the access is brutally direct. Throughout, Kinsella repeats the refrain articulated in the opening section of "Nightwalker" (from *Nightwalker, and Other Poems*): "I only know things seem and are not good." This line strikes a number of characteristic Kinsella notes. Its unrelieved, declarative immediacy is a feature that becomes increasingly pronounced as his verse matures. There is a sense of the unfitness of things, of evil, of times being out of joint.

The speaker is strikingly committed to his subjective view. The line contains a representative Kinsella ambiguity, depending on whether the reader pauses heavily after "seem." Is "are not good" entailed by, or opposed to, "seem"? Readers familiar with Kinsella will hear the line announce a telltale air of threat and of brooding introspection. There is also, perhaps, a faint suggestion of meditative quest in "Nightwalker," which occurs in other important Kinsella poems from the 1960's (such as "Baggot Street Deserta" from *Another September*, and "A Country Walk" and "Downstream" from *Downstream*). Such an undertaking, however, is hardly conceived in hope and does not seem to be a quest for which the persona freely and gladly volunteers. Rather, it seems a condition into which he has been haplessly born.

It is not difficult to understand Kinsella's confession that his vision of human existence is that of "an ordeal." In fact, given the prevalence in his verse of ignorance, darkness, death, and the unnervingly unpredictable tidal movements of the unconscious—all frequently presented by means of apocalyptic imagery—there is a strong indication that the poet is doing little more than indulging his idea of "ordeal," despite the prosodic virtuosity and furious verbal tension that make the indulgence seem an authentic act of soul baring. Such an evaluation, however, would be incomplete. Also evident is the poet's desire to believe in what he has called "the eliciting of order from experience." Kinsella's verse is a continuing experiment in the viability of the desire to retain such a belief and a commitment to negotiate the leap of artistic faith that alone is capable of overcoming the abyss of unjustifiable unknowing that is the mortal lot. The possibility of achieving that act of composed and graceful suspension is what keeps Kinsella's poetry alive and within the realm of the human enterprise.

Although Kinsella's oeuvre exemplifies, to a dauntingly impressive degree, persistence and commitment in the face of the virtually unspeakable abyss, it has gone through a number of adjustments and modifications. Taken as a whole, therefore, Kinsella's output may be considered an enlarged version of some of its most outstanding moments, a sophisticated system of themes and variations. In the words of the preface to *Wormwood*, "It is certain that maturity and peace are to be sought through ordeal after ordeal, and it seems that the search continues until we fail."

One of the most important adjustments to have occurred in the development of Kinsella's poetic career is his emergence from largely private, personal experience. His early poems, particularly those collected in *Another September* and *Downstream*, seem too often to conceive of experience as the struggle of the will against the force of immutable abstractions. While these poems respect the necessarily tense and tentative character of experience, they seem also to regard mere experience as a pretext for thought. These poems share with Kinsella's later work the desire to achieve distinctiveness through allegories of possibility. However, their generally tight, conventional forms have the effect of limiting their range of possibilities. In addition, the typical persona of these poems seems himself an abstraction, a man with only a nominal context and without a culture.

DOWNSTREAM

By *Downstream*, such isolation was being questioned. The concluding line of this collection's title poem—"Searching the darkness for a landing place"—may be taken (although somewhat glibly) as a statement emblematic of much of Kinsella's early work. However, the collection also contains poems that, while painfully acknowledging the darkness, consider it as an archaeological redoubt. One of the effects of this adjustment is that the poet's personal past begins to offer redemptive possibilities. In addition, and with more obvious if not necessarily more far-reaching effects, a generalized past, in the form of Irish history, becomes an area of exploration. It is not the case that Kinsella never examined the past prior to *Downstream* ("King John's Castle" in *Another September* is proof to the contrary). Now, however, to the powerful sense of the past's otherness that "King John's Castle" conveys is added a sense of personal identification.

The poem in *Downstream* that demonstrates this development in Kinsella's range is "A Country Walk." Here, the persona, typically tense and restless, finds himself alone, explicitly undomesticated, with nothing between him and the legacy of the past discernible in the landscape through which he walks. The poem does not merely testify to the influential gap between present and past (a crucial preoccupation in all modern Irish writing) but also enters into the past with a brisk openness and nonjudgmental tolerance. "A Country Walk" reads like a journey of discovery, all the more so since what is discovered is not subjected to facile glorification. The fact that the past is so securely embedded in the landscape of the poem suggests that history is in the nature of things and that there is as much point in attempting to deny its enduring presence as there is in trying to divert the river which is, throughout the course of the poem, never out of the poet's sight. The poem ends, appropriately, on a note of continuity: "The inert stirred. Heart and tongue were loosed:/ 'The waters hurtle through the flooded night. . . .'"

If anything, the present is circumvented in "A Country Walk." To ensure that the reader is aware of this, Kinsella daringly uses echoes of William Butler Yeats's "Easter 1916" to show how antiheroic is contemporary Ireland and to emphasize that the country is still, to paraphrase a line from Yeats's "September 1913," fumbling in the greasy till. This moment in "A Country Walk" prefaces the understandable admission "I turned away." The interlude, however, draws attention to a noteworthy feature of Kinsella's verse: its satire. From the outset, Kinsella's work was capable of excoriation. The addition of local, often contemporary, Irish subject matter has created the opportunity for some scalding satirical excursions.

NIGHTWALKER, AND OTHER POEMS

Perhaps the most notorious of these sallies is to be found in the long title poem of *Nightwalker, and Other Poems*, a poem that, in many ways, is an illuminating counterpart to "A Country Walk." Here, the setting is urban, contemporary Dublin, and the speaker, lacking the briskness of his opposite number in "A Country Walk," refers to himself as "a vagabond/ Tethered." The demoralizing spectacle of modern life is the poem's subject. Nothing is spared. In particular, Kinsella's years in the civil service are the basis for a damning portrait of national ideals stultified and betrayed. This portrait goes so far as to include figures from Irish public and political life who, although distorted by the poet's satirical fury, remain eminently recognizable and still occupy the highest positions in the land. Each of the poem's numerous scenarios is exposed as a hollow social charade, and in direct contrast to the sense of release felt at the end of "A Country Walk," this poem concludes on a note of anticlimax: The speaker fails to find anything of redemptive value in current conditions.

NOTES FROM THE LAND OF THE DEAD, AND OTHER POEMS

Although Kinsella has by no means forsaken the satirical mode (as *Butcher's Dozen*, Peppercanister's first publication, makes vividly clear), his career has developed more fruitfully through exploring the pretexts and presuppositions of his need that poetry be a salvage operation, acknowledging existence's many disasters and the intimacy of their wreckage and through acknowledgment saving face. Thus, in *Notes from the Land of the Dead, and Other Poems* and also in the later *New Poems*, the past is personal and the poems seem like diagnoses of memory and origins. Just as the setting for many of these poems is the poet's childhood home, so the poems reveal what has to be internalized for the sake of comprehending one's native land. In these poems, the speaker is the absorbed witness of others' agony, not only the agony of the deathbed but also the equally unrelenting travail described in "Tear": "sad dullness and tedious pain/ and lives bitter with hard bondage."

The poems in *Notes from the Land of the Dead, and Other Poems* are also noteworthy for their degree of interaction with one another. Earlier, in *Wormwood*, Kinsella produced a strict yet supple poetic sequence. Now, the idea of sequence reemerges and takes more fluid form, a technique that can be seen embryonically in the interrelated sections of "Nightwalker" and that finds mature embodiment in many of the Peppercanister poems. This greater access to range and flexibility has enabled the poet to be less dependent on the singular effects of the dramatic lyric, where, as noted, there seemed to be a considerable degree of pressure to will experience to denote purpose. As a result of an increasing commitment to formal and metrical variety, Kinsella's voice has become more authentically meditative, its brooding habit engendering a measure of containment rather than disenchantment. This voice is present not only in such important Peppercanister collections as *One, A Technical Supplement*, and *Song of the Night, and Other Poems* but also in some of the superb individual poems these books contain, notably *Finistere* (*One*) and "Tao and Unfitness at Inistiogue on the River Nore" (*Song of the Night, and Other Poems*).

BUTCHER'S DOZEN

It is not clear, however, that Kinsella established Peppercanister with the expectation that such wonderful poems would result. On the contrary, the press came into being because of the need to publish an uncharacteristic Kinsella production, a poem written for a particular occasion. The poem in question, *Butcher's Dozen*, was written in response to the killing in the city of Derry, Northern Ireland, of thirteen civil rights demonstrators by British troops. This event took place on the afternoon of Sunday, January 30, 1972, a day that will live in infamy in the minds of Irish people. The poem's immediate occasion is the horrifying event, but its subtitle, "A Lesson for the Octave of Widgery," clarifies the line of attack taken by Kinsella. The subtitle names the Lord Chief Justice of the United Kingdom, Lord Widgery, chairman of the essentially whitewashing court of inquiry set up to examine the event. Thus, *Butcher's Dozen* is a critique not only of the troops' action but also of the mind-set such actions denote. The poem's incisive and abrasive couplets enact an alternative language and disposition to that of the Lord Chief Justice's report. While, from an aesthetic standpoint, *Butcher's Dozen* is hardly Kinsella's greatest poem, its significance as a cultural document is indisputable and is reinforced by the explanatory background notes that Kinsella wrote to accompany it.

A SELECTED LIFE AND VERTICAL MAN

The other occasional poems contained in the Peppercanister series also have to do with significant deaths. In order of appearance, the poems are *A Selected Life*, *Vertical Man*, *The Good Fight: A Poem for the Tenth Anniversary of the Death of John F. Kennedy*, and *The Messenger*. It has become standard practice to regard *A Selected Life* and *Vertical Man* together, two independent but intimately related treatments of the one event, the untimely death of the poet's friend, Seán Ó Riada. Again, the issue of cultural significance arises. Ó Riada, as well as being an accomplished composer of classical music (*Vertical Man* is the title of one of his compositions for orchestra), was also an extraordinary influence on Irish folk musicians. His conception of the rich tradition and important heritage of Irish folk music was the direct inspiration of the internationally acclaimed group the Chieftains. More relevant to the development of Kinsella's career, Ó Riada's scholarly, pleasure-giving rehabilitation of a dormant legacy is an important counterpart to the poet's explorations in Irish-language poetry. As the penultimate stanza of *Vertical Man* has it: "From palatal darkness a voice/ rose flickering, and checked/ in glottal silence. The song/ articulated and pierced."

THE GOOD FIGHT

In the light of the public demeanor assumed in *Butcher's Dozen* and the greater degree of interplay between textural openness and formal control contained in both Ó Riada poems, Kinsella undertook his most ambitious public poem, *The Good Fight*. Not only is the poem's subject matter ambitious, in particular given how rare it is for Irish poets to seek subjects outside the ambit of their own culture and tradition (a rarity that later Irish poets such as Derek Mahon would work to dismantle), but also, formally speaking, *The Good Fight* is one of Kinsella's more daring experiments.

As in the case of earlier Peppercanister poems on public themes, *The Good Fight* has an author's note attached, which begins with the remark, "With the death of Kennedy many things died, foolish expectations and assumptions, as it now seems." In a sense, the poem is a collage of contemporary desires, a view borne out by the numerous allusions to and quotations from Kennedy speeches and other sources from the period. However, such a view is contradicted by two other features of the poem. The most obvious of these are the various quotations from Plato's *Politeia* (fourth century B.C.E.; *Republic*, 1701) and *Nomoi* (fourth century B.C.E.; *Laws*, 1804), which are used to counterpoint the poem's development. This classical reference has the effect of measuring Kennedy's fate against some nominal yet conventionally uncontroversial standard of age-old wisdom. This feature in turn is seen in terms of the pervasive sense of unfulfilled aftermath that pervades the poem. It seems remarkable that this achievement is so little known.

THE MESSENGER

The significant death in *The Messenger* is not that of a well-known figure but of the poet's father. This immensely moving document testifies to Kinsella's growth as an artist. The poem's subject, death, has been a constant presence in his work since "A Lady of Quality," in *Poems*, and has been treated variously in such accomplished and representative poems as "Dick King" and "Cover Her Face" (both from *Downstream*). *The Messenger*, however, dwells more on celebrating the life that preceded its occasion than on the death of a man desiring to possess his culture: "The eggseed Goodness/ that is also called/ Decency." The poet's redemptive power and his cultural as well as personal responsibility to discharge it are seen to consummate effect in this powerful, moving work.

BLOOD AND FAMILY

Blood and Family, Kinsella's first publication from a major publisher since the 1979 *Peppercanister Poems, 1972-1978*, is a reprint of later Peppercanister publications. The volume contains *The Messenger*, *Songs of the Psyche*, *Her Vertical Smile*, *Out of Ireland*, and *St. Catherine's Clock*. The decision to open the volume with a reprint of *The Messenger* is a good one, given that it sets the cultural tone and prosodic idiom for the remainder of the poems. At the same time, it may be said that this volume consolidates rather than enlarges Kinsella's reputation, not merely because of the familiarity of some of its contents but also because of the tension that its title invokes. The sense of belonging to two disjunctive collectives, family and nation, is here articulated thematically but also in terms of form and metrics. The result is an emphatic, diverse restatement of themes of brokenness and incompleteness that have informed the poet's vision from virtually its inception. Although these themes are addressed and expressed with Kinsella's typical vehement, tight-lipped energy, the impression remains one of ground being reworked as worked anew, of a poet revisiting old preoccupations in search of unfamiliar nuances.

POEMS FROM CENTRE CITY

In *Poems from Centre City*, however, there is evidence of a slightly different Kinsella. The poems in this Peppercanister pamphlet address the state of contemporary Dublin in a much more direct way than hitherto, lacking the range and ambition of, for example, "Nightwalker," and presenting themselves more intimately, as more the products of occasions, than is customary with this poet. Metrically simple and verbally direct, they attempt to come to terms with the decay—physical, moral, and institutional—of Kinsella's native place. Decay as a subject is no stranger to Kinsella's imagination. However, despite the comparatively fresh perspective on the poet's concerns that *Poems from Centre City* provides, it should not be assumed that the collection is intended to be thought of as a polemic. The inclusion of a poem on W. H. Auden, one of Kinsella's most permanent influences, may be understood as a caution against the reader's comprehending *Poems from Centre City* as a narrowly activist set of statements on, for example, an environmental theme.

At the same time, the diagnostic—or at least exploratory—thrust of much of Kinsella's work is once again in evidence in this small sampling of his work. The formal range is restricted; the subject matter is largely drawn from the immediacy and adventitiousness of an attentive citizen's experience. A number of the poems are suggested by memory, though all succeed in avoiding either moralizing or sentimentality. In terms of accessibility and immediate effectiveness, *Poems from Centre City* is among the most appealing of Kinsella's later works.

THE PEN SHOP

The 1990's found Kinsella publishing a number of poetry collections, often slight in size but heavy in themes and recollections. *The Pen Shop*, a small volume consisting of two sections titled "To the Coffee Shop" and "To the Pen Shop," focuses on the renewal of a poetic career late in the poet's life. Readers find Kinsella strolling through the streets of Dublin, visiting favorite haunts—the General Post Office, Grafton Street, the Guinness brewery, Trinity College—and seeing the specter of his father in every turn. He meanders to Nassau Street for "some of their best black refills" from the pen shop, and then finds himself at Bewley's, the city's famed tea and coffee shop. Rather than partake in tea or coffee, he instead consumes pills from a tin, needing the black draft of medicinal inspiration to enter his system "direct" with its taste of death, "foreign and clay sharp"; for only in this way may he be jolted into imaginative life and become the grand instrument of his muse's spectral writing: "The long body sliding in/ under my feet." Only then may he no longer be, like the other old men in Bewley's, "Speechless." Indeed, only then may he, like the first voices, "rising out of Europe," become "clear in calibre and professional,/ self chosen,/ rising beyond Jerusalem."

THE FAMILIAR

In 1999, Kinsella issued two short books simultaneously. *The Familiar* consists of the longer title poem and three short poems, all erotically charged and intimate, a style familiar to Kinsella readers. However, here the familiarity is of the flesh, with some mythical overtones. In the title poem, there are "demons over the door" and he has a "Muse on [his] mattress." When he goes to relieve himself during a night of lovemaking, he sees "three graces above the tank." The love scene ends with Kinsella invoking, in the volume's three short poems, a saint in "St. John's," a bride in "Wedding Night," and "Iris," the messenger of the gods.

GODHEAD

Godhead consists of two short poems and a longer title poem. It has little in common thematically with *The Familiar*, since the two short poems are American seascapes ("High Tide: Amagansett" and "San Clemente, California: A Gloss") and the title poem is an evocation of the Holy Trinity of Father, Son, and Spirit. However, both collections share a continuity in their terse, grainy, and stark poetic styles. His poems display a characteristic Irish style in their mythical and religious approach, yet at the same time are startlingly concrete and even irreverent. To speak of the crucifixion as "The Head hanging on one side,/ signifying abandonment" is gruesomely effective, while to end with the line "Dust of our lastborn" seems anticlimactic but haunting.

COLLECTED POEMS, 1956-2001

Toward the end of any poet's career comes the need to produce a complete works. Inevitably, earlier work will have gone out of print, and the poet may experience a need to revise and re-arrange early poetry in the light of later developments. In Kinsella's case, there had been attempts to produce selected works in 1973 and 1979, but by 1990, much of his earlier work had gone through a period of comparative neglect, as other Irish poets, most obviously Seamus Heaney and Paul Muldoon, came to the fore. This resulted in most of his earlier work being largely unavailable.

The production of *Collected Poems, 1956-1994* in 1996 was a major rehabilitation for Kinsella and made his work known to the general public for the first time in many cases. What was significant about the collection was the enormous revision that the earlier poetry had gone through at Kinsella's hand. This only emphasized what students of his writing always knew: that he regarded all his poetry as work in progress, as opposed to, say, Muldoon, who refused to revise his poetry, saying he had no more right to revise it than his readers did.

Kinsella had cut out many of the more Romantic, florid gestures from the earlier poetry, pointing toward the style he was now adopting of simpler, ungestured statement. He had also rearranged some of the poems, and a sense of unity about the oeuvre as a whole was beginning to emerge. Also incorporated were the more or less final version of many of the Peppercanister poems.

The 1996 edition was published by Oxford University Press, one of Kinsella's main publishers. However, in 1999, Oxford University Press decided to cut poetry from its publishing list. This meant little for Kinsella's new work, as the Peppercanister Press was handling that, but it left the *Collected Poems, 1956-1994* high and dry. After some negotiation, Carcanet Press, based in Manchester, England, agreed to produce *Collected Poems, 1956-2001*. It was published in 2001 in the United Kingdom, but copyright did now allow for distribution in the United States. In 2006, Wake Forest University Press published an American version.

Perhaps for the first time, the *Collected Poems, 1956-2001* clearly showed Kinsella's development as being in many ways parallel to that of his great predecessor Yeats. An initial lyrical period, full of imagery, was followed by periods of more political commitment and ironic statement and by more symbolic, very complex personal statements of belief, often drawing on Jungian psychology. Finally came a reversion to a more settled, simpler style, where any form of poetic pretentiousness was avoided.

The other development that can be traced is Kinsella's move to the United States, which resulted in a freeing from traditional bonds of expectation and expression; however, unlike with Muldoon, Kinsella's themes, imagery, and subject matter remain rooted in his Irishness. The depths found by fellow Irish writer James Joyce are mediated through such American poets as William Carlos Williams and in particular Robert Lowell. Kinsella's poetry thus becomes more and more Western mainstream and less and less stereotypically Irish, a move that did not meet the approval of all critics.

OTHER MAJOR WORKS

NONFICTION: *Davis, Mangan, Ferguson? Tradition and the Irish Writer*, 1970 (with W. B. Yeats); *The Dual Tradition: An Essay on Poetry and Politics in Ireland*, 1995; *A Dublin Documentary*, 2006 (poetry and prose); *Prose Occasions: 1956-2006*, 2009 (Andrew Fitzsimmons, editor).

TRANSLATIONS: *The Breastplate of Saint Patrick*, 1954 (revised as *Faeth Fiadha: The Breastplate of Saint Patrick*, 1957); *Longes mac n-Usnig, Being the Exile and Death of the Sons of Usnech*, 1954; *Thirty-three Triads, Translated from the Twelfth Century Irish*, 1955; *The Táin*, 1969 (of *Táin bó Cuailnge*); *An Duanaire, 1600-1900: Poems of the Dispossessed*, 1981 (with Sean O Tuama).

EDITED TEXT: *The New Oxford Book of Irish Verse*, 1986.

BIBLIOGRAPHY

Abbate Badin, Donatella. *Thomas Kinsella*. New York: Twayne, 1996. An introductory biography and critical interpretation of selected works by Kinsella. Includes bibliographical references and index.

Fitzsimmons, Andrew. *The Sea of Disappointment: Thomas Kinsella's Pursuit of the Real.* Dublin: University College Dublin Press, 2008. Produced to honor Kinsella's eightieth birthday, this book analyzes Kinsella's work and career, especially his thematic and structural developments.

Harmon, Maurice. *The Poetry of Thomas Kinsella*. Atlantic Highlands, N.J.: Humanities Press, 1974. The author provides an overview of many of Kinsella's achievements, as well as helpful background information. Kinsella's preoccupation with the Irish language is also dealt with, and close readings of the major poems are offered. In addition, the poet's prosodical originality is analyzed. A valuable introductory guide.

_____. *Thomas Kinsella: Designing for the Exact Needs*. Dublin: Irish Academic, 2008. This volume offers a comprehensive examination of Kinsella's works, looking at them chronologically and grouping them based on similar styles and attitudes. The themes of his poems are also discussed along with his focus on politics and life in Dublin.

Jackson, Thomas H. *The Whole Matter: The Poetic Evolution of Thomas Kinsella*. Syracuse, N.Y.: Syracuse University Press, 1995. A comprehensive overview of Kinsella's achievement.

John, Brian. "Irelands of the Mind: The Poetry of Thomas Kinsella and Seamus Heaney." *Canadian Journal of Irish Studies* 15 (December, 1989): 68-92. An analysis of the cultural implications of the two most important Irish poets of their generation. Kinsella's severe lyricism is contrasted with Heaney's more sensual verse. The two poets' senses of place, time, and history are also examined. The visions of Ireland produced are important evidence of the contemporary debate about Irish national identity.

_____. *Reading the Ground: The Poetry of Thomas Kinsella*. Washington, D.C.: Catholic University of America Press, 1996. A comprehensive study of Kinsella's poetry. John explores the poet's development within both the Irish and the English contexts and defines the nature of his poetic achievement.

Johnston, Dillon. "Kinsella and Clarke." In *Irish Poetry After Joyce*. Notre Dame, Ind.: University of Notre Dame Press, 1985. Kinsella's debt to his most important Irish poetic mentor is discussed. The origins and thrust of Kinsella's satirical tendencies are identified and analyzed. The poet's standing in the tradition of modern Irish poetry is also evaluated.

Skloot, Floyd. "The Evolving Poetry of Thomas Kinsella." Review of *Collected Poems, 1956-1994. New England Review* 18, no. 4 (Fall, 1997): 174-187. Skloot examines

Kinsella's evolving style and themes. Offers a good retrospective look at Kinsella's body of work.

Tubridy, Derval. *Thomas Kinsella: The Peppercanister Poems*. Dublin: University College Dublin Press, 2001. A study of the poetry Kinsella has published with his own press.

George O'Brien; Sarah Hilbert
Updated by David Barratt

GEORGE MACBETH

Born: Shotts, Scotland; January 19, 1932
Died: Tuam, County Galway, Ireland; February 17, 1992

PRINCIPAL POETRY

The Broken Places, 1963
A Doomsday Book, 1965
The Colour of Blood, 1967, 1969
The Night of Stones, 1968
A War Quartet, 1969
The Burning Cone, 1970
Collected Poems, 1958-1970, 1971
The Orlando Poems, 1971
Shrapnel and a Poet's Year, 1973, 1974
In the Hours Waiting for the Blood to Come, 1975
Buying a Heart, 1978
Poems of Love and Death, 1980
Poems from Oby, 1982
Published Collections, 1982
The Long Darkness, 1983
The Cleaver Gardens, 1986
Anatomy of a Divorce, 1988
Collected Poems, 1958-1982, 1989
Trespassing: Poems from Ireland, 1991
Patient, 1992
Selected Poems, 2002

OTHER LITERARY FORMS

In addition to his numerous volumes of poetry, George MacBeth published poetry pamphlets, chapbooks, and limited-edition books. Many of these, initially published in small editions, became parts of larger books and have thus been incorporated into the mainstream of MacBeth's work. MacBeth also published children's books, novels, plays, and an autobiography, and he edited several volumes of poetry.

The sheer volume of MacBeth's production reveals his almost obsessive dedication to writing and the breadth of his interests. Among his publications other than poetry, the autobiography *My Scotland* (1973) probably holds the greatest interest for the reader of his poetry because of what it reveals about MacBeth's background and development. MacBeth himself described the book as a nonlogical, nonnarrative, massive jigsaw of autobiographical bits, a collection of about two hundred short prose pieces about being Scottish.

ACHIEVEMENTS

A corecipient of Sir Geoffrey Faber Award in 1964, George MacBeth was one of the most prolific poets of twentieth century Britain. Volume alone, however, did not account for his significance as a poet; rather, he earned his stature for the diversity of his writing. He was, in the best sense of the word, an "experimental" poet: absolutely fearless in his willingness to attempt new forms and take on unusual subjects, yet simultaneously fascinated by traditional meter and rhyme, as well as by material that has fueled the imagination of poets for centuries. *Poems of Love and Death* contains poems ranging from the dangerously romantic "The Truth," with its didactic final stanza that includes the lines "Happiness is a state of mind,/ And grief is something frail and small," to the satiric "The Flame of Love, by Laura Stargleam," which mocks the dime-novel story line that it exploits. MacBeth is as likely to write about a missile commander as about evening primroses, and the reader familiar with his writing is not at all surprised to find these disparate topics dealt with in a single book, in this case *Buying a Heart*. In fact, it is the sense of discovery and the vitality of MacBeth's imagination that continues to attract many readers.

BIOGRAPHY

Born in Scotland near Glasgow, George Mann MacBeth lived the greater part of his life in England. This circumstance had a substantial impact on his poetry, leading him to view himself as something of an exile. Although he felt comfortable in England, he did not regard himself as English and remarked on the sensation of detachment, of living and working in a foreign country. The Scotland he left as a child remained in his mind as a lost world, a kind of Eden that could never be regained, and his sense of loss helped make him, in his own evaluation, "a very retrospective, backward-looking poet." Perhaps more significantly, his detachment, or rootlessness, enabled him to embrace a larger part of the world than is available to most writers.

Another significant element of MacBeth's life was his long-term association with the British Broadcasting Corporation, where he worked as a producer of poetry programs. This position bought him into contact with the leading poets in England and around the world and exposed him to everything that was happening in poetry. MacBeth himself acknowledged that his close work with a broad variety of poets over the years influenced his writing, particularly in the areas of technique and structure. Always careful not to become too involved in purely "English" writing, he consciously tried to keep in touch with poetic developments in the world at large, and his accomplishments as a poet can be measured most accurately if they are considered in the context of that endeavor.

By the late 1980's, MacBeth had moved to Ireland, continuing to work there as a freelance broadcaster, a teacher, and a writer, and traveling frequently to give readings of his poetry abroad. His life was tragically cut short when, in 1992, he died of motor neuron disease, in Tuam, County Galway.

George MacBeth once remarked that he considered the word "experimental," often used to describe his work, to be a term of praise. Although he acknowledged the possibility of failing in some of his excursions into new forms and new subjects, he obviously felt the risk to be justified. His strongest impulse as a writer was to test the bounds of poetry and, wherever possible, extend them.

This daring push toward the limits of his craft is nowhere better revealed than in the fourth section of his *Collected Poems, 1958-1970*, where MacBeth employs his no-holds-barred approach and enjoys doing it. Indeed, the sense of pleasure that MacBeth manages to communicate, his pure delight in the shape of language on the page, is essential to readers because it helps carry them through poems that at first glance may repel rather than attract.

"LDMN ANALYSIS OF THOMAS NASHE'S 'SONG'" AND "TWO EXPERIMENTS"

Two such forbidding poems that challenge the analytical mind in satiric fashion are "Two Experiments" and "LDMN Analysis of Thomas Nashe's 'Song.'" The first of these poems, divided into two sections, presents a "Vowel Analysis of 'Babylonian Poem' from the German of Friederike Mayröcker" and a "Numerical Analysis of 'Brazilian Poem' from the German of Friederike Mayröcker." If the ponderous and unlikely subtitles are not enough to warn the reader not to be too serious, the actual text should be sufficiently illuminating. The first section is a listing of vowels, ostensibly from the Mayröcker poem, presented in the following fashion: "U EE-EI A I AE-IIE-EIE UE EOE U EI; E." Thus runs the first line, and the second section begins in the following way: "(. .2 2 6 2 3 5: 2 3 3-6 3 8: 3." Clearly, these representations are meaningless, but they do make a point, not a very positive point, about the analytical approach to poetry: that critical analyses of poetry may make no more sense than these vowel and number analyses. A similar statement is made in "LDMN Analysis of Thomas Nashe's 'Song,'" which offers an arrangement of *L*'s, *D*'s, *M*'s, and *N*'s, presumably as they might be extracted from the Nashe poem.

As might be expected, the response to such experimentation has not been universally positive, and a number of readers have questioned whether such strategies can properly be called poetry. Ironically, this may be the very question that MacBeth wants the reader to ask, the ultimate critic's question: "What is poetry?" MacBeth himself is as sincere as any reader in his search for an answer, for he offers no dogmatic views of his own; he merely tosses out experiments in an effort to determine where the boundaries lie.

"FIN DU GLOBE" AND "THE SKI MURDERS"

Other poems that are somewhat less eccentric but nevertheless experimental are "The Ski Murders" and "Fin du Globe." The first is an "encyclopaedia-poem" consisting of twenty-six individual entries, one for each letter of the alphabet. The entries themselves are written in a prose style that might have been taken from a spy novel, and the reader is invited to construct his own story by piecing the vignettes together in whatever fashion he wishes. The second poem is presented as a game containing fifty-two "postcards" and four *"fin du globe"* cards. The players (the readers) are instructed to deal out the cards as in an ordinary deck and to read, in turn, the brief postcard message printed on each. When a *fin du globe* card is turned up, the game is over. Again, the question arises—Is this poetry?—and once again MacBeth is challenging the reader while exploring the limits of his craft and trying to extend his artistic territory. Even the most skeptical readers can find pleasure in these and similar experiments, for they are clever and entertaining, and one can sense the pleasure that MacBeth himself must have experienced in giving free rein to his imagination.

"A POET'S LIFE"

Among MacBeth's most successful comic poems is "A Poet's Life," which first appeared in *In the Hours Waiting for the Blood to Come* and has since developed into a kind of serial poem published in various installments. In its original form, the poem consists of twelve episodes focusing on various aspects of the poet's life. The point of view is third person, to permit MacBeth as much distance as possible from his subject, himself. The result is a poem, which avoids the gloomy seriousness of typical introspection and yet focuses on some serious themes, showing the poet to be as human as anyone else. The first section of the poem is representative of MacBeth's technique; it shows the poet at home, trying to write and jotting down the following lines: "today I got up at eight, felt cold, shaved,/ washed, had breakfast, and dressed." The banality here reflects a larger tedium in the poet's life, for nothing much happens to him, except in his imagination. It is not surprising, then, when his efforts to write lead nowhere and he turns to the television for an episode of the *Avengers*, a purely escapist adventure show.

Viewed almost as a specimen or as a caged animal might be viewed, the poet is an amusing creature, sipping his "peppermint cream" and sucking distractedly on his pencil; and yet he is also pitiable. There is, in fact, something of the fool about the poet, something reminiscent of Charlie Chaplin's little tramp, for although he evokes laughter or a bemused smile there is something fundamentally sad about him. The poignancy comes from the realization that the poet, no matter how hard he tries to blend into the common crowd, must always remain isolated. It is the nature of his craft; writing poetry sets him apart. Consequently, when he goes to the supermarket, dressed in "green wranglers" to make himself inconspicuous, he still stands out among the old women, the babies, and the old men. He is "looking/ at life for his poems, is helping/ his wife, is a normal considerate man," and yet his role as poet inevitably removes him from the other shoppers and from the world at large.

Technically, "A Poet's Life" is rather simple and straightforward, but several significant devices work subtly to make the poem successful. The objective point of view enables MacBeth to combine the comic and the pathetic without becoming maudlin or self-pitying; this slightly detached tone is complemented by MacBeth's freewheeling, modernized version of the *Don Juan* stanza. It is typical of MacBeth to turn to traditional forms for inspiration, to borrow them and make them new.

"How to Eat an Orange"

Not a poet to break the rules without first understanding what the rules are, MacBeth is fascinated by traditional forms as well as by those that are new and experimental. It is a measure of his poetic temperament that he is able to take a traditional form and incorporate it into his general experimentation. The reader often encounters regular rhyme and meter in MacBeth's work and occasionally recognizes something like a sonnet or sestina. Invariably, though, the standard form is modified to conform to MacBeth's urge to experiment. "How to Eat an Orange" is as nearly a sonnet as it can possibly be without actually being one. It has fourteen lines and a Shakespearean rhyme scheme, including the final couplet; but it lacks the iambic pentameter. In fact, it has no regular meter at all, although the iambic does surface from time to time like a theme played in the background. Form, then, is not an end in itself but a means to an end, and MacBeth employs whatever forms he finds useful, including the traditional, in communicating his ideas.

"What Metre Is"

MacBeth's attitude toward form is captured most provocatively in a poem titled "What Metre Is." A tour de force of technique, this poem stands as the poet's manifesto. The controlling idea is that the poem itself will provide examples of various poetic devices while they are being discussed. For example, when alliteration is mentioned, it appears in the context of the following passage: "leaping/ long lean and allusive/ through low lines." The uses of prose are considered in this fashion: "Prose is another possibility. There could be three/ sentences in the stanza. This would be an example of/ that." Other aspects of metrics discussed and illustrated in the poem are syllabics, free verse, word and interval counting, internal rhyming, rhythm, assonance, and finally, typography, "its mos/ t irrit/ ating (perhaps) manif/ estation." Irritating and mechanical it may be, representing the voice of the typewriter and the "abdic/ ation of insp/ iration," but still the poet feels compelled to say "I li/ ke it." He likes it because it is "the logica/ l exp/ ression o/ f itsel/ f." Having gone through his paces, the way a musician might play the scale or some well-known traditional piece just to prove he can, MacBeth turns finally to the experimental, which, despite its flaws, holds some irresistible attraction for him. He can manage traditional metrics, and he illustrates this ability in the poem, but he can also handle the riskier, less traditional devices. This poem, then, embodies on a small scale the range of poetic techniques one is likely to encounter in MacBeth's poetry: the traditional, often with modifications, and the experimental, always with MacBeth's own particular daring.

CHILDHOOD, WAR, AND VIOLENCE

If MacBeth takes chances with the form of his poems, he also takes considerable risks with the content. Many of his poems are violent or sexually explicit, and some readers have found his subject matter objectionable. Perhaps the chief characteristic of the content of his poetry is a fascination with fear and violence, which MacBeth feels can be traced to his childhood. As a boy during World War II, MacBeth lost his father and experienced the bombing of his house. He collected shrapnel in the streets after air raids, spent night after night in the shelters, and grew up surrounded by physical violence and the threat of death. This kind of environment affected him strongly, and MacBeth felt that it led ultimately to a kind of obsession with violence that finds an outlet through his poetry.

The connection between his childhood experience of the war and such poems as "The Sirens," "The War," and "The Passing Ones" is obvious because these poems are explicitly about that experience, about "those bombed houses where/ I echoed in/ The empty rooms." Other poems, such as "Driving West," with its apocalyptic vision of a nuclear war, are less concerned with the actual experiences of World War II than with the nightmare vision it instilled. MacBeth's childhood fear of bombs has been translated into an adult's vision of the end of the world: "There was nothing left,/ Only a world of scrap. Dark metal bruised,/ Flung soup of blood, anchors and driven screws." This is the inheritance of Hiroshima and Nagasaki, a vision of the potential that humanity has to destroy itself and the entire planet.

"THE BURNING POEM"

The same influences are operating, though less obviously, in "The Burning Poem," which ends with the following passage: "Burning, burning,/ and nothing left to burn:/ only the ashes/ in a little urn." Here the violence has been freed of its war context with only a passing reference to suggest the connection: "rice paper, cartridge-paper,/ it was all the same." The merging of art, as represented by the rice paper, and war, represented by the cartridge paper, suggests the relationship between MacBeth's experiences of the war and his poetry. He is, in effect, "Spilling petrol/ on the bare pages." There is a sense in which many of MacBeth's poems are burning with the effects of remembered violence.

"A CONFESSION"

Inevitably, the violence loses its war context entirely and becomes associated with other things, just as it must have been absorbed into MacBeth's life. In "A Confession," for example, the topic is abortion, and the woman who has chosen to abort her child remembers the procedure as "the hard cold inrush of its killer,/ Saw-teeth, threshing fins, cascading water,/ And the soul spat like a bubble out of its head." The act was not clinical or antiseptic but personal and highly violent. The woman, in the course of her dramatic monologue, reveals an obsessive guilt and an inability to deal with what she has done. She wonders, finally, what her punishment might be "For crucifying someone in my womb." In this case MacBeth is somewhat removed from the poem because he uses the persona of the woman, but in "In the Hours Waiting for the Blood to Come" and "Two Days After," he approaches the topic of a lost or aborted child in a much more personal way, considering the impact of the death on the people involved in the relationship. In "Two Days After," the couple make love, but the act has less to do with love than with guilt and a kind of spent violence.

Often, MacBeth's images seem designed specifically to shock the reader, to jolt him or her out of complacency. It is important, however, to realize that MacBeth employs violent and sexually explicit passages for more than merely sensational purposes. He wants to consider the darker side of human nature; violence and fear are alive in the world, and acknowledging their existence is a first step toward coming to terms with them.

"THE RED HERRING"

It would be a mistake to regard MacBeth as merely a poet of sex and violence, for he has more dimensions than those. MacBeth himself seems bothered by the attention that has been given to the more sensational aspects of his poetry to the exclusion of other elements, and has remarked that he does not find his poetry any more violent than anyone else's. In terms of his total body of work, he is right, but the shocking and explicit poems inevitably call more attention to themselves than those that are more subdued in tone and subject matter, especially the very fine children's poems and MacBeth's engaging forays into the fantastic or surreal.

"The Red Herring" is a good illustration of MacBeth's poetry for children. The elements of the poem are a dried red herring, a bare wall, a ladder, and a man with a hammer, a nail, and a long piece of string. After the man has tied the red herring to the string suspended from the nail in the top of the wall and gone away, the poet addresses the question of why he would bother to make up such a simple story: "I did it just to annoy people./ Serious people. And perhaps also/ to amuse children. Small children." Undoubtedly, a child could take pleasure in this poem, but it is not entirely limited to the child in its appeal. The adult who is able to put off his seriousness for a moment or two will find himself smiling at the poem because of its saucy tone and at himself because he was probably gullible enough to enter the poem with a serious mind, even though the title itself warned him that things were not what they seemed. The playfulness here is characteristic of MacBeth's sense of humor, and, as usual, it is designed to make a serious point as well as to please.

"SCISSOR-MAN"

Related to the children's poems are MacBeth's trips into the fantastic, as reflected in "Scissor-Man." The speaker, a pair of scissors used to cut bacon rind, contemplates his position in life, grousing about being kept under the draining board rather than in the sink unit. Further, he worries about what might be going on between the nutcrackers and the carrot grater and vows that if he should "catch him rubbing/ those tin nipples of hers/ in the breadbin" he will "have his/ washer off." Clearly, this is not meant to be children's poetry, but it is, perhaps, a kind of children's poetry for adults, for it engages the imagination in the same way that nursery rhymes and fairy tales do. In this case, MacBeth's humor seems designed to be an end in itself, an escape into the purely fanciful.

If one were to compile a list of adjectives to describe MacBeth's poetry, it would include at least the following: experimental, traditional, humorous, serious, violent, compassionate. The fact that these adjectives seem to cancel one another out is significant, for MacBeth is possessed of a vital desire to encompass everything. In all his diversity, MacBeth is an original and important contemporary poet, a risk-taker who is continually trying to extend the boundaries of his art.

OTHER MAJOR WORKS

LONG FICTION: *The Samurai*, 1975; *The Transformation*, 1975; *The Survivor*, 1977; *The Seven Witches*, 1978; *The Born Losers*, 1981; *The Katana*, 1981; *A Kind of Treason*, 1982; *Anna's Book*, 1983; *The Lion of Pescara*, 1984; *Dizzy's Woman*, 1986; *Another Love Story*, 1991; *The Testament of Spencer*, 1992.

PLAYS: *The Doomsday Show*, pr. 1964; *The Scene-Machine*, pr., pb. 1971 (music by Anthony Gilbert).

NONFICTION: *My Scotland*, 1973.

CHILDREN'S LITERATURE: *Noah's Journey*, 1966; *Jonah and the Lord*, 1969; *The Rectory Mice*, 1982; *The Book of Daniel*, 1986.

EDITED TEXTS: *The Penguin Book of Sick Verse*, 1963; *Penguin Modern Poets VI*, 1964 (with J. Clemo and E. Lucie-Smith); *The Penguin Book of Animal Verse*, 1965; *Poetry, 1900-1965*, 1967; *The Penguin Book of Victorian Verse*, 1968; *The Falling Splendour*, 1970; *Poetry for Today*, 1983; *The Book of Cats*, 1992 (with Martin Booth).

BIBLIOGRAPHY

Booth, Martin. *Travelling Through the Senses: A Study of the Poetry of George MacBeth*. Isle of Skye, Scotland: Aquila, 1983. A brief assessment of MacBeth's poetic work.

Dooley, Tim. Review of *Collected Poems, 1958-1982*, by George MacBeth. *The Times Literary Supplement*, January 26, 1990, p. 101. According to Dooley, the poems in the volume under review reveal a healthy development: "Formal scrupulousness replaces formal daring and self-examination replaces self-regard." Dooley praises the "new tenderness" that accompanied MacBeth's increasing attention to form.

Ries, Lawrence R. "George Macbeth." In *Poets of Great Britain and Ireland Since 1960: Part 2, M-Z*, edited by Vincent B. Sherry, Jr. Vol. 40 in *Dictionary of Literary Biography*. Detroit: Gale Research, 1985. A judicious appreciation that calls attention to MacBeth's black humor and dexterity as a "trickster." Some biographical facts are given, but the piece is primarily a survey of the achievements (and disappointments) of MacBeth's poetry through *Poems from Oby*.

Robinson, Peter. "Keep on Keeping On: Peter Robinson Salutes Two Collections by Poets Whose Stock May Have Fallen but Who Never Gave Up." Review of *Selected Poems*, by George MacBeth, and *Residues*, by R. S. Thomas. *The Guardian*, March 8, 2003, p. 25. In this review of two books of poetry, including the MacBeth collection by Anthony Thwaite, Robinson argues that MacBeth's poetry, while uneven, does not deserve to fade from memory.

Rosenthal, Macha Louis. *The New Poets: American and British Poetry Since World War II*. New York: Oxford University Press, 1967. Rosenthal discusses MacBeth in the context of all English language poets in the last half of the twentieth century. MacBeth, a prolific and experimental poet, defined his times as well as being a product of them. Contains a bibliography.

Schmidt, Michael, and Grevel Lindop. *British Poetry Since 1930: A Critical Survey*. Oxford, England: Carcanet Press, 1972. A useful overview that places MacBeth's poetry in context. MacBeth gave shape to the alienation of modern life by being one of the most fecund and experimental of modern poets.

Thwaite, Anthony. *Twentieth-Century English Poetry: An Introduction*. New York: Barnes & Noble, 1978. Discusses MacBeth as a member of the Group, with only a very brief characterization of his poetry itself but providing an overview of the twentieth century British poetry that can serve as a context for a student of MacBeth. Contains a bibliography and an index.

Neal Bowers

LOUIS MACNEICE

Born: Belfast, Ireland (now in Northern Ireland); September 12, 1907
Died: London, England; September 3, 1963
Also known as: Louis Malone

PRINCIPAL POETRY

Blind Fireworks, 1929
Poems, 1935
Poems, 1937
The Earth Compels, 1938
Autumn Journal, 1939
The Last Ditch, 1940
Poems, 1925-1940, 1940
Selected Poems, 1940
Plant and Phantom, 1941
Springboard: Poems, 1941-1944, 1944
Holes in the Sky: Poems, 1944-1947, 1948
Collected Poems, 1925-1948, 1949
Ten Burnt Offerings, 1952
Autumn Sequel: A Rhetorical Poem in XXVI Cantos, 1954
The Other Wing, 1954
Visitations, 1957
Eighty-five Poems, 1959
Solstices, 1961
The Burning Perch, 1963
The Collected Poems of Louis MacNeice, 1966 (E. R. Dodds, editor)

OTHER LITERARY FORMS

Although he was a poet first and foremost, Louis MacNeice (mak-NEES) published a number of important works in other genres. His only novel, *Roundabout Way* (1932), not very successful, was published under the pseudonym Louis Malone. MacNeice's only other venture into fiction was a children's book, *The Penny That Rolled Away* (1954), published in England as *The Sixpence That Rolled Away*.

An area in which he was no more prolific, but much more successful, was translation. The combination of his education in classics with his gifts as a poet led him to do a successful translation of Aeschylus's *Agamemnon* in 1936. E. R. Dodds, an eminent classics professor at Oxford and literary executor of MacNeice's estate, calls the translation "splendid" (*Time Was Away*, 1974, Terence Brown and Alec Reid, editors). W. B.

Stanford agrees that in spite of the almost insurmountable difficulties of Aeschylus's text, MacNeice succeeded in producing an eminently actable version, genuinely poetic, and generally faithful to the original. MacNeice's translation of Johann Wolfgang von Goethe's *Faust: Eine Tragödie* (pb. 1808, 1833; *The Tragedy of Faust*, 1823, 1838) for radio presented very different problems—in particular, his not knowing German. The radio medium itself also produced problems in terms of what the audience could follow. MacNeice collaborated with E. L. Stahl on the project, and on the whole it was successful. According to Stahl, MacNeice succeeded in rendering the work's unusual combination of the dramatic with the lyric, producing excellent versions of the various lyrical passages.

MacNeice wrote several plays for the theater and nearly one hundred radio scripts for the BBC. Except for *The Agamemnon of Aeschylus*, his theatrical works are not notable, although *Station Bell* was performed by the Birmingham University Dramatic Society in 1937, and a similar play, *Out of the Picture*, was performed in 1937 by the Group Theatre in London, which had also done *Agamemnon*. The verse play was accounted a failure, while having its moments of very good poetry and wit. It was similar to the plays that W. H. Auden and Christopher Isherwood were producing for the Group Theatre in the 1930's: cartoonish parodies in the service of leftist political views. MacNeice's play does, however, show a serious concern with love. Much later, in 1958, MacNeice wrote *One for the Grave* (pr. 1966), patterned on the medieval morality play. It exemplifies his growing interest in allegory, described in *Varieties of Parable* (1965). During World War II, MacNeice wrote documentary dramas for radio, contributing much that was original, though not of lasting literary value, to the genre. His later radio dramas, such as *Out of the Picture*, and his late poems tend toward allegory and quest motifs. *The Dark Tower* (published in *The Dark Tower, and Other Radio Scripts by Louis MacNeice*, 1947) is the most successful of these dramas in its equilibrium between realism and allegory.

MacNeice also wrote an unfinished prose autobiography, published posthumously as *The Strings Are False* (1965); several works of mixed poetry and prose, most notably *Letters from Iceland* (1937) with Auden; and several volumes of literary criticism. These works illuminate MacNeice's poetry, offering insight into the self-conscious relationship of one poet to his predecessors and his craft. *Modern Poetry: A Personal Essay* (1938) is significant as a manifesto of one of the new poets of the 1930's, who believed that poetry should speak directly to social and political issues. *The Poetry of W. B. Yeats* (1941), written before the major scholarly commentaries on William Butler Yeats, offers lucid insights into particular poems, as well as illuminating MacNeice's own goals as a poet. *Varieties of Parable*, a posthumous printing of MacNeice's Clark Lectures of 1963, elucidates his concern with writing poetry that operates on two levels simultaneously, the realistic and the symbolic, moral, or allegorical.

ACHIEVEMENTS

Louis MacNeice is most notable as an exemplar of Socrates' maxim that the unexamined life is not worth living. The major question surrounding his reputation is whether he ranks as a minor or a major poet, whether his poems show a progression of thought and technique or an essential similarity over the years. No one would deny that his craft, his mastery of prosody and verse forms, is of the highest order. Most critics agree that in his last three volumes of poems MacNeice took a new point of departure. Auden asserts in his memorial address for MacNeice (*Time Was Away*) that posterity will endorse his opinion that the later poems do advance, showing ever greater craftsmanship and intensity of feeling. Auden claims that of all his contemporaries, MacNeice was least guilty of "clever forgeries," or dishonest poems. This honesty, combined with an ingrained temperamental skepticism, is at the root of both his major contributions to poetry and what some people see as his flaws. MacNeice is a philosophical poet, Auden says, without a specific body of beliefs, except for a fundamental sense of *humanitas* as a goal and standard of behavior. He is a harsh critic of general systems because he is always faithful to the complexity of reality.

MacNeice's achievements as a poet are paradoxical: He combines an appeal to large audiences with highly learned allusions, and he focuses on everyday events and political issues while also exploring ultimate metaphysical questions. Most interesting is his transition from the 1930's view that the poet is chiefly a communicator, almost a journalist, to the belief that poetry should operate on two levels, the real and the allegorical. It is these contradictory qualities, along with the literary-historical value of recording a thoughtful person's ethical responses to the trials of modern life, that will ensure MacNeice's poetry a lasting reputation.

BIOGRAPHY

Louis MacNeice was born Frederick Louis MacNeice on September 12, 1907, in Belfast, the son of a well-respected Church of Ireland rector. Because his early childhood experiences inform the imagery and ideas of almost all his work, the details of MacNeice's early life are important. His father, John Frederick MacNeice, and his mother, Elizabeth Margaret, were both natives of Connemara in the west of Ireland, a bastion of wild tales and imagination. Both parents communicated to their children their strong attachment to the Ireland of their youth as opposed to the stern, dour, Puritanical atmosphere of Ulster. MacNeice's father was extraordinary among Protestant Irishmen in his outspoken support for Home Rule and a united Irish republic. Thus the young poet started life with a feeling of displacement and a nostalgia for a culture and landscape he had never seen. Life in the rectory was, of course, pervaded by religion and a sense of duty and social responsibility. MacNeice had a sister, Elizabeth, five years his elder, and a brother, William, in between, who had Down syndrome and therefore did not figure heavily in the other children's play. The children were fairly isolated and developed many imaginative games. Louis showed a tendency toward gothic preoccupations in his fear of partially hidden statues in the church and in the graveyard that adjoined his garden. Of special significance is his mother's removal to a nursing home and subsequent death when Louis was seven. She had provided comfort and gaiety in the otherwise secluded and stern life of the Rectory. Louis, the youngest, had been particularly close to her, and his poetry reflects the rupture in his world occasioned by her loss. Without their mother and intimidated by the misery of their father, the MacNeice children became particularly subject to the influences of servants. On one hand, the cook, Annie, was a warm Catholic peasant who spoke of fairies and leprechauns. On the other hand, Miss MacCready, who was hired to take care of the children when their mother became ill, was the antithesis of both Mrs. MacNeice and Annie, a puritanical Calvinist, extremely dour and severe, lecturing constantly about hell and damnation.

In 1917, MacNeice's father remarried. Though she was very kind and devoted, the new Mrs. MacNeice had a Victorian, puritanical outlook on life that led to further restrictions on the children's behavior. Soon after the marriage, MacNeice was sent to Marlborough College, an English public school, further confusing his cultural identity. From this point on, England became his adopted home, but the English always regarded him as Irish. The Irish, of course, considered him an Anglo-Irishman, while he himself always felt his roots to be in the west of Ireland. Both at Marlborough and later at Merton College, Oxford, MacNeice was in his milieu. At Marlborough he was a friend of Anthony Blunt and John Betjeman, among others. He flourished in the atmosphere of aestheticism and learning. At Oxford he encountered Stephen Spender and the other poets with whom he came to be associated in the 1930's. MacNeice studied the classics and philosophy at Oxford, and these interests are second only to the autobiographical in their influence on his poetry. He graduated from Oxford with a double first in Honour Moderations and "Greats."

Having rebelled against his upbringing by drinking heavily and rejecting his faith at Oxford, MacNeice in a sense completed the break by marrying a Jewish girl, Mariette Ezra. Together they moved to Birmingham, where he was appointed lecturer in classics at the University. In Birmingham, MacNeice encountered the working class and taught their aspiring children at the University. He had always been protected from the lower classes of Belfast and in English schools had lived among the upper classes. The new contact with working people led to a healthy respect for the ordinary man and a broadening of MacNeice's social awareness. At the same time, he was becoming recognized as a member of the "poets of the thirties," with Auden, Isherwood, Spender, and Cecil Day Lewis, whose sense of social responsibility led them to espouse Marxism. MacNeice never became a communist, but he did write about social issues and questioned the comfortable assumptions of traditional English liberalism. While at Birmingham, MacNeice became friendly with E. R. Dodds, who was later to become his literary executor. In 1934, he and his wife had a son, Dan, and in 1936, his wife abruptly left her son and husband to live with an American graduate student at Oxford, Charles Katzman. This abandonment, parallel to the death of his mother, haunted MacNeice for many years and is reflected in his poetry. In the later 1930's, MacNeice traveled twice to Spain, reporting on the Spanish Civil War, and twice to Iceland, the second time with Auden. In 1936, he became lecturer in Greek at Bedford College for women at the University of London. In 1939 and 1940, he lectured at colleges in the United States, returning to what he felt to be his civic responsibility to England following the outbreak of World War II.

From 1941, MacNeice worked for the British Broadcasting Corporation as a scriptwriter and producer, except for the year and a half in 1950-1951 that he served as director of the British Institute in Athens, Greece. In 1942, he married a singer, Hedli Anderson; they had a daughter, Corinna, the following year. In the 1940's and 1950's, MacNeice traveled extensively, to India, Greece, Wales, the United States, Africa, Asia, France, and Ireland. His premature death in 1963 was the sort of paradoxical experience he might have used in a poem on the irony of life. He was going far beyond the call of duty for the BBC by descending a chilly manhole to check the sound transmission for a feature he was producing. He suffered from exposure, contracted pneumonia, and died. Such a death appears to represent the antithesis of the poetic, yet for MacNeice, poetry spoke about the ordinary as well as the metaphysical and it was intended to speak to the ordinary man. His death resulted from the performance of his ordinary human responsibility, his job.

ANALYSIS

Louis MacNeice was an extremely self-conscious poet. He wrote several books of literary criticism, gave lectures on the subject, and often reflected on the role of the poet in his poems. In an early essay, written in 1936, he reveals his allegiance to the group of poets represented by W. H. Auden, who believed their chief responsibility to be social rather than purely artistic. MacNeice divided art into two types: parable and escape. William Butler Yeats and T. S. Eliot, while unquestionably great, represent the latter, the less valid route. MacNeice always retained his belief in "parable-art," that is, poems that appear naturalistic while also suggesting latent moral or metaphysical content—although he came to realize in later years that journalistic or overly realistic art has its defects while "escape-art" often addresses fundamental problems. MacNeice's lasting conception of the poet's task is remarkably close to William Wordsworth's in the preface to the *Lyrical Ballads* (1798): The poet should be a spokesperson for and to ordinary men. To communicate with a large audience, the poet must be representative, involved in current events, interested in the news, sports, and so on. He must always place the subject matter and the purpose of his art above a pure interest in form. In *Modern Poetry*, he echoes Wordsworth's dictum that the poet must keep his eye on the object. A glance at the titles of MacNeice's poems reveals the wide range of his subjects; geographical locations, artists, seasons, classical and mythical figures, types of people, technological objects, and types of songs are a few representatives of the plurality embraced by his poems. Furthermore, like Wordsworth, MacNeice studies external objects, places, and events closely, though his poems often end up really being about human consciousness and morality, through analogy or reflection on the experience.

TELLING VS. SHOWING

Thus, MacNeice's fundamental approach to poetry also resembles Wordsworth's. Many of his poems are a modernized, sometimes journalistic version of the loco-descriptive genre of the eighteenth century, arising from the description of a place, object, or event, followed usually by a philosophical, moral, or psychological reflection on that event. Although MacNeice attempts to use a plain, simple style, his training in the classics and English literature tends to produce a rich profusion of allusive reverberations. The relationship between the topical focus of the poem and the meditation it produces varies from association to analogy to multiple parallels. In technique, MacNeice differs from the Imagistic, Symbolist thrust of T. S. Eliot, Ezra Pound, and the modern American poets influenced by them. The framework of MacNeice's poems is primarily expository; he tells rather than trying to show through objective correlatives.

POET OF IDEAS

As Terence Brown argues in *Louis MacNeice: Sceptical Vision* (1975), MacNeice is most notable as a poet of ideas. In his study of Yeats, he emphasizes the importance of belief in giving substance to a poet's work. Many critics have mistakenly criticized Mac-Neice's poetry on this basis, finding it superficial and devoid of philosophical system. Brown argues cogently that MacNeice is deceptively philosophical because he remains a skeptic. Thus the few positive beliefs underlying his poetry appear negative. Many of his poems question epistemological and metaphysical assumptions; depending on one's interpretation, MacNeice's "final" position may seem positive or negative. Many of his poems represent what might loosely be called an existentialist position. Although he never stops evaluating the validity of religion, MacNeice ceased to believe in God in his late teens, after being brought up in the home of a future Anglican bishop. The loss of God and Christianity left a huge gap in the metaphysical structure of MacNeice's thought, and he resisted replacing it with another absolute system such as Marxism. He retained a strong sense of moral and social duty, but he found no objective sanctions for value and order. In his poems, he explores the conflicting and paradoxical facts of experience. For example, he believes that a new social order will benefit the masses, but he is honest enough to admit his fondness for the privileges of the elite: good education, clothes, food, and art. He remains obsessed with the Heraclitean theory of flux, that we can never step into the same river twice. Yet when we face the absence of certainty, belief, and absolute value, we can celebrate plurality and assert ourselves against time and death. Brown distinguishes the modernity of MacNeice in "a sceptical faith, which believes that no transcendent reality, but rather non-being, gives being value."

STYLISTICS

The most striking technical features of MacNeice's poems evince his sometimes conflicting concerns with reaching a large audience of ordinary people and with reflecting philosophically on experience. In line with the former, he attempts to use colloquial, or at least plain, language, and often to base his rhythm and style on popular musical forms, from the folk ballad, nursery rhyme, and lullaby to modern jazz. His concern with contemporary issues, coupled with his classical training, makes irony and satire inevitable. Like the English Augustans (with whom he did not want to be identified), MacNeice cannot help contrasting reality with the ideals of past literature, politics, and belief systems. His satire of contemporary society tends to be of the urbane, gentle, Horatian type, only infrequently becoming harsh and bitter. Other stylistic features mark his concern with metaphysical issues. He uses analogy and paradox, accreting many resonances through classical and biblical allusions, usually simultaneously. Many poems pose unresolved questions and problems, circling back on their beginnings at the end. The endings that repeat initial statements or questions would seem to offer closure, or at least a definite structure, to the poems, but paradoxically they do not. Rather, they emphasize the impossibility of answering or closing the issue.

Another stylistic feature that recurs throughout MacNeice's work is the list, similar to the epic catalogs of Homer. Rather than suggesting greatness or richness as they usually do in epics, MacNeice's catalogs represent the irreducible plurality of experience.

EVOLUTION VS. STASIS

In addition to the question of his belief system or lack thereof, critics have disagreed over whether MacNeice's work develops over time or remains essentially the same. The answer to this question is sometimes viewed as a determinant of MacNeice's rank as a poet. An argument can be made for both positions, but the answer must be a synthesis. While MacNeice's appreciation of the complexity of life, its latent suggestions, grows as his poetry develops, certain interrelated clusters of themes and recurring images inform his work from beginning to end.

For example, the places and events of his childhood shape his problematic identity and worldview, including his obsessions with dreams and with Ireland as a symbol of the more gothic, mysterious, and mystical sides of experience. Connected with his upbringing in the home of an Anglican rector is a preoccupation, mentioned above, with disbelief in God and religion, and faith in liberal humanism. The disappearance of God results in complex epistemological and moral questions that also pervade many poems. Another related thematic cluster is a concern with time, death, and Heraclitean flux. Closely related to this cluster is an increasing interest in cycles, in repetition versus renewal, reflected in many poems about spring and fall.

Although these themes, along with recurring images of train journeys, Ireland, stone, dazzling surfaces, and time represented as space, among others, continue to absorb MacNeice's attention, the types of poems and emphases evolve over time, particularly in response to changes in the political temper of the times. His juvenilia, written between 1925 and 1927, reflects the aesthetic focus of his student years, playing with sound and rhetorical devices, musing on sensation, death, God, and self-consciousness. MacNeice did not really emerge as a poet until the 1930's, when his teaching, marriage, and life among the workers of Birmingham opened his eyes to the world of social injustice and political reality. At that point he was influenced by Auden, Spender, and Lewis, and came to see the poet's role as more journalistic than purely aesthetic.

FROM POLITICAL TO PHILOSOPHICAL

The poems of the 1930's reflect his preoccupation with the disheartening political events in Spain and Germany and his belief that the existing social order was doomed. The poetry of this period is more leftist than at any other stage in MacNeice's career, but he never espouses the dogmas of Marxism. During World War II, his poetry becomes more humanistic, more positive in its treatment of man. MacNeice's faith in human nature was fanned by the courage and generosity he witnessed in his job as a fire watcher in London during the war.

After the war, his poems become at first more philosophical, reflecting a revaluation of the role of art and a desire for belief of any kind, not necessarily in God. At this point, the poems express an existential recognition of the void and a disgust with the depersonalization of England after the war; they also play with looking at subjects from different perspectives. His last three volumes of poems, published in 1957, 1961, and posthumously in 1963, represent what most critics consider to be the apotheosis of MacNeice's career. The lyrics of his latest poems are austere and short, often using tetrameter rather than pentameter or hexameter lines. Many of these poems are "parable-poems" in the sense that MacNeice described in his Clark Lectures of 1963, published as *Varieties of Parable*; that is, they use images to structure a poem that is in effect a miniature allegory. The poems appear to be topical or occasional, but they hold a double or deeper meaning.

"THE KINGDOM"

Because MacNeice was essentially a reflective, philosophical poet, his poetry records an ongoing dialectic between the shaping forces of his consciousness and the events and character of the external world. Thus certain techniques, goals, and preoccupations tend to recur, though they are different in response to historical and personal developments in MacNeice's life. Since he was a skeptic, he tends to ask questions rather than give answers, but the more positive values that he holds become clearer by the last years of his life. In particular, the idea of a kingdom of individuals, who lay claim to their freedom and create their lives, is implicit in many of the later poems, after being introduced in "The Kingdom," written around 1943. The members of this kingdom counteract flux and fear by their genuineness, their honest seeing and feeling, their incorruptibility. The Greek notion of *arête*, sometimes translated as virtue or excellence, but without the narrowly moral meaning usually attached to "virtue," comes to mind when one reads the descriptions of exemplary individuals in "The Kingdom." This kingdom is analogous to the Kingdom of Christ, the ideal Republic of Plato, and the Kingdom of Ends in Immanuel Kant's moral system. Yet it does not depend on absolutes and thus it is not an unattainable ideal but a mode of life that some people manage to realize in the ordinary course of life. Moreover, the members of this kingdom belong by virtue of their differentness, not because they share divine souls or absolute ideas of reason.

"BLASPHEMIES"

MacNeice sees himself in terms of stages of development in such poems as "Blasphemies," written in the late 1950's, where he describes his changing attitude toward God and belief. The poem is a third-person narrative about his own feelings toward religion since his childhood. In the first stanza, he is seven years old, lying in bed pondering the nature of the unforgivable sin against the Holy Ghost. In the second stanza, he is seventeen, striking the pose of a blasphemer, parodying prayers. The middle-aged writer of the autobiographical poem mocks his earlier stance, seeing the hollowness of rebellion against a nonexistent deity. The third stanza describes how, at thirty, the poet realized the futility of protest against an absence and turned to a new religion of humanism and realism, facing facts. The mature MacNeice undercuts these simple new faiths by ending the stanza with a question about the nature of facts for a thirty-year-old. Stanza 4 finds the poet at forty attempting to appropriate the myths of Christianity for purely symbolic use and realizing that their lack of absolute meaning makes them useless to him. At the age of forty, he has reached a crisis of sorts, unable to speak for himself or for humankind. The final stanza sums up MacNeice's ultimate philosophical position: that there are no ultimate beliefs or postures. He finally throws off the entire issue of Christianity, finding divinity neither above nor within humankind.

The irreducible reality is that he is not Tom, Dick, or Harry, some archetypal representative of ordinary man. He is himself, merely fifty, a question. The final two lines of the poem, however, in typical MacNeice fashion, reintroduce the problem of metaphysics that he has just dismissed. He asserts that although he is a question, that question is as worthwhile as any other, which is not saying too much. He then, however, uses the word "quest" in apposition to the word "question," reintroducing the entire issue of a search for ultimate meaning. To complete the confusion, he ends with a completed repetition of the broken-off question that opens the poem: What is the sin against the Holy Ghost? The repeated but augmented line is an instance of the type of incremental repetition used in folk ballads such as "Lord Randall," and it suggests the kind of dark riddle often presented in such songs. The final question might be just idle intellectual curiosity or it might imply that ultimate questions of belief simply cannot be escaped by rationality.

"To Hedli"

MacNeice's dedicatory poem, "To Hedli," which prefaces the 1949 *Collected Poems, 1925-1948*, serves as a good introduction to his technique and themes. The poem is clearly occasional and autobiographical, using the first-person point of view that he often eschews in later poems. While employing fairly plain diction, the poem is a sestina, a highly restrictive verse form made up of six stanzas, each having six lines ending with the same six words throughout the poem. In addition, the final word of each stanza is repeated as the last word of the first line in the succeeding stanza. MacNeice takes a few liberties, adding a tercet, or half-stanza, at the end, and substituting the word "returning" for "turning" in stanza 4. The poem is typically self-reflective, calling into question the poetic efforts represented in the collected poems, regretting the unanswered question present in the volume. The content of the poem thus radiates out from a highly specific event, the collecting of MacNeice's poems from 1925-1948, and their dedication to the listener of the poem, his second wife, Hedli. From this focus the poem reaches back to the poet's past practices and beliefs and outward to suggest a broad metaphysical stance. The poem is therefore typically occasional, personal, and philosophical. Although the poem does not make explicit reference to World War II, its recent horror is implicit in the anger of those who believed they knew all the answers and the "grim past" that has silenced so many poets.

Two recurrent themes that pervade this poem are the need for belief and the motif of repetitive cycles, with the question of renewal. The sestina form, so highly repetitive, mirrors the concern with cycles. Stanza 1 calls the poetic moments in the collection "April Answers." In MacNeice's works, spring and fall always signal, on one level, the cycles of time and life. In "Day of Renewal," he says he has measured all his experience in terms of returning autumns. The answers that come in April are the positive side of cycles; they herald renewal if not rebirth. The poems, or answers, implicitly compared to perennial plants, seem to have "withered" off from their bulbs or roots, their questions. The questions, or sources of the poems, are akin to the frozen barrenness of winter, perhaps representing despair. Stanza 3 picks up the metaphor implicit in the word "withered" by comparing the "Word" to a bulb underground. MacNeice is writing this poem during the period when he began attempting to deal with religious matters symbolically, so it is clear that "Word" has no literal Christian significance. It is rather the source of true poetry, informed by some body of belief. The cycles of renewal in MacNeice's past work are contrasted with a larger cycle in which this word is awaiting a new generation of poets who will produce "full leaf" and "bloom" of meaning and image.

The alternating stanzas, two and four, criticize more clearly what MacNeice sees as his own weaknesses as a poet. He has lived too much in the present, in a no-man's-land of belief, between unknown gods to come and the rejected gods of his ancestors. This position parallels, though without the defined system of belief, Yeats's prophecy in "A

Second Coming." There is a milder sense than Yeats's of the crumbling of the old order in the outpouring of angry sound from those who knew the answers, perhaps enthusiasts for communism. Stanza 4 explains MacNeice's past contentment with "dazzle," the poetic mirroring of intense moments in the flux of life, and with chance gifts washed up by the sea of life. These gifts were fragments from older castaways who could never return. This statement suggests that while nature repeats its cycles endlessly, men die. The final half stanza suggests that the poet is growing older and has nothing but half answers; his end is in sight. Stanza 5 begins with the word "But," clearly contrasting the poet's past contentment with his present goals. He refers to the autumn in which he is writing this dedicatory poem (November, 1948) and parallels the leaves' turning brown with the gilt's flaking off his poetic images. The poem ends with a definite desire for some fundamental answers to metaphysical questions. Unlike later poems, "To Hedli" at least implies that such answers may exist.

"AN ECLOGUE FOR CHRISTMAS"
Among the earlier poems in the 1949 collection, "An Eclogue for Christmas" (December, 1933) marks an early point of departure, a turning toward serious poems of social commentary. In his fragmentary prose autobiography, *The Strings Are False*, MacNeice describes his absorption in his home life during the early 1930's. His sister, in "Trees Were Green" (*Times Was Away*), comments on the special pleasure Christmas always represented for her brother. MacNeice explains that when he had finished writing this poem he was taken aback by the depth of his despair over Western culture's decay. Like many of the poems of this period, "An Eclogue for Christmas" combines colloquial language with a classical form, the eclogue, which is a dialogue between shepherds, often on love or poetry, or the contrast between city and country life. The two speakers of MacNeice's poem, A. and B., represent the city and the country, the country in this case being the world of the landed gentry in England. There is no disagreement between the two speakers; they mirror each other's prophecies of doom in terms of the societies they represent. Neither city nor country escapes the horrors of the times. B., the representative of country life, tells A. not to look for sanctuary in the country. Both places are equally bad. The poem describes a time like that in Yeats's "A Second Coming," but in a more dominant way than "To Hedli." It seems that MacNeice could clearly see the coming of World War II. The poem satirizes contemporary upper-class British society as mechanistic, slick, and superficial. The rhythms of jazz pervade the hectic and chaotic life of the city, and people like A. become automatons. Rather than being individuals like those in MacNeice's later "The Kingdom," people are grotesque in their efforts to be unique.

The motif of cyclical return is what motivates the poem, the reflection on Christ's birth as represented by "old tinsel and frills." This is a hollow repetition, not a renewal or rebirth. The elaboration of technological "improvements" has alienated people from the

151

genuine reality of life. The cyclicity of history is suggested in the metaphor of the Goths returning to silence the pneumatic drill. Yet MacNeice is such a skeptic that he is unable to make a wholesale condemnation of modern industrial society. He admits that a narcotic beauty can be perceived in the lights and bustle of the city, which he here calls an "organism" rather than a machine. *B.* attacks the country gentry in Marxist terms, as a breed whose time is about to end. He alludes to the destruction of the "manor wall" by the "State" with a capital "S," and also to private property as something that is turning to "poison and pus." Much of this part of the dialogue is carried on in questions, so it is difficult to assign a positive attitude to either speaker, let alone the author. *A.*, who seems closer to MacNeice, counters the Marxist-inspired questions of *B.* with questions about the results of violent revolution. *A.* is clearly the skeptic who sees the problems inherent in capitalist society but cannot accept the Marxist solution. *A.* interrupts *B.*, telling him not to "gloat" over his own demise, suggesting the irony of an upper-class communism. The poem ends with self-mocking assertions on the part of both speakers; they have no choice but to cling to the few good, real things they have in life.

Like so many of MacNeice's poems, this one circles back to its opening occasion, the significance of Christmas. The ending holds out a somewhat flippant hope for renewal, but it is extremely "ephemeral," like the few positive ideas in the last part of the poem. Thus, "An Eclogue for Christmas" shows MacNeice facing an "evil time," the discord and injustices of modern industrial society, but unwilling and unable to accept the premises of a new regime founded on violence and the subordination of the individual to the state. This skepticism sets him apart from the group of poet-friends surrounding Auden.

AUTUMN JOURNAL

In the fall of 1938, MacNeice wrote *Autumn Journal*, a long poem in twenty-four cantos, commenting specifically on the depressing political events of the time: the Munich Pact and the Spanish Civil War. In a prefatory note, he categorizes the poem as half lyric and half didactic, hoping that it presents some "criticism of life" with some standards beyond the "merely personal." The poem, however, is a journal (as the title states) and its record of events is tinged by fleeting personal response. It is a huge, complex version of his shorter poems in its intertwining threads of autobiography, travel, politics, philosophy, morality, and poetics. The personal-ethical response to political events is the strongest of these threads, coloring the entire poem. Because it takes its impetus from the private and public events of the days and months of late 1938, from late August until New Year's Eve, it does not have an overall architectonic structure; each individual canto rounds itself out as a separate unity that is enhanced by its relationship to the whole.

The poem as a whole is given closure by the parallels between the dying summer at the beginning, the dying year at the end, and the threatened death of European civilization from the impending world war throughout. The narrative is basically chronological, following the poet's first day of the fall term, through trips to Oxford and finally to Spain. The narrative technique resembles stream of consciousness, the thoughts and memories of the poet creating the subject matter. The poem is more fluently lyrical than many of MacNeice's poems, which have been criticized as being "flat." It uses an alternating rhyme scheme like that of ballad stanzas (*abcbdefe . . .*), but the effect resembles terza rima.

As in most of MacNeice's works, the meditations are rooted in specific observations of actual times, places, and events. Canto 1 begins with a catalog of concrete images of summer's end in Hampshire, ordinary people leading ordinary lives, insulated within their families. The poet-narrator is in a train, as in so many of his poems. The train ride comes to symbolize the journey of life, the time line of each individual. In an ambiguous tone, MacNeice mentions his dog lying on the floor of the train, a symbol of lost order. This is picked up both more seriously and more ironically in canto 7 when the dog is lost while political treaties are dying and trees are being cut down on Primrose Hill to make an antiaircraft station. The loss of the dog is the close of the "old regime." In MacNeice's personal life, the "old regime" represents his marriage to Mariette, but in larger terms, it is the demise of traditional Western capitalist society. At the end of this canto, the speaker tries to work up enthusiasm for a war that he cannot romanticize. He realizes exactly what it is, yet he also realizes that he may have to become uncritical like the enemy, like Hitler propagandizing on the radio.

Canto 8 builds, through satirical popular song rhythms, to a climax of fear about the outbreak of war. At the end of the canto the poet learns that the crisis is averted through the sacrifice of Czechoslovakia. He does not explain his response directly except to say that he has saved his own skin as an Englishman in a way that damns his conscience. The poet-narrator feels a terrible conflict between a natural desire to avert war and a sense of duty, which might in earlier times have been called honor, to face up to the threat of Hitler and defeat him. This conflict is implicit until canto 12, in which he describes people, himself included, lacking the heart to become involved in ethics or "public calls." In his private debate with his conscience, MacNeice recalls the soldiers training across the road from his home when he was a child during World War I. Having described the beginning of classes in canto 9, cynically and mockingly stating that *we* are safe (although the Czechs are lost), the poet is reading Plato in preparation for teaching his philosophy course. The ethical differences between Plato and Aristotle form an important context for the progress of MacNeice's feelings and thoughts in the poem. In canto 12, he rejects Plato's ideal forms as a world of capital initials, preferring instead the Heraclitean world of flux, of sensation. He admits at the end of canto 12 that his desire is to be "human," in the fullest sense, to live in a civilized community where both mind and body are given their due. He undercuts this desire by satirizing the professors of humanities who become "spiritually bankrupt" snobs, yet conceding his own willingness to take the comforts that such a profession provides. Though the connection is not explicitly made here, the reader must keep in mind the overwhelming threat to civilization that forms the background of these reflections. *Autumn Journal* traces MacNeice's emotional and moral journey from reluctant self-interest to reluctant determination to do his share to protect humanity in the impending war.

Canto 13 is a mocking, slightly bitter rejection of the elitist education, particularly in philosophy, that MacNeice has received. The bitterness arises from the disjunction between the promise and world of thought and the real world he must inhabit. He must be happy to live in the world of appearances and plurality, life in the particular rather than the eternal and ideal realm. The poet's synthesis between skepticism and moral and civic responsibility is revealed in the next canto where he describes a trip to Oxford to help drive voters to the polls. While he cannot commit himself to political ideologies, he does mobilize himself to act for a "half-believed-in principle." Imperfect though it is, the parliamentary system is England's only hope for political progress. Here MacNeice comes to the important realization that to shun politics for private endeavor is to risk the conditions that support or allow that private endeavor. As he drives back to London at the end of canto 14, MacNeice has a new understanding of the need for all Englishmen to unite against the threat of fascism. This new resolution allows the cheerful final image of the sun caressing the plurality of nature, wheelbarrows full of oranges and apples. This serenity is undercut in the following canto by a nightmarish effort to escape through drink the horrors that threaten, horrors associated in MacNeice's mind with his childhood fears and bad dreams.

In canto 17, at nine o'clock on a November morning, the poet savors a moment of almost Keatsian escape in a bath, allowing responsibility to die. Metaphorically he speaks of the ego merging into the bath, thus leading himself into a meditation on the need of man to merge, or at least interact, with those outside himself. Significantly, MacNeice affirms Aristotle's ethical notion that humankind's essence is to act, as opposed to Socrates' idea that humankind's crowning glory is to think. The canto ends with his refusal to "drug" himself with the sensations of the moment. This climactic decision to act is followed by cantos satirizing industrialized England, implying, as William Blake does in *Songs of Innocence* (1789) and *Songs of Innocence and of Experience* (1794), that church and state conspire to allow social injustice. While MacNeice is not a communist, he fairly consistently condemns *laissez-faire* economics as an instrument of evil. Although canto 18 is very bitter about England's social and political failure to act, it ends with the affirmative statement that the seeds of energy and choice are still alive. Canto 20, trying to sound bitter, relaxes into a nostalgic longing for Christmas, a week away, a "coral island in time." This beautiful image is typical of MacNeice's conflation of space and time. Any poem about consciousness exists in the stream of time, but to be comprehensible the passing of time must be anchored to spatial reference points. MacNeice frequently concretizes this space/time relationship by metaphorically imaging time as a geographical space. Christmas here is an ideal moment, described through an allusion to the lotus eaters of the *Odyssey* (c. 725 B.C.E.; English translation, 1614). The remainder of the canto speaks respectfully of Christ but ends on a satirical note about people exploiting the season to beg for money. This carries additional overtones, however, because if one remembers the spirit of Christmas rather than the selfish pleasures it brings, nothing is more appropriate than to celebrate Christ's birthday by giving money to beggars.

Canto 21 returns to the notion of canto 17, that one must live a life beyond the self, in spite of the wish to quit. The poem, like the year, ends with MacNeice's train journey through France to Spain. Significantly, the poem skips Christmas, implying that neither the hollow religion of Christianity nor the personal pleasures of the holiday have a meaningful place in the ethical and political events at hand. MacNeice goes to face the New Year in Spain, a place where metaphorically all Europe may soon stand in time. He goes to confront his duty as a man of action and a citizen of a free country. His New Year's resolutions, detailed in the penultimate canto, reveal his self-criticisms and determination to seek the roots of "will and conscience," to participate. The final canto is a sleep song, gentle in tone, allowing some peace after the hard-won resolutions of canto 23. MacNeice addresses himself, his parents, his former wife, and all people, to dream of a "possible land" where the individual can pursue his natural abilities in freedom and understanding. He tells of his hope to awaken soon, but of his doubts to sleep forever.

VISITATIONS, SOLSTICES, AND THE BURNING PERCH

Most critics agree that MacNeice's final three books of poems, *Visitations*, *Solstices*, and the posthumous *The Burning Perch*, achieve new heights of technical precision and depth of meaning. The themes of flux and renewal become even more prominent than in the past. According to his own statements in literary criticism, MacNeice was attempting to write more "parable-poems." The use of the train journey and of Christmas Day in *Autumn Journal* exemplifies the multiple layers of meaning he could achieve in describing an actual event, object, or place. In these later poems, there is more respect for the mysterious, the dark side of experience. The focus on life as a paradox is playfully yet darkly expounded in poems resembling folk ballad riddles, poems such as "A Hand of Snap-shots," "The Riddle," and parts of "Notes for a Biography." In particular, the poems of *The Burning Perch* give brief nightmare sketches of the gothic side of experience. Connected to the motifs of riddles and paradoxes is a new concern with perspective or various ways of knowing, as in Part I of "Jigsaws," "The Wiper," "The Grey Ones," and perhaps "Budgie."

"The Wiper," from *Solstices*, is a perfect example of the kind of "parable-poem" MacNeice sought to write in his later years. On the literal level, it starts with a concrete description of the driver's and passengers' perspective of the road from inside the car on a dark, rainy night. The first stanza portrays the glimpses of the shiny asphalt when the windshield wipers clear the window, only to blur it when they move back the other way. The focus shifts to the nature of the road and then to an outside view of the wet cars on the road. The fourth stanza turns to the memory of the car's passengers, to the relationship between past and present, while the final stanza looks not very invitingly to the "black future," literally the dark night ahead on the road. Only through subtle double meanings does MacNeice suggest the allegorical or symbolic nature of the poem. The words "mystery" and "always" in stanza 2 and "black future" in stanza 5 are the only obvious indicators of a level of meaning beyond the literal.

The poem symbolizes life as a journey with the potential of being a quest, a potential limited by the restrictions of partial blindness. The riders in the car can see only brief snatches of a black road, a mysterious road with unknown dimensions. The darkness of night, the meaningless void of existence, is broken intermittently by the lights of other people insulated and partially blinded in their own "moving boxes." Significantly, while each driver is able to see very little through the dark and rain, his or her car gives off light that illuminates the way for other drivers, if only transiently. The dials in the cars measure speed and distance covered. In Aristotle's terms, these are indicators of efficient causes, but the final cause, the destination and the daylight, is not indicated. The final line of the poem is highly characteristic of MacNeice in its qualified, pessimistically positive assertion. In spite of ignorance and clouded perceptions, living in a world of night and rain, the drivers manage to stay on the road.

MacNeice is a poet of contradictions, a learned classicist who sought to write in a colloquial idiom and appeal to a broad audience, a man who sought belief but was unable to accede to the dishonesty of systematizing. His poems are above all honest. They study life in the fullness of its antinomies and paradoxes.

OTHER MAJOR WORKS

LONG FICTION: *Roundabout Way*, 1932 (as Louis Malone).

PLAYS: *Out of the Picture*, pr., pb. 1937; *Station Bell*, pr. 1937; *One for the Grave*, pr. 1966; *Selected Plays of Louis MacNeice*, 1993.

RADIO PLAYS: *Christopher Columbus*, 1944; *The Dark Tower, and Other Radio Scripts by Louis MacNeice*, 1947; *The Mad Islands and The Administrator*, 1964; *Persons from Porlock, and Other Plays for Radio*, 1969.

NONFICTION: *Letters from Iceland*, 1937 (with W. H. Auden); *I Crossed the Minch*, 1938; *Modern Poetry: A Personal Essay*, 1938; *Zoo*, 1938; *The Poetry of W. B. Yeats*, 1941; *Astrology*, 1964; *The Strings Are False*, 1965; *Varieties of Parable*, 1965.

TRANSLATIONS: *The Agamemnon of Aeschylus*, 1936; *Goethe's Faust, Parts I and II*, 1951 (with E. L. Stahl).

CHILDREN'S LITERATURE: *The Penny That Rolled Away*, 1954.

BIBLIOGRAPHY

Brown, Terence. *Louis MacNeice: Sceptical Vision.* New York: Barnes & Noble, 1975. Concerned with the themes in MacNeice's poetry. Argues that the poet's real contribution is as a proponent of creative skepticism. The result is a dependable, authoritative study. Contains a good bibliography and notes.

Brown, Terence, and Alec Reid, eds. *Time Was Away: The World of Louis MacNeice.* Dublin: Dolmen Press, 1974. A collection including personal tributes, reminiscences, and evaluations of MacNeice's work. Several pieces are of interest, including one by MacNeice's sister that contains personal biographical information. Other selections look at MacNeice's Irishness, his poetry, and his reaction to his mother's death. Includes W. H. Auden's "Louis MacNeice: A Memorial Address."

Devine, Kathleen, and Alan J. Peacock, eds. *Louis MacNeice and His Influence.* New York: Oxford University Press, 1998. Essays by leading experts on MacNeice's work examine the range and depth of his achievement, including his influence on Michael Longley, Derek Mahon, Seamus Heaney, and Paul Muldoon. Includes bibliographical references and index.

Longley, Edna. *Louis MacNeice: A Study.* London: Faber & Faber, 1988. The first complete study after MacNeice's death. Explores the dramatic nature of MacNeice's poetry, stresses the importance of his Irish background, and credits William Butler Yeats's influence, hitherto downplayed. This piece of historical criticism moves chronologically, linking MacNeice's life and times. Special attention is given to his English, war, and postwar poems. Bibliography.

McDonald, Peter. *Louis MacNeice: The Poet in His Contexts.* New York: Oxford University Press, 1991. An examination of MacNeice in the context of Northern Ireland and its poets. W. J. Martz, reviewing for *Choice* magazine, notes the author's "need to see MacNeice as MacNeice . . . in his contexts rather than those that have hitherto been thought to be his." Bibliography, index.

Marsack, Robyn. *The Cave of Making: The Poetry of Louis MacNeice.* New York: Oxford University Press, 1982. This book looks at MacNeice as a poet of the 1930's and focuses on despair and disillusionment in his work. Contains commentary on the poet's craft and process based on papers, drafts, and notes made available to the author. Extensive notes and an excellent bibliography.

Moore, Donald B. *The Poetry of Louis MacNeice.* Leicester, England: Leicester University Press, 1972. This descriptive study traces the poet's development chronologically. Tracks themes such as self, society, and philosophy through MacNeice's work. The final chapter gives a retrospective and general critical overview. Includes a select bibliography with citations of related works.

O'Neill, Michael, and Gareth Reeves. *Auden, MacNeice, Spender: The Thirties Poetry.* London: Macmillan Education, 1992. A close analysis of the major works of three giants of 1930's English poetry.

Stallworthy, Jon. *Louis MacNeice*. New York: W. W. Norton, 1995. Stallworthy produces the first full-scale biography of MacNeice, a tour de force "not likely to be superseded," according to W. J. Martz of *Choice* magazine. Includes pictures and copies of manuscript pages, each dated. Bibliography, notes, index.

Wigginton, Christopher. *Modernism from the Margins: The 1930's Poetry of Louis MacNeice and Dylan Thomas*. Cardiff: University of Wales Press, 2007. The author looks at the poetry of MacNeice and Dylan Thomas, placing their works in the Auden-dominated 1930's and discussing their poetry in relation to modernism.

Eve Walsh Stoddard

JAMES CLARENCE MANGAN

Born: Dublin, Ireland; May 1, 1803
Died: Dublin, Ireland; June 20, 1849

PRINCIPAL POETRY

Poems, by James Clarence Mangan, with Biographical Introduction, by John Mitchel, 1859
Poems of James Clarence Mangan (Many Hitherto Unpublished), 1903 (D. J. O'Donoghue, editor)
Poems, 1996-1999 (4 volumes; Jacques Chuto, editor)
Selected Poems of James Clarence Mangan, 2003

OTHER LITERARY FORMS

James Clarence Mangan (MAN-gahn) is known primarily for his poetry and verse translations from more than twenty different languages, including Gaelic. However, he also wrote and translated witty, humorous prose works, articles, stories and essays, most of which appeared between 1832-1849 in different Irish periodicals, such as the *Comet, Irish Penny Journal, Dublin University Magazine, Vindicator, Nation,* and *Irish Monthly Magazine.* During the last year of his life, Mangan wrote a series of articles called "Sketches and Reminiscences of Irish Writers," published in *The Irishman.*

ACHIEVEMENTS

The biggest distinction any mid-nineteenth century Irish poet could hope to achieve was to be called a national poet. James Clarence Mangan, one of the Young Ireland poets, won this "title" through versatile and prolific poetic production. Although written in English, most of his poetry absorbed distinctly Gaelic patterns and rhythmical structures and effectively revived the tone and imagery of the ancient bardic verse. Mangan's work inspired a whole generation of Irish writers—among them William Butler Yeats and James Joyce—to find their own voice and, thus, continue the process of de-Anglicization of Irish literature and culture, which had been the goal of the first Celtic Revival at the end of the eighteenth century, by means of antiquarian explorations of the ancient Celts' heroic past. Haunted by a sense of cultural inferiority and lost identity caused by the country's colonial dependence on the British Empire, Mangan's poetry responded to the pressing demand in nineteenth century Ireland for a national literature. His authentic, powerful counterimages would help Ireland resist and repair the cultural rupture and discontinuity caused by the colonial intervention.

BIOGRAPHY

Remembered by his contemporaries as a bohemian, James Clarence Mangan was a victim of morbid melancholy, opium, and alcohol. He was prone to painful introspection, which, intensified by his Catholicism, led to frequent withdrawals from friends, family, and society. This, combined with his recurring financial difficulties and physical neglect, resulted in a troubled, though artistically intensive, life and an early death at the age of forty-six.

The poet was born in Dublin, where he spent his whole life. His father gave up his position as a schoolteacher to run the grocery business he had inherited through his wife. He sent James to a Jesuit school where the boy started learning Latin, Spanish, French, and Italian—languages that would determine to a great extent the course of his career. A rather eccentric child, he experienced severe difficulties dealing with the "outside" world and withdrew into an eight-year-long state of blindness, allegedly caused by excessive exposure to rain. His relatives found him hard to reach and considered him "mad."

Mangan was fifteen when he became the family's breadwinner—his father had gone bankrupt. The first job he took was at a scrivener's office. It was at this time that he started publishing his first poems in the *Grant'*s and *New Ladies'* almanacs and when his mysterious blindness disappeared. Two years later, however, in 1820, an illness and a severe emotional disturbance led to a diagnosis of hypochondriasis. His poetic apprenticeship ended in 1826, but his ill health persisted. By this time, Mangan had moved away from his family and had started publishing nationalistic poetry. He continued earning a meager living by doing clerical work. In 1833, he supported a parliamentary petition for repeal of the Act of Union between Ireland and Britain. His political activism motivated him also to start learning Gaelic and establish close contacts with Gaelic scholars.

In 1834, the *Dublin University Magazine*, Ireland's most prestigious periodical at the time, started accepting Mangan's poetry for publication. This marked the beginning of a long-term collaboration; in *Dublin University Magazine*, the twenty-two chapters of Mangan's *Anthologia Germanica = German Anthology: A Series of Translations from the Most Popular of the German Poets* (1845), as well as numerous other "translations" from various languages, would appear for the next twelve years. The following few years were also eventful: In 1836, Mangan met Charles Gavan Duffy, the future founder of the nationalist Young Ireland Party and its weekly magazine *The Nation*, both active advocates of physical-force politics as the only means to achieve Irish independence.

Two years later, Mangan was hired by George Petrie, a famous antiquarian, to work at the Ordinance Survey Office. The project involved surveying and remapping the whole of Ireland for the purposes of the British government. This was arguably the most enabling experience in Mangan's life as, on one hand, it strengthened his contacts with

Gaelic scholars and, on the other hand, allowed him to get acquainted with numerous historical sources and manuscripts, and through them, with Ireland's ancient past. Touched by concrete visions of the glory of the ancient Celts, Mangan began reworking Eugene O'Curry's prose translations of Irish bardic verse, gaining confidence in the strength of his own artistic voice. These poems, "translations" from the Irish, appeared in the *Irish Penny Journal*, founded in 1840 with the task of popularizing the country's Gaelic past.

Although the late 1830's marked a very fruitful period in Mangan's artistic life, they had detrimental effects on his health, which worsened to such an extent that friends started referring to him as "poor Mangan." They also realized that he had become addicted to opium (later to be substituted by alcohol) in an attempt to deal with his attacks of "intellectual hypochondriacism." He denied the fact, refusing to take an abstinence pledge. His finances worsened when the Ordnance Survey Office was closed in December of 1841. It took Petrie a few months to find Mangan a new job—this time at the Trinity College Library. The poet experienced relative financial stability for a few years, but the solitary nature of his work made it hard for him to publish. As biographers point out, his artistic production in *Dublin University Magazine* alone had declined from an average of one hundred pages annually, between 1835 and 1839, to about thirty during each of the following five years.

Having been unemployed for about six months, in 1845, Mangan resumed his job at Trinity Library. It was a half-time position, which meant increased financial difficulties for the poet. The years 1845-1846, however, were marked by remarkable creative achievements and the publication in *Nation* of his most passionate nationalistic verse. He declared his readiness, as his biographer Ellen Shannon-Mangan pointed out, "to devote [himself] almost exclusively to the interests of [his] country." However, his desire to join openly the physical-force politics led by Duffy was repeatedly thwarted by the latter's refusal to admit Mangan in the Irish Confederation. As the great Famine intensified in Ireland, so did Mangan's bad health. In December of 1847, ill and homeless, he took to drinking again, although he had tried to give it up for a number of years. The remaining year and a half of his life was characterized by bad health and poverty, despite the isolated attempts by few of his friends to help him. Still, Mangan continued to write and publish poetry.

In May, 1849, he contracted cholera. In June, having allegedly recovered from it, he was found dying in a street cellar. He was taken to a hospital, where he died a week later.

ANALYSIS

As an Irish Romantic poet, James Clarence Mangan was aware of a loss of innocence, a feeling central to Romantic subjectivity in general, which was intensified by the poet's attempts to cope with the feeling of being trapped in a present corrupted by Britain's colonial power. The poet's search for an alternative, natural and pure self (individual, cultural, national) was therefore colored by a search for an appropriate medium for its expression. Until the beginning of his ardent nationalism in the mid-1830's, Mangan relied primarily on translation from various European and Middle Eastern languages as a means of escaping his oppressive environment, both personal and social. Through acts of imagination, translation transported him to various, often exotic lands. However, his biographers emphasize repeatedly that Mangan had no knowledge of most of the languages from which he "translated." He often transformed his originals by saturating them, especially Oriental verse and that of the minor German Romantics, with rhetorical and stylistic effects typical for his own nationalistic poetry. When Duffy criticized him once for a rather loose Moorish "translation," Mangan pointed out instead its relevance to the Gaelic Revival, responding in his own witty way: "Well, never mind, it's Tom Moorish."

There were also cases when Mangan attributed his own verse to foreign poets. "Twenty Golden Years Ago," he claimed, was originally a German poem by Selber (German for "himself"). Other works were attributed to a Persian poet by the name of Hafis ("half-his"). It is true that, in the absence of an Irish literary tradition in English, a poet like Mangan had greater chances to support himself by publishing translations from languages with rich and firmly established literary traditions, such as German, or from cultures that were distinctly non-English, such as Turkish, Persian, or even Serbian. Translation, therefore, offered Mangan a means of release from his personal anguish and a means of pulling himself away from English Romanticism, which represented for all Irish the culture of the colonizer. Poems such as "Siberia" demonstrate eloquently Mangan's idea of the devastating effects his country's colonial history had had on Irish consciousness. He translated the poem, which originally voiced Freiligrath's impressions of an Icelandic landscape, into a metaphor with distinct political overtones pointing to the inhuman conditions in Ireland during the Famine: "Blight and death alone./ No summer shines." The year was 1846:

> Pain as in a dream,
> When years go by
> Funeral-paced, yet fugitive,
> When man lives, and doth not live,
> Doth not live—nor die.

"O'Hussey's Ode to the Maguire"

Mangan never learned enough Gaelic to be able to translate Irish verse. Therefore, he relied primarily on the "translation" strategies he had already acquired. His wide access to old numbers of *Dublin University Magazine* allowed him to benefit from Samuel Ferguson's and other antiquarians' prose translations from the 1820's and 1830's. Mangan's creative imagination and acute ear for melody and rhythm completely transformed them into remarkable pieces of poetry. "O'Hussey's Ode to the Maguire" serves as a poignant example. Compare the opening stanzas of Ferguson's translation (1834) with Mangan's poem (1846). The speaker is Eochaidh Ó Heodhussa, chief bard of the Maguire Hugh. Hugh, himself, is in the Irish province of Munster, waging war against the colonizing enterprise of Queen Elizabeth I:

> Cold weather I consider this night to be for Hugh!
> A cause of grief is the rigor of its showery drops;
> Alas, insufferable is
> The venom of this night's cold.

> Where is my Chief, my master, this bleak night, mavrone!
> O, cold, cold, miserably cold is this bleak night for Hugh,
> Its showery, arrowy, speary sleet pierceth one through
>   and through,
> Pierceth one to the very bone!

Although Mangan preserved the four-line stanza of Ferguson's translation, his poem reveals a psychological intensity not readily audible in Ferguson's version. Partly because each of the poets chose to emphasize different sides of the native Irish character— Ferguson stressed its profound sense of loyalty to a leader, while Mangan singled out its pure, natural force and strength—the two texts convey different political messages. Ferguson, representative of the Anglo-Irish Ascendancy, strives to bring England's attention to the respect and loyalty with which the Old Irish address their leader, a quality the Crown should value in its subjects if the prosperity of both England and Ireland is to be secured. By 1846, however, the physical-force politics as a means to achieve Irish independence had gathered considerable momentum. That is why Mangan's regular *abba* rhyme is opposed to variations in line length and beat, from iambs to dactyls or anapests, to produce a singular explosive power.

"KATHALEEN NY-HOULAHAN"

This poem of 1841 refers to an Irish sovereignty myth, very much like Mangan's most famous poem, "Dark Rosaleen." Ireland is personified as a beautiful young queen ("Ny" is the feminine equivalent of the masculine "O," as in O'Neill), whose beauty and youth fade in sorrow, while waiting for her land and people to be delivered from the distress the enemy has inflicted upon them. Only masculine strength and sacrifice can again transform the "ghostly hag" into a maiden-queen. Mangan based the poem on a literal translation from the Irish by O'Curry and, although its immediate context relates to a particular historical event, the eighteenth century Jacobite rebellions, it is beyond doubt that the contemporary readers saw it on another level: the pressing need for decisive action, if Ireland's prosperity was to be restored. In a subtle way, very much as in

"Dark Rosaleen," the poem establishes a contrast between a glorious past and a rather bleak present carried across by the conditional in line four below:

> Think her not a ghastly hag, too hideous to be seen,
> Call her not unseemly names, our matchless Kathaleen:
> Young she is, and fair she is, and would be crowned a
>   queen,
> Were the king's son at home here with Kathaleen
>   Ny-Houlahan!

The poem contains another major theme—homelessness and wondering—introduced and elaborated upon by the framing effect of the first and last quatrains. The implicit comparison between the Irish and God's chosen people justifies the cause of Ireland's independence and renders distinctly optimistic both the end of the poem and the struggle against Britain.

"THE NAMELESS ONE"

Published in 1849, after Mangan's death, this ballad is often interpreted as the poet's farewell to his country. It is worth noting that it was one of Joyce's favorite poems, and it is not difficult to see why. In the very first stanza, the poet creates a host of images that are distinctly Irish and at the same time transcend the narrow, nationalistic notion of Irishness that Joyce found oppressive: The "song," like the salmon, one of Ireland's ancient symbols, has started its journey to the sea, mature and full of hope. The identity of the singer, his "soul," is no longer to be separated from the "song," his art. The restraining power of history and tradition, language and ideology—the name—means no more. All that matters is the cycle of life itself, encompassing both God (first stanza) and hell (last stanza), birth and death.

OTHER MAJOR WORKS

NONFICTION: *Autobiography*, 1968.

TRANSLATIONS: *Anthologia Germanica = German Anthology: A Series of Translations from the Most Popular of the German Poets*, 1845 (2 volumes); *The Poets and Poetry of Munster: A Selection of Irish Songs by the Poets of the Last Century, with Poetical Translations by James Clarence Mangan*, 1849.

MISCELLANEOUS: *The Prose Writings of James Clarence Mangan*, 1904 (D. J. O'Donoghue, editor); *Prose*, 2002 (2 volumes; Jacques Chuto, editor); *Selected Prose of James Clarence Mangan*, 2004.

BIBLIOGRAPHY

Chuto, Jacques. *James Clarence Mangan: A Bibliography*. Portland, Oreg.: Irish Academic Press, 1999. This bibliography, by an editor of Mangan's poems, lists the works of the poet, his contributions to magazines, as well as works written about him. Contains a index of titles and first lines.

Lloyd, David. *Nationalism and Minor Literature: James Clarence Mangan and the Emergence of Irish Cultural Nationalism.* Berkeley: University of California Press, 1987. Mangan's literary production is examined in terms of its "failure" (in the positive sense of "resistance") to comply with imperial narrative models of cultural development. Focus is on the political and cultural effects of colonialism on Irish nationalist ideology and the emerging Irish aesthetic culture.

MacCarthy, Anne. *James Clarence Mangan, Edward Walsh, and Nineteenth-Century Irish Literature in English.* Lewiston, N.Y.: Edwin Mellen Press, 2000. This study of nineteenth century Irish literature in English compares and contrasts the works of Mangan and Walsh.

Shannon-Mangan, Ellen. *James Clarence Mangan: A Biography.* Dublin: Irish Academic Press, 1996. Excellent, detailed study of Mangan's life and works, relying on extensive use of primary materials. Includes short analyses of Mangan's most significant work.

Welch, Robert. "James Clarence Mangan: 'Apples from the Dead Sea Shore.'" In *Irish Poetry from Moore to Yeats.* Irish Literary Studies 5. Totowa, N.J.: Barnes & Noble, 1980. Examines Mangan's literary achievements within the context of the emerging Irish national literature in English. Welch compares Mangan's Romantic nationalism with works of English and German Romantic poets. The chapter contains stylistic and rhetorical analyses of about twenty original poems, translations, and prose works.

Miglena Ivanova

JOHN MONTAGUE

Born: Brooklyn, New York; February 28, 1929

PRINCIPAL POETRY

Forms of Exile, 1958
Poisoned Lands, and Other Poems, 1961 (revised as *Poisoned Lands*, 1977)
A Chosen Light, 1967
Tides, 1970
The Rough Field, 1972, 1989
A Slow Dance, 1975
The Great Cloak, 1978
Selected Poems, 1982
The Dead Kingdom, 1984
Mount Eagle, 1988
New Selected Poems, 1989
About Love, 1993
Time in Armagh, 1993
Collected Poems, 1995
Chain Letter, 1997
Smashing the Piano, 1999
Drunken Sailor, 2004

OTHER LITERARY FORMS

John Montague (MAHNT-uh-gyew) has published short stories, a novella, a memoir, a collection of his essays, several volumes of poems translated into English (some in collaboration with others), and several anthologies of Irish literature.

ACHIEVEMENTS

John Montague is one of the preeminent poets writing in English in the past several decades, perhaps best known for his poems about the Troubles (past and present) in Ireland and about personal relationships. Among his many awards and prizes are the Butler and O'Shaughnessy Awards from the Irish American Cultural Institute (1976), the Marten Toonder Award (1977), the Alice Hunt Bartlett Award from the Poetry Society of Great Britain (1978), a Guggenheim Fellowship (1979-1980), the Hughes Award (1987), the American Ireland Fund Literary Award (1995), a Festschrift, *Hill Field*, in honor of his sixtieth birthday, and the Vincent Buckley Poetry Prize (2000). He received honorary degrees from the State University of New York, Buffalo (1987); University College, Cork; and the University of Ultser, Coleraine (2009). A signal honor was being named, and serving as, the first Ireland Professor of Poetry (1998-2001).

166

BIOGRAPHY

John Patrick Montague was born in Brooklyn of Irish parents in 1929. His father, James Terence Montague, had gone there for employment in 1925, joining a brother who ran a speakeasy. James's wife, Mary (Molly) Carney, and their two sons joined him in 1928; John, the third son, was produced by this reunion. In 1933, the three brothers were sent to County Tyrone in Northern Ireland, the older two moving in with Carney relatives in Fintona, the youngest staying with two unmarried Montague aunts in Garvaghey. John's mother returned to Ireland in 1936, settling in Fintona (his father did not return until 1952).

Montague was reared apart from his mother and brothers, though he spent some holidays with them. He excelled at local schools, developed a stammer that would persist through his life, and won a scholarship to a boarding school in Armagh. He spent summer holidays during World War II with cousins in the South of Ireland. Having enrolled at University College, Dublin, he received a B.A. in history and English in 1949. He traveled in Austria, Italy, and France; in 1952, he received his M.A. in Anglo-Irish literature.

Montague traveled to the United States in 1953, spending a year at Yale University, a summer at Indiana University, and a year in the University of Iowa Writers' Workshop, where he received a master of fine arts degree in 1955. There he met Madeleine de Brauer. They were married in her native France before returning to Dublin in 1956.

He worked for the Irish tourist board for three years (1956-1959), became associated with Liam Miller's Dolmen Press, helped found Claddagh Records, and published his first book of poems before moving to Paris in 1961, where for two years, he was correspondent for the *Irish Times*. He lived in Paris during most of the 1960's, but also in the United States (teaching during 1964-1965 at the University of California, Berkeley) and Ireland. His first marriage ended in divorce; in 1972, he was married to Evelyn Robson, a French woman.

They settled in Cork, where Montague taught at University College, Cork (1972-1988) and where they reared their daughters, Oonagh (born 1973) and Sibyl (born 1979). For much of the 1990's, Montague spent a semester each year in residence as distinguished professor in the New York State Writers Institute at Albany. He separated from his second wife. He and his new partner, American-born novelist Elizabeth Wassell, made their home at Ballydehob, County Cork, Ireland.

ANALYSIS

The subjects of John Montague's poetry are Ireland, family, and love. He writes about people and places he knew growing up in County Tyrone, about sectarian strife in Ulster and its historical sources, and about relatives, especially his parents, seeking to understand them and his relationships with them. He has examined love from all angles: from outside and within, as desired and feared, found and lost, remembered in joy and pain.

FORMS OF EXILE

If Ireland, family, and love are Montague's main subjects, his main theme is loss, a theme clearly seen in his poems about exile, a topic he has explored thoroughly. The title of his first book of poems, *Forms of Exile*, points to this preoccupation. "Emigrants," the shortest of its poems, confronts a major fact of Irish life since the 1840's: economic exile. Its "sad faced" subjects could be Montague's own parents, bound for Brooklyn.

"Soliloquy on a Southern Strand" looks at another sort of exile. After many years in Australia, an Irish priest reflects disconsolately on what has become of his life. He feels cut off from Ireland, alienated from the young people around him on the beach, discouraged about his vocation. In "A Footnote on Monasticism: Dingle Peninsula," Montague thinks about "the hermits, lonely dispossessed ones," who once lived on the peninsula. He feels a degree of kinship with these "people hurt into solitude/ By loss of love." Dispossession, another form of exile, and "loss of love" appear in this early poem to be equivalent.

More than half the poems in *Forms of Exile* allude to religious belief and practice, a subject seldom mentioned in Montague's later books. Clearly, despite his sympathy for the Irish priest in Australian exile and his qualified empathy with the Dingle hermits, Montague is distancing himself from the more parochial aspects of Irish Catholicism. "Rome, Anno Santo" looks unsympathetically at "the ignorant Irish on pilgrimage." "Incantation in Time of Peace" expresses doubt whether prayer can prevent the coming of "a yet more ominous day" in Ireland.

"Cultural Center" (later retitled "Musée Imaginaire") contemplates artworks from different cultures in a museum, each representing a civilization's values. Among them, commanding the speaker's attention and that of a nun in the museum, is a "minatory" Catalan crucifix. The "rigid figure" on the cross, its "sharp body twisted all awry," bespeaks a religion harsh but undeniably real. At the nun's waist swings a miniature crucifix: "a minute harmless god of silver plate," as "inoffensive . . . and mild" as the nun herself. Given these "conflicting modes" of imaging Catholicism, clearly Montague prefers the strength and authenticity of the "lean, accusing Catalan crucifix"; yet his misgivings about the values it represents are obvious.

Although love would develop into one of Montague's chief subjects, there is more fear than love in *Forms of Exile*. When love does appear, it is merely observed, not actually experienced: in "Irish Street Scene, with Lovers," for example, and "Song of the Lonely Bachelor."

"The Sean Bhean Vocht" introduces an old woman who, symbolically, is Ireland personified, a repository of "local history" and "racial memory." "As a child I was frightened by her," Montague says, but it is not entirely clear what has replaced fear: fascination, respect, perhaps a hint of affection. Montague's ambiguity in this regard suggests that he has only begun to work through his feelings toward Ireland.

POISONED LANDS, AND OTHER POEMS

Poisoned Lands, and Other Poems overlaps with *Forms of Exile*: 40 percent of its poems appeared in the earlier book. In its new poems, Montague continues to write about Ireland, reflecting on his relation to it and its relation to the world. Several of these poems attempt to shape and understand childhood memories. "The Water Carrier" describes the chore of fetching water with precisely rendered details, then stops short. "Recovering the scene," Montague says, "I had hoped to stylize it,/ Like the portrait of an Egyptian water-carrier:/ Yet halt, entranced by slight but memoried life." Realizing that he cannot be that detached from memory, he concludes,

> I sometimes come to take the water there,
> Not as return or refuge, but some pure thing,
> Some living source, half-imagined and half-real
>
> Pulses in the fictive water that I feel.

Memory itself is that "fictive water," a resource on which to draw.

"Like Dolmens Round My Childhood, the Old People" evokes the lives of country neighbors. As megalithic structures dot the Irish countryside, mysterious and yet matter-of-factly present, so these figures populate the landscape of the poet's memory. "For years they trespassed on my dreams," he says, "until once, in a standing circle of stones,/ I felt their shadow pass// Into that dark permanence of ancient forms." He has commemorated the old people without sentimentality and made peace with their memories.

The outside world began to impinge on his local world when he was a schoolboy, as he recalls in "Auschwitz, Mon Amour" (later retitled "A Welcoming Party"). Newsreel images of concentration-camp survivors brought home to him the irrelevance of Ireland's "parochial brand of innocence." Having learned something about evil in the wider world, he has yet to comprehend what he has seen. For now, there is nothing to do but return to school and toss a football. The "Irish dimension" of his childhood, he says, came from being "always at the periphery of incident."

In poems such as "Auschwitz, Mon Amour" and the sarcastic "Regionalism, or Portrait of the Artist as a Model Farmer," Montague's disaffection with Irish provincialism gives him an exile's sensibility, in the tradition of one of his masters, James Joyce. "Prodigal Son" reflects on his annual visits to Ulster: It is a nice place to visit, but he would not want to live there. (Montague is well aware that the self-selected exile of the artist has little in common with exile imposed by economic circumstance, such as he alludes to in the opening poem of *Poisoned Lands, and Other Poems*, "Murphy in Manchester.")

Within the new poems in this collection, the subject of religion all but disappears. Love is alluded to occasionally, mostly in passing; yet the volume does include Montague's first full-fledged love poem, "Pastorals." It is a dialogue between two lovers, a cynic who sees love as but the "movement of unlawful limbs/ In a marriage of two whims" and an idealist who views it as a sanctuary where "hearts long bruised . . . can trace/ Redeeming patterns of experience."

A CHOSEN LIGHT

The first section of *A Chosen Light* is a gathering of love poems. "Country Matters" and "Virgo Hibernica" recall love unspoken; the inhibiting shyness of adolescence. The latter acknowledges "the gravitational pull/ of love," but the former concludes that "the word of love is/ Hardest to say."

"All Legendary Obstacles" memorializes the reunion of separated lovers. A number of subsequent poems in the section draw on less ecstatic (less "legendary") experiences, including the strains within a marriage. "Loving Reflections," for example, moves in its three parts from tenderness to an angry argument to grim determination to hold on to the relationship.

Montague begins to explore family connections seriously in *A Chosen Light*, particularly in "The Country Fiddler" and "The Cage." His uncle and godfather John Montague, for whom he was named, had been a country fiddler, but his "rural art [was] silenced in the discord of Brooklyn," and he died in American exile. His nephew, born there, became his uncle's "unexpected successor" when sent to Ireland at age four to live. Montague also sees his craft, poetry, as "succession" to his uncle's "rural craft" of music.

In "The Cage," Montague calls his father "the least happy/ man I have known," who drank himself to "brute oblivion." When he finally returned to Ireland in 1952, after twenty-seven years in Brooklyn, he and his son were briefly reunited; by then, however, the son was but an occasional visitor to Tyrone and would soon head for the United States himself. Mingled in the poem are Montague's conflicting feelings toward his father: pity, revulsion, respect, affection.

"The Road's End" grew out of one of Montague's visits home. He retraces childhood steps, noting changes: overgrown thorns, a disused well, abandoned homes. "Like shards/ Of a lost culture," he says, "the slopes/ Are strewn with cabins, emptied/ In my lifetime." His sense of loss is strong.

TIDES

In *Tides*, only two poems allude to Montague's blood kin, "Last Journey" and "Omagh Hospital," and both move from their specific subjects to the larger world of Northern Ireland. The former is subtitled "i.m. James Montague," but salutes Ulster's, as well as his father's, memory, citing the "placenames that sigh/ like a pressed melodeon/ across this forgotten/ Northern landscape." In "Omagh Hospital," Montague's dying Aunt Brigid pleads to be taken home, but he pictures her house, "shaken by traffic/ until a fault runs/ from roof to base." The house that has become uninhabitable is not only the family home but also the whole province, rent by a grievous "fault."

Tides has an increased proportion, and a stunning variety, of love poems. The first two of the book's five sections concentrate on the darker side of love. "Premonition" and "The Pale Light" provide horrific, nightmare images. "Summer Storm" scales down to the more prosaic hell of a couple arguing, Montague returning here to his theme of love gone sour. "Special Delivery," in which "the worm of delight/ . . . turns to/ feed upon itself," reinforces this theme. The two poems in these sections that actually celebrate love are those that, at first glance, might seem least capable of doing so: "The Wild Dog Rose" and "The Hag of Beare." "The Wild Dog Rose" focuses on a haggish woman who has lived a solitary life of few expectations and fewer pleasures. Her one encounter with a man was a terrifying attempted rape. However, love is not absent from this apparently loveless life: The poem ends with a glimpse of transcendent, absolutely selfless love. The poem elicits not pity for the old woman but admiration for her great heart. In "The Hag of Beare," another crone comes to a higher love, at the end of a life utterly different from that briefly sketched in "The Wild Dog Rose." Having known all fleshly pleasures, now denied by age and infirmity, the Hag of Beare expresses her willingness to welcome "the Son of Mary," like so many men before, "under my roof-tree."

The middle section of *Tides* introduces a frankly erotic note into Montague's love poetry. "A Dream of July" celebrates "Ceres, corn goddess," whose "abundant body is/ Compounded of honey/ & gold," and similar imagery of honey and gold can be found in "The Same Gesture" and "Love, a Greeting" (as earlier it was found in "Virgo Hibernica"). Love here is primarily physical, exuberant, largely unassociated with responsibilities, and—as in the title poem, "Tracks"—without commitment.

THE ROUGH FIELD

Poems in Montague's first two books of poems are not randomly arranged, but a greater degree of order obtains in books three and four, which group poems into thematically related sections. Moreover, in *Tides*, the fourth book, sea imagery, often metaphorical, helps unify the volume as a whole. Montague's fifth book, *The Rough Field*, is more highly organized still. Though it contains a number of individual poems capable of standing on their own (eight appeared in previous Montague books), in fact it is one long poem composed of many parts.

Montague began work on *The Rough Field* in the early 1960's, concluding it a decade later, after a new outbreak of sectarian violence struck Ulster. Montague says that he began with "a kind of vision . . . of my home area, the unhappiness of its historical destiny." Violent confrontations in Belfast and Derry gave added point to the project and contributed materials that Montague incorporated into the completed work: "the emerging order/ of the poem invaded," as he says in part 9, "by cries, protestations/ a people's pain."

"Rough Field" translates the name of the townland, Garvaghey, where Montague grew up: "Rough Field in the Gaelic and rightly named/ . . . Harsh landscape that haunts me." He weaves together family stories, incidents from his childhood, and episodes from Irish history since the sixteenth century. The book is populated by members of his family, people from Tyrone whom he knew growing up, and historical figures from Hugh O'Neill (1545-1616) to Bernadette Devlin (born 1947). It evokes the landscape and dwells on the place-names of Tyrone, and of Ulster in general, sites of ancient or recent historical significance. Interspersed among Montague's poems, often with ironic effect, are a variety of "found" texts: excerpts from historical documents, memoirs, letters, newspapers, and the like. The "conversation" among the various voices in *The Rough Field* (Montague's several voices and these "found" voices) contributes to the book's multilayered complexity.

Its complexity notwithstanding, the book is unified by its steady focus on one place (and the continuity of its problems) as well as by recurring images—the rough field, houses, swans—and recurring concerns: home, inheritance, exile; memory; dreams; loneliness; things lost; things broken, shaken, scattered, shattered, including buildings, families, lives, dreams, tradition, a culture, a province. *The Rough Field* is further unified by successfully linking the personal, the familial, the regional, the national, and the global, Montague's Garvaghey becoming a microcosm of "the rough field/ of the universe." Finally, it is unified by successfully linking past and present: generation joined to generation ("This bitterness/ I inherit from my father"), century to century (contemporary exile in the United States and the seventeenth century "Flight of the Earls"). *The Rough Field*, treating a serious theme with artistry and authority, is widely considered Montague's greatest work.

A SLOW DANCE

A Slow Dance is a rich mixture, its five sections linked by recurring images: warmth and cold and, especially, dance. The slow dance, Montague has said, is the "dance of death and life," and this volume reveals a heightened sense of both mortality and vitality.

Section 1 takes the reader "back to our origins"—individually to the womb, collectively to primordial cave—and there the dance of life and death begins. "The humid pull/ of the earth" is immediate; the dance begins "in . . . isolation" but ends in complete identification with the natural world, human "breath mingling with the exhalations of the earth." The section collapses time and dissolves distinctions between civilizations, so that legendary poet-king Sweeny coexists with Saint Patrick, and (in "For the Hillmother") the Christian Litany of the Blessed Virgin provides the form for a pagan invocation to nature as the source of life. The section is about life, with death only hinted at.

Section 2 opens with a birth, but in "Courtyard in Winter," the poet meditates on the suicide of a friend. Montague grieves that he could not "ease the single hurt/ That edged her towards her death," but he does not give in to guilt or despair. Rather, "I still affirm/ That nothing dies, that even from/ Such bitter failure memory grows." Much of the rest of the section consists of lyrical evocations of nature, of which "Windharp" is perhaps the best known.

The opening section collapses time and telescopes civilizations in the service of life; the third does the same in the service of death, "The Cave of Night" substituting for the womb/cave. Ancient Celtic blood sacrifice is juxtaposed to armed struggle in Belfast. Killing with sword and rifle, the slaughtering of a pig in a farmyard and of soldiers on a battlefield, are essentially the same in this hellish section, ruled over by the "Black Widow goddess." The section ends, fittingly, with a poem called "Coldness."

The reader turns with relief in the fourth section to the warmer world of family. Problems here—parents unable to live together, a child denied "the warm circle" of its mother's company—are problems that can be comprehended, sometimes even dealt with. Loneliness is here (it is never far in Montague's poetry), but "human warmth" is, too.

The final section of *A Slow Dance* is Montague's eulogy for his friend the composer Séan Ó Riada. The "slowly failing fire" dies out, and the book ends with a cry of anguish:

> a lament so total
> it mourns no one
> but the globe itself
> turning in the endless halls
>
> of space.

The book, which begins by celebrating "The whole world/ turning in wet/ and silence," thus ends lamenting the same turning world. The "globe itself/ turning" enacts the "slow dance" of life and death.

THE GREAT CLOAK

The Great Cloak focuses on love—no poems here are about growing up, family, or Ireland. Montague examines the breakup of one marriage, the beginning of another, and the interval between. The poems are short (averaging about half the length of those in *A Slow Dance*), uncomplicated, accessible. Their imagery is predominantly visual (attentive to the play of light and shadow) and tactile (hands touching, caressing).

In the first section, sexual encounters are brief respites from loneliness. Loneliness and worse—nothingness, the void—seem implicit in the ominous image that closes the section: "profound night/ like a black swan/ goes pluming past."

The second section, less self-absorbed, sadly sifts through the fragments of a broken marriage. It is an inventory of losses. "Darkness" finds Montague trying to understand his estranged wife's feelings, and in four other poems, he goes so far as to speak with her voice: "I sing your pain/ as best I can," he says, in his own voice. The longest and best poem in the book, "Herbert Street Revisited," returns to the Dublin street where, newly wed, Montague and his wife made their first home. It is a generous-spirited celebration of the love they shared.

"Anchor," title of the last section, expresses a wish; the new relationship Montague explores here seems less fixed, less certain, than the title suggests. "Walking Late," for example, ends with the couple circling "uncertainly/ towards a home." Only in "Protest," which records the birth of their child, and the handful of poems that follow it does the tone of voice become confident enough to warrant the section's title.

SELECTED POEMS

Montague's *Selected Poems* draws from all his previous books of poems and includes a few that would appear later in *The Dead Kingdom* or *Mount Eagle*. Some poems, particularly early ones, show substantive revisions, and the order in which they appear is not always that of the earlier books.

THE DEAD KINGDOM

Like *The Rough Field*, *The Dead Kingdom* is a single long poem—an arrangement of shorter poems, ten of which appeared in previous books. Unlike *The Rough Field*, *The Dead Kingdom* has a narrative line. It begins when news arrives in Cork that Montague's mother has died. "The 'thread' or plot," Montague has written, "is the long drive North" to attend her funeral.

The drive north takes Montague through the Midlands, calling up bittersweet memories of summers in County Longford. More than half the poems in the book's first two (of five) sections connect with "this neutral realm." "Abbeylara" affectionately recalls summers with Carney relatives, but now they are dead, their house abandoned, their carefully tended garden gone wild. The small piece of land to which they gave order is "reverting to first chaos/ as if they had never been."

Two poems in section 1 meditate on transience itself. In "Process," "time's gullet devouring" all that people value becomes an abyss of "fuming oblivion," across which one can but cast "swaying ropeladders" such as "love or friendship,/ an absorbing discipline." "Gone" recalls things great and small that have been "hustled into oblivion" and stoically salutes "the goddess Mutability,/ dark Lady of Process,/ our devouring Queen." Terms such as "chaos," "oblivion," and "the void" spatter the first half of the book, and the metaphor of "time's gullet" and the "devouring Queen" is reinforced by multiple references to appetite, feeding, and digestive organs.

In section 3, the border of Northern Ireland revives thoughts of violent conflicts there. Weather and mood alike turn cold and dark as the poet returns to the "bloody ground" where he was raised. More despairing than in *The Rough Field*, Montague can but "sing a song for the broken/ towns of old Tyrone" and "for the people,/ so grimly holding on." He calls his wish for "an end to sectarianism" a "forlorn hope."

As in *A Slow Dance*, the almost unrelieved gloom of section 3 gives way to the warmer (even when painful) images of family in section 4. In a series of flashbacks, Montague reviews his parents' lives, together and apart (a photograph of the young couple introduces the section).

Music has woven its way through all of Montague's books, but none of them is as filled with music as *The Dead Kingdom*, which invokes everything from popular songs ("Kathleen Mavourneen," "Paddy Reilly") to Mary Mulvey's music box and "the sound/ of bells in monastic/ sites." Montague himself calls for song in several poems (for example, "sing a song for/ things that are gone"). The principal singer, however, is his father, teaching his son the words to "Ragtime Cowboy Joe"; singing "Molly Bawn" to his own Molly, after his long-delayed return to Ireland; lending his "broken tenor" to Christmas carols in midnight Mass. Montague understands that, back in Brooklyn, his "father's songs/ couldn't sweeten the lack of money" that had contributed to the family's fragmentation. However, Montague recognizes that "the healing harmony/ of music" had been his father's rope ladder across oblivion, and he regrets that his mother's funeral is "without music or song" to "ease the living" and "sweeten our burden."

Montague continues to examine the subject of exile in its various forms, under its various names: "emigration," "transportation," "diaspora," "dispossession." At last, his mother dead, he brings himself to mention the form of exile he himself has experienced most painfully: being rejected by his mother in childhood. "You gave me away," he says to her posthumously ("The Locket"), "to be fostered/ in Garvaghey" ("A Muddy Cup"), "to be fostered/ wherever charity could afford." This, he says, was the "primal hurt," to be "an unwanted child": "All roads wind backwards to it" ("A Flowering Absence").

"It is hard to work so close to the bone," Montague has said of these poems about his mother. After a lifetime of excavating the strata of his life, Montague has finally reached emotional bedrock. To have been "fostered" is to have been exiled most radically. Nevertheless, "The Locket," "a last song/ for the lady who has gone," ends with a "mysterious blessing": The poet learns, after his mother's death, that the locket she had always worn contained an old photograph of "a child in Brooklyn."

His responsibilities in Tyrone finished, Montague turns his attention to the living woman in his life

> I place my hopes
> beside yours, Evelyn,
> frail rope-ladders
> across fuming oblivion

and heads "back across the/ length of Ireland, home."

MOUNT EAGLE

Mount Eagle is neither arranged as a coherent whole, like *The Rough Field* and *The Dead Kingdom*, nor organized into distinct sections, like *A Chosen Light, Tides, A Slow Dance*, and *The Great Cloak*. Rather, like Montague's first two books, *Forms of Exile* and *Poisoned Lands, and Other Poems*, it is something of a miscellany, though its poems are generally arranged by subject. The volume includes a quartet of poems related to the Troubles in Northern Ireland, each rendering a sharply etched vignette. There is a late harvest of childhood memories, usually recalled, not for their own sake, but for a connection Montague wishes to draw with something in later life. "The Leap," for example, draws an analogy between daring jumps years before across the Garvaghey River and, referring to his second marriage, a new "taking off . . . into the uncertain dark." Four poems are culled from a father's affectionate observation of his young daughter's investigations of their world. Only one poem alludes to Montague's father, and then in passing; none mentions his mother.

Perhaps a third of the poems could be classified under the general heading of "love." "Fair Head" recalls an early, unconsummated love; several other poems, more characteristically, commemorate consummations. "The Well-Beloved" muses on the process by which smitten lovers, each idealizing the other, descend into married life, and wonders what it takes to "redeem the ordinary." The startling "Sheela na Gig," inspired by the grotesquely sexual female figures carved on medieval Irish churches, synopsizes male human behavior in terms of "banishment" from "the first home" at birth and then a lifetime of trying "to return to that [anatomical] first darkness." Birth, too, is banishment: the first experience of exile.

The most interesting development in *Mount Eagle* is its attention to nature. "Springs" expresses the ecologically correct wish to "erase/ from this cluttered earth/ our foul disgrace." "Peninsula" is a much more appealing celebration of "Dame Nature's self-/ delighting richness." Several poems draw on Native American nature myths, including the title poem, wherein an eagle trades its freedom to disappear into, and become "the spirit of," a mountain. The poem seems to encode Montague's own intent to dedicate himself to a new sort of poetry: less subject to the buffeting of life's winds, perhaps less confessional, more abstract. (Montague has privately acknowledged that "Mount Eagle" is a homonym for his own name.) The last seven poems in *Mount Eagle*, which include "Luggala" and "The Hill of Silence," reflect this new direction in his work.

ABOUT LOVE

Montague followed *Mount Eagle* with another collection of selected poems, *New Selected Poems*. Somewhat different selections in this published-in-Ireland volume distinguish it from the 1982 *Selected Poems*, published in the United States. The next collection, *About Love*, is a generous compilation of Montague's love poems, all but three of them previously published (about a third of them drawn from *The Great Cloak*). The variety of the poems is remarkable. They examine love of many kinds, at many stages, and in diverse moods; they examine love coolly and in heat (cerebrally and passionately), with regret and gratitude, bitterness and bemusement, longing and contentment. Mostly, they celebrate love, although that emotion is often shaded with darker feelings: jealousy, guilt, loneliness. The book amounts to a learned treatise on love, Montague's anatomy of love.

TIME IN ARMAGH

Time in Armagh is a small, well-focused collection that recalls its author's years at boarding school (St. Patrick's College, Armagh), from 1941 until 1946. World War II is a presence in five of the volume's twenty-six poems, but its emphasis is on "the harshness of our schooling," as Montague says in the preface. The harshness is evident in the physical violence administered both by the priests who ran the school (seven poems, as well as the book's epigraph from Juvenal, allude to canes or beatings) and by fellow students. The harshness is also evident in the absence of tenderness or love. Although there are moments of humor and even of nostalgia in the volume, the prevailing feelings are anger and bitterness, undimmed after half a century. In his preface, Montague compares his school years with those that Joyce recorded in *A Portrait of the Artist as a Young Man* (1916). When he writes about the beatings administered by the priests at St. Patrick's, most notably in "Guide" and the title poem, "Time in Armagh," Montague's language echoes that of the pandybat scene in Joyce's novel.

COLLECTED POEMS

Collected Poems, a magisterial assemblage, brings together more than three hundred poems, the best work of the first forty years of Montague's output. It is divided into three sections. The first, a bit more than half the book, consists of the three great volumes from the 1970's and 1980's, all symphonically orchestrated (each conceived of as a single, integrated work): *The Rough Field, The Great Cloak*, and *The Dead Kingdom*. The second section, constituting nearly 40 percent of the book, contains poems from *Forms of Exile, Poisoned Lands, and Other Poems, A Chosen Light, Tides, A Slow Dance*, and *Mount Eagle*. Section 3, less than 10 percent of the book, contains poems from *Time in Armagh* and the previously uncollected long poem "Border Sick Call" (1995). Montague has revised some poems, omitted some poems, and included a few poems translated from the Irish and originally published in *A Fair House: Versions of Irish Poetry* (1973).

SMASHING THE PIANO

Few poets in old age write with undiminished power. William Butler Yeats was one; Montague is another. *Smashing the Piano* is a great follow-up to his *Collected Poems*: not merely a curtain call but a real encore. The collection contains forty-one poems, but since several of these are sequences of lyrics (individually titled and each capable of standing alone), by another way of reckoning the collection contains sixty-five poems.

Unavoidably, many of the poems in this gathering reintroduce themes and characters introduced in earlier books. The opening half dozen poems, for example, recall figures and incidents from a County Tyrone childhood: Aunt Winifred ("Paths"), Aunt Brigid ("Still Life, with Aunt Brigid"), and children who died young ("Kindertotenlieder"). This group segues naturally into a sequence about Montague's own children, "Prayers for My Daughters." The title is deliberately Yeatsian, but the tender domesticity of these poems owes nothing to Yeats.

A sequence of short love poems, "Dark Rooms," recalls many of Montague's earlier love poems, but "Postscript," the sixth of the seven lyrics in the sequence, introduces a new situation: An old poet, having been supplanted by "another, younger man," struggles to contain his rage in the constraining form of a poem—such as this one, more regularly rhymed than most Montague poems. Other poems also demonstrate that this volume is the work of advanced years, most notably "Talking with Victor Hugo in Old Age." The untitled brief poem that serves as the volume's epigraph connects youth and age in a wholly suitable way:

> Fierce lyric truth,
> Sought since youth,
> Grace my ageing
> As you did my growing,
> Till time engraves
> My final face.

A number of poems scattered through *Smashing the Piano* seem to be extensions of the impulse, seen in *Mount Eagle*, to write about nature: "Starspill" even refers to "Mount Eagle." "Between" is a gorgeous meditation on the yin and yang of nature as observed in the Gap, where County Waterford and County Tipperary meet.

The longest sequence in the collection, the eight-part "Civil Wars," reengages political themes that Montague has dealt with memorably before. There are updates here, however: memorializing hunger striker Bobby Sands, excoriating British prime minister Margaret Thatcher, speaking of "the unspeakable" Omagh bombing, respectfully addressing (in conclusion) his own father, once politicized, now dead. "Your faith I envy," he tells his father, though

> Your fierce politics I decry.
> May we sing together
> someday, Sunny Jim,
> over what you might
> still call the final shoot-out:
> for me, saving your absence,
> a healing agreement.

Though in this collection there is the usual great range of subjects and feelings characteristic of Montague's best books of poems, this one is marked with unwonted serenity. This should not be mistaken for a sign of diminished inspiration or power; it is an added, and most welcome, quality: a late blossoming, a late blessing.

OTHER MAJOR WORKS

LONG FICTION: *The Lost Notebook*, 1987.

SHORT FICTION: *Death of a Chieftain, and Other Stories*, 1964 (revised as *An Occasion of Sin*, 1992); *A Love Present, and Other Stories*, 1997; *A Ball of Fire: Collected Stories*, 2009.

NONFICTION: *The Figure in the Cave, and Other Essays*, 1989; *Myth, History, and Literary Tradition*, 1989 (with Thomas Kinsella and Brendan Kennelly); *Company: A Chosen Life*, 2001; *The Pearl Is Ripe: A Memoir*, 2007.

TRANSLATIONS: *A Fair House: Versions of Irish Poetry*, 1973 (from Irish); *November: A Choice of Translations from André Frénaud*, 1977 (with Evelyn Robson); *Selected Poems*, 1994 (of Francis Ponge; with C. K. Williams and Margaret Guiton); *Carnac*, 1999 (of Eugène Guillevic).

EDITED TEXTS: *The Dolmen Miscellany of Irish Writing*, 1962; *The Faber Book of Irish Verse*, 1974 (*The Book of Irish Verse*, 1976); *Bitter Harvest: An Anthology of Contemporary Irish Verse*, 1989.

MISCELLANEOUS: *Born in Brooklyn: John Montague's America*, 1991 (poetry, short fiction, and nonfiction).

BIBLIOGRAPHY

Irish University Review 19 (Spring, 1989). This special issue, edited by Christopher Murray, includes an interview with Montague, seven articles on his work, an autobiographical essay by Montague ("The Figure in the Cave"), and Thomas Dillon Redshaw's checklist of Montague's books.

Kersnowski, Frank. *John Montague*. Lewisburg, Pa.: Bucknell University Press, 1975. The first book-length study of Montague's work (actually a slim monograph), this work surveys his career through *The Rough Field*. Its chief value may be its readings of individual poems and stories.

Montague, John. *Chosen Lights: Poets on Poems by John Montague in Honour of His Eightieth Birthday*. Edited by Peter Fallon. Loughcrew, Oldcastle, Ireland: Gallery Press, 2009. Poets such as Paul Muldoon, Seamus Heaney, Eavan Boland, and Eamon Grennan comment on poems by Montague.

_____. *Company: A Chosen Life*. London: Duckworth, 2001. The first volume of Montague's memoirs, focusing mainly on the 1950's and 1960's. Provides entertaining and often illuminating accounts of his encounters with Samuel Beckett, Brendan Behan, Theodore Roethke, and many others. The book's most memorable portrait, however, is that which emerges indirectly of the author himself. The warmth, wit, intelligence, generosity, and humor of his sensibility inform the book.

_____. *The Pearl Is Ripe: A Memoir*. Chester Springs, Pa.: Dufour Editions, 2007. The second volume of Montague's memoirs, similarly warm and witty, takes up where the author left off in *Company*. Recounts his dealings with Allen Ginsberg, Patrick Kavanagh, and the composer Séan Ó Riada.

Redshaw, Thomas Dillon, ed. *Well Dreams: Essays on John Montague*. Omaha, Nebr.: Creighton University Press, 2004. Eighteen essays examine successive aspects of Montague's career. The most substantial work published on Montague.

Richard Bizot

PAUL MULDOON

Born: County Armagh, Northern Ireland; June 20, 1951

OTHER LITERARY FORMS

Unlike many other contemporary Irish poets, Paul Muldoon is, generally speaking, content to let his verse speak for him. Hence his production of articles and reviews is small and not very helpful in coming to terms with his poetry. His most notable contribution to Irish literary culture has been his idiosyncratic, and in some quarters controversial, editing of *The Faber Book of Contemporary Irish Verse* (1986). Muldoon has also published translations of a small number of poems by the important contemporary Irish-language poet Nuala Ní Dhomhnaill. The distinctive character of Muldoon's own verse invites the conclusion that translating is much closer to his imaginative inclinations than editing. He has also edited *The Scrake of Dawn: Poems by Young People from Northern Ireland* (1979), *The Essential Byron* (1989), and *Contemporary Irish Poetry* (2006). His lectures of poetry have been collected in *To Ireland, I* (2000) and *The End of the Poem: Oxford Lectures* (2009).

ACHIEVEMENTS

Although Paul Muldoon regularly publishes book-length collections and has become an increasingly familiar presence internationally, particularly in the United States, he remains somewhat overshadowed by older, more celebrated poets from Northern Ireland. Muldoon's fluency and inventiveness have been constants since the publication of his precocious volume *New Weather* in 1973. As a result, it has been easier to take pleasure in his method than to chart the development of his aesthetic and thematic concerns. It is possible that the poet himself has experienced some of this sense of occlusion and that this has accounted, at least in part, for his increasing tendency to write unfashionably long poems. The publication of the book-length poem *Madoc* in 1990— a work that in many senses is a typically quirky yet not wholly unexpected product of the longer poems in *Why Brownlee Left, Quoof,* and *Meeting the British*—provides a pretext for an interim report on the attainments, challenges, and difficulties of the most original Irish poet to emerge since the 1930's.

While the critical jury may still be out as to the overall significance of Muldoon's work, there is no doubt that his poetry signifies an impressive departure from the work of his immediate predecessors among Northern Irish poets (such as Seamus Heaney, John Montague, and Michael Longley) and that Muldoon diverged from the conception of Irish poet as cultural watchdog and keeper of the national conscience, promoted and embodied by the founder of modern Irish poetry, William Butler Yeats.

Certainly the number of awards Muldoon has received suggests a critical acceptance of his work. Some of the accolades he has received include the Eric Gregory Prize (1972), the Sir Geoffrey Faber Memorial Award and the T. S. Eliot Prize for Poetry (both in 1994), the Award in Literature from the American Academy of Arts and Letters and the Bess Hokin Prize from *Poetry* magazine (both in 1996), the *Irish Times* Literature Prize (1997), the Pulitzer Prize and the Griffin Poetry Prize for *Moy Sand and Gravel* (both in 2003), the American Ireland Fund Literary Award and the Shakespeare Prize (both in 2004), the Aspen Prize for Poetry (2005), the European Prize for Poetry (2006), and the John William Corrington Award for Literary Excellence from Centenary College of Louisiana (2009-2010). He has been elected to a Fellowship of the Royal Society of Literature and became a member of the American Academy of Arts and Letters in 2008.

BIOGRAPHY

Paul Muldoon was born on June 20, 1951, in the remote rural community of The Fews, County Armagh, Northern Ireland. Shortly afterward, his family moved to the no less remote area of The Moy, County Tyrone. The poet, therefore, comes from a background that is similar in many external respects to those of Northern Ireland poets such as Seamus Heaney and John Montague, who have done much to put that part of the world on the literary map. This point is relevant because Muldoon's response to his background is very different from that of his illustrious near-contemporaries.

After secondary education at St. Patrick's College, Armagh, Muldoon read English at Queen's University, Belfast, and was graduated with a B.A. in 1971. Like many writers from Northern Ireland, particularly those of an older generation, he worked as a talks producer for the Northern Ireland regional service of the British Broadcasting Corporation in Belfast. He resigned this position in 1986 and began working as a visiting professor in a number of American universities. He has taught at Columbia University, the University of California, Berkeley, and the University of Massachusetts, and in 1990, he began teaching at Princeton University. In 1993, he became director and founding chair of creative writing at Princeton's Lewis Center for the Arts. In 1999, he was elected professor of poetry at Oxford, succeeding James Fenton in this five-year honorary appointment, and he continues at Oxford as fellow of Hertford College. At Princeton, he was elected to the Howard G. B. Clark '21 Professorship and became involved with academic administration as well as teaching. He is a professor emeritus at the University of St. Andrews, Scotland. He has taught on the summer Bread Loaf program of creative writing. In 2007, he became poetry editor for *The New Yorker.*

In his private life, his first marriage to Anne-Marie Conway, an Irish woman, broke up in 1979. After an affair with Mary Ann Powers came to an end with her death, he married the American novelist Jean Hanff Korelitz, a Jewish woman, by whom he has had two children, Dorothy and Asher. The family settled in New Jersey near Princeton. As a hobby, he joined a rock band, Rackett, and has been writing lyrics for its songs.

ANALYSIS

Although direct environmental influences on the growth of the imagination are impossible to prove, it does seem relevant to point out that Paul Muldoon's coming to consciousness coincided with the disintegrative threats to the social fabric of his native province. These threats of violence to civilians and forces of law and order alike, to property and the general communal infrastructure of Northern Ireland, date from 1969, when Muldoon was a freshman at Queen's University, Belfast. The threats have been both carried out and resisted. Disintegration of families, neighborhoods, and institutions has occurred, yet those entities continue to survive. Codes of self-protective speech have arisen, and things are no longer necessarily what they seem on the surface. It would be fanciful to argue that such characteristics of the poet's outer world are precisely what Muldoon's poetry reproduces, since, to begin with, such an argument overlooks the inevitable significance of form in his work. At the same time, however, there is such a degree of unpredictability, play, and opacity in his poetry that it is tempting to consider it an attractive, exuberant, puzzling, and blessedly harmless parallel universe to that of bombers and demagogues.

This does not mean that Muldoon has not addressed poems to the trials and tribulations of the Northern Ireland of his adult life. Poems such as "Anseo" in *Why Brownlee Left* (*anseo* is the Irish word for "here," meaning "present" in the poem), "The Sightseers" in *Quoof*, and the arresting and unnerving title poem of *Meeting the British*—to name well-known instances—confront in ways that are not particularly euphemistic the euphemistically named Troubles. However, it is equally, if not more, revealing of Muldoon that he would name a collection of poems for "our family word/ for the hot water bottle" ("quoof"), particularly since the reader has only the poet's word for it that this is what "quoof" actually means. More than any other Irish poet of his generation, perhaps, Muldoon demands to be taken first and foremost, and if possible, exclusively at his word.

Muldoon's slightly surreal, slightly whimsical, very subjective, and very oblique view of his material—his almost perverse conception of what constitutes "material" itself—sits at a seemingly crazy but refreshing angle to the modern Irish poetic tradition. Muldoon is concerned more with the making of verses than with the making of statements, and his work is airy, reckless, private, and provocative. Many of his poems are as much teases as they are texts in the predictable sense, yet they can also be seen as indebted to a more intriguing tradition of Irish poetry than that inaugurated by Yeats. Muldoon's implicit rejection of the public, vatic role of the poet, his frequent absorption in the minutiae of the natural world, his deployment of fragmented narrative, his use of pastiche, his finding himself equally at ease with foreign or domestic themes, his playfulness, and the challenge of his cunning superficiality have—among numerous other devices and resources—provided a valuable counterpoint to the more solemn, preoccupied, and fundamentally historicist poetry of his Northern Irish elders.

NEW WEATHER

New Weather, the title of his early work, has become over time a helpful phrase to describe the surprising novelty of Muldoon's poetry and its place in the canon of modern Irish verse. The poem in which the phrase "new weather" occurs, "Wind and Tree," is in one sense not particularly representative of Muldoon's work, with its talk of love and its unironic, somewhat sheepishly attention-claiming "I." The poem's elaborate metaphorical conceit of lovers being injured as trees are by wind heralds one of the most conspicuous elements in Muldoon's distinctive art, his generally shape-changing propensity, of which metaphor is a primary feature. "Wind and Tree" also provides the revealing lines, "Most of the world is centred/ About ourselves," often availed of by readers struggling for a foothold in some of the poet's less hospitable works.

Much more instructive of things to come in Muldoon's work is "Hedgehog," for the economy and distinctively contemporary quality of its imagery ("The snail moves like a/ Hovercraft, held up by a/ Rubber cushion of itself"), the outrageousness of its conceits (the hedgehog is referred to as "the god/ Under this crown of thorns"), and the possibility that the poem overall is a metaphor for communal and interpersonal division and defensiveness both in Northern Ireland and beyond. As in "Our Lady of Ardboe" (from *Mules*), "Who's to know what's knowable?"

MULES

By the time of the publication of *Mules*, the question of knowability in Muldoon's work was not strictly rhetorical—rather, to be Muldoonish about it, it was strictly rhetorical, meaning that it was built into the nature of the poem, rather than occurring every so often as a detachable line from a given poem. "Lunch with Pancho Villa," with its mysterious quality and the novelty of being written by an Irish poet, is not merely a witty imaginative adventure, expressive of the poet's range and restlessness. The poem interrogates, in a tone that is all the more incisive for lacking solemnity, the consequences of violence, and it questions whether the poet's duty is to respond to what the world contains or to the contents of his own imagination.

"CUBA"

One answer to this question—a question that may be used as a means of investigating Muldoon's increasingly complex mapping of his subjectivity—may be found in "Cuba" (from *Why Brownlee Left*). Here a remembrance of family life and common usages, both domestic (a father's predictable anger) and communal (an erring daughter goes to Confession), is placed in the context of the Cuban missile crisis of 1962, revealing the quirky, intimate, and reassuringly unresolved and unmechanical manner in which personal and public history overlap. This poem, ostensibly a simple narrative elaborating a vignette of memory, is a delicate essay in remoteness and intimacy, last things and initial experiences, innocence and eschatology. The poem's open rhythm (often captured by Muldoon through direct speech) leaves the reader in no doubt that the poet stands for the tender insignificant moments of the human realm rather than a melodramatic characterization of the machinations of history.

"WHY BROWNLEE LEFT"

A comparable sense of openness, of life as new beginnings and deliberately unfinished business, is provided by the title poem of *Why Brownlee Left*, in which the material achieves significance by—as the title implies—being neither a question nor an answer. Who Brownlee is seems irrelevant. The emphasis is on what has remained "a mystery even now." The point is the leaving, the possibility of pastures new, lyrically recapitulated by the absconder's horses at the end of the poem, "gazing into the future."

"IMMRAMA"

Perhaps Brownlee wanted to be able to say, like the narrator in "Immrama" (from *Why Brownlee Left*), "I, too, have trailed my father's spirit"—even if the trail leads to an inconclusive and implausible end for both father and son. Conclusion is less important than continuity. Analogously, Muldoon's work suggests that a poem's happening—the multifarious activities of the words contained by and excited within a prosodic framework (itself various and informal, though necessarily final)—is of more consequence than the poem's meaning. At an elementary level, which the reader dare not overlook, perhaps the happening is more lifelike, by virtue of its free play and variety, its sometimes outrageous rhymes and syncopated rhythms, than the meaning. Though quest as a motif has been present in Muldoon's work from the outset—"Identities" in *New Weather* begins "When I reached the sea/ I fell in with another who had just come/ From the interior"—it becomes more pronounced in the collections after *Why Brownlee Left*. The unusual title "Immrama" draws attention to this fact, as presumably it is meant to. It is the plural form of *immram*, the name in Irish for the genre of medieval Irish romances (including tales of travel to the other world) and a word that in the singular provides the title of Muldoon's first important long poem, which also appears in *Why Brownlee Left*.

In "Immrama," Muldoon releases the possibilities latent or implied not only in the quirky lyrics of *Why Brownlee Left* but also in his overall body of work. Using narrative in order to subvert it—a strategy familiar from, for example, "Good Friday, 1971, Driving Westward" in *New Weather*—Muldoon brings the reader through a somewhat phantasmagorical, surreal adventure that pantomimes the style of hard-boiled detective fiction. Set in Los Angeles, the story itself is too erratic and effervescent to summarize. As the title of the poem is intended to suggest, however, the material maps out a territory that is rich and strange, which may be the landscape of dream or of vision or the objective manifestation of the psychic character of quest. Lest the reader be merely exhausted by the extent of the poem's literary high jinks—"I shimmied about the cavernous lobby./ Mr. and Mrs. Alfred Tennyson/ Were ahead of me through the revolving door./ She tipped the bell-hop five dollars"—there are important themes, such as identity, fabulation, and rootlessness, and an alert meditation on the hybrid nature of writing as an imaginative process, of which "Immrama" is a helpful rehearsal.

"THE MORE A MAN HAS THE MORE A MAN WANTS"

Much more allusive, spectacular, and demanding is Muldoon's next adventure in the long poem "The More a Man Has the More a Man Wants" (from *Quoof*). Here, an increasingly prominent interest on the poet's part in the lore and legends of Native American traditional literature comes influentially into play. In particular, the various legends of jokers and shape-changers, particularly those of Winnebago literature, are availed of, not in the sense of overt borrowings or new translations but with a respect for and fascination with their spirit. Muldoon is not the first poet to pay homage to these mythical figures. The English poet laureate Ted Hughes employed them in one of his most cele-brated works, *Crow: From the Life and Songs of the Crow* (1970, 1972). The results are so different, however, that it is tempting to think of "The More a Man Has the More a Man Wants" as Muldoon's response to the senior poet.

The subject of the poem is change. As in the case of "Immrama," scenes shift with confusing rapidity, and the inherent transience and adaptability of the persona is once again a central, enabling concern. The thematic mixture is far richer, however, in "The More a Man Has the More a Man Wants." In particular, the nature of change is not con-fined to Muldoon's familiar deployments, such as travel, quest, and dream. Violence as an agent of change is also explored and its consequences confronted. Here again, a cer-tain amount of frustration will be experienced by the reader, largely because the poem, though promising to be a narrative, becomes a variety of open-minded narrative op-tions, while the integration of the material takes place by virtue of the reader's ability to explore the possibilities of congruence within the widely diversified settings and per-spectives. Sheer verve, inventiveness, unpredictability, and impenitent originality make "The More a Man Has the More a Man Wants" the poem that most fully illustrates the scope of Muldoon's ambitious aesthetic energies, through which all that is solid—including, perhaps particularly, the legacy of history—is transformed into airy, insub-stantial, but memorable surfaces.

MADOC

Any claim for the centrality of "The More a Man Has the More a Man Wants" must be made in the awareness of Muldoon's book-length poem *Madoc*. This poem is in ef-fect prefaced by a handful of lyrics recognizably in the mode of, say, those in *Quoof*, among which is the superb elegy "Cauliflowers" (the incongruousness of the title is a typical Muldoon maneuver). "Madoc" itself, however, consists of a sequence of rather impenetrable lyrics, all of which are headed by the name of a philosopher. Subtitled *A Mystery*, it is certainly a baffling poem. Once again, the assertion and denial of narrative are fundamental to the poet's procedures.

The source of the poem is a work of the same name written by the English Romantic poet Robert Southey, drawing in a manner vaguely reminiscent of Sir Walter Scott on the heroic legends of one of Great Britain's marginal peoples, in this case the Welsh. Muldoon, without adapting Southey's theme or prosody, seems to have adapted, in a sa-tirical vein, Southey's method. His *Madoc* looks back to an adventure in which Southey was involved—namely, the establishment of a pantisocratic community on the banks of the Susquehanna River in Pennsylvania. The inspiration for this ill-fated scheme was the major English Romantic poet Samuel Taylor Coleridge. Casting his own mind back over the historic, not to mention romantic, dream of community, Muldoon reproduces his own puzzlement with such a project, articulating not the self-deceiving confidence of Coleridge's thought (and, by invoking the names of philosophers, of thought generally) but the fact that so little that is clear remains of what such thought asserted. In turn, or rather concurrently, a disquisition on the knowability of the world, a surreal satire on the inevitable insubstantiality of ideals, and a narrative poem whose most submerged feature is its storytelling, *Madoc* is clearly Muldoon's most sustained and substantial work, though most readers will find it easier to admire than it is to enjoy or decipher.

"INCANTATA"

Muldoon's reputation for mischief making, obfuscation, and intellectual pyrotechnics can lead the reader to forget that he is also a poet of considerable lyric skill and occasionally deep feeling. "Incantata" (from *The Annals of Chile*) is written in memory of Mary Farl Powers, a former lover, who died of cancer in 1992. It is loaded, as usual, with recondite material, but somehow gets out from under its wittiness to reveal, if often in a sideways gesture, his feeling for Powers, often in the context of her work as an artist:

> I saw you again tonight, in your jump-suit, thin as a
> rake,
> your hand moving in such a deliberate arc
> as you ground a lithographic stone
> that your hand and the stone blurred to one
> and your face blurred into the face of your mother.

The form of the poem (an eight-line stanza) is taken from Abraham Cowley, the seventeenth century Royalist poet. Muldoon quietly traces the history of the affair, sometimes sadly and sometimes with comic gusto, as in their encounter with a priest who objected to their living together outside marriage. "Who came enquiring about our 'status', of the hedge-clippers/ I somehow had to hand, of him running like the clappers." Through the superfluity of references, the feeling rings true:

> . . . the day your father came to call, of your
> leaving your sick-room
> in what can only have been a state of delirium,
> of how you simply wouldn't relent
> from your vision . . .
> that fate governs everything . . .

It is a poem that disproves the complaint that Muldoon is often "too clever by half" while, at the same time, showing how clever he is.

"ANONYMOUS: MYSELF AND PANGUAR"

"Anonymous: Myself and Panguar" (from *Hay*) shows how relaxed and direct Muldoon can be if the subject is right. In this poem about the poet and his cat, Panguar, the idea is to compare his cat's search for mice with his own search for the right word:

much as Panguar goes after mice
I go hunting for the precise

word.

The poem is light, simple, and without show of the virtuoso flashiness that Muldoon
possesses:

Panguar going in for the kill
with all his customary skill
while I, sharp-witted, swift and sure,
shed light on what had seemed obscure.

He may be teasing with the last line, aware, as he is, of the criticism of his sometime obscurity.

POEMS, 1968-1998

Several collections of Muldoon's poems had been published in 1986, 1987, and
1996. However, as some of the earlier volumes went out of print, Muldoon decided to
publish a collection including everything he had written through 1998. *Poems, 1968-
1998* brought together eight volumes: *New Weather, Mules, Why Brownlee Left, Quoof,
Meeting the British, Madoc, The Annals of Chile,* and *Hay.* For the first time, it was possible to trace Muldoon's development clearly and to see some of the particular features
that mark his poetry.

This collection highlighted Muldoon's tendency to put a long poem at the end of
each volume; his long poems have gradually begun to be seen as his best work. The long
poem, generally unpopular in modern poetry, was reinstated by Muldoon as a large canvas on which to explore a number of concurrent themes and motifs that intertwine with
each other and gradually come together as the associations become spelled out. In the
last poem in the collection, "The Bangle (A Slight Return)," motifs of his father's possible emigration to Australia run alongside a ferry crossing from Ireland to Scotland, to a
slap-up meal in Paris (for which there is no hope of payment), to sections of Vergil's
Aeneid (c. 29-19 B.C.E.; English translation, 1553). There is a postmodernist sense of
"all is as the poet wills," and one word or episode can be read instead of another, as if it
might somehow be an *erratum* that can be corrected.

The long poems show Muldoon's debt to James Joyce, both as a modernist and as a
precursor to postmodernism. At all times, Muldoon engages in free association, backed
by his vast and eclectic learning, which, as with Joyce, leaves the reader groping to locate the source and subtext. In terms of other influences, one of the interesting things to
see overall in the collection is the way Muldoon marries Irish and American influence.
Unlike Heaney, whose American sojourns left almost no dint in his Irishness, Muldoon's *Madoc,* one of his first offerings after his transatlantic translation, suggests a

grasping at Americana. His is the new Southey, actually settling in the United States and exploring the landscape. However, what follows is a judicious blend of Irish-themed poetry and a distinctly American poetry. The influence of Robert Frost is obvious, but also the voices of Walt Whitman, Robert Lowell, and John Berryman are discernible.

Perhaps what does become more obvious, and not always for the good, is the influence of creative writing programs, master of fine arts versification, where any associative imagery is rewarded for originality, even genius, regardless of how little relationship to real human value or experience it has. In committing himself to teach courses in creative writing, Muldoon takes a professional risk. However, some of Muldoon's long poems, such as "Incantata," "Yarrow," and "Third Epistle to Timothy," suggest that the associative method allows Muldoon to work out experiences and emotions lodged deep within his psyche, making these poems quite moving and major contributions to the modern long poem.

Perhaps the obvious absence is any sense of the spiritual and a great sense of the more human aspects of sexuality. Muldoon's own experience of Ulster religion seems to have blocked off any ability to explore other forms of spirituality, and he can only recount acts of random violence in some effort to make peace with his past. Thus whole swathes of human experience are excluded from these poems, and the sheer technical brilliance of a poetic mind pouring out startling word associations is never going to compensate for such absence. This, of course, is not to deny Muldoon's achievements, only to suggest that as with the prolific Victorians Elizabeth Barrett Browning or Alfred, Lord Tennyson, a multitude of words in itself does not make for greatness.

MOY SAND AND GRAVEL

After the major collection of poems taking him up to 1998, Muldoon's next volume, *Moy Sand and Gravel*, perhaps might seem a bit of an anticlimax. He gathers poems written between 1998 and 2002, giving the collection the title of one of the very minor poems in it, a sort of Muldoon joke. The Moy, being his childhood village in Ulster, might suggest the poems are reminiscences of childhood memories, and indeed a few, including "The Misfits," "Beagles," "Tell," and "Homesickness," deal with his early life.

Other poems—"Unapproved Road," "Guns and Butter," and "A Brief Discourse on Decommissioning"—also go back to Ireland, but the Northern Ireland of the Troubles. More complex poems return to grapple with the Irish American experience and Muldoon's own uneasy relationship with earlier immigrants. They, like his father, were men of the soil and manual labor: he, by contrast, is part of the "ruling class," the elite and privileged. Thus he writes "outsider" poems such as "The Loaf" (a particularly powerful poem as it touches on past famines), "Summer Coal," "The Stoic," and "As." In "As," everything gives way to something else. Muldoon makes no value judgments as to whether this is a good or a bad thing, but there is, among the joking, a pervasive sense of guilt.

A further complexity has arisen for Muldoon, however, in that his second wife and mother of his son is Jewish. Her family also has experienced immigration, and Muldoon interweaves the Jewish and the Irish experiences to form a new note in this collection, especially in "Cradle Song for Asher," "The Ancestor," and "The Grand Conversation." The collection's high point comes in the one long poem of the collection, "At the Sign of the Black Horse, September 1999." This truly is a great poem, raising the collection into one of significance, and the main reason the collection was awarded a Pulitzer Prize in 2003.

"At the Sign of the Black Horse, September 1999" is written in a series of forty-five eight-line stanzas (a form Muldoon used earlier in "Incantata"), rhyming *aabbcddc*, with line lengths from four to eight feet. Each stanza is run into the next. It can perhaps be best seen as a series of meditations caused by the birth of his son, after the earlier loss of a daughter. It echoes especially Yeats's "Prayer at the Birth of My Daughter," with its echoing of Yeats's phrase "radical innocence" no less than four times. However, it also belongs to a much longer tradition of poems written on the birth of poets' children, going back to William Wordsworth and Coleridge particularly. The occasion makes the poets wonder what sort of world their child is being born into, and for Muldoon, as for Yeats, raises problems of preserving the child's innocence.

The birth shortly preceded Hurricane Floyd, and so flood and deluge imagery becomes significant, as in references to Noah and Ararat, especially as it is shifted to the Holocaust experiences that are part of the child's Jewish heritage. Both Irish and Jewish heritages are fraught, retain a strong identity, and deal with the tragic past with black humor, which runs throughout the poem. In terms of literary tradition, Muldoon's humor is Joycean rather than Yeatsian, with frequent plays on words and, typical of the whole collection, the pursuit of associations caused by rhymes (for example, otter/blotter in "Otter"). While Yeats had his tower, Muldoon only has a "helter-skelter," a fragile, twisted construct.

The poem deals with the hurricane and its aftermath and the context of the child's Irish and Jewish ancestry; however, it also explores modern American and Western culture, especially as reflected in public and road signs, including "No Way Out" and "Please Do Not Leave Window Ajar." The significance of items is often revealed only in the rhyming word. The prohibitions of these signs meld with particular cultural prohibitions, such as Jewish dietary restrictions. The peccary is seen as a case in point: Is it a pig, and therefore forbidden? Muldoon sees it as being sanitized in an autoclave: Does that make it permissible? These are the sort of tensions he is no doubt feeling from interactions with the child's Jewish relatives: Is the boy going to be brought up Jewish or not? Are the religious conflicts that plagued Muldoon's youth going to pursue him in a different form through the child? Is he merely the "goy from the Moy"? In addition, hints of criminality lie in the past of the now respectable Jewish extended family.

Images and themes that run through other poems in the collection are gathered into this poem. Therefore, Tuaregs (African nomads) and signs of the wanderer and exile appear, as do places such as the Bialystock ghetto, Griggstown ("Summer Coal"), Carrickmacross ("John Luke: *The Fox*"), or the Delaware and Raritan Canal ("The Loaf"), which Irish navvies helped build. This melding of past and present, while making statements on an overall culture at a particular moment of history is reminiscent of Robert Lowell's first draft of "The Quaker Graveyard in Nantucket" (from *Lord Weary's Castle*, 1946), and the poem could take on the iconic status for Muldoon that the other poem did for Lowell.

HORSE LATITUDES

Horse Latitudes represents the work done by Muldoon from 2002 to 2006. Most of it appeared first in an impressively wide range of literary magazines and journals. The title derives from one of the major poems of the volume, a long opening poem centered on the persona of Carlotta. At times, she appears to be a conglomerate of all Muldoon's lovers; at other times, she appears to be dying. Her grandfather also figures prominently, suggesting an agrarian ancestry. The horse latitudes are those areas at sea around the tropics where becalmed sailors would throw their horses overboard or eat them, and certainly horses figure prominently in the poems.

The poem is the nearest Muldoon has come to writing a sonnet sequence, each poem being the name of a battle beginning with the letter "B." As in *Madoc*, the poem titles appear to have their own life as part of an independent categorization. The poems are fourteen lines long, but do not rhyme like sonnets and are not formed with iambic pentameters, but rather with tetrameters. However, the overall feel is certainly of a sonnet sequence.

As is typical of Muldoon, the volume ends with a major long poem, "Sillyhow Stride: *In Memory of Warren Zevon*." The whole volume is dedicated to Muldoon's sister Maureen, who died of cancer in 2005, and it is in this poem that the reader is most aware of her presence, even though technically it is the dead Zevon, a fellow musician, who is addressed. The poem is powerful in that the poet's anger at the death of his sister is a predominating force. The other uniting force is Muldoon's focus on the poetry of John Donne, the seventeenth century poet he long admired for his conceits, striking images, and tropes. He quotes Donne's poetry throughout. However, when a poet invites comparison with another poet, this is not always to the advantage of the writer. Donne's poetic strengths are his remorseless logic and control and his passionate writing on love and religion. These are the very qualities that Muldoon lacks. Certainly Muldoon shares with Donne the ability to force quite disparate ideas and themes together, but at times the poem becomes a rant, a verbal performance, in which his sister's death becomes a mere platform. Like Donne, too, Muldoon is able to take contemporary events and meld them into a poetic statement. Here Muldoon deals with ecological issues and the September 11, 2001, terrorist attacks on the United States, and the rhythms are very much those of hip-hop and reggae. In this way, Muldoon is incorporating the performance-art skills gained from his membership in a rock band into mainstream poetry.

The other poems in *Horse Latitudes* seem to be somewhat of a miscellany. Some, like "Soccer Moms" and "Turkey Buzzards," are instantly accessible and typically American, and will no doubt find their way into many anthologies. Others, such as "At Least They Weren't Speaking French" and "The Old Country," are playful, using repetition and popular idioms to make a point. In "The Old Country," Muldoon seems to be dismissing Ireland and nostalgic Irishness as a joke. "Ninety Instant Messages to Tom Moore" (a popular nineteenth century Irish poet) is a bravura sequence of haiku. Other poems, such as "It Is What It Is" and "Riddle," reflect Muldoon as a family man, living in typical American suburbia. The collection demonstrates that Muldoon is still at the height of his creativity and can turn his hand to whatever form he wishes. It may be that, as some critics claim, that he is freeing modern verse for the twenty-first century; or, it may be that he is just proving that poetry can keep reinventing itself.

OTHER MAJOR WORKS

PLAYS: *Shining Brow*, pr. 1993 (libretto); *Six Honest Serving Men*, pb. 1995; *Vera of Las Vegas: A Nightmare Cabaret Opera in One Act*, pr. 1996 (libretto); *Bandanna*, pb. 1999 (libretto).

NONFICTION: *To Ireland, I*, 2000; *The End of the Poem: Oxford Lectures*, 2009.

TRANSLATIONS: *The Astrakhan Cloak: Poems in Irish by Nuala Ní Dhomhnaill*, 1993; *The Birds*, 1999 (of Aristophanes' play).

CHILDREN'S LITERATURE: *The Last Thesaurus*, 1995; *The Noctuary of Narcissus Batt*, 1997.

EDITED TEXTS: *The Scrake of Dawn: Poems by Young People from Northern Ireland*, 1979; *The Faber Book of Contemporary Irish Verse*, 1986; *The Essential Byron*, 1989; *The Faber Book of Beasts*, 1997; *The Best American Poetry*, 2005 (with David Lehman); *Contemporary Irish Poetry*, 2006.

BIBLIOGRAPHY

Birkets, Sven. "Paul Muldoon." In *The Electric Life: Essays on Modern Poetry*. New York: Morrow, 1989. An assessment of the poet's relationship to his contemporaries on the international scene. Muldoon's originality is identified and appreciated. The provision of a wider context for his work reveals its scope and interest. In particular, Muldoon's distinctive verbal deftness receives attention.

Goodby, John. "'Armageddon, Armagh-geddon': Language and Crisis in the Poetry of Paul Muldoon." In *Anglo-Irish and Irish Literature: Aspects of Language and Culture*, edited by Birgit Bramsback and Martin Croghan. Uppsala, Sweden: Uppsala University Press, 1988. The title comes from Muldoon's poetic sequence "Armageddon." In using the name to pun on the poet's birthplace, the author draws attention to Muldoon's verbal dexterity. His dismantling and reassembling of language is reviewed. These practices are also related to Muldoon's background.

_____. *Irish Poetry Since 1950: From Stillness into History.* New York: Manchester University Press, 2000. Puts Muldoon into the wider context of modern Irish poets. There are three subsections dealing with his development as a poet up until 2000.

Holdridge, Jefferson. *The Poetry of Paul Muldoon.* Dublin: Liffey Press, 2008. Introduces the general reader to some of the main critical discussion around Muldoon's work. Looks particularly at his political stances and the links between suffering and creativity.

Kendall, Tim. *Paul Muldoon.* Bridgend, Wales: Seren, 1996. One of the first full-length studies of Muldoon with individual chapters on all the books up to and including *The Annals of Chile.* A sensible, intelligent reading of the poems in the context of his entire career.

Kendall, Tim, and Peter McDonald, eds. *Paul Muldoon: Critical Essays.* Liverpool, England: Liverpool University Press, 2003. A collection of essays by many experts on contemporary Irish poetry; it gives a rounded picture of Muldoon's achievements.

Osborn, Andrew. "Skirmishes on the Border: The Evolution and Function of Paul Muldoon's Fuzzy Rhyme." *Contemporary Literature* 41 (Summer, 2000): 323-358. A study of Muldoon's rhyme schemes and the semantic and strategic functions in his poetry.

Robinson, Peter. "Muldoon's Humour." In *Politics and the Rhetoric of Poetry: Perspectives on Modern Anglo-Irish Poetry.* Amsterdam: Rodolpi, 1995. The question of how to use humor in serious poems, and otherwise, is examined in the light of Muldoon's reputation for wit.

Wills, Claire. *Reading Paul Muldoon.* Newcastle, England: Bloodaxe Books, 1998. Wills's sensible comments are considerable help in clarifying Muldoon's more difficult texts.

George O'Brien; Charles H. Pullen
Updated by David Barratt

JONATHAN SWIFT

Born: Dublin, Ireland; November 30, 1667
Died: Dublin, Ireland; October 19, 1745

PRINCIPAL POETRY
Cadenus and Vanessa, 1726
On Poetry: A Rapsody, 1733
Verses on the Death of Dr. Swift, D.S.P.D., 1739
The Poems of Jonathan Swift, 1937, 1958 (3 volumes; Harold Williams, editor)

OTHER LITERARY FORMS

Jonathan Swift's major satires in prose are *A Tale of a Tub* (1704) and *Gulliver's Travels* (originally titled *Travels into Several Remote Nations of the World, in Four Parts, by Lemuel Gulliver, First a Surgeon, and Then a Captain of Several Ships*, 1726); both are included in the most useful general collection, *The Prose Works of Jonathan Swift* (1939-1968; 14 volumes.; Herbert Davis, editor); but *"A Tale of a Tub" to Which Is Added "The Battle of the Books" and the "Mechanical Operation of the Spirit"* (1958, A. C. Guthkelch and D. Nichol Smith, editors) is also notable. Swift is also master of the short satiric treatise, as evidenced by *Argument Against Abolishing Christianity* (1708; first published as *An Argument to Prove That the Abolishing of Christianity in England May, as Things Now Stand, Be Attended with Some Inconveniences and Perhaps Not Produce Those Many Good Effects Proposed Thereby*) and *A Modest Proposal for Preventing the Children of Poor People of Ireland from Being a Burden to Their Parents or the Country, and for Making Them Beneficial to the Public* (1729; known as *A Modest Proposal*). Noteworthy as well are his comical satires in prose, best exemplified by the "Bickerstaff" pamphlets against Partridge the Almanac-Maker (such as *Predictions for the Year 1708*, 1708; *The Accomplishment of the First of Mr. Bickerstaff's Predictions*, 1708; and *A Vindication of Isaac Bickerstaff, Esq.*, 1709). Swift's major political diatribes are included in *The Drapier's Letters to the People of Ireland* (1935); other notable political writings include his contributions to *The Examiner* (1710-1711); and the treatise termed *The Conduct of the Allies and of the Late Ministry, in Beginning and Carrying on the Present War* (1711). The letters are assembled in *The Correspondence of Jonathan Swift* (5 volumes.; 1963-1965, Harold Williams, editor). Equally interesting is his chatty and informal *Journal to Stella* (1766, 1768).

ACHIEVEMENTS

By common consent, Jonathan Swift is perhaps the greatest satirist who ever lived. His prose creation *A Tale of a Tub* is clearly one of the densest and richest satires ever

Jonathan Swift
(Library of Congress)

composed. His terse mock-treatise *A Modest Proposal* is considered the most brilliant short prose satire in the English language. The long pseudonarrative of his later years, *Gulliver's Travels*, is acknowledged to be his masterpiece.

For this very mastery, Swift was in his time considerably dreaded and feared. In his case, the pen was mightier than the sword, and politicians trembled and dunces quavered at his power. In many instances, his satire could instantly shade into invective, and Swift wrote many powerful tirades against individuals whom he openly named, reducing them to impotence by powerful mockery and public scorn. At one time, he was the most important political writer for the ruling Tory party; his essays, projects, and analyses were a potent force in the halls of government.

However, all was not terror, violence, and indecorum. In addition to his nasty side— his "serious air"—he could, as Alexander Pope acknowledged, praising him in *The Dunciad* (1728-1743), take his rightful place as a great comedian; he could "laugh and shake in Rab'lais' easy chair." Swift was terribly potent precisely because he could be so terribly funny. He was an absolute master at writing little idiotic mock-solemn invitations to dinner, in composing poetry in pig Latin, in donning masks and voices and assuming the roles of others. He will be remembered as the imitator of the voices of dunces: the perplexed but grandly complacent "Modern" hack writer of *A Tale of a Tub*; the utterly self-satisfied Isaac Bickerstaff (the Astrologer who could See Into and Predict the Future); the ceaselessly chattering poor female servant, Frances Harris; the quintessential public-defender M. B.; the "Patriot" Drapier; and the tautological and ever-to-be-befooled Lemuel Gulliver.

Finally, Swift was a poet of considerable skill. He deprecated his verse; he preferred throughout his career the jog-trot of the octosyllabic line, deliberately avoiding the heroic couplet that was in his day the reigning poetic form. He chose to treat "low" topics and paltry occasions in his verse, and he was ever fond of coarseness: Many of his poems take up nearly unmentionable topics—particularly excrement. For such reasons, Swift was for long not taken seriously as a poet; the staid Victorians, for example, found in him nothing of the Arnoldian "high seriousness" and grim cheerfulness that heralded and endorsed progress. However, there has been a renewed interest in Swift's poetry, and in this realm too, Jonathan Swift is coming to occupy his rightful—and rightfully very high—place.

Biography

Jonathan Swift, as Louis Bredvold has observed, was the "greatest genius" among the Augustan wits, and even more clearly "one of the most absorbing and enigmatic personalities in literature." He was a man of brute talent with the pen, a man with remarkable intensity and drive, yet one who was frequently alienated and rebuffed. Of English parentage, Swift was born in 1667 in Dublin, seven months after his father's death. In straitened circumstances, Swift was reared in Ireland. His father had settled there at the time of the Restoration of Charles II (1660); his paternal grandfather had been an Anglican minister in England. Swift and his mother were dependent on a relatively well-to-do uncle, who did see to young Jonathan's education at Kilkenny Grammar School (at that time, the best in the land). Swift's mother, Abigail, returned to England to live; Swift remained in Ireland, and subsequently, with the help of his uncle, attended Trinity College, Dublin.

Going to England in 1689, Swift obtained a secretaryship under Sir William Temple at Moor Park in Surrey, where he resided with few interruptions for some ten years. Temple had been a major diplomat, an ambassador to The Hague, and a wise conservative who had even arranged for the future King William's marriage. Twice refusing to become secretary of state, he had at last retired with dignity and honor to a rural plot. At the least, Swift could anticipate great instruction and "connections," but he never did realize any actual preferment from this affiliation. It was also at Moor Park that Swift met "Stella" (Esther Johnson), the eight-year-old daughter of Sir William's housekeeper; a compelling and intimate relationship (still not fully fathomed or explained) developed over the years between the two, which led to Stella's following Swift to Ireland and living close to him for the remainder of her life. Neither ever married. In 1694, Swift became an Anglican priest in Dublin, with a remote parish in the isolated countryside at Kilroot. Nevertheless, Swift stayed mostly at Moor Park in England until Temple's death in 1699, whereupon he accepted the chaplaincy to the earl of Berkeley, who was settling in Ireland as Lord Justice. Still, preferment and advancement eluded the young man.

After several false starts in literature, Swift found his true voice—in prose and in verse—as a satirist. He wrote many short, incisive poems in the early years of the new century, and a prose masterpiece, *A Tale of a Tub*, appeared in 1704. The next decade was perhaps the most crucial in his career, for Swift helped the Tories gain office after a lengthy absence, and he became their chief spokesperson, apologist, and potent political satirist (1710-1714). His power and success in London were inordinate; he did not lack glory. During this period, Swift held court with the brightest of the Tory wits in the so-called Scriblerus Club (the most famous of its kind in literary history), which included such distinguished authors as Alexander Pope, John Arbuthnot, Matthew Prior, and John Gay.

Ireland, however, could not be avoided for long. Swift had held (though as an absentee) a post as minister to the parish of Laracor in Ireland, and the most he could extract from his political allies (he had every reason to expect more) was the deanship of St. Patrick's in Dublin. Moreover, there were other reasons for disillusionment: The Tory leaders had taken to squabbling among themselves, and their authority became precarious. Unable to patch up this rift, Swift sadly withdrew from London. The Tories fell resoundingly from power in 1714, with the sudden death of Queen Anne. There were immediate political repercussions: A Whig government even went so far as to seek to imprison the Tory leadership. Swift had already retired—for safety and out of necessity—to Ireland. He would seldom be able to return.

After a period of quiet adjustment to the catastrophe that brought him to exile (1714-1720), Swift finally came to terms with his destiny and entered on a great creative period. From 1719 on, he wrote a great deal of poetry and produced his prose masterpieces, *Gulliver's Travels* in 1726 and *A Modest Proposal* in 1729. His great period culminated with *Verses on the Death of Dr. Swift, D.S.P.D.* and *On Poetry*.

In his old age, Swift was kept busy with cathedral affairs, with overseeing an extensive edition of his "Collected Works" being printed by George Faulkner in Dublin throughout the 1730's, and with polishing old works that he had not previously brought to fruition. His health—never too hardy—commenced rapidly to decline. After what is believed to have been a crippling stroke in 1742, Swift was declared incompetent, and others were assigned by a court to handle his affairs. He died in October, 1745, and was buried in St. Patrick's Cathedral. As a final touch of satiric bravado, Swift in his will left his little wealth for the establishment of a "hospital" or asylum for incurables—both fools and madmen. Jonathan Swift, if he had had the last word, would have implied that among humankind, there are fools and knaves—and little else.

ANALYSIS

In 1689, Jonathan Swift, at the age of twenty-two, came to Moor Park to serve as secretary under Sir William Temple. It was to be Swift's brush with gentility, polite learning, and aristocracy, and it served him well. As a raw, aspiring man of letters, the youthful Swift hoped to make his name as a serious poet, and in this period, he composed a series of rather maudlin and certainly pedestrian poems that sought to soar in the panegyric strain, Pindaric odes in the manner of Abraham Cowley (and of John Dryden in his youth): polite but plodding celebrations and praises—to King William after the Battle of the Boyne ("Ode to the King," 1690-1691), to a supposedly Learned Organization ("Ode to the Athenian Society," 1692), to William Sancroft, to the successful Irish playwright William Congreve, and two effusions to Sir William Temple himself (all in 1692 and 1693). Like many young beginners, he was rather excessively enamored of his own productions ("I am overfond of my own writings . . . and I find when I writt what pleases me I am Cowley to my self and can read it a hundred times over," he tells a relative in a letter of May 3, 1692), but by 1693 even Swift himself recognized the hopeless nature of this stiflingly formal and elevated gentlemanly verse, for he broke off rudely in the midst of his second Ode to Temple and renounced such a Muse forever.

Certainly, *politesse* and officious, gaudy, and Cavalier verse (already a mode passing out of date since the Restoration in 1660) were never to be Swift's forte, yet even in these formal pieces there are some sparks and signs of the later Swift, for he could not restrain periodic outbursts of an inborn satiric temper as in "Ode to the Athenian Society":

> *She seems a Medly of all Ages*
> With a huge Fardingal to swell her Fustian Stuff,
> A new Comode, a *Top-knot*, and a Ruff,
> Her Face patch't o'er with *Modern Pedantry*,
> With a long sweeping Train
> Of Comments and Disputes, ridiculous and vain,
> *All of old Cut with a new Dye. . . .*

In a rather strained posture—even for a satirist—he let himself boast of "*My hate, whose lash just heaven has long decreed/ Shall on a day make sin and folly bleed . . .*" ("To Mr. Congreve"). In his poem to Congreve, in fact, he had recommended that the writer should "*Beat not the dirty paths where vulgar feet have trod,/ But give the vigorous fancy room.*"

ANTIPOETIC PRACTICES

Within a year Swift would take his own advice and relinquish oppressive formal structures and grand studied compliments. Indeed, throughout the remainder of his career as a poet, Swift purposely eschewed all hints of genteel elegance, polite praise, or formal density. Thereafter, his verse was rough, chatty, and colloquial, deliberately informal, low in diction and in subject—scrupulously out of the beaten track of the faddish mode in verse, the heroic couplet. For the rest of his life, Swift's poetry took its measure instead from the witty, learned, and coyly antipoetic practices of Samuel Butler's *Hudibras* (1663, 1664, 1678), making use of the almost singsong, Mother Goose-like octosyllabic couplet, pedestrian subjects, far-fetched rhymes, and coarse mien. In addition, Swift never indulged in the longer epical modes so much in favor in his day; his poems remained prosaic and short.

"VERSES WROTE IN A LADY'S IVORY TABLE-BOOK"

Hence, in the next extant verse of Swift to appear ("Verses wrote in a Lady's Ivory Table-Book"), the new mode is almost fully formulated and matured. He mocks the typical empty-headed young lady whose hall guest book is entirely scribbled over (by suitors and herself as well) with the muck of self-regard and of shallow tastes, flirtatious clichés, and torpid vanities; such "Brains Issue" the poet considers "Excrement"—and real gentlemen are warned to avoid such a tart:

> Whoe're expects to hold his part
> In such a Book and such a Heart,
> If he be Wealthy and a Fool
> Is in all Points the fittest Tool,
> Of whom it may be justly said,
> He's a Gold Pencil tipt with Lead.

A number of strategies in operation here are certainly worthy of note, for they remained Swift's hallmarks throughout his career. First, Swift owes many of his themes to the Restoration and its stage themes of fops, seducers, and fashionable lovers; a frequent topic of his art is the idle, frivolous, vacant, and flirtatious city maiden and her mindless, posturing fop or "gallant." Swift endows these conventional and even humdrum subjects with venomous sting: Such a woman is, in his imagery, no better than a whore, a prostitute of fashion, and her suitors are portrayed as perverse and impotent whore-masters: "tools" "tipt with Lead."

SAVAGE SATIRE

Swift's poetry transforms the polite inanities of social intercourse into monstrosities. His poetry gains all the more telling force precisely because of its seemingly innocuous outer clothing; bobbing along in quaint, informal four-footed lines, and immersed in chatty diction, the verse promises to be no more than light and witty. However, the images soon transform such poetry into a species of savagery. Swift once mildly observed in one of his poems that "*Swift* had the Sin of Wit no venial Crime," and that "Humour, and Mirth, had Place in all he writ. . . ." It is true that Wit and Mirth are featured dramatically in virtually all Swift's creations, but let no reader be lulled into expectations of mild pleasure and repose, for the Dean's poetry often turns wit and humor deliberately sour.

"THE DESCRIPTION OF A SALAMANDER"

A good example of this transformation may be observed in an early lampoon, "The Description of a Salamander," a deliberate cold-blooded attack on Baron Cutts the warrior, who had been nicknamed the "Salamander." In the poem, Cutts is metamorphosized into a salamander and reptile. Swift savors setting up the analogy, and does so with painstaking nicety:

> . . . should some Nymph who ne'er was cruel,
> Like *Carleton* cheap or fam'd *Duruel,*
> Receive the Filth which he ejects,
> She soon would find, the same Effects,
> Her tainted Carcase to pursue,
> As from the *Salamander*'s Spue;
> A dismal shedding of her Locks
> And, if no Leprosy, a Pox.

Although this is an early effort, there is no doubt that Swift is adept at being ruthlessly unkind: words such as *cheap, Filth, Spue,* and *Pox* are staccato-like Anglo-Saxon monosyllables, and only seemingly simplistic. What is more, they are amassed with furious delectation and vigor. Nevertheless, the poem remains tightly contained, purporting throughout to be a calm, disinterested argument, a scientific demonstration, a precise comparison. Swift's robustness arises precisely because he can interfuse the careful language of reasoning with the gross irrationality of nightmarish visions of infectious and loathsome vice and disease.

CLASSICAL INFLUENCES

Needless to say, a number of Swift's poems are less vicious, but there is always in them a certain flickering spark that implies imminent combustion. A number of his early poems are deliberate imitations or paraphrases of Horace, and others follow Ovid in telling a far-fetched story. Swift learns much from both of these classical authors about the manipulation of animal imagery, about the handling of diverse tones, and above all about sophistication: the juggling with diction, the juxtaposition of high and low styles, and the sly use of irony and indirection. Behind these deft usages is the potential adder and spike of the Swiftian assault.

CITY PASTORALS

Two companion pieces in this early period are almost universally admired: "A Description of the Morning" and "A Description of a City Shower." Both are studied presentations, ironic, quiet, and steady, while they also demonstrate another of Swift's strengths: parody. The two poems are species of City Pastoral, a mock-form that laughs at the fad of writing polite bucolic pieces about some never-never land of innocent shepherds and of the happy life in a pristine garden. Swift simply moves eclogues and idylls heavy-handedly indoors—and into the reeking, overcrowded, dirty London of the eighteenth century. The result (a frequent strategy in much of Swift's verse) is polite Vergilian verse that is overcome by gross content: thieving swains, whorish nymphs, and maids and apprentices too lazy to do any work.

EXPOSING AFFECTATION

Swift likes nothing better than to puncture civilization's postures, to divulge what Henry Fielding called affectation, and to blast holes in a nation's language of hypocrisy, concealment, euphemism, and deceit. Such uncovering can take the form of exposé: polite, tedious love-verse that is merely a tissue of clichés is rigorously parodied and exposed by hilarious ineptitudes of language ("A Love Song in the Modern Taste"), or a gross physical deformity is laid bare as a "modern nymph" disrobes and reveals herself to be in the last stages of disintegration from syphilis ("A Beautiful Young Nymph Going to Bed"). Swift would argue that false and impure language is exactly as viciously deceptive as ulcerous and pox-ridden physical reality. Both are instances of human-made corruption. With satiric glee, Swift loves to paint a running sore in technicolor.

Swift is not always savage, cunning, or voracious. Some of his most pleasant verse remains Horatian, and plays quieter games. An early piece, "Mrs. Harris' Petition," reveals his mastery of mimicry; he assumes the voice and exact intonations of a middle-aged busybody servant who has lost her purse—and considers that event the greatest cataclysm since The Flood. (For a similar tone of voice, consult "Mary the Cook-Maid's Letter to Dr. Sheridan"). One of his longest poems in the early years, *Cadenus and Vanessa* is a masterpiece of coy indirection; one Esther Vanhomrigh had indiscreetly pursued the older Swift with some heat and passion: A polite and circuitous allegorical tale is used to cool her down and warn her off.

POEMS TO STELLA

Swift is at times at his most elegant (if such a term may be applied to his hobble-footed, four-stressed, grossly rhymed lines) in a number of poems over the years (1719-1727) to Stella. These are usually poems on slight topics, birthday celebrations, or graver reflections in the later years on her growing illness. They are always light and bantering in style, polite yet quaintly backhanded with compliments, and sometimes almost insulting. Swift was a master not only of the direct attack but also of ironic indirection, and, following Vincent Voiture, he loved what he called "raillery"—a kind of bantering jest that paid compliments by seeming complaints and mock- or near-insults. A good example would be lines from "On Stella's Birth-day 1719":

> STELLA this Day is thirty four,
> (We shan't dispute a Year or more)
> However Stella, be not troubled,
> Although thy Size and Years are doubled,
> Since first I saw Thee at Sixteen
> The brightest Virgin on the Green,
> So little is thy Form declin'd
> Made up so largly in thy Mind.

The jesting continues until that last line, and so do the whimsical inaccuracies: Stella was not thirty-four (but older), and Swift had not first met her when she was sixteen (more likely at eight); she is obviously invited to wince at the trite phrases about bright Virgins, lofty queens, village greens, and sweet sixteens, for these are the pabulum of most pedestrian Muses (even today they thrive in popular lyrics and Hallmark cards). Finally, there is the innuendo about her girth—so paradoxically multiplied but nevertheless "So little . . . declin'd." Swift could not resist in some way speaking the truth. Much of his verse is of this seriocomic, semiprivate nature (and includes epigrams, puns, some pig Latin, invitations to dinner, verse epistles, windowpane scribblings, and merest notes), but all of it has a certain effervescence—and the Stella poems are surely the most accomplished in this vein.

POLITICAL INVECTIVE

Another body of poems, like the verse attacking Lord Cutts, consists of savage political invective, bred of the heat and animosity of factions, contentions, and parties. Some of the most acerb include a potent libel against Richard Tighe in "Mad Mullinix and Timothy," a most vicious portrayal of the duke of Marlborough, the renowned Whig general ("A Satirical Elegy on the Death of a late Famous General"), and, in his strongest poem of this type, a savage libelous attack on the Irish Parliament, in "A Character, Panegyric, and Description of the Legion Club," which indicts the group as a crowd of mad demoniacs. One of the most artful of these politically tinged poems incorporates themes about similar corruptions in the arts: *On Poetry: A Rapsody*. Like Pope's *Peri-Bathos: Or, The Art of Sinking in Poetry* (1727), this poem purports to be a manual of instruction, a how-to handbook guiding one who seeks to become a degenerate modern-day political hanger-on and hack writer. The final implication is that most men are already so degraded, abject, and profligate that there ought to be no one, really, who needs such "helpful" advice. That is exactly Swift's point: The so-called Age of Reason is in reality decimated and dissolute, the last, the Fifth or Iron Age of Vice (in Hesiod's terms): the final stage of creation's decline. Like Juvenal before him, Swift the satirist found it expedient to assume the worst about humankind's propensity for deterioration and debasement.

SCATOLOGICAL POEMS

Perhaps Swift's most renowned poems are his most shocking; they defame women, employ scatology, and have often been considered "obscene" and even "unprintable." They use the typical Swiftian ploy of jolting the reader into paying attention by using paradoxes and coarse language, and they include in their number some of Swift's best verse. On the borderline in this category are such fine poems as "The Progress of Marriage" and "Phillis: Or, The Progress of Love," poems that speak in the crassest terms of ill-matched marriages, and which frankly wage battle against the trifling romantic slogans that presume that "true-love" and "feelings" and "good intentions" and "high hopes" will win out against all practical odds. Rather grimly, Swift shows—in gruesome detail—the fate of such marriages.

The most blatantly offensive of the scatalogical poems include "The Lady's Dressing Room," "A Beautiful Young Nymph Going to Bed," "Strephon and Chloe," and "Cassinus and Peter." Every one of these poems mocks the "double standard" that allows men to be most coarse in their everyday affairs and yet somehow naïve about the single topic of women (whom they place on pedestals in the tradition of courtly love). This self-deception leads inevitably to disillusionment, misery, and the destruction of lives, just as it has made for sheaves of tedious, lackluster love poetry. In Swift's poems, rather dirty modern urban swains are baldly confronted with nymphs who defecate and stink (as do all people) and who in extreme cases are coming apart with syphilis and gonorrhea. The bane of Venus, in short, is that she is fetid and venereal. As a consequence of such a confrontation, the knavish and foolish men in these poems usually run mad—precisely as Gulliver does when he encounters man-as-Yahoo. The lesson applies as well to these dubious Lovers as it does to Gulliver: They are so easily unhinged because their minds never were screwed very well together; they have trained themselves—and society has trained them—to ignore or distort reality, to set up screens and shields and ideals—clouds of obfuscation that cut one off from everyday physical reality. Swift implies that if such men shut out actuality, they deserve the manure and laughter he heaps rather furiously on them. These verses deserve more consideration than they usually receive.

VERSES ON THE DEATH OF DR. SWIFT, D.S.P.D.

Swift's most fruitful years span the period from 1730 to 1733, and special notice should be given to his masterpiece, the 484-line *Verses on the Death of Dr. Swift, D.S.P.D.* In it, the Dean chooses to defend a rather nasty maxim by François La

Rouchefoucauld asserting that adversities befalling our friends do not necessarily displease us. Here is a sterling opportunity to expose human perversity, and Swift rises to the occasion. He points out amicably that all people like to get ahead of their acquaintances, and especially of their friends. Then he commences to use a marvelous example to "prove" his case: the occasion of his own demise. Sure enough, as Swift would have it, all his friends in some way gloat over his passing. Even more curiously, enemies actually lament the Dean's death. Before the poem is through, it is paradoxically worked out that only men "indifferent," absolute strangers, can ever fairly assess one's merits or judge one's worth.

There is a further stickler that the reader should grasp in the thorny thicket of ironies infesting Swift's delightful poem: All men do in some way indulge in self-aggrandizement; a man naturally exalts his ego over others, and does not mind in the least treading on toes (or heads) in the implacable urge to ascend. The last touch of irony includes even Dean Swift, who was so curiously "generous" in consenting hypothetically to "sacrifice" his own life so that he might win this argument. That is the very point: Swift, like the rest of humankind, will stop at nothing to salve his ego or to engineer a victory—even the most trifling triumph in a debate. Men will sacrifice friends, relatives, and even twist and convert enemies, so that they might, in Swift's fond phrase, "lie uppermost." Men are engendered in heaps; it is each one's voracious inclination to climb to the top. Thus stands one of Swift's most pleasing (and yet vexing) conundrums.

CRITICAL RESPONSE

For some two hundred years, Swift's poetry was seldom taken very seriously; it was, after all, not in the mainstream of the poetry of his own day, and much of it was crass and vulgar in the bargain. Swift himself had contributed to this downplaying of his talents, typically paying himself a left-handed compliment: His verse, he reports in a prose addendum to a poem ("A Left-handed Letter to Dr. Sheridan," 1718), is slight, for he composes with his "Left Hand, [when he] was in great Haste, and the other Hand was employed at the same Time in writing some Letters of Business." More and more often, however, recent criticism has been coming to take that self-deprecation with a grain of salt. The truth is that Swift's poetry is both dexterous and sinister—full of easy grace as well as of two-fisted power. His poems are disturbing yet pleasing, and growing numbers of readers are acknowledging that vexation and that pleasure. Perhaps the oppressive reality of warfare, terrorism, and recession has suggested that Swift and La Rochefoucauld came close to putting humanity in its place.

OTHER MAJOR WORKS

LONG FICTION: *A Tale of a Tub*, 1704; *Gulliver's Travels*, 1726 (originally entitled *Travels into Several Remote Nations of the World, in Four Parts, by Lemuel Gulliver, First a Surgeon, and Then a Captain of Several Ships*).

NONFICTION: *A Discourse of the Contests and Dissensions Between the Nobles and the Commons in Athens and Rome*, 1701; *The Battle of the Books*, 1704; *The Accomplishment of the First of Mr. Bickerstaff's Predictions*, 1708; *Argument Against Abolishing Christianity*, 1708 (first published as *An Argument to Prove That the Abolishing of Christianity in England May, as Things Now Stand, Be Attended with Some Inconveniences, and Perhaps Not Produce Those Many Good Effects Proposed Thereby*); *Predictions for the Year 1708*, 1708; *A Project for the Advancement of Religion, and the Reformation of Manners By a Person of Quality*, 1709; *A Vindication of Isaac Bickerstaff, Esq.*, 1709; *The Conduct of the Allies and of the Late Ministry, in Beginning and Carrying on the Present War*, 1711; *A Proposal for Correcting, Improving and Ascertaining the English Tongue, in a Letter to the Most Honourable Robert Earl of Oxford and Mortimer, Lord High Treasurer of Great Britain*, 1712; *The Public Spirit of the Whigs, Set Forth in Their Generous Encouragement of the Author of the Crisis*, 1714; *A Letter from a Lay-Patron to a Gentleman, Designing for Holy Orders*, 1720; *A Proposal for the Universal Use of Irish Manufacture*, 1720; *A Modest Proposal for Preventing the Children of Poor People of Ireland from Being a Burden to Their Parents or the Country, and for Making Them Beneficial to the Public*, 1729; *The Drapier's Letters to the People of Ireland*, 1735; *A Complete Collection of Genteel and Ingenious Conversation, According to the Most Polite Mode and Method Now Used at Court, and in the Best Companies of England, in Three Dialogues*, 1738; *Directions to Servants in General . . .*, 1745; *The History of the Four Last Years of the Queen, by the Late Jonathan Swift DD, DSPD*, 1758; *Journal to Stella*, 1766, 1768; *Letter to a Very Young Lady on Her Marriage*, 1797; *The Correspondence of Jonathan Swift*, 1963-1965 (5 volumes; Harold Williams, editor).

MISCELLANEOUS: *Miscellanies in Prose and Verse*, 1711; *Miscellanies*, 1727-1733 (4 volumes; with Alexander Pope and other members of the Scriblerus Club); *The Prose Works of Jonathan Swift*, 1939-1968 (14 volumes; Herbert Davis, editor).

BIBLIOGRAPHY

Barnett, Louise. *Jonathan Swift in the Company of Women*. New York: Oxford University Press, 2007. This volume takes a look at Swift's relationships with the women in his life and his attitude toward the fictional women in his texts. Barnett explores his contradictory views and illustrates how he respected and admired individual women, yet loathed the female sex in general. She offers a critical, nonjudgmental study of the misogynistic attitude Swift displays in his writing when he expresses his contempt and disgust for the female body.

Ehrenpreis, Irvin. *Swift: The Man, His Works, and the Age*. 3 vols. Cambridge, Mass.: Harvard University Press, 1962-1983. A monumental biography that rejects long-held myths, provides much new information about Swift and his works, and relates him to the intellectual and political currents of his age.

Fox, Christopher, and Brenda Tooley, eds. *Walking Naboth's Vineyard: New Studies of Swift*. Notre Dame, Ind.: University of Notre Dame Press, 1995. The introduction discusses Swift and Irish studies, and the subsequent essays all consider aspects of Swift as an Irish writer. Individual essays have notes, but there is no bibliography.

Glendinning, Victoria. *Jonathan Swift: A Portrait*. New York: Henry Holt, 1998. Glendinning illuminates this proud and intractable man. She investigates the main events and relationships of Swift's life, providing a portrait set in a tapestry of controversy and paradox.

Hunting, Robert. *Jonathan Swift*. Boston: Twayne, 1989. While primarily useful as a source for biographical information, this volume does contain much insightful, if general, analysis of Swift's art. Includes chronology, notes and references, bibliography, and index.

Nokes, David. *Jonathan Swift: A Hypocrite Reversed—A Critical Biography*. New York: Oxford University Press, 1985. Draws heavily on Swift's writings, offering a good introduction for the general reader seeking information about his life and works. Nokes views Swift as a conservative humanist.

Palmieri, Frank, ed. *Critical Essays on Jonathan Swift*. New York: G. K. Hall, 1993. Divided into sections on Swift's life and writings, *Gulliver's Travels*, *A Tale of a Tub* and eighteenth century literature, and his poetry and nonfiction prose. Includes index but no bibliography.

Rawson, Claude. *The Character of Swift's Satire: A Revised Focus*. Newark: University of Delaware Press, 1983. Presents eleven essays by Swift scholars, including John Traugatt's excellent reading of *A Tale of a Tub*, Irvin Ehrenpreis on Swift as a letter writer, and F. P. Lock on Swift's role in the political affairs of Queen Anne's reign.

Real, Hermann J., and Heinz J. Vienken, eds. *Proceedings of the First Münster Symposium on Jonathan Swift*. Munich: Wilhelm Fink, 1985. Includes twenty-four essays on all aspects of Swift's work, each preceded by an abstract. Includes index.

Swift, Jonathan. *The Correspondence of Jonathan Swift*. Edited by David Woolley. New York: Peter Lang, 1999. A collection of letters by Swift that offer insight into his life and work. Includes bibliographical references.

John R. Clark

OSCAR WILDE

Born: Dublin, Ireland; October 16, 1854
Died: Paris, France; November 30, 1900

PRINCIPAL POETRY
Ravenna, 1878
Poems, 1881
Poems in Prose, 1894
The Sphinx, 1894
The Ballad of Reading Gaol, 1898

OTHER LITERARY FORMS

Oscar Wilde wrote a number of plays produced successfully in his lifetime: *Lady Windermere's Fan* (pr. 1892), *A Woman of No Importance* (pr. 1893), *An Ideal Husband* (pr. 1895), and *The Importance of Being Earnest: A Trivial Comedy for Serious People* (pr. 1895). Banned in London, his play *Salomé* was produced in 1893 in Paris with Sarah Bernhardt. Two plays, *Vera: Or, The Nihilists* (pb. 1880) and *The Duchess of Padua* (pb. 1883), were produced in New York after publication in England. Finally, two plays, *A Florentine Tragedy* (pr. 1906) and *La Sainte Courtisane*, were published together in the collected edition of Wilde's works in 1908. Wilde published one novel, *The Picture of Dorian Gray* (1891), serially in *Lippincott's Magazine*. Commercially and artistically successful with a number of his plays and his one novel, Wilde reached his peak in the early 1890's when he wrote little poetry. Wilde also wrote short stories and a number of fairy tales. His last prose work is a long letter, *De Profundis*, an apologia for his life. Parts of it were published as early as 1905, but the full work was suppressed until 1950.

ACHIEVEMENTS

G. F. Maine states that the tragedy of Oscar Wilde is that he is remembered more as a criminal and a gay man than as an artist. Readers still feel overwhelmed by Wilde's life just as his personality overwhelmed his contemporaries. His greatest achievement is in drama, and his only novel–*The Picture of Dorian Gray*—is still widely read. In comparison, his poetry is essentially derivative.

Wilde modeled himself on the poets of a tradition that was soon to end in English literature, and most of his poetry appears in the earlier part of his career. Within this Romantic tradition, Wilde had a wider range than might be expected; he could move from the limited impressions of the shorter poems to the philosophic ruminations of the longer poems. Yet behind each poem, the presence of an earlier giant lurks: John Keats,

Oscar Wilde
(Library of Congress)

William Wordsworth, Algernon Charles Swinburne. Wilde's most original poem, *The Ballad of Reading Gaol*, is not derivative, and its starkness shows a side of Wilde not generally found in his other poems. Wilde's poetry is a coda, then, to the end of a tradition.

BIOGRAPHY
Oscar Fingal O'Flahertie Wills Wilde was born in Dublin, Ireland, on October 16, 1854. Flamboyance, so characteristic of the adult Wilde, was an obvious quality of both of his parents. His father was noted for physical dirtiness and love affairs, one of which led to a lawsuit and public scandal. Something of a social revolutionary, his mother published poetry and maintained a salon for intellectual discussion in her later years. Wilde grew up in this environment, showing both insolence and genius. He was an excellent student at all his schools. He attended Portora Royal School, Trinity College in Dublin, and then won a scholarship to Magdalen College, Oxford. At this time, John Ruskin was lecturing, and Wilde was influenced by Ruskin's ideas and style. More important, he

heard and met Walter Pater, who had recently published his *Studies in the History of the Renaissance* (1873). It is Pater's influence that is most obvious in Wilde's development as a poet. While at Oxford, Wilde visited Italy and Greece, and this trip strengthened the love of classical culture so obvious in his poetry.

In the 1880's, as he developed as a writer, he also became a public personality. He toured the United States for about a year, and in both the United States and England, he preached an aesthetic doctrine that had its origins in the Pre-Raphaelites and Pater. He married in 1883 and had two sons. Wilde serially published his only novel, *The Picture of Dorian Gray*, which immediately created a sensation with the public. Thereafter, he wrote a number of plays, most notably *Lady Windermere's Fan* and *The Importance of Being Earnest.*

Wilde's last decade involved the scandal over his sexuality. His chief male lover was Lord Alfred Douglas, whose father, the marquess of Queensberry, tried to end Wilde's liaison with his son and ruin Wilde socially. Consequently, Wilde sued the marquess of Queensberry for libel but lost the case and also had his sexuality revealed. Tried twice for homosexuality, a crime in England at the time, he was found guilty and sentenced to two years at hard labor. From his prison experiences, Wilde wrote his most famous poem, *The Ballad of Reading Gaol.* Released from prison, he wandered over the Continent for three years, broken physically and ruined financially. He died in Paris at the age of forty-six.

Analysis

Oscar Wilde's poetry derives from the rich tradition of nineteenth century poetry, for, as Richard Aldington shows, Wilde imitated what he loved so intensely in the great poets of his century. Drawing from John Keats, Dante Gabriel Rossetti, William Morris, and Algernon Charles Swinburne, Wilde demonstrated an aestheticism like theirs in his lush imagery and in his pursuit of the fleeting impression of the moment. His poetry tries to capture the beautiful, as the Victorian critic John Ruskin had urged a generation earlier, but generally lacks the moral tone that Ruskin advocated. Wilde's poetry best fulfills the aesthetic of Walter Pater, who, in his *Studies in the History of the Renaissance*, advocated impressionism and art for art's sake. Indeed, Wilde paraphrased Pater's famous line of burning with a "hard, gemlike flame" in several of his poems.

Wilde published many poems individually before 1881, but his *Poems* of 1881 included almost all these poems and many new ones. With this collection, he published more than half of the poetry that he was to produce. The collection of 1881 is a good representation of his aestheticism and his tendency to derivativeness. Wilde avoided the overtly autobiographical and confessional mode in these poems, yet they mirror his attitudes and travels as impressions of his life. The forms he tried most often in the collection were the Italian sonnet and, for longer poems, a six-line stanza in pentameter with an *ababcc* rhyme scheme. The smaller poetic output that followed the 1881 collection consists of a number of shorter poems, two longer poems, and *Poems in Prose*. The short poems break no new ground, *The Sphinx* heralds a decadence and a celebration of pain unequaled in the nineteenth century except by Swinburne a generation earlier. *The Ballad of Reading Gaol*, however, builds on Wilde's earlier efforts. Again, he avoids the confessional mode that one would expect, considering the horrors of incarceration out of which the poem grew. The persona of the poem is no longer an urbane mind observing nature and society, but a common prisoner at hard labor generalizing about the cruelties of humans and their treatment of those they love. In this poem, despite its shrillness and melodrama, Wilde struck a balance between his own suffering and art, a balance that the impressionism of his poetic talents made easier. He dealt, as an observer, with the modern and the sordid as he had dealt earlier with art and nature. *Poems in Prose* is Wilde's effort at the short parable, offering neither the impressionism nor the formal qualities of his other poems, but ironic parables that refute the pieties of his era. Here Wilde is at his wittiest.

RAVENNA

Ravenna was Wilde's first long poem to be published, and it won the Newdigate prize for poetry while he was still at Oxford. Written in couplets, the poem deals with many of the themes that he developed for the 1881 collection; thus, *Ravenna* is the starting point in a study of Wilde's poetry. Like the later long poems, *Ravenna* develops through contrasts: northern and southern European cultures, innocence and experience, past and present, classical and Christian. As a city, Ravenna evokes all these contrasts to the youthful Wilde.

The opening imagery is of spring, with a tendency to lushness typical of Keats. The boyish awe that Wilde felt in Ravenna is tempered, however, by recollection, for in the poem he is recalling his visit a year later. It is through recollection that he understands the greatness of the city, for in his northern world he has no such symbol of the rich complexity of time. What he learns from the English landscape is the passage of seasons that will mark his aging. He is sure, though, that with his love for Ravenna he will have a youthful inspiration despite his aging and loss of poetic powers.

Most of the poem is a poetic recounting of Ravenna's history. Wilde discusses the classical past of the city with reference to Caesar, and when he refers to Lord Byron's stay in the city, by association with Byron's last days in Greece, he imagines the region peopled with mythological figures; but the evening convent bell returns him to a somber Christian world. Recounting the Renaissance history of the city, Wilde is most moved by Dante's shrine. He closes the poem with references to Dante and Byron.

Wilde published twenty-eight sonnets in the 1881 collection, *Poems*, all of them Italian in form. Like his mentor Keats, Wilde used the sonnet to develop themes that he expanded in his longer poems.

SONNETS

"Hélas," an early sonnet not published in the 1881 collection, is his artistic manifesto that sets the tone for all the poems that followed. "Hélas" finds Wilde rhetorically questioning whether he has bartered wisdom for the passion or impression of the moment. In the sonnets that follow, he clearly seems to have chosen such moments of vivid impression.

In several sonnets, Wilde alludes to the poets who molded his style and themes, including two sonnets about visiting the graves of Keats and Percy Bysshe Shelley in the Protestant cemetery in Rome. He identifies himself with Keats as he never identifies with Shelley, and rightly so, for Keats's style and themes echo throughout the 1881 collection. Wilde also refers directly to Keats in another sonnet, "Amor Intellectualis," and to other poets important to him: Robert Browning, Christopher Marlowe, and particularly Dante and John Milton. The sonnet "A Vision" is a tribute to Aeschylus, Sophocles, and Euripides. On a larger scale than the sonnets, the longer poem "The Garden of Eros" presents Wilde's pantheon of poets with his feelings about them.

Some of the sonnets have political themes; in a number of these, Wilde advocates freedom, occasionally sounding like a Victorian Shelley. He is concerned with the political chaos of nineteenth century Italy, a land important to him for its classical past; "Italia" is a sonnet about the political venality in Italy, but it stresses that God might punish the corrupt. In his own country, Wilde idealizes the era of the Puritans and Oliver Cromwell; the sonnet "To Milton" laments the loss of democracy in England and advocates a return to the ideals of the Puritan revolution. In "Quantum Mutata," he admires Cromwell for his threat to Rome, but the title shows how events have changed, for Victorian England stands only for imperialism. This attack on British imperialism informs the long poem "Ave Imperatrix," which is far more emotional in tone than the political sonnets.

A number of Wilde's sonnets express his preference for the classical or primitive world and his antipathy for the modern Christian world. These poems have a persona visiting Italy, as Wilde did in 1877, and commenting on the Christian elements of the culture; "Sonnet on Approaching Italy" shows the speaker longing to visit Italy, yet, in contemplating far-off Rome, he laments the tyranny of a second Peter. Three other sonnets set in Italy, "Ave Maria, Gratia Plena," "Sonnet Written in Holy Week in Genoa," and "Urbs Sacra Aeterna," have Wilde contrasting the grandeur and color of the classical world with the emptiness and greyness of the Christian world. It is in these poems that Wilde is most like Swinburne. In other sonnets, he deals with religious values, often comparing the Christian ideal with the corruption of the modern Church he sees in Italy, or Christ's message with the conduct of his sinful followers. In "Easter Day," Wilde depicts the glory of the Pope as he is borne above the shoulders of the bearers, comparing that scene with the picture of Christ's loneliness centuries before. In "E Tenebris," the speaker appeals for help to a Christ who is to appear in weary human form. In "Sonnet,

On Hearing the Dies Irae Sung in the Sistine Chapel," Wilde criticizes the harsh picture of a fiery day of judgment and replaces it with a picture of a warm autumn harvest, in which humankind awaits reaping by and fulfillment in God.

Wilde's best religious sonnet, "Madonna Mia," avoids the polemicism of some of his other religious sonnets, showing instead an affinity with the Pre-Raphaelite painting and poetry of a generation earlier. This sonnet is Pateresque in its hard impression, and it fulfills the credo suggested by the sonnet "Hélas." The picture Wilde paints in words is detailed: braided hair, blue eyes, pale cheeks, red lips, and white throat with purple veins; Wilde's persona is a worshiper of Mary, as Dante was of Beatrice.

"THE BURDEN OF ITYS"

"The Burden of Itys" is one of several long philosophic poems about nature and God to be found in the 1881 collection. Each of these poems has the same stanza form, a six-line stanza with an *ababcc* rhyme scheme; the first five lines are iambic pentameter, and the sixth is iambic heptameter. The stanza form gives a lightness which does not perfectly fit the depth of the ideas the poems present; it seems a form better suited to witticism than to philosophy.

Set in England close to Oxford, "The Burden of Itys" is similar in imagery and setting to Matthew Arnold's poems "The Scholar Gypsy" and "Thrysis." Wilde piles image on image of the flora of the region to establish the beauty of the setting, suggesting that the beauty of the countryside (and thus of nature in general) is holier than the grandeur of Rome. Fish replace bishops and the wind becomes the organ for the persona's religious reverie. By stanza 13, Wilde shifts from his comparison between Rome and nature to a contrast between the English landscape and the Greek. Because England is more beautiful than Greece, he suggests that the Greek pantheon could fittingly be reborn in Victorian England. A bird singing to Wilde, much like the nightingale singing to Keats, is the link between the persona imagining a revival of classical gods and actually experiencing one in which he will wear the leopard skin of a follower of Bacchus. This spell breaks, though, with another contrast, for a pale Christ and the speaker's religion destroy the classical reverie.

Brought back then to the Victorian world, as Keats was brought back to his world at the end of "Ode to a Nightingale," Wilde philosophizes and fixes the meaning of his experience in a way Keats never would have done. He stresses that nature does not represent the lovely agony of Christ but warm fellowship both in and between the worlds of humankind and animal. Even Oxford and nature are linked to each other, Wilde implies, as the curfew bell from his college church calls him back.

PHILOSOPHICAL POEMS

"Panthea" also works through dissimilarity, this time between southern and northern Europe, passion and reason, and classical and Christian thought. Wilde's rejection of the Church in "The Burden of Itys" is gentle, but in "Panthea" it is blatant. The gods have simply grown sick of priests and prayer. Instead, people should live for the passion and pleasure of an hour, those moments being the only gift the gods have to give. The poem emphasizes that the Greek gods themselves dwell in nature, participating fully in all the pleasures there. Their natural landscape, though, is not the bleak landscape of northern Europe, but the warm rich landscape of southern Europe.

Wilde proceeds to the philosophical theme of the poem, that one great power or being composes nature, and Nature, thus, subsumes all lives and elements and recycles them into various forms. For people to be reborn as flower or thrush is to live again without the pain of mortal existence; yet, paradoxically, without human pain, nature could not create beauty. Pain is the basis of beauty, for nature exists as a setting for human passion. Nature, in Wilde's words, has one "Kosmic Soul" linking all lives and elements. Wilde echoes lines of Keats and Pater, and, uncharacteristically, William Wordsworth; Wilde's affirmation proceeds with lines and images from Wordsworth's "Ode: Intimations of Immortality from Recollections of Early Childhood."

"Humanitad" is the longest of the philosophical poems in the 1881 collection, and it has much less in common with the other two philosophical poems than they have with each other. While spring is imminent, the speaker responds only to the winter elements still persisting. He emphasizes (paraphrasing Pater) that he has no fire to burn with a clear flame. The difference here is with the renewal of spring and spiritual exhaustion, and the speaker must look outside himself for some source of renewal. At one point, the poem turns topical by referring to ideals of simplicity and freedom: Switzerland, Wordsworth, and Giuseppe Mazzini. Wilde invokes the name of Milton as epitomizing the fight for freedom in the past; and, at the same time, he laments that there are no modern Miltons. Having no modern exemplar, Wilde also dismisses death and love as possible solutions for his moribund life. Turning to science, Wilde also rejects it. Wilde then has no recourse, and he faces a meaningless universe until he touches on mere causality after having rejected science.

Causality leads to God and creed, for causality is a chain connecting all elements. Nature, as in "Panthea," cannot help the speaker, for he has grown weary of mere sensation. Accordingly, he turns to the force behind nature (in this instance, God as Christ), although he rejects orthodoxy. He sees modern humanity's creed as being in process, for humanity is in the stage of crucifixion as it tries to discover the human in Christ and not the divine. The persona then sees his emptiness as the suffering leading to renewal. It is the full discovery of Christ's humanity that will make modern human beings masters of nature rather than tormented, alienated outcasts.

THE SPHINX

Just as Wilde drew from classical mythology for many of his poems and then contrasted the gray Christian world with the bright pagan world, he used Egyptian mythology in *The Sphinx* to picture a decadent sadistic sensuality as distinguished from a tortured Christian suffering. The situation in the poem is that a cat has crept into the speaker's room; to the speaker, the cat represents the Sphinx. Now, giving his imagination play, the speaker reveals his own sadistic eroticism, a subject that Wilde had not developed in other poems. The style also represents a departure for him; the stanzas consist of two lines of iambic octameter with no rhyme, resulting in a languorous slow rhythm in keeping with the speaker's ruminations about sensuality and sadism.

The cat as Sphinx represents the lush, decadent, yet appealing sensuality found in Egyptian mythology. In half of the poem, Wilde rhetorically questions the Sphinx about mythological figures of ancient Egypt, asking who her lovers were and at the same time cataloging the most famous myths of Egypt. Wilde settles on Ammon as the Sphinx's lover, but then he discusses how Ammon's statue has fallen to pieces, thus suggesting that the lover might be dead. Yet the Sphinx has the power to revive her lover; Ammon is not really dead. Having earlier referred to the holy family's exile in Egypt, Wilde now mentions that Christ is the only god who died, having let his side be pierced by a sword. Christ then is weaker than Ammon, and, in this way, Wilde suggests that pagan mythology is more vital than Christian mythology. The speaker's reflections on love become orthodox at the end; he feels he should contemplate the crucifix and not the Sphinx. He returns to a world of penitence where Christ watches and cries for every soul, but the speaker sees the tears as futile. The poem then raises the question of whether human beings can be redeemed from their fallen condition.

THE BALLAD OF READING GAOL

Wilde's most famous poem, *The Ballad of Reading Gaol*, is a departure from any of the poems he had published previously. Sometimes overdone emotionally, the poem uses the prison as a metaphor for life and its cruelties. Wilde is the observer rather than the subject; in this way, he distances himself from his own experiences. The poem raises the thematic question of why humans are cruel to other human beings, so cruel that they always destroy what they love. It is through cruelty that people kill or destroy the ones they love, just as the prisoner whom Wilde observes, and who is soon to hang, murdered his lover. The mystery of human cruelty was the mystery of the Sphinx in Wilde's previous poem, but here the issue is the agony of the mystery rather than the decadent glory of cruelty, as in *The Sphinx*.

Wilde exploits the Gothic elements of the situation, dwelling on the macabre details of the grave of quicklime that dissolves the murderer's body. He uses the dread and gloom of the prisoners' lives to heighten the tone, but he often becomes shrill and melodramatic by emphasizing details such as the bag that covers the head of the condemned, tears falling like molten lead from the other prisoners as they observe the condemned, terror personified as a ghost, and the greasy rope used for the hanging. Ironically, the surviving prisoners are bedeviled by terror and horror, while the condemned dies calmly and serenely. Wilde uses a simple six-line stanza for a forcefully direct effect. The short lines alternate three and four feet of iambic pentameter with masculine rhyming of the second, fourth, and sixth lines. The stanza form is not one that suggests a reflective tone but rather a direct, emotional one.

The concluding motif of the poem is religious. The prison is a place of shame, where brother mistreats brother. Christ could feel only shame at what he sees his children do to each other there; but he rescues sinful humankind when he is broken by suffering and death. Even though the body of the hanged had no prayers said over it before interment in the quicklime, Christ rescued his soul. The surviving prisoners, their hearts broken and contrite, also gain salvation from the effects of their suffering.

POEMS IN PROSE

Wilde's *Poems in Prose* was the last collection published of all his poems except *The Ballad of Reading Gaol*, and the reader hears a different voice from that of the other poems, satirical and paradoxical like William Blake's in *The Marriage of Heaven and Hell* (1790). In Wilde's hands, the prose poem is a debonair and provocative parable on religious subjects. More often than not in his six prose poems, Wilde is trying to shock the bourgeoisie out of complacency and religious orthodoxy.

"The Artist" sets the tone of the prose poems; in this piece, the artist forsakes the oppressive sorrow of Christianity for the pursuit of hedonism. It is this kind of ironic reversal that the other prose poems also develop. In "The Doer of Good," Christ returns to find sinners and lepers he has saved or cured delighting in the sin, no longer wrong, from which he saved them. The one person whom Christ saved from death wishes that Christ had left him dead. "The House of Judgment" ironically shows the sinner complaining that his earthly life was hellish, and confronted now with Heaven, he has no conception of it after his life of suffering. The most moving of the six is "The Teacher of Wisdom," in which Wilde shows that the finest act of humankind is to teach the wisdom of God. A hermit, having attained the knowledge of God, refuses to part with it by giving it to the young sinner who is imploring him. Frustrated, the sinner returns to sin, but, in so doing, extracts the knowledge from the hermit, who hopes to turn the sinner away from more sin. Fearing that he has parted with his knowledge, the hermit is consoled by God, who now, for his sacrifice, grants him a true love of God. In this parable, Wilde has transcended the satiric wit of the other parables to teach through irony.

OTHER MAJOR WORKS

LONG FICTION: *The Picture of Dorian Gray*, 1890 (serial), 1891 (expanded).

SHORT FICTION: "The Canterville Ghost," 1887; *The Happy Prince, and Other Tales*, 1888; *A House of Pomegranates*, 1891; *Lord Arthur Savile's Crime, and Other Stories*, 1891.

PLAYS: *Vera: Or, The Nihilists*, pb. 1880; *The Duchess of Padua*, pb. 1883; *Lady*

Windermere's Fan, pr. 1892; *Salomé*, pb. 1893 (in French), pb. 1894 (in English); *A Woman of No Importance*, pr. 1893; *An Ideal Husband*, pr. 1895; *The Importance of Being Earnest: A Trivial Comedy for Serious People*, pr. 1895; *A Florentine Tragedy*, pr. 1906 (one act; completed by T. Sturge More); *La Sainte Courtisane*, pb. 1908.

NONFICTION: *Intentions*, 1891; *De Profundis*, 1905; *The Letters of Oscar Wilde*, 1962 (Rupert Hart-Davis, editor); *The Complete Letters of Oscar Wilde*, 2000 (Merlin Holland and Hart-Davis, editors).

MISCELLANEOUS: *Works*, 1908; *Complete Works of Oscar Wilde*, 1948 (Vyvyan Holland, editor); *Plays, Prose Writings, and Poems*, 1960.

BIBLIOGRAPHY

Belford, Barbara. *Oscar Wilde: A Certain Genius*. New York: Random House, 2000. An examination of Wilde's life with a somewhat revisionist view of Wilde's post-prison years.

Bloom, Harold, ed. *Oscar Wilde*. New York: Bloom's Literary Criticism, 2008. A collection of literary criticism on Wilde's body of work.

Canning, Richard. *Brief Lives: Oscar Wilde*. London: Hesperus, 2008. A biography of Wilde that covers his short life and his works.

Guy, Josephine, and Ian Small. *Studying Oscar Wilde: History, Criticism, and Myth*. Greensboro, N.C.: ELT Press, 2006. This volume attempts to provide a guide to studying the poet that distinguishes between the myth and history as well as provides literary criticism.

Harris, Frank. *Oscar Wilde: Including My Memories of Oscar Wilde by George Bernard Shaw*. 2d ed. New York: Carroll & Graf, 1997. Harris was one of the few friends who remained loyal to Wilde after his downfall. His biography, although highly readable and full of interesting anecdotes, is not always reliable.

McKenna, Neil. *The Secret Life of Oscar Wilde*. New York: Basic Books, 2005. This controversial and groundbreaking biography focuses on how Wilde's homosexuality influenced the writer's life and work. Illustrated.

Nunokawa, Jeff, and Amy Sickels. *Oscar Wilde*. Philadelphia: Chelsea House, 2005. A portrait of Wilde that examines his rise to fame, his sexuality, and the difficulties he experienced, especially after his fall.

Pearce, Joseph. *The Unmasking of Oscar Wilde*. San Francisco: Ignatius Press, 2004. Pearce avoids lingering on the actions that brought Wilde notoriety and instead explores Wilde's emotional and spiritual search. Along with a discussion of *The Ballad of Reading Gaol* and the posthumously published *De Profundis*, Pearce also traces Wilde's fascination with Catholicism.

Stokes, Anthony. *Pit of Shame: The Real Ballad of Reading Gaol*. Winchester, England: Waterside Press, 2007. Looks at Wilde's poem and also the actual jail that held the poet.

Wilde, Oscar. Interviews. *Oscar Wilde in America: The Interviews.* Edited by Matthew
   Hofer and Gary Scharnhorst. Urbana: University of Illinois Press, 2009. A collection of interviews from the time Wilde spent in the United States.

Dennis Goldsberry

WILLIAM BUTLER YEATS

Born: Sandymount, near Dublin, Ireland; June 13, 1865
Died: Roquebrune-Cap-Martin, France; January 28, 1939

PRINCIPAL POETRY
Mosada: A Dramatic Poem, 1886
Crossways, 1889
The Wanderings of Oisin, and Other Poems, 1889
The Countess Kathleen and Various Legends and Lyrics, 1892
The Rose, 1893
The Wind Among the Reeds, 1899
In the Seven Woods, 1903
The Poetical Works of William B. Yeats, 1906, 1907 (2 volumes)
The Green Helmet, and Other Poems, 1910
Responsibilities, 1914
Responsibilities, and Other Poems, 1916
The Wild Swans at Coole, 1917, 1919
Michael Robartes and the Dancer, 1920
The Tower, 1928
Words for Music Perhaps, and Other Poems, 1932
The Winding Stair, and Other Poems, 1933
The Collected Poems of W. B. Yeats, 1933, 1950
The King of the Great Clock Tower, 1934
A Full Moon in March, 1935
Last Poems and Plays, 1940
The Poems of W. B. Yeats, 1949 (2 volumes)
The Collected Poems of W. B. Yeats, 1956
The Variorum Edition of the Poems of W. B. Yeats, 1957 (P. Allt and R. K.
    Alspach, editors)
The Poems, 1983
The Poems: A New Edition, 1984

OTHER LITERARY FORMS

William Butler Yeats (yayts) was a playwright as well as a poet. During certain periods in his career, he devoted more time and energy to the composition, publication, and production of plays in verse or prose than to the writing of nondramatic poetry. These plays, excluding several early closet dramas, were republished singly or in various collections from 1892 through the year of his death. *The Collected Plays of W. B. Yeats* was

William Butler Yeats
(©The Nobel Foundation)

published in 1934, and a "new edition with five additional plays" appeared in 1952 (London) and 1953 (New York), the former being the "basic text." The genuinely definitive publication, however, is the admirably edited *Variorum Edition of the Plays of W. B. Yeats* (1966).

In addition to poems and plays, Yeats published prolifically during the course of his life in almost every imaginable genre except the novel. Numerous prose tales, book reviews, nationalistic articles, letters to editors, and so on far exceeded poems and plays in volume in the early stages of Yeats's career. In 1908, *The Collected Works in Verse and Prose of William Butler Yeats*—including lyrics, narrative poems, stories, plays, essays, prefaces, and notes—filled eight volumes, of which only the first contained predominantly nondramatic poetry. Previously, stories and sketches, many of them based wholly or in part on Irish folk tales, had been collected in *The Celtic Twilight* (1893) and *The Secret Rose* (1897). Rewritten versions of those tales from *The Secret Rose* that featured a roving folk poet invented by Yeats were later published as *Stories of Red Hanrahan* (1904). Similarly, relatively formal critical and philosophical essays were collected and published as *Ideas of Good and Evil* (1903), *The Cutting of an Agate* (1912), and *Essays, 1931-1936* (1937).

A slender doctrinal book, *Per Amica Silentia Lunae* (1918), is generally regarded as something of a precursor to *A Vision* (1925). The first edition of *A Vision* itself, an exposition of Yeats's mystical philosophy, appeared in 1925. A considerably revised edition first published in 1937 has revealed to scholars that while the book unquestionably owes much to his wife's "automatic writing," as avowed, more than a little of its content is generally based on Yeats's or his and his wife's earlier occult interests and contacts. In 1926, Yeats published a volume titled *Autobiographies*. In 1938, an American edition titled *The Autobiography of William Butler Yeats* was released, with the addition of several sections or units that had been published separately or in groups in the interim. Then, in 1955 a final British issue appeared with the original title and one sub-unit not included in the American edition. A posthumous supplement to *Autobiographies* is *Memoirs* (1972), combining the draft of an earlier unpublished autobiography with a complete transcription of the private journal from which Yeats had used only selected portions in the post-1926 versions of his original book. A large and carefully edited collection of Yeats's correspondence, *The Letters of W. B. Yeats*, was published in 1954, and various smaller collections of correspondence with certain people have been published from time to time since the poet's death.

Most of Yeats's major prose, other than *A Vision, Autobiographies*, and his editor's introduction to *The Oxford Book of Modern Verse* (1936), has been collected and republished in three volumes printed simultaneously in London and New York. *Mythologies* (1959) includes *The Celtic Twilight, The Secret Rose, Stories of Red Hanrahan*, the three so-called Rosa Alchemica stories from 1897 (which involve Yeats's fictional personae Michael Robartes and Owen Aherne), and *Per Amica Silentia Lunae. Essays and Introductions* (1961) incorporates *Ideas of Good and Evil*, most of *The Cutting of an Agate, Essays, 1931-1936*, and three introductions written in 1937 for portions of a projected edition of Yeats's works that never materialized. *Explorations* (1962) brings together a number of miscellaneous items, most of them previously not readily accessible. There are three introductions to books of legend and folklore by Lady Augusta Gregory, introductions to some of Yeats's own plays, a sizable body of his early dramatic criticism, the essay "If I Were Four and Twenty," *Pages from a Diary Written in Nineteen Hundred and Thirty* (1944), and most of the author's last prose piece *On the Boiler* (1939), a potpourri including late political philosophy.

As to fiction not already mentioned, two stories from 1891—a long tale and a short novel—have been republished in a critical edition, *John Sherman and Dhoya* (1969), and a fine scholarly edition of Yeats's early unfinished novel, *The Speckled Bird* (published in a limited edition in Dublin in 1974), was printed in 1976 as an item in the short-lived *Yeats Studies* series. In another highly competent piece of scholarship, almost all the previously mentioned early book reviews, nationalist articles, and so on, as well as some later essays, have been edited and republished in *Uncollected Prose by W. B. Yeats*, Volume 1 in 1970 and Volume II in 1976. Finally, the bewildering mass of Yeats's unpublished materials—thousands of pages of working drafts, notebooks, proof sheets, personal and family letters and papers, occult documents, automatic scripts, and the like—were made available on microfilm by the poet's son, Senator Michael Yeats, in 1975. Two sets of these films are housed, one each, at the National Library of Ireland and the State University of New York at Stony Brook. With the generous permission of Yeats's daughter and son, Anna and Michael, scholars are currently studying, transcribing, and editing many of these materials. Several books that employ or reproduce portions of them have been published. Several volumes of Yeats's letters, *The Collected Letters of W. B. Yeats*, trace his life and poetic influences between the years 1865 and 1904. Most of the letters included are from Yeats's twenties, when he was passionately involved with furthering two causes: his own career and Irish literature as a whole.

ACHIEVEMENTS

William Butler Yeats is generally regarded as one of the major English-speaking poets of the "modern" era (approximately 1890 to 1950). Some authorities go even further, designating him the most important twentieth century poet in any language. Although in his late career and for some time thereafter, he was overshadowed by the poetic and critical stature of T. S. Eliot, in the years since Eliot's death, Yeats's reputation has continued to grow whereas Eliot's has declined. Like most modern poets, writing in a period labeled the age of the novel, Yeats has been relatively obscure and inaccessible to the general reader, but among academicians his eminence has flourished, and, even more significant, his influence on other poets has been both broad and deep.

Even though he was never very robust, suffering from chronic respiratory problems and extremely poor eyesight throughout much of his adult life, Yeats lived a long, productive, and remarkably multifaceted life. How one person could have been as completely immersed in as many different kinds of activity as he was is difficult to conceive. Throughout his life, he was involved in occult pursuits and interests of one kind or another, a preoccupation that has long been considered by many authorities (especially early ones) as more an impediment than a contribution to his literary career. Of more "legitimate" significance, he was, with a handful of associates, a leading figure in the initiation of the related movements that have come to be known as the Irish Renaissance and the Celtic Revival. Especially as a cofounder and codirector of the Irish National Theatre—later the famous Abbey Theatre—he was at the center of the literary movement, even aside from his prolific publication of poems, plays, essays, and reviews and the editorship of his sisters' artistically oriented Cuala Press. Moreover, between 1903 and 1932, Yeats conducted or participated in a series of five theater or lecture tours in America, thereby enhancing his renown in English-speaking countries on both sides of the Atlantic.

Major expressions of national and international recognition for such endeavors and achievements were forthcoming in the last decades of Yeats's life in such forms as honorary degrees from Queen's University (Belfast) and Trinity College (Dublin) in 1922, Oxford University in 1931, and Cambridge University in 1933; appointment as senator for the newly established Irish Free State in 1922; and, most gratifying of all, the Nobel Prize in Literature in 1923. Furthermore, in 1935 Yeats was designated editor of the *Oxford Book of Modern Verse*, having declined previously an offer of knighthood in 1915 and an invitation to lecture in Japan in 1919. From young manhood, Yeats had lived and played out the role of the poet in society, gesturing, posing, and dressing for the part. In middle years and old age, he experienced genuine fulfillment of his dream and enjoyed self-realization as "the great man" of Anglo-Irish literature within his own lifetime.

Yeats's greatest accomplishment, however, was the achievement, in both his life and his work, of an astonishing singleness or oneness in the midst of myriad activities. Driven by an obsessive precept that he labeled "Unity of Being," he strove unceasingly to "hammer" his thoughts into "unity." Though never a masterful thinker in terms of logic or ratiocination, Yeats possessed unequivocal genius of the kind recognized by today's psychologists as imaginative or creative, if not visionary. In addition to an almost infallible gift for the precisely right word or phrase, he had a mind awesomely capacious in its ability to conceive and sustain complexly interwoven structures of symbolic suggestion, mythic significance, and allusive associations. He used these abilities to link poems to plays, and oeuvre to a self-consciously dramatic life, which was itself hardly other than a supremely sculpted *objet d'art*. By the time of his death at the age of seventy-three, Yeats had so completely interfused national interests, philosophical convictions, theories of symbolic art, and mythopoeic techniques of literary composition that he had indeed fulfilled his lifelong quest to master experience by wresting unity from multiplicity, achieving an intricately wrought identity of life and work in the midst of almost unimaginably manifold diversity.

BIOGRAPHY

The eldest son of an eldest son of an eldest son, William Butler Yeats was born on June 13, 1865, in Sandymount, Ireland, a small community on the outskirts of Dublin that has since been absorbed by that sprawling metropolis. His father, paternal grandfather, and great-grandfather Yeats were all graduates of Trinity College, Dublin, but only his father, John Butler Yeats, had begun his postcollegiate career in the city where he had studied. Both the great-grandfather and the grandfather had been clergymen of the Protestant Church of Ireland, the latter in county Down, near Northern Ireland, and the former at Drumcliff, near the west-Irish port town of Sligo, with which the poet is so thoroughly identified.

The reason for the identification with Sligo is that John Butler Yeats married the sister of his closest collegiate schoolmate, George Pollexfen, whose family lived in Sligo. Dissatisfied with the courts as a fledgling barrister, J. B. Yeats abandoned law and Dublin to follow in London his inclinations as a graphic artist in sketches and oils. The combination of limited finances and his wife's dislike of urban life resulted in numerous extended visits by her and the growing family of children back to Sligo at the home of the poet's maternal grandfather, a sea captain and partner in a shipping firm. Thus, Yeats's ancestral line doubled back on itself in a sense. In the Sligo area, he became acquainted with Yeats descendants of the Drumcliff rector, and in memory and imagination the west-Irish valley between the mountains Ben Bulben and Knocknarea was always his spiritual home.

Yeats's formal education was irregular, at best. His earliest training was in London at the hand of his father, who read to him from English authors such as Sir Walter Scott and William Shakespeare. He did not distinguish himself at his first school in London or at Erasmus High School when the family returned to Dublin in 1880. Declining to matriculate at Trinity in the tradition of his forebears, he took up studies instead at the Metropolitan School of Art, where he met George Russell (later Æ), who was to become a lifelong close acquaintance. Yeats soon found that his interests inclined more toward the verbal arts than toward the visual, however, and by 1885, he had discontinued his studies in painting and had published some poems. At this same relatively early time, he had also become involved in occult interests, being among the founders of the Dublin Hermetic Society.

In 1887, the family returned to London, where Yeats was briefly involved with the famous Madame Blavatsky's Theosophical Society. The years 1889 to 1892 were some of the most important in this crucially formative period of his life. He was active in the many diverse areas of interest that were to shape and color the remainder of his career. In rapid succession, he became a founding member of the Rhymers Club (a young group of Pateresque fin de siècle aesthetes) and of the Irish Literary Society of London and the Irish Literary Society of Dublin (both devoted to reviving interest in native Irish writers and writing). He also joined the newly established Hermetic Order of the Golden Dawn, a Rosicrucian secret society in which he became an active leader for a number of years and of which he remained a member for more than two decades. In 1889, Yeats published *The Wanderings of Oisin, and Other Poems* and became coeditor of an edition of William Blake's work, an experience that was to influence greatly much of his subsequent thought and writing. No event in this period, however, had a more dramatic and permanent effect on the rest of his life than his introduction in the same year to Maud Gonne, that "great beauty" of Ireland with whom Yeats fell immediately and hopelessly in love. The love was largely unrequited, although Maud allowed the one-sided relationship to continue for a painfully long time throughout much of the poet's early adult life—in fact, even after her marriage and widowhood.

From this point on, Yeats's life was a whirlwind of literary, nationalistic, and occult activity. In 1896, he met Lady Augusta Gregory and John Millington Synge, with both of whom he was later to be associated in the leadership of the Abbey Theatre, as well as in investigation of the folklore and ethos of west-Irish peasants. The purpose of the Abbey Theatre, as far as these three were concerned, was to produce plays that combined Irish interests with artistic literary merit. The acquaintance with Lady Gregory also initiated a long series of summer visits at her estate in Coole Park, Galway, where his aristocratic inclinations, as well as his frequently frail physical being, were nurtured. During parts of 1895 and 1896, Yeats shared lodgings in London briefly with Arthur Symons, of the Rhymers Club, who, as author of *The Symbolist Movement in Literature* (1899), helped to acquaint him further with the French Symbolist mode. Actually, however, through his intimate relationships with Hermetic lore and the English Romantics—especially Blake and Percy Bysshe Shelley—Yeats was already writing poetry in a manner much like that of his continental contemporaries. Later in 1896, Yeats moved in to 18 Woburn Buildings, Dublin, which came to be his permanent residence, except for rather frequent travels abroad, for an extended period.

At about the turn of the century and just after, Yeats abandoned his Pre-Raphaelite aestheticism and adopted a more "manful" style. Not wholly unrelated to this was his more outgoing involvement in the daily affairs of the nationalist theater movement. The fact should be remembered—for it is easy to forget—that at this time Yeats was in his late thirties, already moving into a somewhat premature middle age. In 1909 he met Ezra Pound, the only other major figure in the modernist movement with whom he was ever to develop an acquaintance to the point of literary interaction and influence. The relationship reached its apex in the years from 1912 to 1915, during which Pound criticized Yeats's romantic tendencies and, perhaps more important, encouraged the older poet's interest in the highly stylized and ritualistic No drama of Japan.

In the same years, another important aspect of Yeats's life and interests had been developing in new directions as well. Beginning about 1908-1909, his esoteric pursuits shifted from active involvement in the Order of the Golden Dawn to investigations in spiritism, séances, and "psychical research." This preoccupation continued until 1915 or 1916, at which point some biographers seem to indicate that it ended. Yet, in one sense, spiritism as an obsessive concern simply redoubled itself about this time on the occasion of Yeats's late-life marriage, for his wife turned out to be the "mystic" *par excellence*, through whose mediumship came the ultimate flowering of his lifelong prepossession with occult aspects of human—and superhuman—experience.

After Maud Gonne MacBride's husband was executed for his participation in Dublin's 1916 Easter uprising, Yeats visited Maud in Paris and proposed to her, only to be rejected as on previous occasions years before. He then became attracted to her daughter Iseult and proposed to her in turn. Once again rejected, he decided to marry an English woman whom he had known in occult circles for some years and who was a close friend of mutual acquaintances—Georgie Hyde-Less. On their honeymoon in 1917, Georgie began to experience the first of what came to be a voluminous and almost literally fantastic collection of "automatic writings," the basis of Yeats's famous mystic system, as elaborated in his book *A Vision*.

The various honors that Yeats received in the 1920's and 1930's have been outlined already under "Achievements." Ironically, from these same years, not earlier ones, came most of the poems and collections by which his importance as a major modern literary figure is to be measured. Two interrelated experiences were very likely the chief contributors to the newfound vigor, imagery, and stylistic devices characteristic of these late works—his marriage and the completion of his mystic system in *A Vision*. The nature and degree of indebtedness to the latter of these influences, however, has often been both misunderstood and overestimated. The connection can probably never be assessed with complete accuracy, whereas various other possible factors, such as his renewed interest in the writings of John Donne and Jonathan Swift, should not be ignored or minimized.

In 1926 and 1927, Yeats's health became a genuinely serious problem, and at times in the last dozen years of his life, to live seemed to him to be almost more difficult than to die. There can be little question that such prolonged confrontation with that ultimate of all human experiences is responsible for some of the combined profundity, choler, and—paradoxically—wit of his last poems and plays. During this period, winters were usually spent in various Mediterranean locales for climatic reasons. Death eventually came in the south of France in January, 1939. With characteristic doggedness, Yeats continued working to the very end; he wrote his last poem only a week before his death and dictated to his wife some revisions of a late poem and his last play after the onset of his final illness, only two days before he died. Because of transportation difficulties at the beginning of World War II, Yeats was initially buried at Roquebrune, France. His body was exhumed in 1948, however, and transported aboard an Irish corvette for reburial at Drumcliff Churchyard, as he had specified at the end of his valedictory poem, "Under Ben Bulben." As his friend and fellow author Frank O'Connor said on the occasion, that event brought to its appropriate and symbolic conclusion a life that was itself a work of art long planned.

ANALYSIS

The complexity and fullness of William Butler Yeats's life was more than matched by the complexity and fullness of his imaginative thought. There are few poets writing in English whose works are more difficult to understand or explain. The basic problems lie in the multiplicity and intricacies of Yeats's own preoccupations and poetic techniques, and all too often the reader has been hindered more than helped by the vagaries of criticism and exegesis.

A coincidence of literary history is partly responsible for the latter problem. The culmination and conclusion of Yeats's career coincided with the advent of the New Criticism. Thus, in the decades following his death, some of his most important poems became exercise pieces for "explication" by commentators whose theories insisted on a minimum of attention to the author's cultural background, philosophical views, personal interests, or even thematic intentions (hence their odd-sounding term "intentional fallacy"). The consequence has been critical chaos. There simply are no generally accepted readings for some of Yeats's major poems. Instead, there have been ingenious exegeses, charges of misapprehension, countercharges, alternative analyses, then the whole cycle starting over again—in short, interpretational warfare.

Fortunately, in more recent years, simultaneously with decline of the New Critical movement, there has been increasing access to Yeats's unpublished materials—letters, diaries, and especially the manuscript drafts of poems and plays—and more scholarly attention has been paid to the relationships between such materials and the probable themes or meanings in the completed works. Even so, critical difficulties of no small magnitude remain because of continuing widespread disagreement among even the most highly regarded authorities about the basic metaphysical vision from which Yeats's poetic utterances spring, variously interpreted as atheism, pagan theism, quasi-Christian theism, Theosophy, sheer aestheticism, Platonic dualism, modern humanist monism, and existentialism.

SHIFTING PHILOSOPHIES

Added to the problems created by such a critical reception are those deriving from Yeats's qualities as an imaginative writer. Probably the most obvious source of difficulty is the highly allusive and subtly symbolic mode in which Yeats so often expressed himself. Clearly another is his lifelong practice of infusing many of his poems and plays with elements of doctrine, belief, or supposed belief from the various occult sources with which he was so thoroughly imbued. Furthermore, as to doctrine or belief, Yeats was constantly either apparently or actually shifting his ground (more apparently than actually). Two of his better-known poems, for example, are appropriately titled "Vacillation" and "A Dialogue of Self and Soul." In these and numerous others, he develops and sustains a running debate between two sides of an issue or between two sides of his own truth-seeking psyche, often with no clear-cut solution or final stance made unequivocally apparent.

Related to this—but not simply the same—is the fact that Yeats tended to change philosophical or metaphysical views throughout a long career, again either actually or apparently, and, also again, sometimes more apparently than actually. One disquieting and obfuscating consequence of such mental habits is that one poem will sometimes seem flatly to contradict another, or, in some cases even aside from the dialogue poems, one part of a given poem may appear to contradict a different part of the same poem. Adjacent passages in the major piece "The Tower," involving apparent rejection of Plato and Plotinus alongside apparent acceptance of Platonic or Neoplatonic reincarnation and "translunar paradise," constitute a case in point.

To quibble at much length about Yeats's prevailing metaphysical vision is to indulge in delusive sophistry, however, if his more than moderate pronouncements on such matters in prose are taken at anything approaching face value. What emerges from the prose is the virtually unequivocal proposition that—having rejected orthodox Christianity—

the poet developed his own theistic "religion." His ontology and cosmology are made from many pieces and parts of that almost unimaginably multiplex body of lore— exoteric and esoteric—sometimes referred to as the *philosophia perennis*: Platonism, Neoplatonism, Hermetic symbolism, spiritual alchemy, Rosicrucianism, and certain elements of cabalism. Moreover, as Yeats stated in several essays, he found still further parallel and supporting materials at almost every turn—in Jakob Boehme, Emanuel Swedenborg, and William Blake; in the folklore of the Irish peasantry; in classical mythology, Irish legends, and the seasonal rituals examined by Sir James George Frazer; and in Asian religions, among other places. In two different senses Yeats found in all these materials convincing bases for the perpetuation of his obsession with extracting unity from multiplicity. For one thing, all the similarities and parallels in theme and motif from the many diverse sources constituted in themselves a kind of unity within multiplicity. Furthermore, the "philosophies" involved were largely oriented toward oneness—Plato's idea of the good, alchemy's distillation of the immutable *lapis* from the world of flux, Hermetism's theory of symbolic correspondences (as above, so below), Hinduism's Brahma, and so on.

In both thought and work, however, the unresolved opposites sometimes seem to loom as large as—or even larger than—the union itself. From this context came the so-called doctrine of the mask or anti-self (though not actually wholly original with Yeats). From that in turn, or alongside it, came the concept of the daimon, "guardian genius," or minor deity for each human being, a concept fundamental to a number of the traditional sources already cited. The greatest of all possible unions, of course, was the ultimate one of human beings with God, natural with supernatural, or temporal with eternal. Because of the *scintilla* principle, however, also inherent in parts of the tradition (the universe's permeation with tiny fragments of the godhead), the union of human being and daimon became virtually equivalent to the ultimate divine union. This concept helps to explain a handful of otherwise misleading passages where Yeats occasionally seemed to be rejecting his usually dominant dualism for a momentary monism: For example, in "The Tower," man creates everything in the universe from his own soul, and in "Two Songs from a Play" whatever illuminates the darkness is from man's own heart. Such human wholeness and power, however, are not possible, Yeats would probably say, without communion with daimon.

In spirit, doctrine, or belief, then, Yeats remained preponderantly a romantic and a nineteenth century spiritualist as he lived on into the increasingly positivistic and empirically oriented twentieth century. It was in form, not content, that he gradually allowed himself to develop in keeping with his times, although he abjured *vers libre* and never wholly relinquished his attachment to various traditional poetic modes. In the direction of modernism, he adopted or employed at various times irregular rhythms (writing by ear, declaring his ignorance of the technicalities of conventional metrics), approximate rhymes, colloquial diction, some Donnean or "metaphysical" qualities, and, most important of all, symbolic techniques much like those of the French movement, though not from its influence alone. The inimitable Yeatsian hallmark, however, remained a certain romantic rhetorical quality (despite his own fulminations against rhetoric), what he called passionate syntax, that remarkable gift for just the right turn of phrase to express ecstatic emotional intensity or to describe impassioned heroic action.

   To suggest that Yeats consistently achieved great poetry through various combinations of these thematic elements and stylistic devices, however, would be less than forthright. Sometimes doctrinal materials are indeed impediments. Sometimes other aspects of content are unduly personal or sentimental. At times the technical components seem to be ill-chosen or fail to function as might have been expected, individually or conjointly. Thoroughly capable of writing bad poetry, Yeats has by no means been without his detractors. The poems for which he is famous, however—even those which present difficulties of understanding—are masterpieces, alchemical transformations of the raw material of his art.

"THE LAKE ISLE OF INNISFREE"

   Probably the most famous of all Yeats's poems, especially from his early period and with popular audiences, is "The Lake Isle of Innisfree." A modern, middle-income Dublin homemaker, chosen at random, has said on mention of Yeats's name: "Oh, yes; I like his 'Lake Isle of Innisfree'; yes, I always did like 'The Lake Isle of Innisfree.'" Such popularity, as well as its representative quality among Yeats's early poems, makes the piece a natural choice for initial consideration here.

   On the surface, there seems to be little that is symbolic or difficult about this brief lyric, first published in 1890. The wavering rhythms, syntactical inversions, and colorful but sometimes hazy images are characteristic of much of Yeats's youthful verse. So too are the Romantic tone and setting, and the underlying "escape motif," a thematic element or pattern that pervades much of Yeats's early work, as he himself realized and acknowledged in a letter to a friend.

   The island of the title—real, not imaginary—is located in Lough Gill near the Sligo of Yeats's youth. More than once he mentioned in prose a boyish dream of living on the wooded isle much as Henry David Thoreau lived at Walden Pond, seeking wisdom in solitude. In other passages, he indicates that while homesick in London he heard the sound of a small fountain in the window of a shop. The experience recalled Lough Gill's lapping waters, he says, and inspired him to write the poem. The most important factor for Yeats's emerging poetic vision, however, was his long-standing fascination with a legend about a supernatural tree that once grew on the island with berries that were food for the Irish fairy folk. Thus in the poet's imaginative thought, if not explicitly in the poem itself, esoteric or occult forces were at play, and in a figurative sense, at least, the escape involved was, in the words of the letter to his friend, "to fairyland," or a place much like it.

One of the most notable sources of praise for "The Lake Isle of Innisfree" was a letter from Robert Louis Stevenson in distant Samoa. Stevenson wrote that only two other passages of literature had ever captivated him as Yeats's poem did. Yeats himself said later that it was the earliest of his nonnarrative poems whose rhythms significantly manifested his own music. He ultimately developed negative feelings, however, about his autobiographical sentimentality and about instances of what he came to consider unduly artificial syntax. Yet in late life when he was invited to recite some of his own poems for radio programs, he more than once chose to include "The Lake Isle of Innisfree." Evidently he wished to offer to that audience what he felt it probably wanted to hear. Evidently he realized that the average Irish homemaker or ordinary working man, then as later, would say in response to the name Yeats: "Oh, yes, I like his 'Lake Isle of Innisfree.'"

"LEDA AND THE SWAN"

Technically, "Leda and the Swan" (1923) is a sonnet, one of only a few that Yeats ever composed. The spaces between quatrains in the octave and between the octave and the sestet—not to mention the break in line eleven—are evidently Yeats's innovations, characteristic of his inclination toward experimentation within traditional frameworks in the period of the poem's composition. The story from Greek mythology on which the poem is based is well known and much treated in the Western tradition. In the tale from antiquity, a Spartan queen, Leda, was so beautiful that Zeus, ruler of the gods, decided that he must have her. Since the immortals usually did not present themselves to humankind in their divine forms, Zeus changed himself into a great swan and in that shape ravished the helpless girl. The story has often been portrayed pictorially as well as verbally; Yeats himself possessed a copy of a copy of Michelangelo's lost painting on the subject. There has been considerable critical discussion of the degree of interrelationship between the picture or other graphic depictions and Yeats's poem, but to no very certain conclusion, except that Leda seems much less terrified in Michelangelo's visual version—where perhaps she might even seem to be somewhat receptive—than in Yeats's verbal one.

The poem has been one of Yeats's most widely praised pieces from the time of early critical commentaries in the first decade after his death. Virtually all commentators dwell on the power, economy, and impact of the poem's language and imagery, especially in the opening sections, which seem to be concerned predominantly, if not exclusively, with mere depiction of the scene and events themselves. The poem's apparent simplicity, especially by Yeatsian standards, however, is decidedly deceptive. The greatest problem in interpretation is with the sestet's images of Troy in flames and with Agamemnon's death.

To understand the importance of these allusions to Greek history—and the deeper meanings of the poem—the reader must realize that Yeats intended the poem to represent the annunciation of a new era of civilization in his cyclic vision of history, the two-thousand-year-period of pagan polytheism that preceded the present age of Christian monotheism. As emphasized in Giorgio Melchiori's book *The Whole Mystery of Art* (1961), the poet later imaginatively balanced a second poem against "Leda and the Swan": "The Mother of God," in which another woman, Mary, is visited by another deity, the Holy Ghost, in the form of another bird, the divine dove, to initiate another period of history, the Christian era. The conscious intention of such a parallel between the two poems is attested by Yeats's having printed "Leda and the Swan" at the head of the chapter in *A Vision* titled "Dove or Swan," with a sentence on the next page stating explicitly that he thought of the annunciation that began Grecian culture as having been made to Leda. Equally unequivocal evidences are Melchiori's citation of a letter in which Yeats called the poem a classic annunciation, Yeats's note for the poem that speaks of a violent annunciation, and the fact that the poem's first submission to a publisher was under the title "Annunciation."

This last-mentioned fact relates to another point of critical disagreement. In a note, Yeats says that the poem was written in response to a request from the editor of a political review. As he worked, though, the girl and the swan took over the scene, he says, and all politics fell away. Some commentators have accepted or reaffirmed this assertion, failing to realize that Yeats—intentionally or unintentionally—overstated the case. Bird and woman did indeed so dominate the poet's imagination in the first eight lines that one critical consequence has been undue attention to the language and imagery of the surface there. When one recalls, however, that the pre-Christian era in Yeats's system was governmentally monarchical or totalitarian while the present era was imagined (however erroneously) as predominantly democratic, the perception dawns that the affairs of Leda's progeny, especially Helen as a causal factor in the Trojan war and Clytemnestra as a figure involved in its aftermath, constitute, in truth, "politics" enough. Otherwise, the allusions to the burning city and deceased king would be gratuitous deadwood in the poem, unaccountable anomalies, which is just exactly what they remain in those analyses that disregard them or minimize their importance.

Even recognition and acceptance of the themes of annunciation and history do not reveal the poem's full complexity, however, as the average reader may well sense on perusal of the final interrogative sentence. This concluding question seems to constitute a third unit in the piece, as well as the basis of some third level of significance. The traditional octave-sestet relationship of the Italian sonnet created for Yeats a division into two parts with two different but related emphases. It is his unconventional break in line 11, however, which achieves a tripartite structure at the same time that it introduces the thematic bases for an amalgamating—if not resolving—unity for all three parts of the poem and for all their interrelated levels of symbolic implication.

If the octave can be said to focus predominantly on the "surface" level of "Leda and the Swan," with the allusions to antiquity adumbrating a historical level, then the final question—a real one rather than the rhetorical sort with which Yeats sometimes concluded poems—can be seen as the introduction of a philosophical or metaphysical level. Given the possibility of such consort or interaction between the human and the divine, what supernatural effects—if any—are consequent for the mortal party? This issue, so relevant to the rest of this poem, is raised not only here or a few times in related pieces like "The Mother of God," but rather over and over again throughout the entirety of Yeats's canon. More than that, it is frequently voiced in those other places in surprisingly similar terms.

SEEKING A TRANSCENDENT UNION

The possibility of union between humankind and God, between natural and supernatural, is probably the most persistent and pervasive theme in all of Yeats's oeuvre. It is the strongest of those threads woven throughout the fabric of his work that create the unity within multiplicity previously considered. It was also unquestionably the motivating factor in his relentlessly moving from one occult preoccupation to the other. Moreover, the conviction that artistic inspiration was one of the more readily observable manifestations of such divine visitation on the human sensibility was what made Yeats philosophically a confessed Romantic for life, regardless of what modernist elements of style or technique he may have allowed to emerge in the poetry of his later years.

A major emblem for such miraculous converse, elsewhere in Yeats just as in "Leda and the Swan," is sexual union. In several prose passages, for example, he draws explicit parallels between human interaction with the daimon or semidivine guardian spirit and a man's relationship with his sweetheart or lover. In another place, he conjectures that the "mystic way" and physical love are comparable, which is not surprising in the light of the fact that most of his occult sources employed the same analogy and frequently spoke of the moment of union—mortal with immortal—as the "mystic marriage." Yeats's utilization of this particular sexual symbology is apparent in pieces such as "Solomon and the Witch," "A Last Confession," "Chosen," and *The Player Queen*, among others. Equally relevant is the fact that Yeats repeatedly used birds as symbols of discarnate spirits or deities. Finally, the two motifs—sexual union as an analogue for supernatural union and avian symbolism for the divine—occur together in at least two works by Yeats other than "Leda and the Swan": the plays *At the Hawk's Well* (pr. 1916) and *The Herne's Egg* (pb. 1938), in the latter of which, copulation between a woman and a great white bird is similarly fundamental to the piece's philosophical implications.

In Yeats's imaginative thought, such moments of transcendent union leave behind in the physical world some vestige of the divine condescension—the art object's "immortality" in the case of inspiration, for example. In more portentous instances, however, such as those imaged in "Leda and the Swan" and "The Mother of God"—with clear metaphorical interplay between the phenomena of creation and procreation, even if not voiced in so many words—the remnant is the conception of some demigod or incarnate divinity such as Helen or Christ, whose beauty, perfection, or power is so great that its presence on earth inaugurates a whole new cultural dispensation. What one ultimately finds in "Leda and the Swan," then, is Yeats hammering out, in the midst of manifold antinomy, two kinds of unity at a single stroke. The three somewhat separate parts of the poem are joined in unity with one another, and, simultaneously, the poem as a unified whole is united to some of the most important themes that recur throughout his canon. This unity within multiplicity is achieved through Yeats's ingeniously imaginative manipulation of a single famous myth chosen from many that involve—either or both—godhead manifested in avian form and divine visitation on humankind cast in the image of sexual conjugation.

"THE SECOND COMING"

Almost as synonymous with Yeats's name as "The Lake Isle of Innisfree" is the unusual and foreboding poem "The Second Coming," which was composed in January, 1919, and first published in 1920. It is one of Yeats's few unrhymed poems, written in very irregular blank verse whose rhythms perhaps contribute to the ominous effect created by the diction and imagery. The piece has had a strange critical reception, deriving in part from the paradox that it is one of Yeats's works most directly related to the system of history in *A Vision*, but at the same time appears to offer reasonably accessible meanings of a significant kind to the average reader of poetry in English.

The more obvious "meanings," generally agreed on, are implications of disorder, especially in the first section, in which the falcon has lost touch with the falconer, and impressions of horror, especially in the second section, with its vision of the pitiless rough beast slouching through the desert. In the light of the date of composition, the validity of such thematic elements for both Yeats and his audience is immediately evident. World War I had just ended, leaving the Western world in that continuing mood of despondency voiced also in T. S. Eliot's *The Waste Land* (1922) (which shares with Yeats's poem the desert image) and in Gertrude Stein's—and Ernest Hemingway's—epithet of "a lost generation." In other words, despite the author's considerable further concerns, the piece on this level "caught a wave," as it were, so that it quickly came to be regarded by commentators and the author alike as prophetic—an attitude enhanced, of course, by the richly allusive title.

HISTORY AS SPIRAL

On a deeper level, "The Second Coming" is directly related to the cyclical conception of history that Yeats delineated in *A Vision*. As seen in the discussion of "Leda and the Swan," Yeats envisioned history in terms of two-thousand-year eras, each of which was ushered in by a portentous annunciation of some sort. If Zeus's descent on Leda initiated the period from about 2000 B.C.E. to the year zero, and if the Holy Ghost's descent to Mary initiated the subsequent period from the year zero to approximately 2000 C.E., then in 1919, the poet could speculate that the next such annunciation might occur either just barely within his lifetime or else not very long thereafter. These two-thousand-year periods of culture were characterized, like so many other things in Yeats's imaginative thought, by opposition to each other, with the main oppositions in *A Vision* designated as antithetical (or "subjective") and primary (or "objective"). These labels, or tinctures as Yeats called them, are not always easy to define, but from reading *A Vision* one begins to sense their nature. In general, the antithetical is individualistic (self-centered), heroic, aristocratic, emotional, and aesthetic. It is concerned predominantly with inner being and is symbolized by a full moon. The primary, by contrast, is anti-individualistic (mass-oriented), saintly or sagelike, democratic, rational, and moral. It is associated mainly with external existence and is symbolized by either the sun or the dark of the moon. Yeats identified himself with the antithetical and associated many things that he disliked (such as democracy and "fact-finding" science) with the primary. Thus he favored the polytheistic era of Homeric and classical Greece (antithetical), whereas he rejected or spurned the moral and anti-individualistic monotheism (primary) which began with the birth of Christ.

Borrowing from Swedenborg and other esoteric sources, Yeats conceptualized the growth of these historical movements in terms of gyres or spirals, a feature of the system rather difficult to discuss without reference to diagrams. (One may see *A Vision* for diagrams in great sufficiency.) For the sake of convenience in depiction, the spirals (widening from vertex in larger and larger circles) are imaged as the outer "shells" surrounding them—that is, as cones. Furthermore, for purposes of two-dimensional representation on a book's page, each cone is usually regarded simply in terms of its profile—that is, as a triangle. However, since the entire system of *A Vision* is based on the proposition that the universe consists of numberless pairs of antinomies or contraries, no cone or triangle exists in isolation; instead, everyone is in locked interpenetration with an opposing cone or triangle, each with its vertex or narrowest point at the center of the other's widest expansion or base. Thus, Yeats conceived of the present two-thousand-year era not simply as one set of interlocked cones, but rather as two sets of one thousand years each, as is made quite explicit in the chapter that reviews history under the title "Dove or Swan." Thus, instead of the Christian gyre or cone sweeping outward toward its widest expansion at the year 2000 C.E., as most commentators seem to have assumed, the widest expansion of the triangle representing that primary religious dispensation occurred at about the year 1000 C.E., completely in keeping with the medieval Church's domination of virtually all aspects of life at that time. For the period following 1000 C.E., that religion's declining movement is represented by a contracting gyre, its base set against the base of its predecessor, forming, in two-dimensional terms, a figure that Yeats speaks of as shaped like an ace of diamonds. The Christian dispensation, then, is at dwindling to its cone's or triangle's narrowest point, at the center of the opposing gyre's widest expansion, completely in keeping with the post-Darwinian upheaval in Victorian England about science's undermining the foundations of the Church, subsequent notions of the "death of God," and so on.

What, then, is spiraling outward to its widest expansion in the twentieth century, the falcon's gyring flight having swept so far from the falconer that "the centre cannot hold"? The answer to this question lies in recognition of a point that appears rather clearly at various places in *A Vision*. In Yeats's system of history, every cone representing a religious dispensation has as its interlocking counterpart a cone that represents the secular culture of the same period. Thus, the two movements, religious and secular, live each other's death and die each other's life, to use an expression from Heraclitus that Yeats repeated time and again, in creative pieces as well as in his discursive prose. The birth of Christ came, then, as Yeats indicates with unequivocal clarity, at the time of an antithetical secular or political phenomenon at the very height of its development, at the widest expansion of its cone—the Roman Empire. As the gyre representing the primary Christian religious movement revolved outward toward its widest expansion in the Middle Ages, the power of the Roman Empire gradually declined until it vanished at about 1000 C.E. (Yeats uses the year 1050 in "Dove or Swan"). Then both movements reversed directions, with primary Christianity beginning to dwindle at the same time that a new secular life of antithetical nature started and gyred outward up to the present day. This—the widest expansion of an antithetical secular or political gyre in the twentieth century—is almost certainly what Yeats identified with fascism, not the new annunciation to come. Such a collapsing and reexpansion of the antithetical spirals in the two-thousand-year period since the birth of Christ—two one-thousand-year cones tip to tip—created what Yeats called an hourglass figure superimposed on (or, more accurately, interlocked with) the diamond shape of Christianity's primary religious dispensation.

TINCTURES

The crucial point in interpreting "The Second Coming" is that the annunciation of every new religious dispensation involves what Yeats calls an interchange of the tinctures. In other words, at 2000 B.C.E., at the year zero, and at 2000 C.E., religion changes from primary to antithetical in quality, or vice versa, while secular life and politics change tinctures just oppositely. (Yeats was explicit about identification of the secular with politics.) No such interchange occurs, however, at the initiation of new secular gyres, as at 1000 B.C.E. or 1000 C.E. At those points the expanding or collapsing gyres of both aspects of life—religious and secular—simply reverse directions without their tinctures changing from primary to antithetical or the other way around. The importance of this feature of the system for meanings in "The Second Coming" can hardly be overstated. The interchange is sudden and cataclysmic, causing such strife in human history as the Trojan War soon after the annunciation to Leda from Zeus or the widespread battles of the Roman Empire soon after the annunciation from the Holy Ghost to the Virgin

Mary. The abrupt change near the end of the twentieth century, of the antithetical tincture from secular life's widely expanded cone to religion's extremely narrowed one (and, vice versa, of the primary tincture almost instantaneously from the nearly extinguished religious gyre to the widest expansion of the counterpoised secular or political gyre), could in and of itself be catastrophic enough to warrant most of the portentous imagery and diction in Yeats's poem. Fearful concerns even more specifically related to the system than that, however, were involved in the piece's genesis and evolution. The annunciation of a new religious dispensation, antithetical in nature, would not have been anticipated by Yeats with foreboding, for he simultaneously favored the antithetical tincture and held in low regard the existing primary religious movement which was to be displaced. The only disappointing thing for Yeats about the forthcoming antithetical religion was that it would have no more than its merest beginnings within his lifetime or shortly thereafter, reaching its fullest expansion as a historical gyre not until the year 3000 C.E. The sudden imposition on the world of a primary political system, on the other hand, at its widest expansion from the very outset, was quite another matter.

What might constitute such an ultra-primary or super-"democratic" political phenomenon for the aristocratic-minded Yeats as he looked about the European world in 1919? Other than the last stages of World War I, one particular violent upheaval had just occurred: the Bolshevik Revolution. Communism was for Yeats the horrifying rough beast slouching through the postwar wasteland to be born, its politically primary hour come round exactly as predicted by the gyres and cycles of history available to him from the "automatic scripts" that his wife had begun to write out more than a year before the poem's composition.

Although this interpretational conclusion can be reached through a careful reading of *A Vision*'s sections on history, its validity has been made virtually unequivocal by Jon Stallworthy's publication of the poem's manuscript drafts (originally in his book *Between the Lines: Yeats's Poetry in the Making*, 1963, and again with fuller transcription of some partially illegible passages in the journal *Agenda*, 1971/1972). Along with several other convincing clues in these drafts occurs one line that leaves little to the imagination: "The Germany of Marx has led to Russian Com." Working with these same unpublished drafts as well as other materials, Donald Torchiana has made a persuasive case for the proposition that what upset Yeats most of all was the possibility that Ireland's civil strife in this same period made his country a highly vulnerable tinderbox for the spread of Marxist factions or Communistic forces (*W. B. Yeats and Georgian Ireland*, 1966). A letter by Yeats written later in 1919 makes this thesis virtually incontrovertible. In it the poet states that his main concern was for Ireland to be saved from Marxist values, because he felt that their fundamental materialism could only lead to murder. Then he quotes a catch-phrase that seems to echo lines from "The Second Coming": "Can the bourgeois be innocent?"

The manuscripts reveal much else as well. They show, for example, that from its earliest inception—a brief prose draft of the opening portion—"The Second Coming" was a decidedly political poem, not one concerned with some antithetical religious annunciation. Even the highly effective—though intentionally ironical—religious allusions to Bethlehem and Christ's return emerged relatively late in the poem's development. Moreover, the politics of concern are plainly of the primary tincture; the word "mob" appears repeatedly. When the expression "surely" occurred for the first time, it was followed by "the great falcon must come." Yeats, however, having said in a much-quoted passage elsewhere that he often used large noble birds to represent the subjective or antithetical and beasts that run on the ground to symbolize the objective or primary, realized his momentary drift toward depiction of the birth of an antithetical religious entity and struck the line. Then later came the famous beast, with its blank solar (primary) gaze.

Although it might shock some readers to think that Yeats would identify Christ with a beast, and with a political ideology such as Marxism, the point that should not be overlooked is that while Christ may be alternately sacred or secular in Yeats's imaginative thought, he is always unalterably primary. *A Vision* is quite explicit in several places about Christ's being primary. The poem is therefore, about his second coming, although in a frighteningly unfamiliar secular guise: a mass-oriented and anti-individualistic political materialism that paradoxically corresponds to but simultaneously contravenes his previous mass-oriented and anti-individualistic spiritual teachings. After twenty centuries of religious equality urged by Christ the Lamb, a cataclysmic and leveling social anarchy is about to be loosed on the world by Christ the Lion.

"AMONG SCHOOL CHILDREN"

Composed in 1926 and published in 1927, "Among School Children" is another of Yeats's most widely acclaimed and extensively studied poems. The two most famous interpretative readings are by Cleanth Brooks in *The Well Wrought Urn: Studies in the Structure of Poetry* (1947) and John Wain in *Interpretations: Essays on Twelve English Poems* (1955). Although both essays are almost belligerently New Critical, each sees as the overall theme the relationships between natural and supernatural, or between matter and spirit, and the ravages wrought on humankind by the passage of time. Most other analyses tend to accept this same general meaning for the poem as a whole, although almost inevitably there have been some who see the subject as the triumph of art, or something of that sort. With this poem, the problems and difficulties of interpretation have been not so much with larger suggestions of significance as with individual lines or passages in their relationships—or supposed relationships—to the poem's broadest meanings. Such tendencies toward agreement about the piece's general thematic implications are fortunate since they are in keeping with Yeats's own comments in notes and letters: that physical or temporal existence will waste the youthful students and that the poem is one of his not infrequent condemnations of old age.

The inspirational matrix for the poem was literal enough—a visit by Yeats in his role as senator in the newly established Irish Free State to a quite progressive school administered by a Catholic convent. Given this information, the reader will have no problems with stanza 1. (Any analysis, incidentally, which suggests that Yeats felt that the children depicted were being taught the wrong kinds of things is open to question, for Yeats subsequently spoke to the Senate about the convent school in highly laudatory terms.) The next three stanzas, however, although they are generally thought to be less problematical than the last part of the poem, are somewhat more opaque than the casual-toned and low-keyed opening. In stanza 2, the sight of the schoolchildren suddenly brings to the poet-senator's memory (with little transition for the reader) a scene in which a beautiful woman had told him of some childhood chastisement, probably by a schoolteacher. That memory, in turn, evokes for him a vision of what she must have looked like at such an age, perhaps not too much unlike the girls standing before him in the convent's hall.

There can be little doubt that the beautiful woman in question is the one by whom Yeats's aching "heart" was "driven wild" for a large part of his adult life—Maud Gonne. Time and time again throughout his canon, Yeats compares that special woman's almost divine or superhuman beauty to the beauty of Helen of Troy, who, in Greek mythology, was born to Leda after her visitation by Zeus. This information, then, helps to clarify such characteristically allusive terms in stanzas 2 through 4 as "Ledaean body," "daughters of the swan," "every paddler's heritage," "Ledaean kind," and "pretty plumage." The alteration of Plato's parable (in the *Symposium*, probably one of the middle dialogues, where the basis of love is explained as the desire in divinely separated humankind for reunion in a sphere) to union in the white and yellow of a single egg, rather than the myth's division, also fits into this pattern of Ledaean imagery, at the same time that it looks forward to images and suggestions of generation or birth in subsequent stanzas.

Then, in stanza 4, with still another shift, the beautiful woman's present visage drifts before the poet's eyes. Surprisingly, despite the rather heavily connotative language of lines 3 and 4, along with Yeats's comparison in the second quatrain of his own youth with his present old age (not to mention similar thematic implications in the entire poem), there has been some controversy about line one. The issue is whether Yeats meant to convey a vision of the woman still young and beautiful or, instead, ravaged by time and decrepitude. The word "Quattrocento," denoting fifteenth century Italian art and artists, might be taken to substantiate either side of such a debate, depending on how it itself is construed; but along with virtually everything else in the stanza, the concluding—and later recurring—scarecrow image would seem to lend support to the suggestion of deterioration and decay.

If lines 2 through 4 of stanza 5 were removed, the stanza not only would be completely intelligible, but it would also be a rather concise statement of one of the poem's two main themes—the effects on humankind of time's passage. Since lines 2 through 4 were included, however, along with other characteristically Yeatsian elements akin to them in subsequent stanzas, the poem's real difficulties begin to manifest themselves in its second half. In a note to the poem, Yeats indicates that the honey of generation is an image that he borrowed from Porphyry's essay "The Cave of the Nymphs," almost certainly with an intended symbolic suggestion, on one level, of the pleasures of sexual union. The same note, however, also indicates explicitly that the recollection mentioned is the soul's memory—à la William Wordsworth's "Ode: Intimations of Immortality from Recollections of Early Childhood"—of a prenatal condition higher and freer than earthly incarnation. At this point, Yeats's occult and esoteric beliefs that so many critics have found difficult to accept enter the poem. Brooks's reaction, for example, is virtual incredulity. To make interpretational matters even worse, Yeats evidently employed the honey image ambiguously to relate also to "the drug," presumably physically procreated or temporal existence, which allows or causes the prenatal memory to fade. Both the note and the draft versions of the poem (reproduced in Thomas Parkinson's *W. B. Yeats: The Later Poetry*, 1964) suggest the likelihood of such intentional or semi-intentional ambiguity. All this, along with what is probably the poem's least felicitous line— "sleep, shriek, struggle . . ."—has led to considerable exegetical dispute about who or what was betrayed—mother or shape? The ambiguity seems less intentional in this particular case, however, and the drafts, along with a certain amount of common sense, tend to indicate the child, a soul entrapped in flesh by the mother's generatively honeyed act.

Stanza 6 is perhaps not too difficult once the reader realizes that the final line is, in effect, appositionally related to the main nouns in the other seven lines. In other words, the generally accepted thrust of meaning is that even the greatest and presumably wisest of men come to be, in time, like elderly poet-senators and everyone else, dilapidated old scarecrows. There is, however, a bit more wit and symbolism at work—or at play—in the stanza. For one thing, Yeats has chosen men who were teachers or students or—in two cases—both in turn: Plato, Aristotle, Alexander the Great, and Pythagoras. Furthermore, three of these four men spent their lives contemplating and theorizing about the same crucial and fundamental aspects of human experience which are the subjects of the poem—the relationships between spirit and matter and between being and becoming.

The second half of stanza 7 is the most problematical unit in the poem. The first quatrain, however, gives little trouble. With a pun on the word "images," Yeats refers both to pictures in the maternal mind's eye and to religious icons or statuary. The "Presences" of line 5 are what create interpretational difficulties, again because here Yeats's occult views become involved, views that too few exegetes have been willing to address even as accepted by the poet himself. Yeats's use of a capital *P* and the expression "self-born" (compare "self-sown," "self-begotten," and "miracle-bred" on the very next page of *The Collected Poems of W. B. Yeats*) should be clues that some kind of divinity is being apostrophized in this stanza about worship. That, in turn, can lead to recognition of a third level of meaning for the punword "images." The mask, the antiself, and especially the daimon (not synonymous terms, but kindred ones in Yeats's esoteric thought and vocabulary) were sometimes referred to as the image, for they are, like a mirror image, simultaneously like and yet exactly opposite to the human individual. Furthermore, with the daimon, that special semidivine guiding or misguiding spirit, each man or woman is involved in an exasperating attraction-repulsion relationship which explains the poet's emphasis upon heartbreak and mockery. Fleetingly known—in actuality or by analogy—through such heightened experiences as the earlier stanzas' sexual love (passion), religious love (piety), or maternal love (affection), these hatefully loving guardian geniuses draw man onward from the flesh toward spiritual glory at the same time that they do all they can to frustrate every inch of his progress or enterprise along the way.

The first half of the closing stanza would be much more readily comprehensible if Yeats had retained his draft's version of the opening line, which began with the word "all" instead of "labor." That would have agreed with a draft line relating to the dancer, "all so smoothly runs," and would justify the status *usually* attributed to the concluding quatrain: perhaps the most successful of Yeats's famous passages whose antinomy-resolving symbols or images lift poet, poem, and reader above the strife of physical existence to a condition of triumphant affirmation or realm of artistically perfected unity. Dance and dancer are indivisibly—almost divinely—one. The tree—and the poem—are supremely organic wholes, greater than the sums of their parts. This seems to be Romantic lyricism at its transcendent best.

Such a conclusion, however, is too hasty. When its initial word was "all," the first quatrain of the final stanza rather plainly meant something like "Life in this world is best when and where humankind achieves a balance between body and soul, between spirit and flesh." Yeats's eventual substitution of the word "labor," however, could well have been intended to add, among other things, the idea that such a balance is never easily come by nor readily sustained in this life. That would echo in one sense the feminine persona in "Adam's Curse," who says that women have to labor to become beautiful, as well as her interlocutor's rejoinder that subsequent to Adam's fall nothing very fine can be achieved or created without a great deal of labor. How, then, did the poet move so suddenly from the broken hearts and mockery of stanza 7 to some rhapsodically evoked unity or triumph in the last four lines of stanza 8? Perhaps the poem was never meant to suggest such a leap. There is, after all, no journey in this poem from one realm to another, as there is in "Sailing to Byzantium." The tree and the dancer are still very much in the sensuous physical realm. Perhaps the supposed transition has been only through some strange magic as unsavory to common sense as Yeats's occult inclinations were to the critics who have perpetrated this illusory transmutation. Perhaps, ironically, the unRomantic critics have made Yeats much more Romantic in this particular poem than he ever intended to be. In all fairness, the point must be acknowledged, however, that

Brooks and Wain themselves read the final stanza in much more neutral or negative terms than many of the commentators who have written subsequently. Almost unquestionably the chief influence on numerous analyses of the final stanza in terms of transcendence and artistic unity has been Frank Kermode's book *Romantic Image* (1957), which takes the passage as a virtual epitome of the opposition-resolving powers of the symbolic mode, as the image of the Image.

"Among School Children" has a rather high incidence of puns and intentional ambiguities in addition to the ones already noted. The two most obvious further instances involve the words "labor" and "play," which have been commented on both separately and together. Perhaps insufficient attention has been given, however, to possibilities of multiple meanings in that salient feature, the title. Yeats, an inveterate reviser, was well capable of changing a title if it no longer best suited the interests of his poem. Why would he have retained the title here if it did not fit the finished piece—the whole work as well as the opening portions? Some continuing concern with the symbolic implications of students and teachers has already been observed in stanza 6. Why would not or could not the same kind of thing be appropriate for that very important portion of the poem, its conclusion? Suppose, in contrast to prevalent interpretations of the last quatrain, that the questions asked there are real questions, such as schoolchildren ask, rather than rhetorical ones implying some transcendence or triumph over the rest of the poem's concerns. Like a staring schoolchild, man might well ask—in fact, for centuries he has asked—where the material world ends and the spiritual world begins, and how, in this temporal realm, he can separate the one from the other. The great rooted blossomer, then, may be more an emblem of the puzzles and problems studied in life's schoolroom than of some artistically achieved solution to them. Is man the newborn infant, the adolescent pupil, the youthful procreator, or the white-haired elder statesman—or none of these or all of these or more than all of these? In the face of such conundrums, all men are "among school children," seeking and inquiring, frequently without finding or being given reassuring answers.

"SAILING TO BYZANTIUM" AND "BYZANTIUM"

No work in Yeats's canon has won more renown or elicited more controversy than the so-called Byzantium poems, "Sailing to Byzantium" (1927) and "Byzantium" (1930). Critical opinion as to which is poetically superior has been almost, if not quite, equally divided. There is almost universal agreement, however, that the earlier and more frequently reprinted piece, "Sailing to Byzantium," is the easier to understand.

Several authorities, in fact, have gone so far as to say that "Sailing to Byzantium" explains itself or needs no extensive clarification; but if such were actually the case, the amount of commentary that it has generated would clearly constitute an anomaly. If nothing else, the general reader ought to have some answer to the almost inevitable question, "Why Byzantium?" Though it does not provide every possible relevant response to such a query, a much-quoted passage from *A Vision* indicates some of the more important reasons why and how Yeats came to let that great Near Eastern city of medieval times represent in his imagination a cultural, artistic, and spiritual ideal. He believes, he says, that one might have found there "some philosophical worker in mosaic" with "the supernatural descending nearer to him than to Plotinus even," that in "early Byzantium" perhaps more than at any other time in history "religious, aesthetic and practical life were one." Artists of all kinds expressed "the vision of a whole people," "the work of many that seemed the work of one" and was the "proclamation of their invisible master."

Although there is no question whatever that "Sailing to Byzantium" is a richly symbolic poem, its genesis apparently involved a more or less literal level that, even though it has not been ignored, may not have been stressed in all its particulars as much as might be warranted. Yeats was first exposed to Byzantine art during a Mediterranean tour in 1907 that included Ravenna, where he saw mosaics and a frieze in the Church of San Apollinare Nuovo that is generally regarded as the chief basis of imagery in stanza 3 of "Sailing to Byzantium." Years later, however, two factors coincided to renew his interest, one of them involving a voyage in certain respects interestingly akin to that in the poem. In the first half of the 1920's, Yeats had read rather widely about Byzantium in connection with his work on the historical "Dove or Swan" section of *A Vision*. Then in 1924, nearing sixty years of age, he became somewhat ill and suffered high blood pressure and difficulty in breathing. He was advised to stop work and was taken by his wife on another Mediterranean tour, this time seeking out other Byzantine mosaics, and similar craftsmanship that sharply contrasted art with nature, at places such as Monreale and Palermo, Sicily. As at least one commentator has pointed out, Yeats had no great regrets about leaving home at this time because of dissatisfaction with the political situation and depression about his health. The first legible words in the drafts of "Sailing to Byzantium" are "Farewell friends," and subsequent early portions make unequivocal the fact that "That country" in the finished poem is (or at least originally was) Ireland. Thus, the imaginative and poetic voyage of a sick old man leaving one locale for a more desirable one very probably had at least some of its antecedents in a rather similar actual journey a few years earlier.

Two symbolic interpretations of "Sailing to Byzantium" have been predominant by a considerable margin: Either the poem is about the state of the poet's spirit or soul shortly before and after death, or it is about the creative process and artistic achievement. A choice between the two might be said to pivot on response to the question, "How ideal is the ideal?" In other words, does Byzantium represent this-worldly perfection on the aesthetic level or perfection of an even greater kind in a transcendent realm of existence? A not insignificant amount of the massive critical commentary on the poem (as well as on its sequel "Byzantium") has been in the way of a war of words about the "proper" reply to such a question, with surprisingly inflexible positions being taken by some of the combatants. Fortunately, however, a number of authorities have realized that there is no reason at all why both levels of meaning cannot obtain simultaneously and that, as a matter of fact, the poem becomes much more characteristically Yeatsian in its symbolic complexity and wealth of import if such a reading is accepted.

RETURN TO PHYSICALITY, SEXUALITY

About 1926 or 1927 and thereafter, an apparent major change—with emphasis on apparent—seems to have taken place in Yeats's attitude toward life. On the surface, "Sailing to Byzantium" may look and sound like the culmination of a long line of "escape" poems, while many poems or passages written after it (for example, "A Dialogue of Self and Soul") seem to stress instead a plunge into the physicality of this world, even a celebration of earthly existence. Even though Yeats continued to write poems very much concerned with transcendence, supernaturalism, and otherworldliness, he developed in his late career a "new" kind of poem. These poems were often short, were frequently presented in series or sequences, and were frequently—but not always—concerned with a particularly physical aspect of worldly existence, sex.

These poems also share other attributes, a number of them related to Yeats's revived interest at the time in the ballad form. One group is titled, for example, *Words for Music Perhaps, and Other Poems*, indicating their songlike qualities. In addition to the poems themselves being brief, the lines and stanza patterns are also short, the lines sometimes having as few as two stresses. Diction, syntax, and idiom are—again as in the ballad or folk song—colloquial and uncomplicated. Imagery, too, is earthy, sometimes stark or blunt. At times sound patterns other than rhyme contribute to the songlike effects, and some pieces, although not all, make effective use of the refrain as a device. In these verses, Yeats has come a long way from the amorphous Pre-Raphaelitism of his early lyrics. In them, in fact, he achieves some of the most identifiably "modern" effects in his entire canon.

Related to that modernity is the fact that these late-life songs are anything but simple in content and meaning. Their deceptiveness in this regard has led some early critics to label them—especially the scatological ones—as tasteless and crude. More recent and perceptive analysts, however, have found them to be, in the words of one commentator, more nearly eschatological. What Yeats is doing thematically in such pieces, in fact, is by no means new to him. As in "Solomon and the Witch," "Leda and the Swan," and some other earlier pieces, he is using the sexual metaphor to explore some of the metaphysical mysteries of human existence. One significant difference, however, is that now the sexual experience itself sometimes seems to be regarded as something of a mystery in its own right.

CRAZY JANE POEMS

Almost as well known as Yeats himself is his fictive persona Crazy Jane, evidently based compositely on two old Irish women from the poet's experience, one early, one late. Like Shakespeare's—and Yeats's—fools, however, Jane is usually "crazy like a fox." In her series of poems, in the "Three Bushes" sequence, and in poems such as "Chosen," "A Last Confession," "Her Anxiety," "Consolation," and "The Wild Old Wicked Man," Yeats considers or deals with sexuality and sexual imagery in some six or seven different, though frequently interrelated, ways. At times, the poet seems to vacillate or contradict himself from one poem to another, a habit that at first makes understanding these pieces rather difficult. After a while, however, the phenomenon can be recognized for what it is: Yeats's characteristic technique of shifting ground or altering angle of vision in order to explore his subject the more completely.

One basic use of the sexual image has already been seen: The union of man and woman is parallel to or representative of the union of natural with supernatural, human with divine, or man with daimon. In some of these poems, however, the union seems to be so overwhelming that it almost ceases to be mere symbol and becomes the thing in itself, as in the last stanza of "Chosen" or in an unpublished poem where even the gyres are laid to rest in the bed of love. On the other hand (and at the other extreme) are poems that suggest that sex just does not accomplish very much at all, as in "The Chambermaid's Second Song" (last in the "Three Bushes" sequence), where after mere physical pleasure, man's spirit remains "blind as a worm." A poem of this kind echoes a reported statement by Yeats that the most unfortunate thing about coitus is the continuing "virginity of the soul." In between the two extremes are poems that see sex as little better than a *pis aller*—"Consolation," for example, or "The Wild Old Wicked Man," whose protagonist chooses "the second-best" on "a woman's breast." Then there are poems that contemplate the pleasures or problems of sexuality in this life in the light of a Swedenborgian intercourse of the angels ("A Last Confession" and "Crazy Jane on the Day of Judgment") or the Hermetic paradigm—as above, so below ("Ribh Denounces Patrick," though this piece is not in the ballad tradition). Still other poems in the collection, instead of comparing bodies in this world with spirits in the other world, use sexual symbolism to ponder the conundrums of the body-soul relationship here on earth, a theme reminiscent of "Among School Children." The Lady's three songs in the "Three Bushes" series fall into this category. Finally, Yeats sometimes uses the transience of sexual experience to parallel the ephemeral nature of all human experience, especially such heightened moments as mystic vision or artistic inspiration. Such an ironic self-consuming quality inherent in the sex act is touched on in the first stanza of "Crazy Jane and Jack the Journeyman" and in "Her Anxiety," among other places.

"UNDER BEN BULBEN"

As indicated earlier in the biographical section, Yeats continued to work on poems and plays right down to the last day but one before his death. Although "Under Ben Bulben" was not his last poem, it was written quite consciously as a valedictory or testamentary piece in the summer and fall of 1938, when Yeats knew that death was not far away. Although such a status for the poem has been widely recognized by authorities from a very early date, surprisingly little has been written about it until relatively recently.

Ben Bulben is the impressive west-Irish headland "under" whose shadow Yeats specified that his body be buried in the churchyard at Drumcliff where his great-grand-father had been rector a century earlier. In draft versions, "Under Ben Bulben" had two previous titles: "His Convictions" and "Creed." Furthermore, the opening lines that read "Swear by" in the finished poem originally read "I believe." Here, then, presumably, if anywhere, one should be able to find Yeats's final views on life and the human condition. Because the poem goes on, however, to indicate quite candid belief in the existence of supernatural spirits and, further still, in reincarnation or transmigration of the soul, modern critics who do not accept such quasireligious views have evidently declined to take the piece very seriously. One apparent consequence has been that they have had little adequate basis for understanding or glossing the epitaph with which the poem concludes.

Ironically, the epitaph has been very often quoted: "Cast a cold eye/ On life, on death./ Horseman, pass by!" Exegetical commentary on these three lines, however, has been almost as rare as that on the larger poem. Explication has been so minimal and inconclusive, in fact, that as late as 1974 one spokesperson, Edward Malins, asserted that determination of the epitaph's meaning and its intended audience "is anybody's guess." In terms of the framing poem's thesis of transmigration, however, along with evidence from other sources, the horseman can be identified as Yeats himself, a cosmic journeyer engaged in a vast round of cyclical deaths and rebirths, as outlined in *A Vision*. A cold eye is cast on both life and death because the point of possible release from the wheel of reincarnation to some ultimate beatific state such as that imaged in "Sailing to Byzantium" is at such great distance that the grave is little more than a way station on the cosmic odyssey. Thus, there is time or place for little more than a passing nod or glance toward either life or death. In the words of a passage from *A Vision* that is virtually a prose counterpart of the epitaph's verse, man's spirit can know nothing more than transitory happiness either between birth and death or between death and rebirth; its goal is to "pass rapidly round its circle" and to "find freedom from that circle."

The means of passing rapidly around *A Vision*'s great wheel is to live each incarnation properly "in phase." Failure in this endeavor can cause rebirth again into the same phase, thus slowing progress toward "freedom" or release. From his youthful days as a disciple of Walter Pater, Yeats had long regarded the living of life itself as an art. With the coming of *A Vision*, teleological impetus was added to this aesthetic conviction. In a note on "Sailing to Byzantium" from a radio script and in several poems, Yeats exclaims that he must "make his soul." In the terms of *A Vision*, then, once he knew the prescribed qualities of his current incarnation or phase on the wheel, he must shape and sculpt his very life until it becomes a concrete manifestation of that phase, a mythopoeic *objet d'art*.

In *Autobiographies*, on the other hand, Yeats states that when great artists were at their most creative, the rest was not simply a work of art, but rather the "re-creation of the man through that art." Similarly, in a scrap of verse, he said that whenever he remade a poem, the real importance of the act was that, in the event, he actually remade himself. Thus emerged the ultimate unity. Yeats's life and his work became two sides of the one coin. The phenomena were mutually interdependent, the processes mutually interactive. As he forged his poems, Yeats also created his self. That created self, a living myth, was in turn the image reflected in his poetry, the center of vision embodied in the verbal constructs of his art.

OTHER MAJOR WORKS

SHORT FICTION: *John Sherman and Dhoya*, 1891, 1969; *The Celtic Twilight*, 1893; *The Secret Rose*, 1897; *The Tables of Law; The Adoration of the Magi*, 1897; *Stories of Red Hanrahan*, 1904; *Mythologies*, 1959.

PLAYS: *The Countess Cathleen*, pb. 1892; *The Land of Heart's Desire*, pr., pb. 1894; *Cathleen ni Houlihan*, pr., pb. 1902; *The Pot of Broth*, pr. 1902 (with Lady Augusta Gregory); *The Hour-Glass*, pr. 1903, 1912; *The King's Threshold*, pr., pb. 1903 (with Lady Gregory); *On Baile's Strand*, pr. 1904; *Deirdre*, pr. 1906 (with Lady Gregory); *The Shadowy Waters*, pr. 1906; *The Unicorn from the Stars*, pr. 1907 (with Lady Gregory); *The Golden Helmet*, pr., pb. 1908; *The Green Helmet*, pr., pb. 1910; *At the Hawk's Well*, pr. 1916; *The Dreaming of the Bones*, pb. 1919; *The Only Jealousy of Emer*, pb. 1919; *The Player Queen*, pr. 1919; *Calvary*, pb. 1921; *Four Plays for Dancers*, 1921 (includes *Calvary, At the Hawk's Well, The Dreaming of the Bones*, and *The Only Jealousy of Emer*); *The Cat and the Moon*, pb. 1924; *The Resurrection*, pb. 1927; *The Words upon the Window-Pane*, pr. 1930; *The Collected Plays of W. B. Yeats*, 1934, 1952; *A Full Moon in March*, pr. 1934; *The King of the Great Clock Tower*, pr., pb. 1934; *The Herne's Egg*, pb. 1938; *Purgatory*, pr. 1938; *The Death of Cuchulain*, pb. 1939; *Variorum Edition of the Plays of W. B. Yeats*, 1966 (Russell K. Alspach, editor).

NONFICTION: *Ideas of Good and Evil*, 1903; *The Cutting of an Agate*, 1912; *Per Amica Silentia Lunae*, 1918; *Essays*, 1924; *A Vision*, 1925, 1937; *Autobiographies*, 1926, 1955; *A Packet for Ezra Pound*, 1929; *Essays, 1931-1936*, 1937; *The Autobiography of William Butler Yeats*, 1938; *On the Boiler*, 1939; *If I Were Four and Twenty*, 1940; *The Letters of W. B. Yeats*, 1954; *The Senate Speeches of W. B. Yeats*, 1960 (Donald R. Pearce, editor); *Essays and Introductions*, 1961; *Explorations*, 1962; *Ah, Sweet Dancer: W. B. Yeats, Margot Ruddock—A Correspondence*, 1970 (Roger McHugh, editor); *Uncollected Prose by W. B. Yeats*, 1970, 1976 (2 volumes); *Memoirs*, 1972; *The Collected Letters of W. B. Yeats*, 1986-2005 (4 volumes); *Early Articles and Reviews: Uncollected Articles and Reviews Written Between 1886 and 1900*, 2004 (John P. Frayne and Madeleine Marchaterre, editors).

MISCELLANEOUS: *The Collected Works in Verse and Prose of William Butler Yeats*, 1908; *The Collected Works of W. B. Yeats*, 1989-2008 (13 volumes).

BIBLIOGRAPHY

Chaudhry, Yug Mohit. *Yeats, the Irish Literary Revival, and the Politics of Print.* Cork, Ireland: Cork University Press, 2001. A study of Yeats's political and social views as well as a critique of his writings. Bibliography and index.

Foster, R. F. *W. B. Yeats: A Life.* 2 vols. New York: Oxford University Press, 1997-2003. An excellent, extensive guide to Yeats and his work.

Greaves, Richard. *Transition, Reception, and Modernism in W. B. Yeats.* New York: Palgrave, 2002. In examining Yeats's poetry of 1902 to 1916, Greaves rejects the label of "modernist" and instead analyzes Yeats's poetry from the context of the poet's life.

Grene, Nicholas. *Yeats's Poetic Codes.* New York: Oxford University Press, 2008. Grene examines the key words and habits of speech that shape Yeats's poetry, focusing on poetic technique to understand the work.

Holdeman, David. *The Cambridge Introduction to W. B. Yeats.* New York: Cambridge University Press, 2006. Examines Yeats's poems, drama, and stories in their cultural, historical, and literary contexts.

Howes, Marjorie, and John Kelly, eds. *The Cambridge Companion to W. B. Yeats.* New York: Cambridge University Press, 2006. Yeats scholars from the United States, England, and Ireland contributed eleven essays to this work, illuminating the personal and political events in Yeats's life. Howes and Kelly chronicle his early interests in theater, politics, and the occult, along with the portrayal of these topics in his writing. Includes a detailed time line, bibliography, and index.

Jeffares, A. Norman. *W. B. Yeats: A New Biography.* New York: Continuum, 2001. A biography of Yeats by a leading scholar of the writer.

Ross, David. *Critical Companion to William Butler Yeats: A Literary Reference to His Life and Work.* New York: Facts On File, 2008. A reference work that provides information on his life and critical analysis of his writings.

Vendler, Helen. *Our Secret Discipline: Yeats and Lyric Form.* Cambridge, Mass.: Harvard University Press, 2007. A guide to Yeats' poetry that focuses exclusively on his use of form and the ways in which meaning is derived from it. Useful to scholars and students of poetry.

James Lovic Allen

CHECKLIST FOR EXPLICATING A POEM

A. Before reading the poem, the reader should:
1. Notice its form and length.
2. Consider the title, determining, if possible, whether it might function as an allusion, symbol, or poetic image.
3. Notice the date of composition or publication, and identify the general era of the poet.

B. The poem should be read intuitively and emotionally and be allowed to "happen" as much as possible.

C. In order to establish the rhythmic flow, the poem should be reread. A note should be made as to where the irregular spots (if any) are located.

II. Explicating the Poem

A. *Dramatic situation.* Studying the poem line by line helps the reader discover the dramatic situation. All elements of the dramatic situation are interrelated and should be viewed as reflecting and affecting one another. The dramatic situation serves a particular function in the poem, adding realism, surrealism, or absurdity; drawing attention to certain parts of the poem; and changing to reinforce other aspects of the poem. All points should be considered. The following questions are particularly helpful to ask in determining dramatic situation:
1. What, if any, is the narrative action in the poem?
2. How many personae appear in the poem? What part do they take in the action?
3. What is the relationship between characters?
4. What is the setting (time and location) of the poem?

B. *Point of view.* An understanding of the poem's point of view is a major step toward comprehending the poet's intended meaning. The reader should ask:
1. Who is the speaker? Is he or she addressing someone else or the reader?
2. Is the narrator able to understand or see everything happening to him or her, or does the reader know things that the narrator does not?
3. Is the narrator reliable?
4. Do point of view and dramatic situation seem consistent? If not, the inconsistencies may provide clues to the poem's meaning.

C. *Images and metaphors*. Images and metaphors are often the most intricately crafted vehicles of the poem for relaying the poet's message. Realizing that the images and metaphors work in harmony with the dramatic situation and point of view will help the reader to see the poem as a whole, rather than as disassociated elements.

1. The reader should identify the concrete images (that is, those that are formed from objects that can be touched, smelled, seen, felt, or tasted). Is the image projected by the poet consistent with the physical object?
2. If the image is abstract, or so different from natural imagery that it cannot be associated with a real object, then what are the properties of the image?
3. To what extent is the reader asked to form his or her own images?
4. Is any image repeated in the poem? If so, how has it been changed? Is there a controlling image?
5. Are any images compared to each other? Do they reinforce one another?
6. Is there any difference between the way the reader perceives the image and the way the narrator sees it?
7. What seems to be the narrator's or persona's attitude toward the image?

D. *Words*. Every substantial word in a poem may have more than one intended meaning, as used by the author. Because of this, the reader should look up many of these words in the dictionary and:

1. Note all definitions that have the slightest connection with the poem.
2. Note any changes in syntactical patterns in the poem.
3. In particular, note those words that could possibly function as symbols or allusions, and refer to any appropriate sources for further information.

E. *Meter, rhyme, structure, and tone*. In scanning the poem, all elements of prosody should be noted by the reader. These elements are often used by a poet to manipulate the reader's emotions, and therefore they should be examined closely to arrive at the poet's specific intention.

1. Does the basic meter follow a traditional pattern such as those found in nursery rhymes or folk songs?
2. Are there any variations in the base meter? Such changes or substitutions are important thematically and should be identified.
3. Are the rhyme schemes traditional or innovative, and what might their form mean to the poem?
4. What devices has the poet used to create sound patterns (such as assonance and alliteration)?
5. Is the stanza form a traditional or innovative one?
6. If the poem is composed of verse paragraphs rather than stanzas, how do they affect the progression of the poem?

7. After examining the above elements, is the resultant tone of the poem casual or formal, pleasant, harsh, emotional, authoritative?

F. *Historical context.* The reader should attempt to place the poem into historical context, checking on events at the time of composition. Archaic language, expressions, images, or symbols should also be looked up.

G. *Themes and motifs.* By seeing the poem as a composite of emotion, intellect, craftsmanship, and tradition, the reader should be able to determine the themes and motifs (smaller recurring ideas) presented in the work. He or she should ask the following questions to help pinpoint these main ideas:
   1. Is the poet trying to advocate social, moral, or religious change?
   2. Does the poet seem sure of his or her position?
   3. Does the poem appeal primarily to the emotions, to the intellect, or to both?
   4. Is the poem relying on any particular devices for effect (such as imagery, allusion, paradox, hyperbole, or irony)?

BIBLIOGRAPHY

GENERAL REFERENCE SOURCES

BIOGRAPHICAL SOURCES
Colby, Vineta, ed. *World Authors, 1975-1980*. Wilson Authors Series. New York: H. W. Wilson, 1985.
_____. *World Authors, 1980-1985*. Wilson Authors Series. New York: H. W. Wilson, 1991.
_____. *World Authors, 1985-1990*. Wilson Authors Series. New York: H. W. Wilson, 1995.
Cyclopedia of World Authors. 4th rev. ed. 5 vols. Pasadena, Calif.: Salem Press, 2003.
International Who's Who in Poetry and Poets' Encyclopaedia. Cambridge, England: International Biographical Centre, 1993.
Seymour-Smith, Martin, and Andrew C. Kimmens, eds. *World Authors, 1900-1950*. Wilson Authors Series. 4 vols. New York: H. W. Wilson, 1996.
Thompson, Clifford, ed. *World Authors, 1990-1995*. Wilson Authors Series. New York: H. W. Wilson, 1999.
Wakeman, John, ed. *World Authors, 1950-1970*. New York: H. W. Wilson, 1975.
_____. *World Authors, 1970-1975*. Wilson Authors Series. New York: H. W. Wilson, 1991.
Willhardt, Mark, and Alan Michael Parker, eds. *Who's Who in Twentieth Century World Poetry*. New York: Routledge, 2000.

CRITICISM
Brooks, Cleanth, and Robert Penn Warren. *Understanding Poetry*. 4th ed. Reprint. Fort Worth, Tex.: Heinle & Heinle, 2003.
Day, Gary. *Literary Criticism: A New History*. Edinburgh, Scotland: Edinburgh University Press, 2008.
Habib, M. A. R. *A History of Literary Criticism: From Plato to the Present*. Malden, Mass.: Wiley-Blackwell, 2005.
Jason, Philip K., ed. *Masterplots II: Poetry Series, Revised Edition*. 8 vols. Pasadena, Calif.: Salem Press, 2002.
Lodge, David, and Nigel Wood. *Modern Criticism and Theory*. 3d ed. New York: Longman, 2008.
Magill, Frank N., ed. *Magill's Bibliography of Literary Criticism*. 4 vols. Englewood Cliffs, N.J.: Salem Press, 1979.
MLA International Bibliography. New York: Modern Language Association of America, 1922- .

Nineteenth-Century Literature Criticism. Detroit: Gale Research, 1981-   .
Twentieth-Century Literary Criticism. Detroit: Gale Research, 1978-   .
Young, Robyn V., ed. *Poetry Criticism: Excerpts from Criticism of the Works of the Most Significant and Widely Studied Poets of World Literature.* 29 vols. Detroit: Gale Research, 1991.

POETRY DICTIONARIES AND HANDBOOKS

Deutsch, Babette. *Poetry Handbook: A Dictionary of Terms.* 4th ed. New York: Funk & Wagnalls, 1974.
Drury, John. *The Poetry Dictionary.* Cincinnati, Ohio: Story Press, 1995.
Kinzie, Mary. *A Poet's Guide to Poetry.* Chicago: University of Chicago Press, 1999.
Lennard, John. *The Poetry Handbook: A Guide to Reading Poetry for Pleasure and Practical Criticism.* New York: Oxford University Press, 1996.
Matterson, Stephen, and Darryl Jones. *Studying Poetry.* New York: Oxford University Press, 2000.
Packard, William. *The Poet's Dictionary: A Handbook of Prosody and Poetic Devices.* New York: Harper & Row, 1989.
Preminger, Alex, et al., eds. *The New Princeton Encyclopedia of Poetry and Poetics.* 3d rev. ed. Princeton, N.J.: Princeton University Press, 1993.
Shipley, Joseph Twadell, ed. *Dictionary of World Literary Terms, Forms, Technique, Criticism.* Rev. ed. Boston: George Allen and Unwin, 1979.

INDEXES OF PRIMARY WORKS

Frankovich, Nicholas, ed. *The Columbia Granger's Index to Poetry in Anthologies.* 11th ed. New York: Columbia University Press, 1997.
_____. *The Columbia Granger's Index to Poetry in Collected and Selected Works.* New York: Columbia University Press, 1997.
Guy, Patricia. *A Women's Poetry Index.* Phoenix, Ariz.: Oryx Press, 1985.
Hazen, Edith P., ed. *Columbia Granger's Index to Poetry.* 10th ed. New York: Columbia University Press, 1994.
Hoffman, Herbert H., and Rita Ludwig Hoffman, comps. *International Index to Recorded Poetry.* New York: H. W. Wilson, 1983.
Kline, Victoria. *Last Lines: An Index to the Last Lines of Poetry.* 2 vols. Vol. 1, *Last Line Index, Title Index*; Vol. 2, *Author Index, Keyword Index.* New York: Facts On File, 1991.
Marcan, Peter. *Poetry Themes: A Bibliographical Index to Subject Anthologies and Related Criticisms in the English Language, 1875-1975.* Hamden, Conn.: Linnet Books, 1977.
Poem Finder. Great Neck, N.Y.: Roth, 2000.

POETICS, POETIC FORMS, AND GENRES

Attridge, Derek. *Poetic Rhythm: An Introduction*. New York: Cambridge University Press, 1995.

Brogan, T. V. F. *Verseform: A Comparative Bibliography*. Baltimore: Johns Hopkins University Press, 1989.

Fussell, Paul. *Poetic Meter and Poetic Form*. Rev. ed. New York: McGraw-Hill, 1979.

Hollander, John. *Rhyme's Reason*. 3d ed. New Haven, Conn.: Yale University Press, 2001.

Jackson, Guida M. *Traditional Epics: A Literary Companion*. New York: Oxford University Press, 1995.

Padgett, Ron, ed. *The Teachers and Writers Handbook of Poetic Forms*. 2d ed. New York: Teachers & Writers Collaborative, 2000.

Pinsky, Robert. *The Sounds of Poetry: A Brief Guide*. New York: Farrar, Straus and Giroux, 1998.

Preminger, Alex, and T. V. F. Brogan, eds. *New Princeton Encyclopedia of Poetry and Poetics*. 3d ed. Princeton, N.J.: Princeton University Press, 1993.

Spiller, Michael R. G. *The Sonnet Sequence: A Study of Its Strategies*. Studies in Literary Themes and Genres 13. New York: Twayne, 1997.

Turco, Lewis. *The New Book of Forms: A Handbook of Poetics*. Hanover, N.H.: University Press of New England, 1986.

Williams, Miller. *Patterns of Poetry: An Encyclopedia of Forms*. Baton Rouge: Louisiana State University Press, 1986.

IRISH POETRY

BIOGRAPHICAL SOURCES

Broom, Sarah. *Contemporary British and Irish Poetry: An Introduction*. Illustrated ed. New York: Palgrave Macmillan, 2006.

Sherry, Vincent B., Jr., ed. *Poets of Great Britain and Ireland, 1945-1960*. Dictionary of Literary Biography 27. Detroit: Gale Research, 1984.

_____. *Poets of Great Britain and Ireland Since 1960*. Dictionary of Literary Biography 40. Detroit: Gale Research, 1985.

DICTIONARIES, HISTORIES, AND HANDBOOKS

Broom, Sarah. *Contemporary British and Irish Poetry: An Introduction*. Illustrated ed. New York: Palgrave Macmillan, 2006.

Hogan, Robert, ed. *Dictionary of Irish Literature*. Rev. ed. 2 vols. Westport, Conn.: Greenwood Press, 1996.

Schirmer, Gregory A. *Out of What Began: A History of Irish Poetry in English.* Ithaca, N.Y.: Cornell University Press, 1998.

Tuma, Keith, ed. *Anthology of Twentieth-Century British and Irish Poetry.* Annotated ed. New York: Oxford University Press, 2001.

WOMEN WRITERS

Colman, Anne Ulry. *Dictionary of Nineteenth-Century Irish Women Poets.* Galway: Kenny's Bookshop, 1996.

McBreen, Joan, ed. *The White Page = An Bhileog Bhán: Twentieth-Century Irish Women Poets.* Cliffs of Moher, Ireland: Salmon, 1999.

Weekes, Ann Owens. *Unveiling Treasures: The Attic Guide to the Published Works of Irish Women Literary Writers: Drama, Fiction, Poetry.* Dublin: Attic Press, 1993.

GUIDE TO ONLINE RESOURCES

WEB SITES

The following sites were visited by the editors of Salem Press in 2010. Because URLs frequently change, the accuracy of these addresses cannot be guaranteed; however, long-standing sites, such as those of colleges and universities, national organizations, and government agencies, generally maintain links when their sites are moved.

Academy of American Poets
http://www.poets.org

The mission of the Academy of American Poets is to "support American poets at all stages of their careers and to foster the appreciation of contemporary poetry." The academy's comprehensive Web site features information on poetic schools and movements; a Poetic Forms Database; an Online Poetry Classroom, with educator and teaching resources; an index of poets and poems; essays and interviews; general Web resources; links for further study; and more.

Contemporary British Writers
http://www.contemporarywriters.com/authors

Created by the British Council, this site offers profiles of living writers of the United Kingdom, the Republic of Ireland, and the Commonwealth. Information includes biographies, bibliographies, critical reviews, and news about literary prizes. Photographs are also featured. Users can search the site by author, genre, nationality, gender, publisher, book title, date of publication, and prize name and date.

LiteraryHistory.com
http://www.literaryhistory.com

This site is an excellent source of academic, scholarly, and critical literature about eighteenth, nineteenth, and twentieth century American and English writers. It provides individual pages for twentieth century literature and alphabetical lists of authors that link to articles, reviews, overviews, excerpts of works, teaching guides, podcasts, and other materials.

Literary Resources on the Net
http://andromeda.rutgers.edu/~jlynch/Lit

Jack Lynch of Rutgers University maintains this extensive collection of links to Web sites that are useful to researchers, including numerous sites about American and English literature. This collection is a good place to begin online research about poetry, as it links to other sites with broad ranges of literary topics. The site is organized chronologically, with separate pages about twentieth century British and Irish literature. It also has separate pages providing links to Web sites about American literature and to women's literature and feminism.

LitWeb
http://litweb.net
    LitWeb provides biographies of hundreds of world authors throughout history that can be accessed through an alphabetical listing. The pages about each writer contain a list of his or her works, suggestions for further reading, and illustrations. The site also offers information about past and present winners of major literary prizes.

The Modern Word: Authors of the Libyrinth
http://www.themodernword.com/authors.html
    The Modern Word site, although somewhat haphazard in its organization, provides a great deal of critical information about writers. The "Authors of the Libyrinth" page is very useful, linking author names to essays about them and other resources. The section of the page headed "The Scriptorium" presents "an index of pages featuring writers who have pushed the edges of their medium, combining literary talent with a sense of experimentation to produce some remarkable works of modern literature."

Outline of American Literature
http://www.america.gov/publications/books/outline-of-american-literature.html
    This page of the America.gov site provides access to an electronic version of the ten-chapter volume *Outline of American Literature*, a historical overview of poetry and prose from colonial times to the present published by the Bureau of International Information Programs of the U.S. Department of State.

Poetry Foundation
http://www.poetryfoundation.org
    The Poetry Foundation, publisher of *Poetry* magazine, is an independent literary organization. Its Web site offers links to essays; news; events; online poetry resources, such as blogs, organizations, publications, and references and research; a glossary of literary terms; and a Learning Lab that includes poem guides and essays on poetics.

Poet's Corner
http://theotherpages.org/poems
    The Poet's Corner, one of the oldest text resources on the Web, provides access to about seven thousand works of poetry by several hundred different poets from around the world. Indexes are arranged and searchable by title, name of poet, or subject. The

site also offers its own resources, including "Faces of the Poets"—a gallery of portraits—and "Lives of the Poets"—a growing collection of biographies.

Representative Poetry Online
http://rpo.library.utoronto.ca

This award-winning resource site, maintained by Ian Lancashire of the Department of English at the University of Toronto in Canada, has several thousand English-language poems by hundreds of poets. The collection is searchable by poet's name, title of work, first line of a poem, and keyword. The site also includes a time line, a glossary, essays, an extensive bibliography, and countless links organized by country and by subject.

Voice of the Shuttle
http://vos.ucsb.edu

One of the most complete and authoritative places for online information about literature, Voice of the Shuttle is maintained by professors and students in the English Department at the University of California, Santa Barbara. The site provides countless links to electronic books, academic journals, literary association Web sites, sites created by university professors, and many other resources.

Voices from the Gaps
http://voices.cla.umn.edu/

Voices from the Gaps is a site of the English Department at the University of Minnesota, dedicated to providing resources on the study of women artists of color, including writers. The site features a comprehensive index searchable by name, and it provides biographical information on each writer or artist and other resources for further study.

ELECTRONIC DATABASES

Electronic databases usually do not have their own URLs. Instead, public, college, and university libraries subscribe to these databases, provide links to them on their Web sites, and make them available to library card holders or other specified patrons. Readers can visit library Web sites or ask reference librarians to check on availability.

Canadian Literary Centre
Produced by EBSCO, the Canadian Literary Centre database contains full-text content from ECW Press, a Toronto-based publisher, including the titles in the publisher's Canadian fiction studies, Canadian biography, and Canadian writers and their works series; *ECW's Biographical Guide to Canadian Novelists*; and *George Woodcock's Intro-*

duction to Canadian Fiction. Author biographies, essays and literary criticism, and book reviews are among the database's offerings.

Literary Reference Center

EBSCO's Literary Reference Center (LRC) is a comprehensive full-text database designed primarily to help high school and undergraduate students in English and the humanities with homework and research assignments about literature. The database contains massive amounts of information from reference works, books, literary journals, and other materials, including more than 31,000 plot summaries, synopses, and overviews of literary works; almost 100,000 essays and articles of literary criticism; about 140,000 author biographies; more than 605,000 book reviews; and more than 5,200 author interviews. It contains the entire contents of Salem Press's MagillOnLiterature Plus. Users can retrieve information by browsing a list of authors' names or titles of literary works; they can also use an advanced search engine to access information by numerous categories, including author name, gender, cultural identity, national identity, and the years in which he or she lived, or by literary title, character, locale, genre, and publication date. The Literary Reference Center also features a literary-historical time line, an encyclopedia of literature, and a glossary of literary terms.

MagillOnLiterature Plus

MagillOnLiterature Plus is a comprehensive, integrated literature database produced by Salem Press and available on the EBSCOhost platform. The database contains the full text of essays in Salem's many literature-related reference works, including *Masterplots, Cyclopedia of World Authors, Cyclopedia of Literary Characters, Cyclopedia of Literary Places, Critical Survey of Poetry, Critical Survey of Long Fiction, Critical Survey of Short Fiction, World Philosophers and Their Works, Magill's Literary Annual*, and *Magill's Book Reviews.* Among its contents are articles on more than 35,000 literary works and more than 8,500 poets, writers, dramatists, essayists, and philosophers; more than 1,000 images; and a glossary of more than 1,300 literary terms. The biographical essays include lists of authors' works and secondary bibliographies, and hundreds of overview essays examine and discuss literary genres, time periods, and national literatures.

Rebecca Kuzins; updated by Desiree Dreeuws

CATEGORY INDEX

SUBJECT INDEX